MATTERS OF CONSCIENCE

L. Jackson Newell and Sterling M. McMurrin in conversation.

(Photo by J. A. B. Photography.)

MATTERS OF
CONSCIENCE

Conversations with Sterling M. McMurrin
on Philosophy, Education, and Religion

STERLING M. McMURRIN
and
L. JACKSON NEWELL

SIGNATURE BOOKS
SALT LAKE CITY

To our children

Trudy, Joe, Jim, Laurie, and *Melanie*
and
Chris, Jennifer, Eric, and *Heather*

Each has had an important effect on how we think and
all deserve to know we know it.

———

The introduction and epilogue are based on essays by the author first
appearing in *Dialogue: A Journal of Mormon Thought* 28 (Spring 1995):
1-17, and in *Sunstone* 19 (Sept. 1996): 10-11.

Dust jacket design by J. Scott Knudsen

∞ *Matters of Conscience* was printed on acid-free paper and was
composed, printed, and bound in the United States.

2000   99   98   97   96   6   5   4   3   2   1

McMurrin, Sterling M.
      Matters of conscience : conversations with Sterling McMurrin
on philosophy, education, and religion / by L. Jackson Newell.
            p.   cm.
      Includes index.
      ISBN 1-56085-087-6 (cloth)
      1. McMurrin, Sterling M.—Interviews.   2. Church of Jesus Christ
of Latter-day Saints—Doctrines.   3. Mormon Church—Doctrines.
4. Philosophy.   5. Education—Philosophy.   6. Religion—Philosophy.
I. Newell, L. Jackson.   II. Title.
BX8695.M345A3   1996
289.3'092—dc20
      [B]   96-18068
                                                            CIP

Contents

Sterling Moss McMurrin
died in St. George, Utah, on April 6, 1996.
Matters of Conscience
was in press at the time of his passing.

Foreword

J. Boyer Jarvis

Jackson Newell has engaged Sterling McMurrin in many remarkable conversations over a number of years, recording and arranging them for us all to enjoy. In doing so, he has made available to the interested reader—and there are many good reasons to be interested—the personal story of one of Utah's most distinguished native citizens.

This book defies our usual categories. It is neither biography nor autobiography, though it has characteristics of both forms. To be sure, Sterling McMurrin speaks in his own voice and this is a strength. But the typical weakness of the autobiographical form is absent in this work: McMurrin is not in complete control of his own story. In a spirit of genuine repartee and deep friendship, Jack Newell often probes, occasionally challenges, and constantly draws Sterling McMurrin out as he tells the story of his life and reflects upon his wide-ranging experiences.

Rich in insight and humor, this remarkable dialogue captures the sweep and depth of McMurrin's thought as Newell engages him in revealing and discussing his approaches to philosophy, education, and religion—as well as his perspectives on institutions that have grown up to serve them. This book is as extraordinary in content as it is unusual in form.

Presented in an intertwined chronological-topical pattern, these conversations bring to life the important positive influence of McMurrin's parents, and of his maternal and paternal grandparents, in establishing the fundamentally wholesome values and abilities that have been the foundation of his intellectual development and of his career of service to the State of Utah and to the nation.

Beyond his close family ties and his impressive stature as a scholar, three aspects of McMurrin's adult life are especially noteworthy: (1) his participation in the progress and evolution of the University of Utah over the span of more than half a century; (2) his involvement nationally and internationally as a consultant to educational institutions and major corporations, and as a high official of the government of the United States; (3) his unique service to the Mormon church.

As an undergraduate student at the University of Utah in the mid-1930s, Sterling McMurrin was employed by President George Thomas to locate and assemble information regarding the history of the university from its founding in 1850 to its financial crisis during the Great Depression.

After earning his Ph.D. in philosophy at the University of Southern California and serving there as a full-time faculty member, McMurrin accepted an invitation to return to his alma mater in 1948 as a professor of philosophy. In cooperation with his faculty colleagues in the Department of Philosophy, he established a scintillating series of public lectures on Great Issues in Philosophy that generated intense interest both on the campus and in the community.

As a teacher, McMurrin appealed especially to highly motivated students who were continually impressed by the comprehensiveness of his knowledge and his uncommon ability to present elegantly crafted class lectures entirely without notes.

From the mid-1950s to the mid-1980s, Sterling McMurrin was a diligent and effective representative of the university faculty in the academic administration of the University of Utah. Serving successively as dean of the College of Letters and Science, academic vice-president, provost, and dean of the Graduate School, he was a reliable champion of academic freedom, fairness, high standards, and due process.

Professor McMurrin's unique value to the University of Utah has been acknowledged in many ways. He was the first appointee to the rank of Distinguished Professor in 1964 and first recipient of the coveted Rosenblatt Prize in 1984. In his honor, and through the generosity of others, the University of Utah has endowed the Sterling M. McMurrin Distinguished Visiting Professorship in Liberal Education, the Sterling M. McMurrin Chair in Religious History in the Department of History, and the Sterling M. McMurrin Lectures on Religion in the Obert C. and Grace A. Tanner Humanities Center. In 1988 Obert Tanner and Sterling McMurrin were jointly awarded the first Utah Governor's Award in the Humanities.

As a summer lecturer and moderator for the Aspen Institute in the Humanities at Aspen, Colorado, beginning in the mid-1950s, McMurrin became acquainted with a great many officers of major corporations, labor unions, foundations, educational institutions, and state and federal governments. As a consequence of some of those encounters, McMurrin was invited to serve as a consultant for IBM and AT&T, as a trustee of the Carnegie Foundation, as a consultant to the Fund for the Advancement of Education, and as an adviser to the Princeton University Department of Philosophy.

In 1961 McMurrin was appointed to serve as United States Commissioner of Education in the administration of President John F. Kennedy. During the two years of his leadership in the U.S. Office of Education, he was in the forefront of federal efforts to assist the progress of integration in public schools across America. He addressed the need for better preparation of school teachers and greater rewards for their service, particularly in problem-plagued inner-city schools. He worked constructively with members of Congress, with other officials in various federal departments and agencies, and with representatives of the major national organizations concerned with education.

After leaving his position as U.S. Commissioner of Education and returning to the faculty of the University of Utah, McMurrin continued to serve the federal government in a number of special assignments related to workers' training and science and technology. For several years he was a consultant to the Committee for Economic Development (CED) and produced a series of reports on the importance of education for the economic well-being of the nation.

Sterling McMurrin's lifelong interest in religion is evidenced by his first employment. After completing his M.A. degree at the University of Utah, he was appointed a high school seminary teacher for the Mormon church, which led to his appointment as director of the LDS Institute of Religion at the University of Arizona from 1943 to 1945.

The importance of his service to the Mormon church, however, does not rest upon his performance as an employee of its educational program or as a holder of any ecclesiastical position. That importance grows out of his solidly grounded writings about the philosophical and theological foundations of Mormonism, as well as his highly creditable commentaries on the Mormon church through the years in response to frequent inquiries from reporters for national and international news media. While his comments to the media are on the public record, he also at times has supported the church in important ways that were, and will remain, confidential.

As a leading scholar in the field of philosophy, McMurrin continues to be widely sought as a lecturer. He has spoken at nearly a hundred universities and colleges from coast to coast and around the world. He was associated with Obert C. Tanner in establishing the world-renowned Tanner Lectures on Human Values.

Since their first meeting in the mid-1930s as students at the University of Utah, Sterling and Natalie, his wife for nearly sixty years, have been devoted companions. Together they have reared five children with whom they maintain strong ties of love and loyalty. They now enjoy the bountiful harvest of their productive lives of study and service to their family, to their community, and to their nation.

Preface

L. Jackson Newell

Enviably free. Among the qualities that characterize Sterling McMurrin's life and mind, perhaps the most notable is the freedom with which he has spoken his views on both the sacred and the profane. His intellectual integrity—coupled as it almost always is with his humane instincts and innate fairness—has simultaneously confounded and earned the respect of his critics in established institutions. It has also delighted his many friends in Utah, the nation, and around the world.

Spending his life in the service of three institutions—religion, government, and education—Sterling McMurrin has not only retained his independent judgment, but his observations on these institutions have become at once more stark and more understanding through the years. Thus, this former religion instructor and lay leader in the Mormon church, United States Commissioner of Education, and Distinguished Professor at the University of Utah has been admired and vilified—and frequently envied—by others who have led or served in these institutions.

It is no secret that Sterling McMurrin has few equals as a conversationalist and teller of stories. It is not surprising, therefore, that David Catron, then director of the University of Utah Press, and Dr. Stephen Hess, director of Media Services, approached the two of us in 1984 about the possibility of doing a book to be called *Conversations with Sterling McMurrin*. The press had recently published its successful *Conversations with Wallace Stegner* (1983; 2nd ed., 1990), and Catron and Hess thought we might do a similar volume. Across eight months Stegner and Richard Etulain had engaged in ten two-hour conversations and then published their well-known and respected book in less than three years.

McMurrin and I had been good friends before commencing this project, but I looked forward to getting to know his life and thought more intimately. I gradually discovered the full scope of his extraordinary experiences, and learned that no question posed to him is answered without lively detail. Nor is any discussion brief. We began by approaching his life and thought chronologically; at the end of ten conversations we had not yet gotten him through graduate school.

We conversed in Sterling's office in the early stages, but increasingly we worked at the McMurrins' home in Salt Lake City, and eventually even at their cabin on Kolob Plateau overlooking Zion National Park. At the beginning of each two-hour session, we set the tape recorder in motion and invariably continued for two hours—pausing only to turn or replace the audio cartridge. We had each tape transcribed promptly, and the written record grew steadily. Within a year it was clear that we had commenced a massive oral history project from which I would extract a book. Before we finished our formal conversations, we had engaged in nearly fifty two-hour recorded sessions, spanning eight years. The transcripts of these conversations constitute a stack in my study more than sixteen inches thick. This record will eventually be deposited with the McMurrin Collection in the archives of the University of Utah's Marriott Library.

As the years and our conversations progressed, three things stood out. First, the precision of Sterling's memory: I began as a skeptic, wondering how he could remember the details of a 1952 correspondence with Henry Eyring, or the names of people deep in his past who had played only passing roles in his experience. Early on I resolved to verify some of these details by going through his official papers to read documents or letters to which he made reference. I learned that his memory is astonishingly accurate. I continued to check historical details to insure the accuracy of this volume, but I rarely needed to make corrections.

Second, as our conversations evolved from one year to the next, so did my understanding of the forces that have shaped Sterling's ideas. As I gained greater insight concerning what questions to ask and where to probe, our explorations together went deeper and reached higher. If we had produced this book in two or three years, as originally hoped, it would have lacked much of the richness and texture I believe it now possesses.

Third, unlike many prominent citizens in their senior years, Sterling McMurrin has not become cautious about what he says or protective of his own work. Autobiographies, for instance, often get thinner as publication dates draw nearer—their authors paring back what they say to cloak their pasts in finery and mask their relationships with niceties. In contrast, Sterling has never ducked my most probing questions, nor exerted the slightest pressure on me to temper my editing of our manuscript or slant its substance in one direction or another.

What we have here, then, is a work of uncommon candor; the essence of a long and earnest conversation. I have extracted from the full record of our discussions those passages that are most pertinent to the interests of the general reader. While I have taken responsibility for content selection, we have worked together to refine the text. To illuminate the origins and evolution of McMurrin's thought, the fifteen chapters that follow are generally organized in chronological sequence.

This book, of course, is not the first place that conversations with Sterling McMurrin have been captured and presented to the public. Blake Ostler interviewed McMurrin concerning his views on history and philosophy for the *Seventh East Press*—an independent student newspaper at Brigham Young University—which appeared in the 11 January 1983 issue. The printing of that interview precipitated a crackdown on unofficial student newspapers by the BYU administration, and the closing of the *Seventh East Press* that spring. A description of the incident, together with an expanded version of the interview, appeared in the spring 1984 issue of *Dialogue: A Journal of Mormon Thought*.

More recently, Sterling and I engaged in a ninety-minute televised conversation aired on KUED-TV in 1989, and in a two-hour plenary session conversation at the Sunstone Symposium in Salt Lake City in August 1993. Laurie DiPadova Stocks interviewed McMurrin in a sequel to this conversation at the 1994 Sunstone Symposium. Both Sunstone events were aired live on KCPX-FM Radio.

Sterling McMurrin joins me in acknowledging the many individuals who have helped with the birthing of this book. David Catron and Stephen Hess, as noted above, broached the idea and were instrumental in getting us started. (Since their initial push, changes at the university press, both in personnel and editorial emphasis, convinced Sterling and me to pursue publication with Signature Books.) Janice Crellin skillfully transcribed most of our recorded conversations and assembled a working index for them. Marilyn Damron White invested hundreds of hours transcribing our more recent conversations, organizing the mass of material, and inveigling the computer to accept a seemingly endless string of editing refinements as McMurrin and I labored to eliminate overlapping segments and fill gaps in the flow of our original conversations. During the early years of this project, Ann Blanchard and Jacqueline Jacobsen were our respective assistants at the University of Utah. Each provided valuable support as we proceeded—often shifting other appointments or arranging our busy schedules so as to keep us going. As McMurrin and I moved on to other roles at the university, Jackie and Ann continued to encourage our progress with this work.

Many able people read chapters of this book in manuscript form and offered helpful observations for their improvement. They include Lowell L. Bennion, Joyce and Kenneth McDermott, Anthony W. Morgan, Linda K. Newell, Thomas D. Pederson, Katherine C. Reynolds, Karen I. Spear, David J. Sperry, and a number of my graduate students.

Five individuals read the entire manuscript and made especially valuable contributions to the final edition: Lavina Fielding Anderson, J. Boyer Jarvis, Trudy McMurrin, Laurie DiPadova Stocks, and Marilyn Damron White. This book has benefited greatly from their keen interest, candid suggestions, and seasoned passion for words and ideas. I take full responsibility for any remaining flaws in the work.

Our most heartfelt thanks go to Natalie Cotterel McMurrin and Linda King Newell, who often indulged us as we pursued this project and unfailingly encouraged us to carry on. Their positive influence is evident throughout our conversations.

Introduction
Sterling Moss McMurrin: A Philosopher in Action

L. Jackson Newell

Sterling M. McMurrin, a man of letters, has spent most of his life in the world of affairs. A distinguished professor of philosophy at the University of Utah for four decades, he held key academic leadership positions at this university both before and after his service as United States Commissioner of Education under President John F. Kennedy. I offer here an overview of Sterling McMurrin's life so that the reader will have a context for understanding our extended conversation in subsequent chapters.

McMurrin's paternal grandfather, Joseph W. McMurrin, was a noted Mormon orator and one of the Seven Presidents of the Seventy, a lifelong appointment in the Mormon hierarchy ranked just after the Quorum of the Twelve Apostles. He was at the height of his powers in the late 1920s when McMurrin was growing up. It was something of a shock to Sterling as a child, then, when his father told him of his solemn and decorous grandfather's 1885 gun battle with a deputy federal marshal in Salt Lake City.

Polygamy was still officially sanctioned and practiced by the Mormons at that time, and federal officers were pursuing the church's leaders. McMurrin's grandfather was then a bodyguard for the Mormon church president, John Taylor, who was in hiding. President Taylor was meeting secretly with his top assistants in Salt Lake City's Social Hall when Deputy U.S. Marshal Henry F. Collin appeared outside, prepared to make the arrest of his career. He encountered Joseph McMurrin, not for the first time, and their tempers flared. The two reached for their sidearms. McMurrin took three slugs and nearly died. Collin escaped unscathed; but fearing mob retaliation, he took refuge at the Fort Douglas army post on the east side of Salt Lake City (see entries for November 28, December 2, and December 8, 1885, in Journal History of the LDS church, microfilm, Marriott Library, University of Utah).

This incident, which reverberated in Utah's consciousness for decades, became a matter of national concern. Anticipating a Mormon uprising, the federal government strengthened its garrison at Fort Douglas.

Sterling McMurrin reflected recently on the impact this family revelation had on him as a small child: "From a kid's perspective, it's a story about a federal marshal trying to kill your grandfather because of his religion." He continued with a chuckle, "This tends to give you certain impressions about both the government and your religion."

This story provides a key to understanding McMurrin's eventful career: he served institutions—religious, governmental, and educational—in many ways, but especially by keeping his eyes on, and giving voice to, their essential values. He has always placed his hope in liberal education and his trust in individual freedom.

Now in his eighties, Utah's E. E. Ericksen Distinguished Professor of Philosophy and History, Emeritus, has retired from the university, but not from his habits of thinking and writing . . . nor from practical effort.

ORIGINS AND IDEAS

The third of four sons, Sterling Moss McMurrin was born in Woods Cross, Utah, just north of Salt Lake City, in 1914. His McMurrin grandfather was, in those years, a man of great stature in the Mormon hierarchy, a defender of the new faith. The McMurrin clan was very much a part of Utah's cultural and religious elite. Sterling's father, Joseph Jr., was a school teacher and probation officer, but Sterling characterized him as "a misplaced university professor." He loved good books, entertained diverse ideas and had his son reading Plato, Darwin, and Dante as a youth. He, himself, pursued a lifelong passion to reconcile the claims of reason and religion.

McMurrin described his mother, Gertrude Moss McMurrin, as "completely open-minded and approachable, a person whose company I always delighted in." She hailed from ranch country, though hardly from humble circumstances. Her father, William Moss, was co-founder and general manager of the Deseret Land and Live Stock Company, one of the largest and most successful ranching operations in the Great Basin. The Mosses were educated, practical people seasoned in the rough-and-tumble of frontier agriculture and business. A cattle baron who was also president of a bank in northern Utah, "Bill Moss was in charge wherever he went," his grandson recalls. "People stood back as he walked along the street."

McMurrin describes himself as growing up "half ranch kid, half city kid." At age nine he began wrangling horses for his Grandfather Moss, and two summers later he was pulling his own weight among the ranch hands of the far-flung cattle and sheep operation. He returned home each autumn—not when school started but after the cattle and sheep were brought down from their summer ranges in the high country.

From his early teens, McMurrin was completely at home with ranch hands, physical labor, and practical challenges, just as he was with books, ideas, and Utah's privileged class. His boyhood experience was both physically and intellectually robust. "I think it is true," he reflects, "that I grew up with an essentially critical, but not cynical, approach to the world."

Although McMurrin continued to work for the Deseret Live Stock Company each summer, his family moved to Los Angeles when he was fourteen, and he attended and graduated from Manual Arts High School. Asthma attacks threatened his health during his first year at the University of California at Los Angeles (UCLA). He returned, therefore, to the drier climate of his native state, where he enrolled at the University of Utah in the autumn of 1933. George Thomas, by then University of Utah president for twelve years, appointed him to work on a history of the university. Stimulated by Professor E. E. Ericksen, among others, McMurrin took his bachelor's degree in history and political science in 1936 and his master's in philosophy in 1937.

Sterling met Natalie Barbara Cotterel in the University of Utah library when they were both undergraduates. He was immediately taken with her, and they courted one another for several years. She converted to Mormonism, and church apostle David O. McKay married them in the Salt Lake temple on June 8, 1938. They have five children. Natalie has been central to Sterling's life and work for more than half a century.

During the seven years following receipt of his master's degree, McMurrin taught in the Mormon church's seminary and institute system, which has provided religious education for high school and college students as an adjunct to their secular studies since the 1930s. Students flocked to him, astonished by his theological knowledge and intellectual daring. His former seminary supervisor, Lynn Bennion, remembers McMurrin's classroom atmosphere: "No theological claim was too sacred to be challenged, and no idea was too wild to merit consideration. At the same time Sterling knew more about Mormon theology, and the whole history of Christianity, than anyone in our system, before or since" (conversation on October 22, 1987). J. Boyer Jarvis, a student of McMurrin's at the University of Arizona, has remarked to the same effect.

McMurrin's experience as a teacher in the Utah, Idaho, and Arizona seminaries led to his appointment as director of the LDS Institute of Religion across the street from the University of Arizona. While McMurrin's intellectual courage brought him increasingly into conflict with his ecclesiastical superiors, he began investing his summers in further graduate study in philosophy and religion at the University of Southern California. His escape from the tightening institutional church environment was in the making.

Approaching thirty, McMurrin took a leave from his educational position with the LDS church and devoted himself to full-time doctoral study at USC. He received his Ph.D. in May 1946. The preface to his dissertation—which explored the relationship between positivism and normative value judgments—revealed more than such documents ordinarily do about a scholar's philosophy. He began:

> The moral crisis that characterizes our time is . . . the wide disparity . . . between man's technical attainment in the control of his environment and the effectiveness of his moral and spiritual idealism. It is increasingly imperative that the conduct of men and nations be brought under the dominion of a moral ideal. As a practical issue, this is . . . a responsibility of religion, education, and politics. But the integration of fact and value, necessary to both personal and social character, demands a theoretical foundation which will give meaning and direction to practical effort ("Positivism and the Logical Meaning of Normative Value Judgments," p. 1).

In more than 250 articles, books, and essays on philosophy, education, and religion, McMurrin has continued to explore the themes manifest in this early study: Human institutions must advance human dignity and respect individuality. Ethics must keep pace with technology.

These ideas emerged and were nurtured by the circumstances of McMurrin's family, youth, and early career experiences, but the larger historical backdrop of his formative years should not be overlooked. During McMurrin's college and graduate school years, he witnessed the global depression, Nazi holocaust, fascist and communist totalitarianism, World War II, and the birth of the atomic age.

While eschewing affiliation with any particular school of philosophy, McMurrin is an existentialist without the angst. He has a tragic sense of history, fears for the human prospect, and writes and speaks doggedly in pursuit of his ideal of social justice. He values individuality, and he treasures liberal education as the best hope for liberating the human race from ignorance, bigotry, and violence. While he harbors no illusions about the future, McMurrin personally finds comedy in almost every situation—a gentle, ironic humor.

ACADEMIC CAREER

Even before receiving his doctorate, McMurrin was appointed to the philosophy faculty of the University of Southern California. After three years, however, his health again began to suffer from the California climate. The University of Utah beckoned once again, and he joined its faculty as professor of philosophy in the fall of 1948. There he taught, except for occasional short-term assignments, until 1988.

As a young philosophy professor at Utah, McMurrin enjoyed the same success—and controversy—that he had as a seminary teacher a decade earlier. He was an intellectual lightning rod from the start. Frequently invited to give public addresses and scholarly lectures, McMurrin addressed himself to a great variety of social and philosophical issues. Always concerned with human dignity and freedom, he became a spirited defender of academic freedom on campus and an early activist in the field of civil rights in the community. He spent the 1952-53 academic year on the east coast as a Ford Foundation Faculty Fellow, lecturing and pursuing scholarly interests at Columbia University, the Union Theological Seminary, and Princeton University.

In 1954 McMurrin co-edited *Contemporary Philosophy: A Book of Readings* with James L. Jarrett, and the following year he joined B. A. G. Fuller in expanding and rewriting the third edition of *A History of Philosophy*. The latter was published both as a single-volume and as a two-volume set, and appeared subsequently in Polish translation. By now, as we shall see, McMurrin was "deaning," and his energies were already being diverted from his scholarship. His internal struggle between ideas and action had been joined.

During the academic year 1957-58, however, another old theme resurfaced. McMurrin was invited to give a lecture on "The Philosophical Foundations of Mormon Theology" at Ohio State University. Published by the University of Utah Press in 1959, this treatise remains the most penetrating explanation of Mormon philosophy available. McMurrin extended this theme with a series of lectures in 1965 that resulted in the University of Utah Press publication later that year of *The Theological Foundations of the Mormon Religion*. It remained in print thirty years and is scheduled for republication by Signature Books.

Understanding and explaining Mormon theology was by no means the same thing as accepting that theology or supporting the policies of the Mormon church. For his persistent criticism of specific church practices, especially for its denial of priesthood ordination to males of African descent, McMurrin was regarded by many leaders and members as a dangerous heretic.

In 1954 a Mormon leader of McMurrin's congregation, encouraged from church headquarters, initiated excommunication proceedings (see "An Interview with Sterling M. McMurrin," *Dialogue,* Spring 1984, pp. 18-43; also "McMurrin's Heresies, History and Humor: A Conversation with Sterling McMurrin," *Sunstone,* April 1995, pp. 55-62). When David O. McKay, then president of the Mormon church, heard the news, he called McMurrin on the phone and arranged to meet him that same afternoon at the University Union. When the two men sat down, McKay exclaimed: "They can't do this to you. They can't *do* this to you! If they put you on trial, I will be there as the first witness in your behalf." After a long and cordial discussion, President McKay ended the conversation with heartfelt advice: "Sterling, you just think and believe as you please." Sterling did. The charges were dropped. And, through five successive Mormon presidents, the church has continued to endure McMurrin's criticism—and benefit from his loyalty. He remains a fierce defender of the LDS church, its leaders and members, except on specific matters of doctrine and practice where he differs in principle.

I think I have told enough of Sterling McMurrin's story to provide a sense of his character and style. He has a remarkable capacity to disagree without being disagreeable, to form authentic friendships and comfortable relationships with people of vastly differing perspectives. He has never eschewed controversy. These qualities continued to characterize him as he moved toward the center of American intellectual and political life. The crucible of his own culture and the American West had prepared him to move easily and effectively in wider and wider circles.

THE PATH TO WASHINGTON

Sterling McMurrin's success as a teacher, author, and social critic led inevitably to responsibilities in academic administration—as well as to teaching at higher and higher levels. The two sides of the man—the thinker and the actor—continued to vie with one another, and it was the combination of the two that propelled him to Washington.

Just six years after joining the University of Utah faculty, he was appointed dean of the College of Letters and Science, a position that he held until 1960, when he became vice-president for academic affairs. In these administrative posts, McMurrin delegated generously and reserved his own energies for setting directions and recruiting internationally respected scholars to the faculty. He created a university environment rich in academic freedom and intellectual opportunity.

Walter Paepcke, a wealthy Chicago business executive, established the Aspen Institute for Humanistic Studies in that future Colorado ski resort at about the same time that McMurrin was assuming his deanship at the University of Utah. Looking for a scholar-teacher who could help lead his executive seminar program for high public officials and prominent citizens, Paepcke had apparently been advised by mutual friend Meredith Wilson that McMurrin might be an ideal person. Wilson, then secretary of the Ford Foundation, had recruited McMurrin to the University of Utah faculty when he was dean there. Paepcke simply called McMurrin on the phone, interrupting a luncheon meeting, and secured his agreement to affiliate with the Aspen Institute.

From 1954 to 1962 Sterling, Natalie, and their children spent part of every summer at Aspen, where he led one group of distinguished leaders after another in reading classic texts and considering the saliency of ideas contained in them to contemporary national and world affairs. Just as he had entranced undergraduates, he now stimulated and prodded Walter Paepcke's invited guests: Supreme Court justices, Cabinet officers, foundation presidents, foreign ambassadors, U.S. diplomats, labor leaders and heads of international corporations. McMurrin made them think, and he made friends. Among many others, he formed lasting bonds with Walter Reuther, William Brennan, and Byron White, and got to know Eric Sevareid, Thurgood Marshall, and Russian physicist George Gamow. Attorney General Robert Kennedy proved a source of some irritation. His bare feet in the seminar buildings, McMurrin thought, took "Aspen's generally informal environment a step too far."

More completely at ease with ideas and with people of stature than ever, but largely unconscious of his notoriety, McMurrin was now acting on a national stage. In 1958 the Department of State invited him to go as a special envoy to Iran, where he spent five months as an adviser to the chancellor of the University of Tehran. His responsibilities were to work on stemming the tide of communism among the students by improving relations between them and the faculty and administration. Both before and after that sojourn, Columbia University had tried to lure him to New York with an endowed chair in philosophy in their Graduate School of Business. McMurrin was widely sought for advice in national policy circles concerning public education, higher education, and national human resource needs.

On the Wednesday night before John F. Kennedy's inauguration in

January 1961, McMurrin received a telephone call from Alvin Eurich, vice-president for educational programs at the Ford Foundation. Eurich explained that he and several colleagues had been asked by the new administration to propose someone to be United States Commissioner of Education. "I want to put you forth for that position and would like to know, first, whether you will accept it?" (John W. Gardner, who was then president of the Carnegie Corporation and the Carnegie Foundation, also nominated McMurrin.) McMurrin had never been active in politics, nor had he ever publicly advocated the election of any local or national candidate. Nonetheless, he told Eurich that if asked to serve he would do so. Because of his asthma condition he had not served in the military during World War II and, he explained later, he felt this would help to dispatch an obligation he owed his country.

The day of John F. Kennedy's inauguration, McMurrin received a telephone call from the new Secretary of Health, Education, and Welfare, Abraham Ribicoff. He told McMurrin of his wish to have the president appoint him Commissioner of Education and asked how soon he could come to Washington to talk it over.

In Washington, Ribicoff and McMurrin met briefly and quickly established rapport. Before they finished their initial meeting, Ribicoff sent a message to Ralph Dungan, JFK's special assistant for administrative appointments, who shortly arrived from the White House. He joined the interview with McMurrin, then asked him to step outside the room while he called President Kennedy.

Moments later Dungan and Ribicoff congratulated McMurrin and said the president would announce his appointment that evening. McMurrin was not asked if he would accept, nor was he told what his salary would be. But Ribicoff made it clear from the outset that HEW was a huge department and that he would run the health and welfare ends of it if McMurrin would take care of education. Said the former governor and future U.S. Senator from Connecticut: "Sterling, let's give them hell: and if it doesn't work out, you can go back to teaching philosophy and I'll go back to selling neckties."

The commissioner-elect went to work immediately—commuting weekly to and from Salt Lake City. It was all informal at first, of course, until after Senate confirmation—which did not occur until April due to the flood of nominations from the new administration.

When the confirmation hearing finally commenced, Senator Joseph S. Clark of Pennsylvania asked McMurrin if, as a Mormon, he could support desegregation in the public schools. He responded: "I'd like the committee to know that I do not agree with the policies of the Mormon church with respect to Negroes, and I have made my position very clear to the leadership of the Mormon church. I'm 100 percent in favor of desegregated schools." Clark and others were highly supportive of McMurrin, and his appointment won swift approval from the Senate. And, indeed, desegregation of education, the equalization of educational opportunity, and federal aid to public schools were priorities McMurrin pursued vigorously as commissioner.

The National Education Association was at odds with the new commissioner from the start, but did not oppose his appointment. The conflicts were predictable, especially because of McMurrin's advocacy of merit pay for teachers. Further, he had come out of higher education, he had no previous relationship or membership in the National Education Association, and he did not intend to continue the rather cozy relationship that had long existed between the NEA and the U.S. Commissioner's office. McMurrin did not know until later that one of President Kennedy's criteria for selecting a new commissioner was that he or she *not* come from NEA's membership.

Setting the sights for New Frontier and Great Society education policy, and illustrative of McMurrin's relationship with the NEA, was an early incident involving Admiral Hyman G. Rickover. In the wake of the Soviet Union's launching of the Sputnik satellite in 1957, the father of America's nuclear Navy had become concerned about the state of U.S. education and took a series of trips abroad to compare our system with those of other nations. He wrote extensively about what he regarded as the evils of progressive education and attracted much attention with *Education and Freedom* in 1959 and *Swiss Schools and Ours: Why Theirs Are Better* in 1962.

In the midst of all this, Congressman John E. Fogarty, who chaired the House Appropriations Subcommittee on Labor and Education, invited Rickover to state his views for the benefit of Congress. The admiral did not think American education was competing with Soviet education, and he launched a volley of criticisms at our system. Later Congressman Fogarty asked Commissioner McMurrin for his views on the condition of American education, pointing out that Congress already had such a statement from Admiral Rickover, as well as from McMurrin's predecessor, Lawrence Derthick.

Pleased to respond, McMurrin had begun preparing his thoughts for the assignment when his deputy commissioner approached him and said that the NEA and the Office of Education, as with past assignments of this type, would work together through a joint committee to compose the requested document. Shocked, McMurrin replied, "If it is my views

Congressman Fogarty wants, then it will be my views, and no one else's, that he gets." Reminding the commissioner that the deadline for submission was short, his aide pushed a bit further, suggesting that McMurrin could probably use some help. "I'll have it on time," McMurrin declared, and he did.

McMurrin wrote the essay longhand in one evening, had it typed by his secretary, and then spent a few days tinkering with it as his schedule permitted. He delivered the statement to the House Appropriations Committee, and Congressman Fogarty ordered the U.S. Government Printing Office to publish 100,000 copies. An abbreviated version appeared almost immediately in the *Saturday Review* as "A Crisis of Conscience: A Report on the State of American Education" (September 16, 1961, pp. 58-78).

"A Crisis of Conscience" was pure McMurrin, and it set the tone and framed the agenda for federal education policy during both the Kennedy and Johnson administrations. "In education we are facing a crisis of conscience and collectively we are experiencing a sense of national guilt," he charged:

> We cannot deny that today we would command far more knowledge and have far more creativity, civic character, and national strength if our schools had been more rigorous in their intellectual discipline and . . . more adequately structured to the needs of our society. We have with lavish prodigality wasted the talent and energy of countless persons.

He said that the aims of education cannot be defined in narrow or nationalistic terms, nor does education serve national security primarily through technological and scientific training. Without a "world-minded" citizenry, McMurrin wrote, "we cannot hope to satisfy the obligation of world leadership that history has conferred upon us." He called for better education across the board, urging that we:

> . . . guard against the tendency to suppose that our national well-being is served primarily by advances in technology, however important and timely these may be. . . . The study of politics, history, and philosophy is fundamental to our cultural life, and no nation can achieve a lasting strength unless its character is expressed in great literature, art, and music.

McMurrin called upon the federal government to provide sound leadership for American education "as well as material support," while not interfering with the tradition of local and state control over curricula and teaching. He proposed a new policy of *general* federal financial support for education, but one that avoided national control of schooling or educational and economic planning—which might infringe upon individual choice of educational pursuits.

Specifically, McMurrin offered this agenda for improving American educational practice:

★Raise expectations for student performance, with more emphasis on solid material, less on "trivial studies and activities."

★Set new standards of teacher preparation, including a bachelor's degree in liberal education prior to specializing in teacher education.

★Select teachers according to higher intellectual standards, including stronger preparation in the subjects to be taught.

★Bring teacher education into the mainstream of university intellectual life, rather than keeping it apart.

★Base teacher education on a wide range of academic disciplines, relying less on psychology as the knowledge base for the profession.

Finally, he admonished the nation to "turn a deaf ear to those reactionaries among us who are forever insisting that we abandon our democratic ideal and model our education on the aristocratic patterns of some European nations" (p. 78).

This essay was the expression of one mind; it was anything but the product of a committee. The commissioner sought consciously to put the education of teachers, and educational standards, in the forefront and talked chiefly about ends. He left economic issues like teacher salaries to follow as means. It was not a statement the NEA would have made. It appears that the content of the essay, more than the rebuff of their offer to help write it, put McMurrin in increasing conflict with this union.

"A Crisis of Conscience," republished in several places, won laurels from policy makers across the country and inspired much debate and a fair amount of federal legislation. Like the president he served, McMurrin's ideas were bold and clear, his language graceful and compelling.

Telling the story of McMurrin's *actions* as U.S. Commissioner of Education and assessing his influence on educational policy will be my task in a subsequent publication. Here I am concerned chiefly with his *ideas*, where they came from, and how the philosopher and the actor in McMurrin competed for his energies. Suffice it to say here, he worked diligently for higher standards in education and teacher preparation, general federal aid to education, desegregation of schools and colleges, and the simplification of the federal education establishment. The NEA objected to much of what he tried to do, with comparatively little effect.

RETURN TO UNIVERSITY LIFE

After less than two years as U.S. Commissioner, McMurrin submitted his resignation. Several factors seemed to have played into this decision. Still in his forties, McMurrin had children in school, and he and Natalie did not enjoy having their lives scattered across the country from the Potomac to the Great Salt Lake. He also missed teaching and writing, having been in one administrative post or another since assuming the deanship at the University of Utah in 1954. To go home to Salt Lake City would be to go home to his scholarship for the first time in many years.

The catalyst for McMurrin's decision was HEW Secretary Ribicoff's announcement that he planned to resign as Secretary of the Department of Health, Education, and Welfare in order to run for the U.S. Senate in Connecticut. McMurrin and Ribicoff had worked well together, and that relationship would clearly be missed. In late summer 1962 McMurrin announced that he would also be leaving the administration. Secretary Ribicoff objected to his decision strenuously but fruitlessly.

Abraham Ribicoff had advocated splitting HEW apart and creating a new Cabinet-level Department of Education. He intended to propose legislation to achieve this change and told McMurrin that he expected the president to appoint him U.S. Secretary of Education if the Cabinet-level department was established. McMurrin strongly favored Cabinet-level status for education but had no interest in moving to such a post himself.

Before leaving office, McMurrin had a session with Ralph Dungan, still President Kennedy's appointments chief. Dungan said the president wanted McMurrin to suggest the names of a few people who might be qualified to succeed him. The retiring commissioner gave Dungan three names in rank order: Francis Keppel, professor of art and dean of faculty of education at Harvard, James E. Allen, New York Commissioner of Education, and Harold Howe III, superintendent of a New York school district.

The degree to which McMurrin's judgment continued to affect federal education policy throughout the 1960s is illustrated by subsequent events. The three distinguished educators he nominated turned out to be his three successors as commissioner. President Kennedy appointed Frank Keppel (1962-65); President Johnson appointed Harold Howe (1965-69); and President Nixon appointed James Allen (1969-70).

Sterling and Natalie McMurrin left Washington, D.C., in September 1962, resuming their lives in Salt Lake City and his professorship at

the University of Utah. It was not, however, to be a quiet period for
them. He turned down a number of college and university presidencies,
endowed professorships, and board memberships—including a high
position with the Ford Foundation. But he accepted appointments to a
number of national and international commissions for the improvement
of education and human resource development. For fifteen years
McMurrin was affiliated with the Committee for Economic Development as an adviser on research and director of the committee's projects
on education. During this period he was also a trustee of the Carnegie
Foundation.

In 1964 McMurrin was appointed E. E. Ericksen Distinguished
Professor of Philosophy at the University of Utah. But he was inveigled
back into the administration in 1965, presiding over the institution's
educational affairs as provost. Within a few months of this appointment,
however, Henry Eyring, dean of the Graduate School, announced his
retirement, and McMurrin let the president know that he would prefer
to serve in that capacity. He never liked budgets or personnel administration, and the move to the graduate dean's office in 1966 relieved him
of those burdens, by and large. He served in that role for twelve years,
teaching a course every academic term throughout this period.

I came to the University of Utah in the middle of McMurrin's years
as graduate dean. I was a youthful newcomer as dean of Liberal Education and my introduction to McMurrin and his thinking was twofold.
First, I remember receiving "Communique No. 4" to all faculty from the
graduate dean. I was taken aback by the imposing title of McMurrin's
proclamation and remarked to that effect to a veteran faculty colleague.
"Oh, that's just Sterling having fun," was the quick reply. "He seldom
writes a memo, but when he does he makes the most of it."

My second encounter with McMurrin was over a piece I wrote
about the aims and purposes of liberal education. He read it and sent me
a critique (see letter dated May 5, 1975, University of Utah Archives,
Box 6338 H265). I still call his letter my "Well now, young man"
initiation. McMurrin pointed out that I had pitted liberal education and
career education against one another—a most unfortunate mistake. The
reasons for liberal education go far beyond economic considerations, my
senior colleague pointed out, but critical thinking, broad understanding,
and other values associated with liberal education do, in fact, have
enormous economic benefits. And these benefits accrue both to the
individual and to the society. McMurrin, of course, was right on all
accounts.

As graduate dean, McMurrin pioneered a process for combining the use of internal committees and external scholars for evaluating the quality of graduate programs and academic departments. This method played a major role in raising the stature of the University of Utah, and it has been widely emulated by research universities throughout the nation. He retired from the deanship in 1978 but remained active in the history department as the E. E. Ericksen Distinguished Professor until 1988.

RETROSPECTIVE THOUGHTS

As he looks back over his career, McMurrin has said on a number of occasions that he regrets having spent "so damn much time in administration." Then why did he spend more than twenty years at high levels of leadership? I have no doubt that he always enjoyed being in the thick of university, state, or national issues. While it is true that he never enjoyed the routine acts of administration—directing the work of other people, building and presiding over budgets, and writing memoranda—he very much enjoys being in a position to formulate broad policies and cut through bureaucratic nonsense. And, unquestionably, he enjoyed the tangible benefits of administrative office: highly skilled assistants, discretionary funds, and a forum from which to affect university and community directions and values.

Sterling McMurrin is clearly a man of quick and independent intellect, a philosopher by nature and disposition. He lives in a world of ideas, he thinks in terms of principles and ideals, and, beyond the sheer force of his mind and personality, he has never been oriented toward, or particularly good at, practical politics. But he is a builder of institutional sagas, a steady and felicitous voice who reminds members and leaders alike that educational and religious organizations exist not to perpetuate themselves but to advance knowledge, support learning, and promote human dignity.

A prolific lecturer, writer, and teacher, McMurrin has never thought of himself as anything but a professor. A professor doing a stint in administration much of the time, but a professor still. As his administrative career wound down, his scholarship picked up significantly, lending further credence to the depth of his professorial identity. Since 1980 he has written or co-authored two books on philosophy and religion (*Religion, Reason and Truth: Essays in the Philosophy of Religion* and, with O. C. Tanner and Lewis M. Rogers, *Toward Understanding the New Testament*), written and edited several other volumes, and published dozens of articles. The nature of the influence and leadership that McMurrin exercised throughout his career, the scholar-in-action who forged institutions primarily through the strength of his ideas—and his courage in expressing and acting on them—continues to have enormous appeal. To whatever extent this kind of leadership ever flourished, however, it is clearly more difficult now than in the past. Bureaucracies are bigger, hierarchies are more complex, and external regulations are more confining than ever before—making leadership increasingly mechanical, reactive, and politically driven.

In universities this shift has made deans, vice-presidents, and presidents increasingly career administrators once they are appointed. They must still start as academics; but once in administration, the die is often cast within two or three years, after which a return to teaching and writing is increasingly difficult and eventually unlikely. As a result, their orientation shifts inevitably away from education and knowledge. The university administration itself, and the advancement of their own careers, become the ends. The parallels with contemporary church leadership—Mormon, Protestant, or Catholic—are compelling.

A careful analysis of McMurrin's leadership makes it clear not only that his career peaked in a different era, but, more importantly, that he was able to orchestrate his administrative appointments in such a way as to occupy those rare positions such as graduate dean where he could still keep the real ends of education—thinking, teaching, and writing—at the forefront. Leaders with McMurrin's orientation and temperament are clearly needed in all institutions today, religious, educational and governmental. The question is whether the evolution of these institutions has significantly reduced the probability of the emergence of leaders who possess a moral vision . . . and retain the capacity to act on it.

Contributing no doubt to Sterling McMurrin's success in keeping two kinds of lives going simultaneously, one of reflection and one of action, were his powerful childhood heroes and experiences. His grandfathers flourished in sharply contrasting walks of life, he revered them both, and as a teenager he fully tasted each way of embracing the world. Man of ideas, man of affairs: McMurrin refused to choose one over the other. At the age of eighty-two, he is writing books and essays in Salt Lake City and breeding horses in St. George.

CONCLUSION

From his earliest adult experiences and professional writing, Sterling McMurrin was drawn to the clash between authentic individuality and institutional loyalty. The moral and spiritual idealism about which he continues to speak and write is prompted by a deeply felt concern about a widening chasm between actual community, corporate and organizational practices, and those conditions that advance human dignity and individual liberty. In McMurrin's view, the unfortunate convergence of increasing organizational size and rising technological complexity has pushed our major social institutions further and further from ethical accountability for their actions and, consequently, diminished the realm within which individuals can make and execute moral judgments of their own.

The development of moral and ethical principles, therefore, and the critique of institutional behavior, have interested and concerned McMurrin throughout his life. Further, education and religion, the chief institutions that have conveyed moral ideals among past generations (and powerfully influenced McMurrin in his youth), have been noticeably weakened in their moral influence throughout the twentieth century.

This schism between technology and morality, between organizational conduct and organizational ideals, was the force that animated McMurrin's protest of the Mormon church's earlier proscription of priesthood ordination to males of African descent and that drove his efforts to reform American education and religion. Neither religion nor education has been spared the awful dichotomies of displaced institutional values and bureaucratic abominations, but McMurrin has remained devoted consistently to the improvement of both of these institutions—to the end that they might make their badly needed offerings to a society he sees in serious decline.

Sterling M. McMurrin's lifelong intellectual leadership springs from strongly held and clearly stated ideas about human nature, formal education, and social organizations. Since his early adulthood, he has devoted himself to the refinement of religion, education, and government. Sorting out ends and means within his own cultural heritage as a youth and as a young scholar put a distinctive stamp on his leadership that has served him and his institutions well. He has never seen himself as a servant of the institutions themselves. Rather, McMurrin has been, and continues to be, a trustee of the ideals they were created to advance. In the fifteen chapters that follow we will explore in conversation the themes identified here, as well as a wide variety of events that have shaped and punctuated Sterling McMurrin's beliefs, thoughts, and actions.

1.
Growing Up Moss and McMurrin

Newell: Sterling, you describe yourself as having been both a city kid and a ranch kid. How so?

McMurrin: Well, my father, Joseph W. McMurrin, Jr., was from the city, and my mother, Gertrude Moss McMurrin, was from the country, and from the time of my birth in 1914 until I was in college, I lived part of the year in the city going to school and part of the year—summers, often encroaching upon school time in both spring and fall—I lived on a ranch associating with sheep, cattle, and horses.

So you led a double life?

That's right. It *was* a double life. And I've never entirely outgrown it. My father was very much an urban person. My three brothers and I—no sisters—were like my mother, at home in both city and country.

What city was that?

Ogden, Utah, in my very early years, and then Los Angeles—in its better days. My father was a teacher at Ogden High School—completely an urban man, as I said. In the late twenties our family moved to Los Angeles, where he was a probation supervisor, first for the state of California and later for Los Angeles County.

Then the ranch belonged to your mother's people?

My mother's father, William Moss, and his father were the chief founders of the Deseret Live Stock Company, a huge ranching operation—the largest in this part of the country. It was founded in 1891 and embraced a considerable number of large ranches. Except for a very short time when he was on an LDS mission in England, my grandfather was the general manager of the company until just before he died in 1933 at the age of seventy-eight. The central or home ranch is now owned by the LDS church.[1] It was an enormous sheep and cattle

---

1. This Home Ranch still includes 220,000 acres in northeastern Utah. Bought by the LDS church in 1983, it was recognized nationally as a

operation, and that's where I was reared during the summer season every year until I was twenty. The "home ranch" was really home to me—and still is.

What did you take from those years on the ranch? What effect did they have on your later life?

Experience like that keeps a person close to nature, close to the real world, in a way that urban life doesn't. It taught me the lessons you learn only from really hard work. We all had to work from as early as I can remember—you know, kid's work, but real work. When I was nine, I started to do ranch jobs for a few days at a time that would ordinarily be given to a man. When I was ten, it stepped up to a few more days at a stretch. Then when I was eleven, I was doing a man's job full time. One of the benefits of that, of course, was that I got a man's wages. It was two dollars a day plus room and board while I was nine and ten; but when I was eleven, I got the full ranch hand's wage—two-fifty a day. There I was, an eleven-year-old kid with a bank account. In those days a dollar would go a long way. If you wrote out a check for a dollar, it would last you about as long as a hundred dollars would last you today. I would accumulate well over a hundred dollars during a summer. That meant I could buy some new clothes in the fall and have some spending money for a bicycle, a baseball, or a ball mitt and funds for recreation until the next summer.

This work and pay made you partially self-sufficient, even at an early age. Can you characterize the life you had there or the work you were doing?

Well, as a kid, I was involved to a considerable extent in the sheep end of the Deseret Live Stock Company. Even a child can help to corral sheep and work with them and get dust in his hair and his eyes and mouth. Deseret Live Stock was heavily involved with sheep. At times it had eighty thousand head running in herds of 2,800 to 3,200. Sheep, in many ways, are more interesting than cattle—not as smart as cattle, but they have better memories. It was an exciting time for kids—shearing in the spring, then the fall drive when they're separated, some being driven in herds to the winter ranges, others shipped off for sale.

The Live Stock's winter range was in Skull Valley, Utah, where

---

model cattle ranch, receiving U.S. President George Bush's "Take Pride in America Award" in 1989. It includes a game preserve for buffalo, elk, moose, deer, and other large animals. See Jean Ann McMurrin, *The Deseret Live Stock Company: A Brief History, 1891-1991* (Woodruff, UT: Deseret Land and Livestock, 1991), 1-11; *Arizona Republic*, Chart, Sunday, June 30, 1991, 5.

there was a large ranch and extensive range land. The Deseret Live Stock Company purchased from the LDS church the town and holdings at Iosepa, after the church's Skull Valley Polynesian colony was abandoned. The summer sheep range was over two hundred miles east in the Wasatch Mountains—the area known as Monte Cristo and Lost Creek. The shearing corral was a huge operation three miles west of the Wahsatch Station on the Union Pacific Railroad, about twelve miles this side of Evanston, Wyoming, at the head of Echo Canyon. I don't know for sure how many people worked with the sheep at shearing time—probably about ninety altogether. There were twenty-two shearers with power-driven equipment. I doubt that even Australia or New Zealand had larger shearing operations than that. I understand that it was the largest in the United States.

Moving sheep all the way from Skull Valley up into the Monte Cristo country and back each summer was a major operation. I remember herding sheep along the south end of the Great Salt Lake, right through where the Salt Lake International Airport is now. This would have been during the early 1920s. There were a couple of small hangars there with two small biplanes in them. It was a rare thing to see an airplane in those days. We climbed up and looked in through the windows to see them.

I was never seriously involved with the sheep trailing, however, because by the time I got old enough to be really useful, most of the transportation was by rail from Skull Valley up to Wahsatch and return.

Did you work in other ranch operations as a teenager?

After age eleven, yes. It was on the cattle end of the operation—fixing fences, chasing stray cattle, wrangling horses, and especially putting up hay. The company had many thousands of acres of hay for winter feeding of cattle. I even worked on a surveying crew. The main cattle range was in Utah, running roughly from Echo up the Union Pacific Railroad to the Wyoming border—even over it a little—but mostly running along the border toward Woodruff, Utah, and then cutting back up into the mountains toward Ogden—an enormous operation. I don't know how many acres the ranching operation covered, all told, but up there it went into five counties. The winter sheep range in Skull Valley and Cedar Mountain was also very extensive. I've heard estimates all the way from three-quarters of a million to a million acres, including grazing rights on public land. In some places the company owned every other section—like a checkerboard—so it was a much larger operation than simply the land owned outright. The company owned the sections where there was water so that nobody else had any inclination to homestead the dry sections.

You're talking about a huge business operation.

I don't know much about the finances, but of course you're right. The company acquired the land by accretion, a little like the movies where a big outfit takes over small outfits. When I rode through the range with my grandfather, he would often show me the remnants of ranches—remnants of ranch buildings after the sheepherders had trashed the buildings for firewood, tops of posts sticking out of the ground. I remember him saying on one occasion, "That's where old Sutton had his ranch. These are the remains of his corrals." Anyway, to make a long story short, that's what I did and where I was much of the first twenty years of my life.

Sterling, were you close to your brothers during these years?

Oh yes, we were all in it together—brothers, cousins, uncles. Blaine and Keith are older and Harold is younger. We all followed the same pattern. Two or three people owned most of the stock in the Deseret Live Stock Company: mainly my grandfather and his cousin James H. Moyle. Of course, other relatives and friends bought in. My mother's mother, Grace Ann Hatch Moss, had Hatch relatives who owned stock. Grandfather lived in Woods Cross, just north of Salt Lake in Davis County, and most of the stockholders were relatives and friends who lived in Davis County.

What did you learn growing up in two environments that were so completely different?

Well, living life on the ranch in the summer and in town in the winter I noticed that people reared in rural areas are more conservative in matters of morals than those in urban areas. Ranch kids didn't use as much foul language. They were not so fascinated by violence and pornography. Of course in those days we had no TV, and the movies were in their infancy. The closest I ever came to pornography was the lingerie section of the Sears-Roebuck catalog, which was much tamer then than now. I was reared among ranch hands, some of whom had lived all over the country. There were occasional dirty songs; but by and large their language was cleaner than what one finds in many urban settings.

Did you miss much by being away from your school friends every summer?

By being up on the ranch all summer, I always had to pick up with my school friends again in the fall, if they were still around. We'd start playing sandlot baseball in the spring as soon as the mud dried, but summers were when kids got really serious about baseball—played for hours at a time. I missed much of this. I was either gone or would go the very next day after school ended in the spring.

Your grandfathers were a study in contrast. Joseph W. McMurrin was a man of the cloth—a Mormon church authority, and William Moss was a man of affairs—an influential businessman. They must have made very different impressions on you.

Well, I was definitely closer to my Grandfather Moss, owing especially to those long summers on the ranch and frequent visits to his home in Woods Cross, where I was born. Grandfather McMurrin was a member of the First Council of the Seventy of the LDS church, one of the Seven Presidents of the Seventy.[2] In those days these seven men had far more status than the present Seventy have in the leadership of the church. When I was five, my grandfather became president of the California Mission, which included California, Arizona, and Nevada, before there were local organizations in those states. California and Arizona especially were very important places for the church. He was president from 1919 until his health failed. He was released as mission president in 1931 or 1932 but stayed in California and died in Los Angeles a few months later. Except when I was very young, the only times I even saw him before we moved to California were when he returned to Salt Lake City for church conferences or other business. When he came to Ogden, it was very much like having a visiting church authority in our home.

When my grandfather was in Salt Lake City for meetings, my father would take me and the others with him to Salt Lake on the electric interurban line, the Bamberger, so we could hear Grandfather speak in general conference which was, then as always, held in early April and October. He would usually meet us afterward and take us over to the

---

2. The ecclesiastical hierarchy of the Church of Jesus Christ of Latter-day Saints (Mormon) in Joseph W. McMurrin's day consisted of the first-ranked First Presidency (the president of the church with a first and a second counselors), the second-ranked Quorum of the Twelve Apostles, headed by the senior apostle, and the third-ranked First Council of the Seventy, consisting of seven presidents ranked by seniority. In 1976 the First Council of the Seventy was dissolved and replaced by the First Quorum of the Seventy, consisting of a potential seventy members headed by the seven-man Presidency of the First Quorum of the Seventy. Joseph McMurrin was sustained (approved by a vote of a semiannual general conference) as one of the seven presidents on October 5, 1897, when he was thirty-nine. This appointment was a full-time, lifetime "calling."

Hotel Utah for lunch.

Do you have many personal memories of him?

Those conference talks made a great impression on me. Grandfather was a very powerful figure, a tremendous force in the Mormon church, and a very influential orator. Those were the days before microphones and loudspeakers, radio, and television. Oratory really counted for something, and my grandfather was a power. He would move the audience from tears to laughter. This doesn't really happen anymore, you know; there simply aren't people in the church now who understand the power of the spoken word and how to use it like my grandfather, B. H. Roberts, J. Golden Kimball, and others of that time. Conferences in the Mormon church in those days were really great, moving experiences.

A lot of the power came from the spontaneity of the speakers?

Of course it did. It's hard not to feel manipulated by a text that someone sat down and prepared in cold blood, thinking about the effect it will have. But in those days before radio and television, it was all spontaneous—the speaker developing an idea as it came to him, the audience following along, their own eagerness and understanding inspiring the speaker and his own skills and power and the fresh emotion of the moment further captivating the audience. It would have been outrageous for a person to read his sermon or even to use notes. That just wasn't done. The speaker was supposed to be moved by the Spirit; and if he wrote his stuff and read it, this would be an indication that the Spirit wasn't in the picture. I mean that quite seriously.

And they were really *moved* in no uncertain terms, both speaker and congregation. The great oratory of these earlier years has been replaced by the boredom of prepared texts and teleprompters. There isn't the powerful message and the tremendous emotional impact on the people that there once was.

So you knew your grandfather mainly as a public figure?

Yes, but I don't want to imply that it was a distant or impersonal relationship. My Grandfather McMurrin would always send a dollar bill to each grandchild on his or her birthday. A dollar bill was a lot of money in those days. I'll tell you a funny story. When I was in about the sixth grade, one of my teachers, who I presume was a Mormon—although it never occurred to me to even wonder whether my teachers were Mormons or not—told me that she would like me to write my term paper about my Grandfather McMurrin. I wrote to him about the assignment and asked him to send me information about his life. He wrote back, included a dollar bill, and said, "This is for writing to me. You are the first grandchild who ever wrote me a letter."

Your writing career received encouragement from the very beginning! How did the composition turn out?

He wrote, "I don't think it's a good idea to write about me because I'm not important enough for that, but there's a young man visiting me who is important, and his name is John A. Widtsoe."[3] He gave me a lot of information about John A. Widtsoe, and I wrote my theme on him. He had recently been president of the University of Utah and was then a brand-new apostle. Despite this diverting of my intentions, I had a great deal of affection for my grandfather, great admiration for him. My father was very close to him, and I learned a great many things from him about church affairs.

The McMurrin family closeness wasn't just sentiment. It was almost tribal. My Grandfather McMurrin and my grandmother, Mary Ellen Hunter McMurrin, had seven children. Ultimately all of them followed their parents to California. At one time, all of my aunts and uncles and all of their children lived within the city of Los Angeles. My own family moved to Los Angeles in 1928, when I was fourteen. In California I became much closer to my grandfather and better acquainted with his thought and attitudes. In California he *was* the Mormon church.

So that was more an intellectual relationship, in contrast to the task-oriented relationship with your Grandfather Moss?

That oversimplifies my relationship with my Grandfather Moss a bit. My relation with him was very intimate, partly because I spent so much time with him but mainly because he was a remarkable human being. He and his son, my Uncle Ralph, who was foreman of the cattle ranches, were John Wayne types. They were big men, tremendously powerful in their influence on people—models of integrity. I don't know what your image of a businessman is, Jack, but there was my grandfather—a rancher, head of an enormous agribusiness operation, and also president of a bank from the day it was organized until the day he died. He kept the bank solvent during the Great Depression. He was very tough, a person of remarkable integrity and equally remarkable generosity. No one ever approached him in need without receiving assistance.

---

3. John A. Widtsoe, born January 31, 1872, in Norway, was ordained an LDS apostle in 1921 at age forty-nine and died in Salt Lake City on November 29, 1952.

I was present several times when women in Davis County came to my grandfather needing money because their husbands were going to have operations or something and asked him to buy their stock in the company. He just gave them whatever they needed and told them to keep their stock so they'd have some income in the future.

And he was rigorous in matters of morals. We might be on horseback or in a pickup truck, and he would suddenly say, "Now, don't you ever take a nickel that doesn't belong to you." That kind of talk can have a tremendous impact on a young kid, you know.

He wasn't a Mormon ecclesiastical officer, of course, like your Grandfather McMurrin. What was his relation to the church?

Oh, he was a believing Mormon, but he didn't wear his religion on his sleeve as some do. His Mormonism was simply an inherited property, like the color of his eyes. It was just unthinkable that he could be anything else. He was a genuinely devout person. I'll just give you one example. I worked with Everett Cooley to collect the papers of the Deseret Live Stock Company for the University of Utah Library. The minutes of the early years show that before it declared dividends, the company paid tithing on its profits. I guess the stockholders paid tithing on their dividends, too, so the church probably collected twice.

But the church didn't own him. My grandmother insisted that he go on a mission after his children were getting along. Missionaries were often married men in those days. He was well-to-do, so there were no financial problems with serving a mission for a couple of years. I'm not really sure why he agreed to go.

He didn't want to, I take it, but perhaps his leaving was the only form of birth control your grandmother knew!

You're probably right! He went to England, and he didn't like it one bit. I have a letter that he wrote home to my grandmother. He said, "Dear Sister Moss"—married couples often called each other by their surnames then, you know—"I find no satisfaction or anything to be desired in missionary work . . . and I am disapointed [sic] although I am not surprised for it is just what I antispated [sic]." He just wanted to come home and get back to the sheep, cattle, and horses.

Well, now, we'll test my theory. Did she send him the money to come home on?

Absolutely not. She didn't send him the money, so he stayed there to finish his mission. After he came home, he served for several years as bishop of West Bountiful Ward. Thereafter he was always called "the Bishop." He was a great man, in my opinion. Beyond my own parents, he was the main influence on me.

Back to your Grandfather McMurrin for a moment. You said he had enormous influence on the LDS church. What ideas or principles were particularly important to him? What did he stand for as a leader?

Well, he was probably best known for his power and influence as a missionary. He had been involved in missionary activities for the church before he became president of the California Mission. In fact, that was the major assignment for the Seventies in those days. He had been either president or counselor to the president of the European Mission as a younger man and had worked for the church all of his life. As a matter of fact, he was one of the stone masons who helped construct the Salt Lake temple. He simply grew up with the church, but it was missionary activity that occupied most of his interests.

Anything more on the personal side of his life?

Perhaps I should tell you of his run-in with a federal marshal. I didn't ever hear my grandfather comment on this, but my father told me of it, and it is in the histories of Utah and the church. The newspapers of the time were full of it. It happened in November 1885 when my father was about eight years old.

Just five years before the Woodruff Manifesto officially ending polygamy, then.

Yes, when things were very hot between the church and the government. My grandfather was not a polygamist. Neither of my grandfathers was, but three of my four great-grandfathers had two wives each. A deputy federal marshal named Henry F. Collin was snooping around identifying polygamists for prosecution; and he and my grandfather, who was a bodyguard of sorts for the First Presidency, apparently went the rounds—nothing physical, I gather, but some pretty rough words. Apparently it was understood by both men that the next time they saw one another they would finish it off. And the next time they encountered each other was at the old Social Hall that used to stand just south of Hansen Planetarium on State Street, where Social Hall Avenue is now. The First Presidency, who were all, of course, on the under-ground—hiding out from the feds who wanted them for polygamy—were having a secret meeting; and Grandfather was standing guard at the rear of the Social Hall when Collin came along.

The showdown . . .

Exactly. It appears that they both went for their guns, but Collin pulled a dirty trick. He had his hand on the pistol in his coat pocket and simply shot through his coat, fired two or three rounds. My grandfather later said that he shot at Collin, too, but his gun had not been fired. I presume he intended to fire but was a little slow on the draw. He was shot two or three times in the body and they carried him to his house on Sixth South, between State and Main, expecting him to die. He was administered to—given a blessing of healing by the Mormon elders; and he lived. That has been regarded by some ever since as one of the miracles of the church, because he was very near death. He carried those bullets in his body for the rest of his life.

That story must have made quite an impression on you as a boy!

I suppose it did. From a boy's perspective, it's a tale about your government trying to kill your grandfather because of his religion. Tends to give you certain impressions about both institutions. But when I came back to that story as a young man, I saw it as a rather complicated affair, the way reality always is.

What brought you to this realization?

When I was a student at the University of Utah, President George Thomas assigned me to work on a history of the university, for which they paid me the going rate, 25 cents an hour. So I studied all the newspapers in the library, looking for items about the university; and I ran on to the reports of the Collin-McMurrin affair in the *Deseret News* and *Salt Lake Tribune*. I knew the family version, of course, and had read different versions in the various histories of Utah; but it was fascinating to read a running account with each day's new developments. The *Tribune* actually reported him killed, but of course he didn't die. Nevertheless, the *Tribune* later claimed to be the only newspaper that accurately reported the story of "Bad Boy McMurrin."

What finally happened? The U.S. government didn't let the incident drop, did it?

No. He was expected to be indicted for an attack on a federal marshal, so as soon as he could travel, the church smuggled him out of Salt Lake to England, where he stayed for some time as a missionary. After he returned from England, he gave himself up and the charges were dropped.

What was the local response?

The case has some importance in state history because there was such a great public outcry. The government thought that the Mormons might rise up in rebellion. They put Collin in protective custody at Fort Douglas for fear he'd be lynched, and telegraphed to Washington to strengthen the garrison—which was done. But there was no uprising.

Quite a big deal.

There's a curious postscript to this affair. My father's two sisters were attending a social event in Los Angeles about 1940 when a woman whom they had never met began telling the story of how her father, a deputy U.S. marshal named Collin, had shot one of those Mormons in the early days. An amazing coincidence.

Yes. I understand your grandfather had a very good library. Did you inherit it?

In his Salt Lake home was a library with books from the floor to the ceiling. That always fascinated me as a child, all those books. Some time after my grandmother died, the LDS Institute of Religion at the University of Utah was being built; so I asked Lowell Bennion, who was the founding head of the institute, whether he'd like me to collect my grandfather's religious books for their library. My grandfather's library had already been divided up, but I talked with my brothers, my mother, and my aunts and uncles, and they all made contributions; and his collection is still housed in specially built locked glass bookcases at the institute library.

What kinds of things did he have in the collection?

Oh, he had wonderful stuff. Some very important classical things that you can't obtain now. Also much Mormon material, such as first-edition volumes of the *Journal of Discourses*. He also had important volumes on the history of religion, on theology, and by English divines.

Sterling, you speak affectionately but somewhat less extensively of your grandmothers. Did they have an important role in your growing up years?

They certainly did. My grandmothers were of two types. Both were very impressive women, really very impressive. My mother's mother, Grace Ann Hatch Moss, had been reared in Davis County, one of eight children, with both her father and her husband as ranchers. I'd characterize her as a typical stalwart pioneer type with those rough-hewn, simple frontier virtues. These were people of great integrity. She was a really remarkable person. She was very close to her children and would not tolerate any one of them criticizing any of the others in her presence. For her, family loyalty was one of the prime virtues.

My father's mother, Mary Ellen Hunter McMurrin, was—well, I'd describe her as queenly. She was a very beautiful woman, but it was her manner as much as her appearance. I felt that I was in the presence of royalty when I was with her, an amazing thing. Everyone seemed to feel the same way about her.

So family visits really took two different forms?

Right. When we would go to see my McMurrin grandparents, it was a rather formal occasion. There were very frequent family gatherings when all seven of the children and all of their children were living in Los Angeles—and I mean *in* Los Angeles, not in the suburbs. I still remember the remarkable deference these adult children showed their mother. It was almost as if she were holding court when her sons and daughters and their families would visit. She was very affectionate—I don't want to imply any stiffness by saying it was formal, but, well, I think of adjectives like *courtly* or *gracious* in connection with her. Even when we were adults, when Natalie and I came into the room where my grandmother was holding court, looking very regal, we would go over, kiss her, and then sit down and behave ourselves.

Visits to my mother's outfit were entirely informal. They had a very large, beautiful home in Woods Cross, a generous, capacious home, where I was born. It was a place that accommodated everybody of whatever ages. Even in the winters, we were often there. We'd come in, greet people, and make ourselves as much at home as if we were in our own home. There were usually a few cousins around, and we kids would have the run of the place—a beautiful farm, now covered with homes. The barn, now upgraded to carriage house, has been transformed into apartments.

How long did your grandparents live?

I really have strong memories of them. Joseph McMurrin, the first of my grandparents to die, passed away in 1932, when I was eighteen, William Moss when I was nineteen, and Grandmother Moss the next year, when I was twenty; but my Grandmother McMurrin lived almost ten more years. She died in the early forties.

It must have been a jolt to lose them all so fast, at your age.

Let me tell you about my Grandfather Moss's death. Kind of an interesting story. When I was a student at the University of Utah in the fall of 1933, he was seventy-eight years old and was in Holy Cross Hospital for an operation. Almost every day I would walk down from the university and visit with him. He would tell me all kinds of stories about his life; if I'd had any sense, I'd have taken notes. We didn't have such a thing as a tape recorder then. When he left the hospital, he returned to his home in West Bountiful to convalesce. I was with him one afternoon when he was going through some of his papers from the bank. He was set up in style in his bed in the living room, with a fire in the fireplace. One of the items was a back issue of the *Deseret News*, all folded up, with a full-page article on the hereafter by Apostle James E. Talmage. He said to me, "I didn't see any point in reading this until I was ready to die, so I put it in the bank vault; but now I guess I'd better read it." He sat there and read it and two days later he died.

I hope Talmage's words were comforting. What are your most vivid memories of your mother?

I was very close to my mother. I loved to spend time with her from my childhood until she died in 1965. She was a very beautiful woman, a person of true nobility, and very talented as a teacher and leader. She was involved in a few civic projects; but most of her activities beyond the circle of us children and the extended family were with the church. She was very active in the women's auxiliary and the organization for the teenage girls—the Relief Society and the YWMIA—and so forth. Beyond these formal positions, she was also very kind—constantly ministering to the poor and those who were in need in one way or another. She was very generous with her time and talents. She was deeply religious but not extreme in her religious views. She was a person of very, very good sense and very open. I could talk to her about anything, more so than with my father, who tended to be more formal and conservative.

Can you give me an example?

She would say, "Do you believe all that stuff about the Book of Mormon?" That would make us think, you see. Or she'd make a statement that sounded dogmatic, like, "I expect my sons to be good Latter-day Saints and good Republicans." But then she'd kind of smile. Frankly, she didn't know the difference between a Republican and a Democrat. What she did know was that her father was a Republican, and that settled the question for her. But she was completely open-minded and approachable, a person whose company I always delighted in. In her later years she and I traveled around Europe together and visited Oxford and Cambridge universities.

When Natalie and I were in graduate school at USC during the summers of 1938 to 1945, we had no children and lived with my parents, who had plenty of room. It was a very congenial arrangement. Later, when we had our own place, we would never think of not including my parents in parties or dinners with friends. My brothers who lived in Los Angeles were the same way. Our parents were just a part of everything. Natalie and I wouldn't so much as go to a movie without inviting my mother and father. We were a very close-knit family. We now have that same close relationship with our children and grandchildren.

And did you stay close to your brothers as adults?

Yes, we're very close to this day. We have much in common. My brothers are liberals in both politics and religion, and we share our ideas freely. My brother Blaine died in late 1992. He and I had much in common. We had traveled together in Europe in the fifties when he and his family lived in Germany where he was a high-ranking civilian with the U.S. Air Force. He later moved to Los Angeles.

What about your father?

My father was a bit more formal than my mother. I would say that he had two major influences on me. First, he was a person of strong, even puritanical morals. There's no question but what that has had a very strong influence on me. I'm really old-fashioned in my conceptions of what is right and wrong. I am constantly shocked by what passes today in language and behavior. His second influence was intellectual. He had me reading stuff at a very early age that had a very strong impact on me. My discussions with my father centered on religion and the church more than on society and social problems, though as a probation supervisor he was much involved with personal behavior and social issues.

Were you and your brothers actively involved in church as kids?

We were churchgoers in Ogden, at least on Sunday morning; then as we would sit around the table at our Sunday dinner, our conversations always centered primarily on religion. They were quite open conversations about what the speaker and teachers had to say. We were openly critical within limits. My father didn't encourage rigorous criticism of general authorities or what you would call fundamental criticisms of the church. Nevertheless, he encouraged serious thought about what was said and how it was said. Mormons then paid a lot of attention to forensics and public discourse. Most Mormon kids took classes in public speaking in the MIA and participated in speech contests. So if someone spoke in our ward or stake meetings whose style or grammar weren't very good, he got a good working over around the dinner table at our house. For my father, grammar was a matter of morals.

You said that this was in Ogden. Was it different in California?

Well, I'd have to admit that in California we became regular churchgoers, as opposed to irregular churchgoers. That was largely for social reasons. All of a sudden, church became immensely attractive, because here you would find people from home. That's a much more powerful thing than most people who haven't experienced it would realize. Some Mormons, of course, in moving to California, wanted to get away from the church. In the big city, they became anonymous. But they were in the minority. A much larger number were pulled into the church and would show up every time there were lights on in the meetinghouse.

Your experience was more of the pulled-in type?

That's right. At first we attended the Adams Ward—the oldest of the California Mormon wards, which no longer exists—and later the Wilshire Ward. There were close ties with Salt Lake City. In fact, there used to be a list posted on the bulletin board in the lobby of the Adams Ward keeping track of how fast you could drive to Salt Lake. People would come back and write their names on it and indicate how many hours it took. No freeways then! The roads were graveled from Nephi to Barstow; and through the corner of Arizona they weren't even graded!

But in terms of our family discussions about what went on at church, the pattern was already set by the time we moved to California. It was open, honest, and usually quite critical.

A way of teaching, was it?

It taught, of course; but I don't think that was the intent. It was rather a natural thing—that you thought about, talked about, analyzed what was happening to you. In those early days the *Deseret News* used to list the speakers in some of the Salt Lake City and Ogden wards for sacrament meeting. My father always looked for speakers who were especially competent intellectually and often took me with him to other wards. He did this all the time I was growing up in Ogden. During my teen years in Los Angeles, he was a great hand to ferret out interesting lectures at the universities or the Los Angeles library.

So he had personal intellectual needs that these activities nourished?

When our family went to Los Angeles, we didn't miss a thing. If there was anything going on—lecture, theater, opera—we were there. My father became a thoroughgoing Angeleno. You know, Jack, I think my father was really a kind of misplaced university professor. He should have been a professor of English. He had literary talents and was a competent grammarian who paid close attention to language. But in Utah he landed in high school. In Ogden High School he taught English and mathematics and, I think, geography sometimes. But he really had the temperament and talents to have been in a university, very strong intellectual interests. He would pick out books for me to read; and when I was through with one, there would be another one.

Would you rather have had more? It sounds as if you had intimate discussions with your mother but the intellectual discussions were mainly

with your father.
   That's quite true.

What kinds of things did you read?
   The Harvard Classics, of course, along with a lot of other good stuff
and all of the better church books. Because my father handed me books,
I read a good many things that I otherwise would not have encountered
except by chance. I remember, for instance, that on my tenth birthday
my father gave me a copy of *Science and Belief in God* by Frederick J.
Pack, a professor of geology at the University of Utah. I think it had just
been published then, about 1924. I've lost my copy, I'm sorry to say.

Wasn't that considered pretty advanced for its time?
   I'd say it still is, Jack, considering the conservative direction the
church took from the 1940s on with Joseph Fielding Smith and Bruce
R. McConkie. I'd say Pack's book is still the best book in defense of
evolution by an accepted Mormon. I've encouraged Pack's son, Alvin,
to see about reprinting it. If anything, Mormons have been intellectual
backsliders since the early thirties.

Did your family have any feelings about evolution one way or the other?
   Oh yes. I grew up believing in evolution. It was taken for granted
in our home that evolution was good science, so we didn't go through
the crises that some young people have when they go to school and start
learning different things. Neither I nor my brothers ever experienced
this kind of crisis in our religious thinking, and I think it's due largely
on the one hand to the real common sense of my mother and on the
other to the underlying message my father pounded into us—that science
can be—even should be—harmonized with religion.

And evolution is just one example—
   That's right. In our home, we grew up from our earliest childhood,
as far back as I can remember, talking freely about things having to do
with religion—and religion was simply the center of our lives. That is,
during the school year when we lived in the city. There was nothing
that didn't have some kind of religious connection, whether doctrinal,
historical, ethical, personal—you name it. There were no forbidden
topics. There were no forbidden attitudes. I think it's true that I grew
up with an essentially critical, but not cynical, approach to the world.
When I say "no forbidden topics," I should add that there are subjects
discussed today that we had never heard of. We knew nothing much of
such things as abortion and homosexuality and hadn't the slightest
inkling of premarital sex. We were quite unsophisticated, compared to
teenagers today.

You mentioned your father's moral strictness . . .

Oh, yes. When I say nothing was forbidden, I'll make an exception for our behavior. My parents expected strictly moral behavior—honesty, ethical behavior, and rigorous sex morals. These things were taken for granted throughout my whole extended family.

What other books do you remember your father encouraging you to read that had a particular impact on your thinking?

Well, I remember when I was a kid, maybe eleven or twelve, he had me read H. G. Wells's 1920 volume *Outline of History*. In addition to all the factual information—it was a pretty good liberal education—it exposed me to the idea that you can see patterns in events and attempt, at least, to make meaning out of them. I don't think I ever read the whole thing, but I read a good deal of it. He encouraged me to read Darwin's *Origin of Species* when I was in junior high school.

The Harvard Classics were the great books of that period. They were in my father's library, and he was very fond of them. When I finished one, he'd move me on to the next. I was never very much attracted to the more literary stuff—although I do remember reading Dante's *Divine Comedy*. And, of course, I read lots of church stuff. The church writings my father would give me to read were far superior, in my opinion, to most of what comes out today as church literature. I read B. H. Roberts, James E. Talmage, Orson F. Whitney, and Adam S. Bennion in those days.

And all of this was before you were out of high school! Did you read a lot during the summers?

Well, yes, but not these kinds of books. We wouldn't want to take these volumes out where they'd get dirty or where a horse might step on them. At the ranch I'd encounter things by Jack London and Zane Grey—you know, that sort of thing. They're considered culturally significant writers today, I know; but we didn't put them in the same class as "serious" writers then.

Do you think your father saw himself as consciously countering what might have been some negative influences of the ranch?

I'd never thought about that; but you know, I think that may be the case. When my brothers and I would come down out of the hills in the fall, my father would look us over, haul us off to get haircuts and some new clothes, and then he'd always send us to the books. First, he'd try to make us look like human beings and then try to make sure we had something good to read. He never got an argument from me. I loved to read.

Was there any tension between your immediate family's rather open attitude toward religious questions and your Grandfather McMurrin, the church leader?

No, no tension, as far as I know. But I doubt that my grandfather encouraged as much free thought in his family as my father did. Both of my grandfathers were the imperious type. They were the rulers of their families. The offspring didn't criticize them. Children, even adult children, didn't disagree with them. I don't think it occurred to Grandfather McMurrin that any one of his flesh and blood would have a different opinion from his own. It just wasn't done. When you were in the presence of either of my grandfathers, you realized that they were the bosses. At all those family gatherings in California, the conversation was genteel, interesting, entertaining, significant, courteous—but very deferential. No one ever argued with my grandparents. I have never heard of anybody in the family ever taking issue with them on anything except for my mother, on one occasion, referring to the family failures of B. H. Roberts. Her father-in-law silenced her in no uncertain terms, but she was right and he was wrong.

And your Grandfather Moss was the same way?

I'll say! Frankly, it was a little bit like those movies about cattle barons. He was the head of anything wherever he went. If he went into Evanston or Woodruff, people stood back as he walked along the street. I've seen him with twenty-five or thirty ranch hands—more, sometimes, with the sheep during shearing time; when he walked through a place, I tell you people sat up and took notice. All the ranch hands would fall silent; then they'd start to talk again but they'd speak quietly and be careful what they said. I never heard *anybody* argue with him or take exception to anything he had to say.

During one shearing season when I was just a kid helping run the sheep in for the shearers, I recall a discussion about whether or not there was a "higher power." One of them finally ended the discussion by saying, "Anyone who has ever worked for this company knows that there is a higher power, and that's Bill Moss."

Did your parents insist on the same deference?

No, not at all. I think my father might have preferred the deference shown to his father, and he did receive full parental respect. But he didn't expect us to treat him as if he were some kind of untouchable.

You mentioned reading B. H. Roberts and also hearing him speak.

Yes, well, he was a friend of my Grandfather Moss. Their children had intermarried. They had great respect for one another, and Roberts would come to the ranch on occasion during the summers. He was also closely associated, of course, with my paternal grandfather. I attended lectures by him in Los Angeles and had several conversations with him. He delivered the eulogy at my grandfather's funeral.

What was the marriage connection?

My Uncle Ralph, my mother's oldest brother, married Hazel Roberts, one of B. H. Roberts's daughters by his second wife, Celia Dibble Roberts. That family lived in Centerville, so they were Davis County people. When I was a kid, we always called B. H. "Grandpa Roberts" and Celia "Grandma Roberts," because I was so close to my cousins who were their grandchildren. It was a very official occasion when B. H. came to Centerville; he'd come there for Thanksgiving and Christmas and carve the turkey. I was in his Centerville home a number of times when I was young. I knew Mrs. Roberts quite well; she was almost like a sister to my own grandmother.

How well did you and your father get along on matters of religion?

My father and I had countless conversations on religion and church doctrine after I was grown. I often took exception to church actions and Mormon beliefs, and at times this bothered him some. This was especially true during the summers when Natalie and I were living with my parents in Los Angeles while I was in graduate school at USC. I remember, once, his saying, "Well, it looks to me like you don't believe anything." But that's the closest to a hassle that we ever had; and when I would get into conflicts with other people over religion, he always came down on my side—even when I expected him to come down on the other side. And then as I became involved in some conflicts with church authorities, he was very strongly on my side.

I honestly don't know whether he believed that the Book of Mormon is authentic, because he would never even mention it. You'd think if it were an important part of his faith he would have brought it up. And another thing, he never saw the inside of the temple after he and my mother were married there. My mother would go occasionally, to accompany her own mother; but my father never did.

Are you saying he was a cultural Mormon? There seems to have been no question about his commitment to the church.

None. As I said, it was a kind of tribal loyalty. But on the issue of ecclesiastical authority, I think I may have witnessed a turning point with him, which is pretty interesting when you consider that he was a general authority's son. I was present—I think it was in 1937—when he and Apostle Joseph Fielding Smith, for whom he had great respect, were discussing whether a bishop can forgive sins. My father was greatly shocked when Apostle Smith insisted that a bishop can forgive sins and added that the difference between Mormons and Catholics on this matter is that Catholic priests take money for it. I think my father never quite recovered from this. It opened up a new avenue for his thinking to discover such nonsense purveyed by the church's leading theologian of that time. On the same day, he discussed the matter with J. Golden Kimball, I remember, and they both had a good laugh over it. Kimball was just senior to his own father in the First Council of the Seventy.

That must have been something of a comfort to him. Did it have any effect on your relationship?

Well, yes, it did. It helped cement a closer relationship between my father and me on ideas about faith and authority. He was no longer so sure that the general authorities knew as much or were in as much agreement as he had taken for granted. He certainly didn't lose his faith, but it wasn't the same kind of naive faith—if I can say that without sounding mean—that he'd had before. After that point, he used to confide things in me that I think he wouldn't mention in front of the other members of the family—things his own father had told him about the inner workings of the church and the relationships among the general authorities. I remember that he once said, "Father has told me that B. H. Roberts has written a book that, if it's ever published, will just blow things sky high." Those were his exact words.

That's the **Studies on the Book of Mormon,** *which Brigham Madsen edited and the University of Illinois Press published in 1985, isn't it?*

I think so, and I've often wondered what my father would have thought of my having had a hand in seeing that it was published. I think he'd be pleased. Of course, it may have been Roberts's *The Truth, The Way, The Life,*[4] which Roberts completed before his death but which the church refused to publish. It includes some of Roberts's speculations on pre-Adamites—a notion which, in my opinion, *is* nonsense and wouldn't blow anything sky high.[5] No, I think it was his Book of

---

4. This work was published independently of the LDS church in 1994 by Smith Research Associates (San Francisco, California) and distributed by Signature Books. Edited by Stanley Larson, it includes an introduction by Sterling M. McMurrin. *Brigham Young University Studies* released its own edited version with commentary the same year. See B. H. Roberts, *The Truth, The Way, The Life: An Elementary Treatise on Theology,* ed. John W. Welch (Provo: BYU Studies, 1994).

5. Postulating the existence of pre-Adamites (or human-like creatures before Adam) was B. H. Roberts's effort to reconcile the scientific theory of evolution with the Genesis creation story.

Mormon manuscripts. Well, my grandfather used to confide a lot of things to my father, rather than to his other sons; and my father would pass them on to me. We spent a lot of time discussing religious matters and other topics right up till the day of his death.

Did you have any sense as you were growing up that your father was investing more energy in his relationship with you than with your brothers?

No. His relationships with my brothers were just as solid as with me. But our relationship was, I think, based more on intellectual issues and interests. My eldest brother, Blaine, was much more interested in athletics in high school and college, and Father had a great interest in his career as an athlete. Keith, the brother who is just older than me, was a serious student of church history, and I well recall his discussions with my father on church stuff. My younger brother, Harold, had musical inclinations, and my father was a competent musician. He had a great deal of natural ability. As a matter of fact, in his early years he taught piano for a living and was constantly on call as a pianist, chorister, and choral leader. That was a bond between the two of them. As a child, I remember my father telling stories about serving his mission in England and then taking the grand tour on the Continent and attending perform-ances, among other places, at the Paris Opera.

It must have been hard for him to satisfy all of his cultural appetites in Ogden. Was it easier in California?

Oh, we went to everything, no matter where we were. The first opera I ever attended was in Ogden. Lucy Gates Bowen, a granddaughter of Brigham Young and a well-known soprano, organized her own opera company, which produced operas in Utah. I still remember going to the Orpheum Theatre to see a performance of *Faust*. I attended with my father and a friend, a music teacher from the high school, I think. It was a great, moving experience for me. It really was. I was especially impressed by the way Marguerite's brother, Valentine, after he had been run through with a sword due to the chicanery of Mephistopheles, lying there dying, could still sing loud enough that we could hear him clear up in the second balcony. My father and his friend were on the orchestra floor. The second balcony at the Orpheum was always fifty cents for major performances.

When John Philip Sousa's band came through, we were there. I was in the second grade, and kids' tickets cost ten cents. The performance was in the Alhambra Theatre in Ogden. What a crime to tear down beautiful theaters like the Alhambra and the Orpheum.

It must have been an unforgettable experience.

It was, it was. I can still remember how moved I was by "The Stars and Stripes Forever."

Did they have chautauquas[6] in Ogden at that time?

I didn't know what a chautauqua was, so I think not. But I used to attend lectures of all kinds. My family were conservative Republicans, as I've mentioned—though not politically involved at all. I took it for granted when I was a little kid that the Democrats were rowdy and the Republicans were respectful. I well remember attending a Democratic meeting at Weber College's auditorium—then an LDS college. Then I went to the Egyptian Theatre for the Republican rally, at which Herbert Hoover, then Secretary of Commerce, spoke. I remember reporting to my father that Republicans were a better-behaved crowd and more intelligent than the Democrats, and I "prophesied" that Hoover would someday be president of the United States.

Not bad at all as a prophecy. Did you also notice that the Republicans had less fun than the Democrats?

Well, what I noticed as a kid was that the Republicans seemed to be more dressed up than the Democrats. But I was terribly naive politically. I don't remember many family discussions about politics at all, even during national crises, until we were living in California.

In your professional and public life you became well known as an advocate for equal rights and a number of causes championed by the Democrats, not by the Republicans. Can you identify when these interests began?

I can't recall being interested in civil rights before I was in high school. I had never heard the term "civil rights." In my environment, we were insulated. We just belonged to the moderate middle class in a small city with no slums that I knew of and no really visible minority populations. And there was no serious concern about human equality in the Deseret Live Stock Company! I was probably in college before I developed much sensitivity to the problems of inequality in America. My social conscience matured very slowly.

Well, Sterling, we've talked a lot about your parents and grandparents; but is there anything you'd like to say about any of your earlier ancestors? You

---

6. Traveling presentations of education and entertainment (lectures, concerts, and plays), often presented outdoors or in tents and named after Lake Chautauqua in western New York, where the idea emerged in 1873. Chautauquas flourished in the late nineteenth and early twentieth centuries.

said that all eight great-grandparents were Mormons.

I don't know much about my paternal ancestors except that they were Scottish and perhaps some British. My great-grandparents were all early Utah pioneers. I understand that one of my maternal forebears worked on both the Kirtland, Ohio, and Nauvoo, Illinois, temples. My mother's mother's father, Orrin Hatch—no relation to Utah's current senator was the youngest member of the Mormon Battalion. He lied about his age to enlist. He was one of the party sent from Los Angeles into the mountains for a tree to use as the pole on which the first American flag was raised in that area. There's a monument there now. His older brother was in the battalion, too; they worked for Sutter at Sutter's Mill after they were mustered out of the Army and were involved in the discovery of gold in 1847. Some of the gold he took to Utah became a wedding ring for my great-grandmother.

Resourceful fellow! Was he one of the three polygamous great-grandfathers?

He had two wives. On my mother's side, both great-grandfathers had two wives. They were mild polygamists, you know—only two wives. I always claimed to be legitimate because I'm descended in each instance from the first wife. Now my mother's ancestors are all British, so I'm virtually a hundred percent from the British Isles. One of my mother's ancestors was William Bradford, the first governor of Plymouth Colony.

So you come by your theological interests genetically?

I've never had more than an academic interest in Puritan theology. But the important thing from my standpoint is that I'm a one hundred percent Utahn. All branches of my family on both sides were in Utah long before the railroad came in 1869.

Sterling, beyond your family, who were your childhood heroes?

You've noticed that my two grandfathers had heroic properties as far as I was concerned. As a typical Mormon kid, I naturally looked with great respect on the LDS general authorities; and as a typical American, I believed that George Washington and Abraham Lincoln could do no wrong. Thanks to my father's reading program for me, I knew quite a bit about ancient history; and I'll have to confess that Alexander the Great and Julius Caesar were, in a sense, heroic figures for me and, in a slightly different way, Augustus Caesar. I did some reading about Napoleon as a kid, but I wasn't much taken with him.

Any scriptural heroes?

Well, you'd certainly think so, wouldn't you. Let's see. I can't really remember any. I read a great deal about Jesus, of course, but I don't remember associating him with heroism as much as with great compassion and representing everything that was ideal. I didn't pay much attention to the Old Testament until I was in college; and I never did have the slightest interest in the Book of Mormon or its heroic figures. I had great respect for Joseph Smith when I was young. As a matter of fact, I remember taking the role of Joseph Smith in the Sacred Grove in some religious pageant when I was eight or ten.

You've said you weren't too much interested in literature, so I don't suppose any of the literary heroes . . .

As a child I read the stories of King Arthur, of course. I can well remember my great respect for Sir Galahad; after all, his strength was as the strength of ten because his heart was pure. I've never known for sure what it means to have a pure heart, but I thought that must be a very good thing. Zelta Ballinger, my English teacher for all three years of junior high in Ogden, spent a lot of time on Greek mythology and Greek culture, and that had a very great impact on me. It introduced me to Plato and Aristotle. My father had me reading some of their stuff, but it was pretty tough for a kid. Still, I respected and admired them. I think, if I were picking out the top three or four, I'd have to say my heroes were Jesus, Plato, Aristotle, and perhaps Alexander the Great.

The twenties were a wild and woolly time in American sports. Did you follow Babe Ruth and Lou Gehrig?

Babe Ruth, but not Lou Gehrig. I was actually a lot more interested in a Utah sports hero like Jack Dempsey. I remember hearing the Jack Dempsey–Gene Tunney fight on the radio. The first radios had come to Ogden when I was about ten, in 1924 or 1925, and some neighbors on the corner had a set. They would put the speaker—it was shaped like a horn—in their window; and in the evenings, people would stand outside their house and listen to the musical broadcasts.

Now for baseball, during the World Series, either the *Deseret News* or the *Salt Lake Tribune* or both had a painted ball diamond fifteen or twenty feet high on the side of the building at South Temple and Main Street in Salt Lake City. As the information came over the telegraph, the diamond would light up, and they would run little models of the balls and players around the field while the announcer described what was happening. People congregated there by the hundreds.

Did you play sports?

I was pretty good at baseball, believe it or not; but this was just the sandlot baseball kids would play wherever you could get enough players together and find an enemy to take on. I also played on our school baseball team. We did as we pleased—no adult supervision, none of this Little League stuff. I used to catch without a mask—dangerous to do but masks cost too much. Never tried football. I played a little intramural basketball in high school and on an LDS ward team. When I went to UCLA in the fall of 1931, I made some impression, as I could run the 220 and the low hurdles at a pretty good rate. They tried to get me to go out for track, but I had to work every day. That very winter I developed a severe bronchial ailment, and I've never been able to run since.

Was that hard on you? Emotionally, I mean?

It was and still is. My Grandfather and Grandmother Moss came to California to visit their daughters every winter. Well, when he saw me with that severe bronchial condition, Grandfather said, "If your folks had stayed in Utah where they belong, you wouldn't be having this trouble." And you know, he was probably right. He meant it kind of morally—that my folks had done something wrong, something that upset the natural order of things in our family by moving to California. But the climate did trigger the bronchial attacks, and that was long before the pollution got bad. He looked at me and said, "You get back to Utah." He told my parents, "I want him back on the ranch this summer, and he needs to stay in Utah," and that was the end of that. Nobody argued with him, and I transferred to the University of Utah for my sophomore year. I was the first of my Grandfather McMurrin's descendants to leave Los Angeles when I came back to Utah to live.

Did that take care of the bronchial condition?

Yes. I was perfectly all right all summer on the ranch. I've managed to get by quite well since then, but the bronchial asthma has always been a problem for me. It kept me out of the military during the Second World War. I tried with no success to enlist in both the Army and Navy. Having been turned down several times by the Army, I didn't try the Air Force. I have had a lot of trouble with asthma again over the last five years.

What kind of dreams did you have as a kid about what your adult life might be like?

Well, I hesitate to confess all these things; but since you're asking, when I was in fifth of sixth grade, my great ambition was to be a railroad engineer. In those days of steam engines, railroading was a romantic affair. I paid a lot of attention to trains; we'd take the train from Ogden to Evanston to go to the ranch. Then there was some experience in loading sheep and wool on trains. Ogden was full of trains in those days, and I spent quite a lot of time around the railroad yard. I remember my fourth- or fifth-grade teacher assigned us to write a theme about what we'd like to be when we grew up, and I wrote about being an engineer. The funny thing is that I thought the term "civil engineer" was a sophisticated term for railroad engineer. The teacher read part of my theme to the class and said, "Now, if you're going to be a civil engineer, you're going to be out in the sun a lot and do a lot of walking." I wondered what was the matter with her.

Well, that was one of my ambitions, but I soon outgrew it. When I was in junior high school in Ogden, ROTC was mandatory. I passed some kind of examination and was made a sergeant. And let me tell you, that was something! I was looked upon as a person of real stature! I developed a great desire for a military career.

And what happened to that ambition?

Oh, then we moved to Los Angeles, and the ROTC there was voluntary. I signed on, but it was so sloppily handled compared to my Ogden unit that I lost interest and dropped it at the end of the year. I was later in ROTC at UCLA, where it was required for all men students.

I had a third great interest. When I think of my lack of talent, it's an embarrassing confession. As a kid and up through high school, I had a pretty good singing voice. Well, I really had a passionate interest in music, especially in symphony and grand opera. I had the lead in my junior high opera in Ogden. The female lead was a beautiful girl, and there we were in this romantic situation, both of us twelve or thirteen. The director, Edna Hardy, a great, no-nonsense teacher, told me to put my arm around the girl as we sang a duet. Well, I'd never put my arm around a girl before. I didn't have the faintest idea how to begin, and of course all the kids were down there giggling and watching. Miss Hardy yelled at me to get at it, and finally, totally embarrassed, I sort of draped my right arm around her neck. Miss Hardy marched over, snatched my arm away, and said, "Haven't you ever put your arm around a girl? Put it around her waist!" And she wrapped my arm around this lovely girl's waist. I'll tell you, Jack, I damn near died.

Well, that opera went really well. In high school in Los Angeles, I had the opera lead again. I'm afraid that for a short time I entertained ridiculous ambitions to be in grand opera. At any rate, this lovely girl in junior high had a marvelous singing voice. My brother Harold had a great voice and was in the New York theater and light opera during the late forties and fifties.

You still like serious music a lot, don't you?

Oh, sure. I used to go to New York almost twice a month in the sixties and into the seventies. The very first thing I'd do when I'd get to a hotel was beat it over to the Metropolitan Opera and get a ticket. It wasn't hard, getting just one. I wouldn't miss an opera if I was in New York and had a free night. Natalie and I never miss a chance to attend the opera—here, in New York, or in Europe when we are there.

Well, those are three noble ambitions.

I suppose a fourth would have been somewhat more practical. When I first entered UCLA, I entertained the idea of studying law, but not with the idea of having a typical legal practice. My interests ran more to international law and the foreign service. That's why I registered as a major in political science. When I transferred later to the University of Utah, I took international law and American diplomacy my first semester from George Emery Fellows, a major scholar who was chair of the history department. I even considered going to George Washington University so that I could get some position with the government while I was going to school. But all the time I was studying philosophy at UCLA and at Utah, and philosophy completely captivated me.

Earlier you described your childhood environment as being preoccupied with religious and LDS church issues. When did your interest in international law emerge?

When I was in high school in Los Angeles. It was stimulated by my father's brother, Everard, who was a brilliant attorney and deputy city attorney for Los Angeles. But I came naturally to the idea and interest in international affairs. I was much interested in problems of government when I was in high school, even to the point of writing several papers on government issues in addition to regular assignments.

Do you remember, as you grew up, having any particular inadequacies or any particular talents?

I certainly recognized plenty of inadequacies, but no special abilities. I thought I had some musical talent, but of course, I was mistaken. I may have thought that I had some talent as a writer, because when I was twelve, I started my first and last novel.

Let me guess. A Western?

Naturally. When I was eleven or twelve, my father gave me some birthday money for a book, and I went downtown and bought Zane

Grey's *Riders of the Purple Sage*. My father never forbade us to read anything—and there was no chance of kids running into pornography those days—but he warned me that Zane Grey was anti-Mormon and liked to use Mormons as villains. I think it's the only thing I ever read of Zane Grey's, but the title intrigued me; and the next summer when I was on the ranch and spending my evenings and nights in a sheep camp with a kerosene lamp, I thought I'd try my hand at a Western novel. The Deseret Live Stock Company's cattle brand, right to this day, is a quarter-circle J—the letter J with a quarter of a circle over it. It had been my grandfather's personal brand. For my title, I chose *Riders of the Quarter Circle J*. I thought that was a great title and I still do. Up in the hills above the Weber River is Francis Canyon, the setting for the opening of Chapter 1. The first sentence was, "It was a dark and dreary night." The second sentence was, "A shot rang out!" Certainly a dramatic opener. But I didn't get to the third sentence, as I couldn't decide just who was the shooter and who was the shootee.

At least it started off with a bang! Do you still have it around somewhere?

I saw it a few years ago—two sentences on a piece of scrap paper—but I don't know what became of it after that. I certainly hope it's lost.

What were you reading that summer?

Well, that's interesting. It wasn't Westerns, as you might have supposed. The sheep foreman, a tremendously impressive person, was William Sorenson from Spring City, Utah. He hired herders and camp jacks from Spring City, some of whom were quite well read.

What's a camp jack?

A camp jack is the herder's assistant. He pulls the sheep camp from one place to another, looks after the dogs and horses, cooks the meals, washes the clothes, and generally keeps house while the herder works with the sheep. Well, that summer, I found in the sheep camp where I was working a copy of Darwin's *The Descent of Man* that a herder or camp jack had left there. Now, my father had already had me read at least a part of Darwin's *The Origin of Species*, so that summer I read *The Descent of Man*.

Heavy-duty stuff for a young man in a sheep camp.

Well, that's all there was to read in the camp—besides, I was writing a book myself, you know!

Do you recall any embarrassments and adversities—social obstacles—that gave you your determination to achieve?

No, my childhood was placid and supportive. My father and mother were very close. It was a very happy family. I think it's probably a deficit to grow up without sisters, but my brothers and I right to this day are just as close as a family could be. My parents are both dead. It was a family of modest means, you understand. High school teachers never did make very much money. My father would joke that my mother had champagne tastes with a beer pocketbook because my Grandfather Moss was quite well-to-do, and she was reared in an atmosphere of plenty. Actually, so was my father. My father's mother had inherited considerable property. Her father, if I'm not mistaken, owned the land on Main Street and Fourth South where the federal court building now stands. So actually, my parents were both reared in conditions of plenty; and even though Father never made much money, I never had a sense of being denied anything.

What did you do for a good time up there on the ranch? There weren't any Little League teams, movies, or other entertainments that kids so often depend on today.

Entertainment? Well, we worked most of the time, even when we were kids. There were always things to be done. But a trip to Woodruff or Evanston was always an event. There were always horses around, if you wanted to ride out somewhere. A little like a sailor's holiday boating on the lake, but those who work with horses sometimes can't get enough of them. After supper, you go out to the barn or corrals, put your foot up on a rail, and just watch the damn things eat. Of course, we would pitch horseshoes, ride calves when we were little, and play baseball when we were older. But there just wasn't a lot of free time. Work was six days a week, and sometimes not even Sundays were off.

But one of the forbidden pleasures—you've seen inside-out granaries?

Where the vertical studs are on the outside of the building?

That's right, so the planks that are holding back all that grain will be pushing against the studs. Otherwise the pressure of the grain would pop the planks off. And there are metal tie rods that span from wall to wall to keep them from bowing out. There were big granaries on the ranch, oats for the horses, and so forth. Well, we kids—my brother Keith and I and two or three cousins who were about the same age—would get out on these rods and then drop into the grain—stark naked so the grain wouldn't get into our clothes. We'd swing along those rods playing Tarzan and miss a rod or crash into each other and fall into the grain. We'd never get hurt, but when our aunts caught us, they'd give us hell. Then there were the ponds to swim in, always naked, of course.

And I'll tell you one more ranch story. They had two commissaries at the ranch. The Deseret Live Stock Company operated a general store at Woods Cross. You could buy anything there—pickles to horse collars. At shearing time in the spring, when the herds were being split up for their summer range, the sheepherders and camp jacks would come to the commissary at the shearing corral to stock up for the summer. It was like a rendezvous, a trappers' rendezvous with lots of visiting and activity and excitement.

But the home ranch kept its own commissaries—one for food and the other for hardware. Well, one summer they had a good supply of black powder. These places were kept locked, of course, but Keith and I and two cousins figured out ways of getting in. We spent the whole summer acquiring small quantities of powder and blowing things up. It's a wonder we didn't kill ourselves. We started out blowing cans in the air.

And then you got braver?

Well, we were just dumb kids. There were some deep washes at the mouth of the canyon, and we'd spread the powder up and down, end in a small cave, then light the trail, and run like hell for fifty yards so we could watch it go off. That was the biggest bang between the Creation and Hiroshima for us. They caught us, of course, and we caught hell. That ended my career as an explosives expert.

Your play was imaginative and spontaneous. Dangerous, sometimes, but generally wholesome?

That's the truth. Oh, yes. There was none of this Little League stuff with parents organizing and supervising and shouting at the kids. Parents had work to do. I think that that independence was good for us.

You had to make your own rules?

Oh, yes. In Ogden we would set up our own diamond, decide who was going to play where, how many innings there would be, and resolve our own conflicts. Sometimes there were fights, but the parents were not in the picture. We had to earn our own money, go down and buy our own mitt, ball, and bat. But my father didn't care much about sports, so the situation may have been quite different in other families.

In many respects you enjoyed an idyllic youth, Sterling. Your experiences were highly stimulating and diverse, you knew freedom and learned responsibility at an early age, and you were part of an extended family that was generous with its love and support.

I was indeed very fortunate.

2.
Education in Utah and California

Sterling, you've spent your life as a teacher, writer, philosopher, and as a leader of educational institutions. I'm interested in your own education. How did your educational experiences shape the perspective you've brought to your professional life?

Well, I must say that if the schools of today are actually as bad as their critics say they are, the schools I attended must have been far superior to them. You hear a lot about great innovations in today's schools, but many of the so-called new things we read about were commonplace in my schools. I had some teachers who weren't so good, but I can remember exceptionally talented teachers all the way from kindergarten through high school. I can't recall a single class in which I didn't learn a great deal.

Let's see. You went from kindergarten through ninth grade in Ogden, Utah.

That's right. Madison and Pingree elementary schools for kindergarten through sixth grade; then Lewis Junior High for grades seven, eight, and nine. Then my family moved to Los Angeles and I attended Manual Arts High School for three years.

You have influenced thousands of students as a philosophy professor, Sterling. Who were the teachers who influenced you?

That would be hard to say, but the best teachers I had were in junior high and high school. Miss Zelta Ballinger was my English teacher and home-room teacher for all three years of junior high. That meant English every school day of the year, writing as well as reading. She was tough and at times could be a little mean, but she saw to it that the kids learned something. The other teacher was Miss Edna Hardy, my music teacher in seventh, eighth, and ninth grades. She pounded music into the kids. She would stand over those classes and make us listen to good music on a wind-up Victrola whether we liked it or not. That's how I became acquainted with the great musicians of the time. Have you ever heard of Madame Schumann-Heink? or Galli-Curci?

I can't say I have.

No? In those days, their names were almost household words. I was, I think, in the third grade when my parents bought a wind-up Victrola with the old 78 rpm records and mechanical amplification. We woke up on Christmas morning to the sounds of Caruso singing "O Sole Mio." That has stuck with me ever since. And we always had a great deal of good music at home. Miss Hardy would pour music into us in such a way that I doubt if there's a kid who was in one of her classes who doesn't remember it now, sixty-five years later. We had music coming out of our ears. She was a great teacher.

The music supervisor for the Ogden schools, Mark Robinson, was a family friend as well as an educator. About twice a year he would visit our music class and really lay down the law about music. He was great. It was like Maurice Abravanel visiting a grade school class. He was a forceful person; and when he got through with our class, we knew that music was something to pay attention to.

How old were these two women? How much teaching experience had they had?

Well, we thought they were ancient, used to call them "Old Lady Ballinger" and "Old Lady Hardy" behind their backs, but I suppose they were only in their twenties. Miss Ballinger was still at Ogden High School when I was U.S. Commissioner of Education thirty-some years later. I remember, because I sent a telegram that was delivered to her at her retirement banquet. She was then an administrator. That's what they do with great teachers—promote them to something else.

Up the ladder and away from students.

I hold Miss Ballinger in such high esteem that I paid tribute to her in the preface of a book of philosophical essays, *Religion, Reason, and Truth,* as a teacher to whom I am greatly indebted.

Did her English class deal with philosophical matters? You've told me that much of your interest in philosophy stemmed from your association with your father.

Yes, but Miss Ballinger's English classes spent considerable time on Greek history and mythology. Several times when I answered questions or recited, I remember her saying, "Your answer has a philosophical character." I didn't know quite what she meant . . .

But you took it as a compliment. Those are nice moments in the life of a school child. Did you also have some bad experiences in school?

Well, one. It's just a little thing, really, but it was a terrible blow to me at the time. My seventh- or eighth-grade American history teacher,

Miss Frye, was a very good teacher. I liked her and liked history, too, so I read a lot outside of class. My father had a good library, not extensive, but we must have had six or eight books at home on American history, and I also got books from the Carnegie Free Library in Ogden. As a consequence, I often came up with stuff in class that wasn't in the textbook. When Miss Frye discovered what was going on, she told me I should quit reading those other books, right in front of the class. I was scarred for life!

Hardly what we hope will happen in schools. You were sometimes late coming down from the mountains in the fall and you left early in the spring. Did that make school difficult? Did you have a lot of homework in elementary and junior high?

We certainly did. We had homework starting about the fourth grade, a great deal of it. And enormous amounts in high school. Going to school was not an easy proposition, but it was a pleasure. And yes, I was usually late entering school.

I recall doing one theme when I was just a little kid, fourth or fifth grade, on driftwood. I'd never seen a piece of driftwood. You must be near the ocean, I guess, to have first-hand knowledge of driftwood. But I read up on driftwood. When it burns, it produces various colors, and I wanted to write about its pretty colors. I spelled it "purdy," and my teacher didn't catch the error. I didn't notice it until several years ago when I encountered the theme in some old papers.

Do you remember other homework assignments?

We did extensive research projects in junior high that involved a great deal of writing. We wrote constantly; and I suspect that the average junior high school student of my generation had more writing skills than many of the students I have had in the university. It was not easy going, but I never did feel that we were excessively burdened.

Could you say whether your elementary and junior high would have been considered progressive for the times?

Well, my understanding is that Utah schools during the 1920s were generally regarded as rather outstanding and progressive. My teachers in California would comment favorably on the reputation of Utah schools. The principal of the high school, Dr. Albert Wilson, showed a great deal of interest in the quality of leadership opportunities offered Mormon youth in church activities. He even used me as an exhibit of what the LDS church does for its kids.

Foreign languages are receiving a lot of emphasis again now. Did they hold a prominent place in the curriculum in your school days?

I started Latin when I was in the ninth grade. We had a choice between Latin and Spanish, as I recall. My teacher, a fairly young woman, was extremely effective, really knew how to teach her subject. She taught nothing but Latin. Latin was certainly the best subject I ever had. Then, in Los Angeles I majored in Latin in high school, so I had four years of Latin and continued with it in college. I wish I had stayed with it even longer. Combined with English, it was extremely valuable.

So much is made today of parents' involvement in schools, of the importance of supporting their children's learning. How involved were your parents?

I think there was quite a bit of parental involvement, but it was probably informal and pretty invisible—not like classroom visits or, so far as I know, regular teacher-parent consultation. My father was a teacher at Ogden High and my mother had been an elementary school teacher, so they took considerable interest in our schooling, but I don't recall them visiting our classrooms except for special parent programs. I think they probably knew some of my teachers. Ogden was a small town, after all. In Los Angeles I had a hassle with a teacher in the tenth grade. I had objected to his insulting a Japanese boy by telling the kid to go back to Japan where he belonged. This led to an encounter which resulted in my father going over to the school and having a little talk with the teacher.

You must have been proud of your father! Did your parents help you with assignments or check your themes or mathematics homework? Would that have been rare or a customary thing?

It wasn't customary, but my father would usually read my themes. I remember he was interested enough in one large writing project that he showed it to our next-door neighbor in Ogden, who was superintendent of the Southern Pacific Railroad. My father wouldn't usually comment on the content, but he'd point out problems with punctuation or grammar.

Getting back to your education, do you have any observations on the curriculum?

I think you could say quite accurately that it was a classical education. We studied Shakespeare's plays. Miss Ballinger saw to it that we had a good grounding in Greek history and mythology. There was Latin. We didn't discuss current issues much as students—certainly not like today's students. I think that was a deficiency in my education. I was in high school in Los Angeles before I encountered the word "psychiatrist." My Latin teacher in high school told me about a lecture by a famous psychiatrist he thought I'd be interested in attending and—I'm embarrassed to say this—I recall asking him what a psychiatrist was. Today a first-grader would know the word.

What are your memories of high school in Los Angeles in the 1930s?

Well, Manual Arts High School was really a great institution, no question about it. It was important enough to receive considerable national attention. It was, I believe, the second high school to be created in the city of Los Angeles, very old, with a campus very much like a college—separate buildings, beautiful arbors, and an excellent gymnasium. It was a very fine school, and I have the fondest memories of my experiences there. First-rate teachers. Some better than others, but generally highly competent.

It emphasized manual arts?

Well, the name is something of a misnomer. The school was very strong in the sciences and liberal and fine arts. It did have all kinds of shops—machine shops, even a foundry where the students would start with pig iron and manufacture things. I remember sheet metal shops, woodworking shops, all kinds of things. And when I was there, a group of students made an honest-to-goodness working airplane.

Sounds like a remarkably well-equipped vocational school.

Very well equipped. Everybody had to take a year of shop. I took machine shop, working with machine lathes and that sort of thing. But before the end of the first semester, the head of the shops department took me into his office as his assistant, so I got machine shop credit for running around town in the high school's truck, picking up orders, and running errands. But that wasn't the side of the school I was really involved with. You wouldn't ordinarily think, for instance, that a person could major in Latin in a school with a name like that.

But you did.

Yes. I'm sure you could major in some manual art, but it was a high-grade liberal arts school. Students were majoring in physics, chemistry, and English. No Greek. Los Angeles High School taught Greek as well as Latin. One of my Latin teachers, Joe Hall, was a classics major at USC. Our high school wasn't far from the University of Southern California campus. He was a brilliant teacher, a wonderful person, and he wanted me to learn Greek as well as Latin, so I made arrangements to be excused from study hall to work with Joe on Greek. He'd generously come to the school an hour before the Latin class every day to teach me Greek.

*Your academic development was well served by your schooling. What about
your social development? What part did student government play in school?*

Well, it was remarkably well organized, student self-government.
That's what attracted national attention. I was involved in a lot of
activities—perhaps a little too much. But my grades were good. To
belong to your school's chapter of the California Scholarship Federation—which was the highest honor a student could receive—you had
to make a certain grade-point average every semester. I recall working
hard but never feeling anxious about whether I'd make it or not. Our
high school had a scholarship president, elected by the whole student
body from the members of the Scholarship Federation. This was different
from the regular student body president and vice-president and other
officers.

This sounds like something you might have done.

Yes, I ended up in the student cabinet as scholarship president, and
that was a pleasant position to hold. The principal and vice-principal of
the school tried to get me to run for student body president, but I didn't
have the slightest interest in doing it. For one thing, a very close friend
of mine, Stan Smith, was going to run and I knew, without any question,
that he would be elected.

So you had no interest and no hope.

Stan was a football star and a wonderful person, very popular. As a
matter of fact, I suspect the principal and vice-principal tried to get me
to run just so there would be some opposition to him, so he wouldn't
be elected by acclamation. It was the principle of the thing—not that
they thought I was so well qualified or because they had anything against
Stan. He was terrific. The last time I saw him he was a professor at West
Point.

*The transition from junior high to high school is often a shock for kids, yet
you went from Ogden to a big city high school with no apparent problems?*

Yes, there were no deficiencies in my Utah schooling. I had to
scramble a bit in Latin, because I went into second-year Latin and some
of the stuff we had studied was quite different from what I ran into. I'll
tell you a tragic story. When I registered at UCLA, I told the head of
my high school language department, Miss Bertha Rutledge, who had
been my main Latin teacher, that I was signed up for a rather advanced
course reading Cicero's De Senectute and *The Menaechmi* of Plautus.
Miss Rutledge said, "Oh don't bother to buy books. I have the books
that you'll need right here," and she gave them to me.

Well, this was extremely kind of her; but in the course I noticed that the other students seemed to be reading and translating with a lot less difficulty than I was having. I couldn't figure it out until most of the way through the year. Then I discovered that the editions they were using had almost everything translated in the notes!

So Miss Rutledge had done you a different kind of favor than you thought.

Yes, I have nothing but praise for her and for the school. It was a great institution. When I was U.S. Commissioner of Education, the principal of Manual Arts High School was chairman of an organization of principals of Los Angeles High Schools and asked me to meet with them about some of the difficult racial problems they were having in the 1960s.

He knew you were a graduate?

Yes, or at least he knew that by the time we met. He arranged for me to have lunch with the faculty, and there were two or three people still there whom I knew as teachers. And they had me address the student body. Most of them were black. It was almost an Anglo-Saxon school when I was there—very few blacks and only a few Japanese students. On a visit a few years ago, I was aware that the faculty also were predominantly black. Did you know that this is where I did my first teaching?

Yes. You taught as a student, didn't you? Seems incredible that a teacher would turn a classroom over to a student in that same class.

Not one, three! All at the same time, the tenth grade, the first year I was in Los Angeles. I don't know how I found the time to do it. I was pretty good in geometry. In fact, I've often thought I should have stayed with mathematics. I might have amounted to something if I had. Everyone had to take some kind of a national test in geometry after the first year. Miss Farnum, the head of mathematics, called me in and told me I was the first person in Los Angeles to get a perfect score on this standardized test in geometry. Well, they had me teach during the second semester in tenth grade. It was kind of a tough class but small, largely students who were having difficulties with geometry.

So you taught during study hall?

Yes. It was very worthwhile because I got a little experience working with kids. And I also taught my English class that same semester.

How did that come about?

Well, my English teacher had a practice teacher—a student teacher from USC; and the two of them decided to do some experimenting. It consisted of turning the class over to one of the kids, and they sat in the back of the room every day and simply observed.

Did a different student teach each day or so?

No, no. I had it for the whole semester. I simply replaced the teacher. We were studying English literature—Alexander Pope and the other major poets. We had a large poetry text. I loved his *Essay on Man*, memorized the first part. It seemed perfectly natural at the time. After the two women set things going the first day, I taught the class, made the assignments, and so on. They would have conferences with me, but I simply ran the class.

What about papers and exams?

I gave the examinations, but I don't remember who graded the papers.

And the third class?

The biology teacher was named Mr. La Tourette. I forget his first name. He was kind of a mean cuss, to be frank with you; and I had trouble with him during the first semester over his insulting that Japanese-American kid, who was born and raised in Los Angeles. That wasn't the only case of his being downright mean to some students. Well, during the second semester, still in the tenth grade, the class continued with the same students. La Tourette had some kind of assignment that took him away for about eight weeks. So they assigned me to teach the class while he was gone.

That's a lot of responsibility for a sophomore.

Well, the problem was to keep ahead of the rest of the kids, and that wasn't too difficult in biology. I just plugged ahead in the text. The school had fine laboratories, but the lab work was something of a problem for me.

I can imagine!

I wasn't working after school and was accustomed to studying way into the night, but I still don't know quite how I was able to handle so much at school.

Did you consult with your parents at home or were you doing this pretty much on your own?

On my own. I talked to my parents a lot about school work, but I didn't ask them for help or advice. I functioned quite independently.

Did you keep on teaching as a junior or senior?

No, I guess they had had their fill of me as a teacher!

Now you were doing ROTC at the same time, weren't you?

Yes, it was voluntary at high school but pretty badly handled compared to Ogden's unit, so I dropped out at the end of the year. If I had remained in Ogden, I would have been in the ROTC for four years.

And maybe transferred right into the university and carried on with it when you got here.

Probably would have. I was very enamored of it. I really might have ended up in a military career. I signed up again as a freshman at UCLA, because ROTC was required for two years; but as a freshman, I was beginning to feel a good deal of independence and had some hassles with the ROTC people. Nothing very serious, but that ended any ambition that I had for a military career. I did learn one very good thing in UCLA's ROTC, though. Part of our drill consisted of racing across a field with rifles, running zigzag, the way you would when you're under fire. That same year I was held up a couple of times in the service station where I worked at night. I was always alone. The first time, the guy was a real professional. He held a gun on me, took the money, and then told me exactly what to do. The service station was on the corner of Budlong and Santa Barbara. He told me to cross Budlong, then turn and walk across Santa Barbara, which was very wide with trees planted on the median. "Don't you turn around," he said. "If you turn around, I'll shoot you."

Los Angeles was a rough place even sixty years ago! What did you do?

I followed his instructions—walked across Budlong and then started across Santa Barbara, but I turned and looked back and he was out on the corner with his gun pointed right at me. If it had been a busy corner, he couldn't have done it. I froze, and he said, "Don't you turn again!"

Well, I went half way across Santa Barbara to where the trees and the streetcar tracks were and thought, "Surely the guy's gone by now." I turned again and he was still there! Well, that's where my ROTC training came in. I thought he'd shoot me for sure, and I'll tell you, I zigzagged just as hard as I could go.

Did he shoot?

No, when I started to run he apparently went the other way. But I've always felt that my ROTC training was worth something. I dashed across that street and into an apartment house. I knocked on somebody's door and borrowed a nickel to phone the cops. The police recognized him from my description, said he was a real professional, had been in prison, and that I was lucky to be alive.

Not a comfortable feeling, walking away knowing there was a gun pointed at your back. What about the second holdup?

Two rank amateurs. They didn't know what they were doing. In the first hold-up, the fellow wasn't nervous at all, completely cool. Both of these guys had guns on me and were nervous as the devil. They began arguing with each other right while I was giving them the money out of the cash register and putting it in the black bag. The first man who had held me up had said, "No pennies," so I asked these guys whether they wanted the pennies. They began to argue about it. I said (this sounds ridiculous), "Can I keep a nickel to call the cops? We only have a pay phone here." And this guy said, "Yeah," and then, "Oh, God, no." Well, after that I always kept a nickel hidden.

What happened?

Oh, they left without killing anybody and I borrowed a nickel and called the cops. They had taken all my change and emptied my pocketbook.

So two hold-ups in one year. Is that right?

Plus one burglary, when somebody broke in at night and stole the money.

Well, we've jumped ahead to your college experiences. Anything else you want to say about high school?

I have absolutely no complaints about high school. It was a great experience. I was treated well, and I worked like a dog. I don't know where I found the time to do what I did. Dozens of nights I spent downtown in the main Los Angeles Public Library. It was a wonderful library.

And you received some scholarship awards when you graduated from high school?

I was made a member of the Ephebian Society and a life member of the California Scholarship Federation. These were the two highest high school honors. They put a gold seal on your diploma. I also received another award—only the boys were eligible for this one. The boy with the highest level of scholarship for his entire school career was given an award and scholarship by the Harvard Club of Los Angeles.

But nothing for the girls?

I think they read out her name or there was some kind of award. Mary Funk, a very close friend of mine, later the valedictorian at USC and a brilliant pianist, had the highest level of scholarship among the girls. But she got nothing and I got the Harvard Award. Not fair at all, but we didn't think about things like that too much. I guess it was a man's world.

But you didn't go to Harvard?

Well, the scholarship wasn't enough to make it possible for me to go. It looked like a pretty good piece of money but not enough to swing the deal.

Did you get the money to spend at UCLA or did you forfeit it?

It was in the form of a tuition grant at Harvard, so I didn't get anything. Except the honor, of course. The emblem of the award was a beautifully bound copy of *The Adams Family* by James Truslow Adams. Very appropriate, considering the Adams family's connection with Harvard. I've always greatly valued that volume. I still have it in our living room bookcase.

Were you a speaker at your high school graduation?

Oh yes, let me tell you about that! My commencement was really something. It was the spring of 1931. There were about 3,500 students in our school; and, for the first time in the history of any high school in Los Angeles, this commencement was held off the campus. They scheduled the Shrine Civic Auditorium, which is adjacent to the campus of the University of Southern California.

I've seen the Shrine Auditorium.

A beautiful theater. Largest in the world—actually larger than the Music Hall in Rockefeller Center in New York. The stage is larger and the place seats more people. Before a basketball arena was built in Exposition Park, which is right next to the campus of the University of Southern California, the USC basketball games were held on the stage of the Shrine Auditorium with bleachers set up at both ends and in the back of the stage so that some people sat on the stage and others out in the auditorium, which accommodated more than six thousand people. For grand operas, they curtained off two-thirds of the stage.

Except for Aida *with the live elephants?*

Nope, live elephants and all, they still didn't use the whole stage. It was too large. Elephants would have gotten lost! I attended Wagner's Ring operas there—the whole thing, complete, with a company from Germany. I never missed an opera in those days. Anyway, the auditorium was an enormous, impressive, and very beautiful place.

So to hold a high school commencement there was certainly a major event. I understand you also had an impressive name for your class?

Yes. We had named ourselves "The Modernists," and at no time did we ever give any thought about what "modernist" meant. I was on the committee that selected the name. We didn't pay the slightest attention to the connotation of the term. It simply sounded good. At any rate, the class commencement speakers were a boy and a girl, who had to try out in an extended speech contest and be selected by a faculty committee. I don't know why I was foolish enough to enter the contest, but I did and was the commencement speaker for the boys. Mary Funk was on the program, playing a concerto with the school symphony. One of the top people from the Los Angeles Philharmonic Orchestra conducted because he was so impressed with her great talents. Now the reason why I mention my speech, apart from the fact that it was something of an event for a kid to address such a vast audience, was that I still have a copy of that paper.

This I would like to read.

I'm not going to let you read it. It's too flamboyant. This was the hundredth anniversary of the founding of the city of Los Angeles and there were all kinds of celebrations around the city that year. It had been determined that these commencement addresses had to have some relevance to the city's centennial. The reason I'm mentioning it is that my speech had to do with Los Angeles in the context of a philosophy of culture and history. The philosophy of history has always been one of my main pursuits. When I ran on to that paper just a few weeks ago, I was startled to find that interest showing up in me so early.

What was the thesis of your remarks?

It had to do with the movement of Occidental culture from Europe across America and the movement of Oriental culture across the Pacific to their meeting on the Pacific Coast. You know, it wasn't a bad idea although the presentation was certainly overly dramatic. But there were these two main interests of mine—philosophy of culture and philosophy of history.

This seems like some pretty significant independent thought in high school?

It's probably a bad sign when you're impressed by the achievements of your own youth. But the fact of the matter is that although I studied very seriously and devoted a lot of time to school work, I still found time to launch out and do a good deal of writing on papers that had nothing to do with school assignments. For instance, I remember writing a long paper on the problems of morality when I was in the tenth grade. I was a puritan then and still am, thanks to the influence of my parents.

Then I wrote a long paper on the Monroe Doctrine. I don't remember how I got interested in that topic, but I spent many evenings in the Los Angeles Public Library studying materials on the Monroe Doctrine. I also found recently a long paper that I had written when in high school on the office of the U.S. president, especially the relation of the president to the Secretary of State. But what these papers have in common is that they were largely philosophical in character—

Rather than historical or religious or political?

That's right. My interest in history and religion and politics always took a philosophical direction.

Now during the summer of 1931, between your high school graduation and entering UCLA, did you go back to the ranch?

Oh yes. I'd go back each summer to the ranch. Because of severe bronchial trouble in Los Angeles, I transferred to the University of Utah in the fall of 1933. My Grandfather Moss died that same autumn. I was very much attached to him; and after that I didn't return to the ranch to work. I had a kind of emotional reaction. The place itself wasn't that different. My uncle, Ralph Moss, was still in charge, but it just wasn't the same for me. I would go for visits, and one or two of my brothers still worked there in the summers; but making my summer home there was over.

Let's move on to college. These were the days of the Great Depression. How did you manage to finance your education?

It was a hard thing to find money anywhere. My father had had a good position as a probation supervisor for the State of California, but it was not a civil service position then. A new governor came in who had been mayor of San Francisco—a politician of the worst order, I might say. He simply threw everybody out of office who could be thrown out and brought in his friends and cronies.

This was during your last year in high school, when you were choosing a college?

Yes, but it was pretty clear all along that it was UCLA for me. My father took a position with Los Angeles County as a probation supervisor several months later. It was a civil service position, and he held it until his death in 1948 at age sixty-seven. But money was in rather short supply in our family during the opening months of my freshman year. That's when I started working after school. My mother had some income from Deseret Live Stock Company stock.

But that was hardly a money-making time for cattle ranchers, either.

Not at all.

Why didn't you consider USC, where you later made connections?

USC was an expensive school in those days, while UCLA was virtually free. If they had both had comparable tuition, I would have probably gone to USC because we lived within walking distance of the campus. It took two hours or more for me to get to UCLA and back.

You took the streetcar?

No, but I could have. It was possible to get all over town on the streetcar and buses. But I rode with a friend of mine from high school, John Donley, who also attended UCLA. I want to tell you about John. He and I ran against each other as high school seniors for the position of scholarship president. I think Donley should have won instead of me, but we became intimate friends and he's still my closest friend from my California days. Well, I learned about a $900 scholarship available from our high school; a woman whose name I can't remember had endowed it. I applied for it, but when I learned that Donley hadn't applied, I went to the vice-principal and told her of Donley's situation. He was very brilliant with a high scholastic record; but his parents were separated— well, actually, his father had deserted the family—and John had to support his sister and mother. He worked in the Blue Goose Market at Crenshaw and Slawson in Los Angeles, and he really knew that business. I told the vice-principal that he should be considered for this scholarship, and she said, "You will probably get the scholarship. If you push for him, he becomes competition to you."

How did you feel about that?

Well, you know I was idealistic in those days. I knew I needed it badly enough, but he needed it worse. So I pressed Donley to go in and sign up for the thing and he got it. He was pleased and I was pleased.

That must have forged a powerful bond between you two.

Yes, he had an old one-seater, and I paid him a little each week, but it covered his gas. I'd get up early—around six-thirty or seven, as I recall—and take a seven-cent streetcar ride out to Donley's part of town, in Inglewood. We would meet at Crenshaw Boulevard and head out toward UCLA. It was a long way to go. Then we'd come back together, I'd take the streetcar back home, get into my white uniform, go over to the service station, and get grease all over it.

Your job was pretty important to you, then!

It certainly was. And it was a good job for the times, not too far from home. I had to start work at the service station by four in the afternoon. Then I worked ten hours on Saturday and all day Sunday.

What kind of money did you make there?

The job paid forty cents an hour, which was good money in those days, and I got five cents for every quart of oil that I sold. Now you're a young man and you don't know how things were in those days, Jack, but Penzoil's premium grade sold for thirty-five cents, Shell Oil for twenty-five cents, and a cheaper grade of Shell Oil for fifteen cents a quart. Regular gas was twelve and a half cents a gallon, and ethyl gas was seventeen and a half cents a gallon. I remember a gas war in which gas got down to five cents a gallon, if you can believe it. Large companies like Shell and Standard just put out a lower octane of gas so it could be sold cheaper, but most cars could still run on the stuff.

I also had a second job my freshman year. A woman who managed a nice apartment house, two stories with maybe ten apartments on each floor, liked the way I cleaned her windshield and checked the battery, so she offered me a job which paid ten dollars a month to come on Saturdays, vacuum the halls, put the papers down a chute into an incinerator, and light the incinerator. Not a complicated job at all, and my income was considerably augmented.

You were spared the worst of the Depression, then.

In personal terms, yes, but less so in terms of the national economy or the social impact. I matured very slowly in my social philosophy. I grew up in a kind, fair family and everybody worked hard, but we didn't see poverty or suffering except the kind that you could quickly do something about as a neighbor. I knew bums on the railroad and factory people, but they were a lot like ranch hands. When I took a course in economics at UCLA, the professor sent us out to talk to the construction workers who were extending Sunset Boulevard—pick and shovel work cutting through the hill. When they knocked off to eat lunch, one guy said to me, "See that fellow over there eating by himself? All he has for lunch is potato peelings." I'll never forget the impact that made on me. I never had a nickel to throw away when I was a student, but I didn't have to eat potato peelings for lunch.

What were your expenses at UCLA?

Believe it or not, the total expense not counting books was ten dollars a semester. This was called a matriculation fee. Physical education was required each semester, so when you registered in the fall, you paid a yearly five-dollar fee which supplied you with a clean gym suit, a sweat suit, and towels every time you went to gym.

Not bad! So the cost of going to UCLA was about twenty-five dollars for the year. And it wasn't an easy place to get into even then.

It was highly selective, and representatives from both USC and UCLA had met with students when we were still in high school to tell us about the entrance requirements. That was no problem in my case.

Both schools selected their students from the top 12.5 percent of the graduating class, as they do today.

What was UCLA like in the 1930s?

It was a very attractive place. It had been founded as the Southern Branch of the University of California—that was its name—and it had a beautiful campus on North Vermont Avenue. The year before I entered as a freshman, it had moved to its present campus at Westwood, a very beautiful place, west of Beverly Hills, between Beverly Hills and Santa Monica. It had built several magnificent buildings, particularly Josiah Royce Hall, which is, I think, the most impressive school building in America. And it had a library, a couple of science buildings, temporary gymnasiums, and a student union. Even during the Depression they were constructing magnificent new buildings.

What kind of a year did you have there?

A good year but a rough year. There was my work schedule, the ROTC business, and I also became very ill.

You mentioned earlier tangling with the ROTC as a freshman at UCLA. What really happened?

It really wasn't anything very serious or even very noble. I was out of school for a couple of weeks with a light case of pneumonia; it triggered very severe bronchial asthma later. But anyway, I missed a couple of weeks and the ROTC required me to make it up—which was all right with me. Now the make-up usually consisted of cleaning machine-guns or some kind of work under the supervision of some Army sergeant. They required that I make up my time late in the afternoon. Well, I worked every afternoon and evening in a service station near my home, and it seemed really unreasonable to me that they wouldn't let me make up the work earlier in the afternoon while I was still on the campus. So I didn't make up the time.

Now they didn't cause a problem over it, but the dean of my college—Letters, Arts, and Sciences—was French and a professor of French civilization or something like that. He called me into his office and gave me a stiff lecture about the beauties of military life. He wanted me to know that he had been in the French army and that military service was the patriotic thing to do, that this was my duty, and so on. Well, I just listened to this guy, feeling more and more disgusted. When he got through, I simply told him that my name had been turned in because I hadn't made up my ROTC time. I told him I was perfectly happy to make it up, but I had to work and there was no reason in the world why they couldn't let me come there during a free period during the day to make up that time. That kind of softened him up a little, and he laid off me.

Did all these conditions, including the ROTC matter, take a toll on your academic work?

Well, it didn't make it any easier, I'll say that! My grades weren't bad but they weren't too good.

But you left UCLA after your freshman year?

During the fall term of my freshman year, I had my first attack of bronchial asthma; and it actually knocked me out of school for two or three weeks.

Is that when you first learned you had asthma?

Yes. I'd never had a problem until after I'd had a mild case of pneumonia; but from then on, I had very severe bronchial asthma. I didn't realize that it was something that stayed with a person. When I was up and around I thought that it was over with, because there was no history of it in my family and I'd had no experience with it. I'm not sure I'd ever even heard the word before.

Did it go away for a time?

It didn't go away. I finished my freshman year, worked on the ranch that summer, then came back in the fall of 1932 to register for my sophomore year. I was standing in line in the fall of '32 in Josiah Royce Hall and had such trouble breathing that I had to leave the line. And I just didn't go back. I spent much of that year—what should have been my sophomore year—sitting up in bed, actually struggling to breathe. My uncle, W. D. Chipman, who was an M.D. in Los Angeles, sent me to specialists of all kinds. I took all kinds of tests, trying to figure out how to treat it. On a number of occasions in the middle of the night, the struggle for breath would get so acute that my mother and I would drive many miles, over to Pasadena and up to Altadena in the foothills below Mount Wilson, where I could breathe. More than once the doctors gave me morphine to enable me to breathe. Wonderful stuff—put me to sleep.

The asthma must have been very scary.

Oh, it was a major ordeal. I simply couldn't manage, and the medicines which I was given were not very effective—much less so than the medicines we have now. That's when my Grandfather Moss told me to get back to Utah where I belonged. So I went off again to the ranch and I was like a new person. Even the doctors didn't make any connection between my condition and the region. But I could certainly tell the difference; so in the fall of '33, after I left the ranch, I registered at the University of Utah.

Now when you came to the University of Utah that fall, what was the place like?

Well, it had fewer than four thousand students. I well remember this because I was here full-time for four years—received my B.A. degree in '36 and a master's degree in '37. I remember the hoopla during the winter quarter of, I believe it was 1934-35, when the enrollment reached four thousand. The only buildings here then were those on the oval and adjacent to it.

The Presidents' Circle?

Yes, although it wasn't called that then. It received that name when David P. Gardner was president in the 1970s.

What was the spirit of the place compared with UCLA?

Well, I think they were comparable; but I'm going to confess to you that when I left UCLA and came here, I felt a little like I was going back to high school.

How so? Was it the academic or the social environment?

More the social side. I was living with an aunt and uncle, Dr. Ezra Waddoups and Ethel Moss Waddoups. Aunt Ethel was my mother's oldest sister. They were gracious and hospitable in every way and had a beautiful home on Normandy Circle within walking distance of the university. My grandfather had arranged it. My uncle was in debt to my grandfather, which wasn't unusual for my grandfather's family, so my living with them was the way my grandfather chose for my uncle to cancel part of this debt and at the same time pay me for my summer's work with him.

Your grandfather helped to finance your education, in effect. How did that work out?

I wasn't sure that I liked the idea, and I'm pretty sure they didn't; but my grandfather had spoken and that settled it. I had never been close to my aunt's family because they lived in Utah while we lived in California; but they had two younger daughters at home, and in no time at all a lasting bond of affection developed among us. I looked for work at the university, but nothing came of it, which was a real disappointment.

Tuition that year was about seventy-four dollars, according to Ralph Chamberlin's history of the university.

That's right. About twenty-five dollars a quarter for everything.

Because my aunt and uncle lived within walking distance of the university, I didn't have any transportation costs. It was mostly vacant lots around the university then, though now, of course, it's all built up. Most of my classes were in the L Building. L for liberal arts. When I was dean of the College of Letters and Science, I got the name changed to Mathematics Building. It's now the LeRoy Cowles Building.

But you didn't feel the same challenge here, as a student?

I have no criticism of the University of Utah, you understand. There was much more of a personal quality in the life here and in my relationships with the administration and the faculty. Everything was pleasant. UCLA was really quite impersonal, and I'm afraid the University of Utah has become more impersonal as it has become larger. But at that time a strong personal quality pervaded the relationships which students had, not just with other students but with members of the faculty. It was a very pleasant place from that standpoint. Professors Ephraim Ericksen in philosophy and Gail Plummer in the speech department, and Dean LeRoy Cowles and his secretary Georgia Harmer became my close friends by the end of the first quarter.

But after your first quarter here, you resolved to go home? You encountered some tough things in life that year.

I did. I was homesick and I didn't want to stay here any longer. Grandfather Moss died during that quarter, and my Grandfather McMurrin had passed away the previous year, so I wanted to be with my family. I packed up my stuff for Christmas—everything I owned fit into two suitcases—and went home for Christmas, fully intending to go back to UCLA.

But I spent the whole vacation struggling to breathe and I had no alternative but to return to Utah. I had gone to Los Angeles by train, but I came back by bus—on Union Pacific Stages. It wasn't a bad trip except for the dirt roads between Nephi and Barstow. There was no pavement on that route, except for a little section through Las Vegas, now the so-called Las Vegas Strip.

How about your academic work?

As preparation for the Foreign Service, I originally majored in political science, but I registered for only one course in political science. I did more work in philosophy, and I sensed right from the beginning that my interests were far stronger in philosophy. I had a course in history and a couple of courses in geology, some Latin, some economics.

Was this all at UCLA?

Yes. But I always liked geology and had several courses of geology after I came here. My main work at the University of Utah was in philosophy, political science, and history.

Was the curriculum quite structured when you came here? Or did you have a lot of room to design your own course of study?

I recall having a lot of options. The curriculum was not, I think, any more prescribed than it is now. You were required to satisfy a stipulated number of hours in science, etc. There was one experience that I had at both places that I simply must describe. It involved freshman English. At UCLA this was called Subject A, Freshman Composition, and everyone entering UCLA, even before the school year began, was required to take a test in English grammar and composition.

Isn't that interesting! The use of pre-tests in composition has been reinvented here and elsewhere in recent years.

Well, I think it's a good thing. Now, Donley and I went out together and took the examination, and we left feeling confident that we had done very well. After all, we had done well in high school and we weren't bad in grammar. But we both received notification that we had failed. This was a terrible blow—the required course fee was ten dollars and the class rendered no credit! He and I had both been made life members of the California Scholarship Federation, we were both candidates for the scholarship presidency of the student body, and now we had both failed that cussed examination! We were certain that we had been swindled. The plain fact was that we didn't have the ten dollars to pay for the course, and we didn't have time to take the course if we had had the money. We were both working.

What did you do?

We sought justice! This Subject A examination had its own staff, and they wouldn't even talk to us. But we learned that the test came under the jurisdiction of the head of the English department. The semester was just starting—this was during registration—so we went to see the chair. She wouldn't talk to us, either. So we sat there in her outer office until it was time for her to leave to go home. When she came out of her office and spotted us, she said, "Are you two still here?" We said, "We are, and we're not going to leave until someone agrees to take another look at our examination papers." So she called up the Subject A office—somebody was still there—and made arrangements to review our papers. We went over there and had a session with the man in charge. He laid out the papers for us and said, "There is absolutely nothing wrong with either of these papers. They're both very, very good, on both the grammar and composition."

I never found out what the problem was—whether it was somebody trying to raise money for Subject A or an honest mistake; but I felt good that we'd been so persistent.

That's quite a story! But you said there was a connection with the University of Utah when you transferred?

Yes, when I came to the University of Utah, the dean of the Lower Division was what later became the dean of General Education.

The predecessor to my previous position as dean of Liberal Education, and the present dean of Undergraduate Studies! The tradition here is to dream up a new title every time the incumbent changes.

Right. And the dean of the Lower Division handled graduation requirements.

And there was a composition requirement?

Yes, there was no examination. Everyone was simply required to take a course in freshman English. Dean Cowles assured me that in view of the fact that I had passed the examination at UCLA and was not required to take freshman English there, I would not be required to take it here. Well, he was the law. But in the middle of my senior year, believe it or not, Professor Neff, who was head of the English department, sent for me. He had a very slow and genteel way of talking. He said, "Mr. McMurrin, we have discovered that you did not ever take a course in freshman English." I said, "That's right," and explained what Dean Cowles had told me. He said, "Oh, but Mr. McMurrin, no one can graduate from this university without taking a course in our department"—just like that. This shows you how things have changed. A student today wouldn't put up with being shoved around like that.

Oh they often do, unfortunately. What did you do?

I did what I was told, of course! He had it all figured out. "Now," he said, "there's no point in your taking a course in freshman English. We don't want you to do that. We will put you in a course in advanced composition with Professor Louis Zucker." Later on, when Dean Cowles discovered this, it made him mad as the devil; and he said, "If you had told me about this, I would have stopped it."

How did the course turn out? It must have been a great experience to study with Professor Zucker?

Yes, he was the leading figure in the state's Jewish intellectual life, but also one of the leading figures in the intellectual life of the university. We became very good friends and remained close right up to the day of his death. I later proposed him for an honorary degree from the university. He was in the hospital, but he learned about the degree before his death. I wrote and read the citation. Louis was a wonderful man.

Freshman English and how universities handle it has always rankled me. Testing procedures are so capricious. Now tell me a little more about Professor S. B. Neff. I know he is a legendary character.

Neff was an Easterner, as I recall; and when he retired from the University of Utah, he went back East—at least, that's what most of us thought. But, perhaps ten years later, during the sixties, I received a letter from the president of a college in Texas who said, "The leading scholar on our faculty, who has his degree from Harvard, was once a professor at the University of Utah, S. B. Neff." You know, I must confess that I didn't know Neff was still living.

But the point of the letter was that Neff was retiring, the college was holding a major celebration in his honor, and Neff had asked that I speak at the faculty banquet honoring him.

Well, this was a great chance to tell that freshman English story on him. Did you?

No, I didn't. I forgave Neff all of his sins and I went down to Texas and gave that eulogy. And you know that man didn't look a day older than when I first met him.

Who had the greatest influence on you as your undergraduate years unfolded?

That's a tough question. Even though I was only at UCLA one year, I had philosophy classes with two leading scholars—Hugh Miller in Greek philosophy and John Elof Boodin, a Swedish philosopher who had been a student of William James, in medieval and early modern philosophy. Boodin must have come to this country when he was very young, because James died in 1916. Perhaps he came as a student and then went back to Sweden for awhile, but his English was always so broken I was surprised that he had been in this country from an early age.

What was his specialty?

Boodin was an idealist who did considerable work in metaphysics. He called himself a realist. He was a great figure with an international reputation. I well remember one class at UCLA—a good-sized lecture class. He was planning to bring Albert Einstein, who was a friend of his, to class, because Einstein was in California doing something at Cal Tech. A couple of students were reading the *Daily Bruin,* the student newspaper, and Boodin got furious at the class. He pounded his pipe on the table and said by damn he wasn't going to invite Einstein to a class like this, and he didn't. So I missed meeting Einstein!

Did you meet him later?

No. When I was spending quite a bit of time at Princeton in the early 1950s, I tried to make connections with him at the Institute for Advanced Study but missed him. Missed Jacques Maritain, too, the leading Catholic philosopher. He was teaching at Princeton University, and we exchanged letters; but when I went to his home, hoping to find him, his housekeeper said he was out of town. Well, later, when I was a graduate student at Southern California, I renewed my association with Professor Boodin, who was either still at UCLA or had just retired. When I was on the faculty at USC, the people in philosophy from that whole region would get together from time to time, usually at USC because of its central location. Boodin and Miller were both advanced in years by then, but it was a great pleasure for me to have that continued association with them.

Even from your first university classes it was perfectly evident that your main interest was in philosophy, though you were thinking of a career in government as a way of earning a living.

True. At the University of Utah, I registered my first quarter for a course in logic from E. E. Ericksen. He was the person who had the largest impact on me of any of the teachers that I had in college. Ericksen was not a great scholar, but he was a very great teacher. On my first exam in his logic class, I must have done well enough to impress Ericksen. After giving back the examinations, he invited me to meet with him. So I walked down to his office with him, and we talked. And we continued to talk for more than forty years.

Obviously, he was a man generous with his time.

Absolutely. I spent thousands of hours with Ericksen. He had a very great impact on me in inducing in me a rational, critical attitude toward problems—not only philosophical problems, but problems of any kind. I was fascinated by the consistency and integrity of his belief in the power of reason and his commitment to critical analysis. He had a mind which, in the best sense of the word, was thoroughly critical. It was from Ericksen, more than from any other person, that I imbibed the spirit of Socrates, that the unexamined life is not worth living. That was what Ericksen was all about. He had remarkable influence on his students— and he was certainly a most important influence on me.

During my senior year and my graduate year, I shared Ericksen's office as his assistant. Those old offices, you know, were pretty good sized. He had a desk, a swivel chair, and a book case put in there for me, and the university paid me twenty-five cents an hour.

That's when you were doing research on the history of the university?

Yes, and I worked hard. But my real pay was being with Ericksen every day. We talked about everything. I got acquainted with the faculty, I'll tell you, through these conversations. My main undergraduate association was with members of the faculty, not other students.

Ericksen was an institution around here. I believe he created the philosophy department. What, if any, were his connections with the LDS church?

I think he came here just after the major controversy about academic freedom and due process in 1915. Of course, Ericksen had plenty of battles; but George Thomas, who became president in 1921, supported Ericksen right on through. Ericksen was a Mormon, thoroughly unorthodox but very devoted to the church, and a valuable church worker. He served on the general board of the Young Men's Mutual Improvement Association—the organization for teenage boys and young men. He'd been there in this volunteer position for many years and had a real interest in a progressive and liberal lesson curriculum, social activism, and so on. He wanted more than anything else to serve the church through his work with young people. But he had his enemies, as you well know, who were determined to get him off the general board and away from the youth program. Soon after I got acquainted with Ericksen, in 1933, he was bounced off the general board by a conservative faction led by John A. Widtsoe, who was then an apostle. He used to tell me in detail about this hassle. Arthur L. Beeley was also on the youth board. Now, you wouldn't have known Beeley . . .

No, I didn't.

Beeley was another institution. He was a British convert to Mormonism, and he cultivated his British personal qualities. He was head of sociology and creator of the university's Graduate School of Social Work, of which he was dean, until his retirement in about 1955 or 1956. He retired at age sixty-five, after I became dean of Letters and Science. Not long after Beeley's retirement, the Council of Academic Deans under President Ray Olpin raised the retirement age to sixty-eight for faculty, although it remained sixty-five for administrators. Beeley took that action quite personally. In his best British accent he told me, "You know, Olpin just waited until I was retired so that he could raise the retirement age to sixty-eight."

Beeley had been an aspirant for the presidency when Olpin was made president; and though he was a highly cultivated professional, in every way a very gracious person, it was perfectly obvious to everyone that there was no love lost between him and Olpin.

So the general board for the Young Men's Mutual Improvement Association had two very distinguished faculty members from the University of Utah on it. Getting rid of them must have created a ruckus.

It was a little difficult for the church to fire them, as you can imagine. They were highly thought of in the community. Their contributions were very well known. So the way the church did it was to dissolve the board and reorganize it, leaving Ericksen and Beeley off. Actually, Ericksen told me that when Beeley discovered that they were going to fire them, he resigned first. I don't know whether that was Beeley's version, but that's what Ericksen said. But Ericksen was determined to stay right there and make them kick him off.

Wasn't going to make it easy for them.

Yes, and after the board was reorganized, everybody was back on it except Beeley and Ericksen. It wasn't very subtle. Waldemer Read told me that George Thomas was giving an address somewhere in the university and, to get at some point he was making, called attention to the fact that the church had dissolved the YMMIA general board to drop Beeley and Ericksen: "They burned down the whole barn to get rid of a couple of rats," was how he put it. Thomas was a kind of crusty character. Now I think that should be preserved; and if it isn't preserved here, I don't know where it will be.

Well, it is preserved here and now!

The reason I'm telling you this story, Jack, is that I want you to see that some of these leading figures in the university were really devoted to the LDS church.

Elder Boyd Packer and a few of his apostolic supporters are waging a more vicious campaign against scholars in the 1990s. I'm thinking, for example, of the excommunications of six prominent intellectuals in the fall of 1993. This sort of grudge against freedom of thought, and those who support it, seems to be a continuing characteristic of Mormon leaders, or at least an episodic one.

Yes, I've seen it happen over and over again. But it is clearly at its worst today.

Wasn't Ericksen near retirement when you came? And wasn't there a symbolic link between his professorship and yours?

His last year was 1947-48. He retired at sixty-five, creating the faculty vacancy to which I was appointed. He went to the University of Nevada at Reno and chaired its Department of Philosophy for several years. He and Edna kept their home here in Salt Lake while they were in Nevada, so after his second retirement they lived for many years on

University Avenue near the bottom of the campus, right across the street from the old library. Mrs. Ericksen died just a few years ago. He had died earlier. She was a beautiful woman, highly talented, with a distinguished career in civic affairs.

You've made the point that it was as a teacher that Ericksen had such great influence. What about his writing, his scholarship?

He produced one of the first real scholarly studies of Mormonism—the best thing he wrote, by far, in my opinion. It analyzes Mormon social, moral, and intellectual life.

That was his dissertation at the University of Chicago?

Yes, *The Psychological and Ethical Aspects of Mormon Group Life*. It was published in a limited edition by the University of Chicago Press and, as I think you know, the University of Utah Press republished it a few years ago.

I've read it. It's excellent. You had something to do with getting it republished, didn't you?

Yes. I felt very strongly that it should be republished. After Ericksen's death, I talked to Mrs. Ericksen about it. She liked the idea and thought it would be a very nice thing; so I negotiated with the University of Utah Press and my colleagues in the philosophy department. Four of us had been students and friends of Ericksen: Waldemer Read, Obert Tanner, Charles Monson, and I. We got our heads together and decided that we should do much more than simply reproduce Ericksen's doctoral dissertation. We wanted to make it the centerpiece of a volume in honor of Ericksen with several essays on his philosophy. It wasn't to be a *festschrift* in the ordinary sense because it was to be a volume of Ericksen's own stuff as well as essays on him and his philosophy. He had published another book, *Social Ethics*, in 1937. I worked with him on that book when I was a graduate student; and Waldemer Read, his former student and by then his colleague in the department, contributed importantly to that book. It's a good book. It's a textbook in ethics with a strong pragmatic flavor. It also has a chapter or two on religion—it's not solely on ethics. We were going to include extensive passages from this book and other publications in our essays on Ericksen's philosophy.

I've never seen this book. What were the essays about?

There's a good reason why you've never seen it. It was never published! I'll get to that in just a minute. The way we divided up the work, Monson was going to write on Ericksen's political thought and, to some extent, his economic thought. That was a particular interest of Monson. Ericksen's degree at Chicago was in economics and philosophy; and he had produced a large manuscript on economic philosophy; but it was never published. As a matter of fact, it was somewhat outdated by the time he had finished it. Obert Tanner was to take Ericksen as a moral philosopher. I was doing his philosophy of religion, and Read wrote a biographical essay. Read had been Ericksen's student and colleague since the late 1920s.

Well, to make a long story short—and it *is* a long story—Read did an extensive essay on Ericksen's philosophical position and his involvement with the LDS church. He wrote that essay on the occasion of the establishment of the E. E. Ericksen Professorship in Philosophy, to which I was appointed. President James Fletcher and the vice-president, Jack Adamson, wanted to have a major event to inaugurate the professorship and asked me to give an inaugural address. It was on the philosophy of history and had nothing to do with Ericksen, but Read, at my urging, agreed to read a paper on Ericksen.

Seems like a good balance.

Well, he gave a terrific paper, it really was great. But it analyzed in considerable detail Ericksen's problems with the Mormon church—or rather, its problems with him. We planned to use this essay in the book. Ericksen was still alive and attended the inaugural evening. I don't know how he reacted to Read's paper. He died before we became involved in doing the book.

Too bad.

In more ways than one. Mrs. Ericksen took exception to several things in Read's essay and felt strongly that they should not be in the book. Read was determined that by damn they *were* going to be in there because if Eph—that's what we always called him, short for Ephraim—were still living, he would want them in. Read just felt that it wouldn't be true to the facts to omit those events, that it would distort the description of Ericksen's personality and his intellectual struggles.

Was he right? And was this conflict the undoing of the book?

Oh, I'm sure he was. I felt the same way. One specific example was a kind of grilling by the local Mormon church authorities when they called Ericksen in and really put him on the spot about his beliefs. Ericksen always called that his "inquisition." It wasn't a formal trial for his membership, you understand, but a rather hostile questioning. Read included Ericksen's own account of that. Mrs. Ericksen didn't want it in the book, and the net result was that the book was never published. I think all of the essays were written with the possible exception of two, one by Jack Adamson and the other by Lowell Bennion. I have them right here in the drawer; but the project was dropped, and I've always been sorry about that.

You decided it wasn't worth creating difficulties with the family?

Yes, we didn't want to do anything that would be offensive to Mrs. Ericksen. She was a very dear friend of all of us. A remarkable woman, a wonderful person; but Read wasn't about to yield and neither would she. Monson, the junior partner, was the editor, so he dealt with Mrs. Ericksen. They were extremely close. I don't know if someone else would have been more effective.

What has become of the collection of unpublished essays for the book, especially Waldemer Read's essay?

I've got the whole set in my files at home, at least all those that were finished. I will donate them to the Marriott Library.

But at least you got the dissertation reprinted?

Yes, much to Mrs. Ericksen's pleasure, I might say. The University Press did a very good job. Both Mrs. Ericksen and the director of the press, Norma Mikkelsen, asked me to write an introduction to the book, so I revamped the essay which I had written for the other volume. That dissertation was a fine piece of work. It deserved to be republished and has received a great deal of attention. Far more, I'm sure, than it received when it was first issued by the University of Chicago Press.

There's no question that Eph Ericksen had a powerful and positive influence on your life as a student and later as a professor. Now what can you tell me about campus life in the 1930s. What was it like here?

Well, campus life here was quite simple in those days compared to what it is now, and the whole operation was much smaller.

I understand that one of the great satisfactions of President Thomas was winning a Phi Beta Kappa chapter for the University of Utah. It was established in 1935, when you were here. Do you remember the ceremonies?

Oh yes, very well. The ceremonies were held at Kingsbury Hall, really the only auditorium that we had in those days. And of course, the students attended things. Today if something like the establishment of Phi Beta Kappa were held, I'm sure they would hold it either in the president's office or in a very small auditorium because you wouldn't expect very many students to show up.

Most University of Utah students were living at home then, just as they are now, which is the reason we give to explain why they don't turn out in large numbers for public events on campus today.

You're quite right. I don't know why except that I think there was more of a sense in those days of being a part of the university, among not only students but faculty. My impression today is that many faculty, much less students, don't see themselves as an integral part of the university. They're off in their own corner. They see themselves as part of their own department—and some barely that. Even down into the 1950s, it seemed to me that the typical faculty man or woman had a strong sense of belonging to the whole institution. And the students felt the same way. The student body numbered less than four thousand in the thirties. You'd know everybody.

Well, I didn't mean to distract you from your Phi Beta Kappa tale.

The granting of the charter is a simple ceremony; but the important thing is that it was the first chapter of Phi Beta Kappa to be established in Utah. BYU doesn't have a chapter even now. Well, the national Phi Beta Kappa officer who presided at the ceremony was a celebrated figure in physics, Robert Milliken, who was then president of the California Institute of Technology and a Nobel Prize winner for his research on cosmic rays. He gave a formal address which made a very considerable impression on me—affected my whole approach to higher education.

What did he say about universities?

He talked about the fundamental importance of research, pointing out that practical applications of science depend on disinterested scholarship. He gave several examples of the general impact of basic research upon the development of technology and how technology, in turn, influences the social structure and the rise and decline of civilizations. If I were to try to examine the origins of my own views about higher education, I would certainly cite Milliken's address as having influenced me.

Did you become involved in the Phi Beta Kappa chapter?

Some of the faculty members in those days were Phi Beta Kappa, but the first student members would have been elected from the graduating class in 1935. I was elected to membership in 1936, my senior year, with some other students. Of course, we already had a chapter here of the general honorary society, Phi Kappa Phi, and I was elected to it.

Do you have any other observations on the quality of intellectual life on the campus?

Well, partly because of the high level of participation by most of the students and faculty in all of the activities that were going on, I'd say that the quality was very high. Classroom performance by students was high. And the university was certainly fulfilling its role of being a window on the wider world by bringing in numerous outstanding speakers and events. Departments and colleges didn't do as much then as they do now, obviously. There wasn't the money to bring people in, but the Extension Division, later Continuing Education, was responsible for some very outstanding things. Its "Masterminds and Artists" series was absolutely first-rate. It strikes me as being somewhat superior to the typical stuff that we have going on now. This series was open to the public as well as to the students, so every few weeks there'd be a program with topflight artists and lecturers, major intellectual figures of world recognition, and a very considerable number of artistic events during the year. Kingsbury Hall would be filled for these occasions.

How were such events funded?

In those days each student received a book of coupons when he or she paid the fees. It contained tickets for all of the athletic and dramatic events; and the tickets for the Masterminds and Artists series were right there, too. I found the same situation at UCLA when I was a freshman. And the very fact that students had these books of tickets encouraged their attendance.

Convenient for dates and group socials, I imagine.

Yes, and they were a sort of student identification. You showed the book when you bought streetcar tickets to get a discount. It cost ten cents to ride the streetcar in those days, but buying them as student books of tickets saved you about three cents a ride. Well, that was a significant saving for a student in those days.

So even though there wasn't as much going on as there might be today, each event would draw broader participation?

That's right. Of course, we have more advanced graduate work now. In those days the university offered only masters' degrees. There was no formally organized graduate school—not until Olpin came two decades later—but there was a division of graduate work with a director of its own. As far as I could tell, it functioned very effectively and very smoothly.

According to Ralph Chamberlin's history, The University of Utah, *this institution granted only fifty-five masters' degrees and no doctorates in 1940, so the amount of graduate work was really quite small.*

If I remember correctly, the first master's degree was awarded about 1907.

What kinds of restrictions were placed on students here in your student days?

Well, let's take smoking. This didn't bother me because I've never smoked, but smoking was permitted only in certain areas of the university—shaded areas, they were called. Maps of the university in the catalog and for visitors would show these shaded areas. It was a source of some amusement to the students and faculty. One of those shaded areas was out behind the Park Building.

So you couldn't smoke in front, but you could slip out behind the barn, so to speak?

That's it. Another shaded area was the steps on the east entrance to the Cowles Building. So between classes there would be a conclave of smokers puffing away. Now, you see, we've gone back to such restrictions and they don't sound as silly as they did fifty years ago.

True, but their reasons were different then. What other rules of conduct were enforced for students?

Smoking didn't bother me much, but one that affected all of the students was the segregation of the sexes. I don't know what they did in gym classes because I never took one. But in the library reading room at the top of the stairs on the third floor of the Park Building, the men and women were not allowed to sit together. Now I don't think it was for moral reasons; it was because they made too much noise visiting. There would be a librarian on patrol to make sure you stayed in your own area. The men had the north end and the women had the south end of the reading room. This sort of segregation was enforced even in the student union building.

Where or what was the center of campus life?

When I came to the university in '33, Kingsbury Hall and Gardner Music Hall were new. Very handsome buildings. I think they still are. Gardner Hall was originally the student union building and it had a touch of real elegance, not only in its architectural quality but in its furnishings. Far superior in most respects, in my opinion, to the present Olpin Union Building. It had a beautiful ballroom on the main floor and lounges on the east and west ends.

Here's where the segregation comes in.

Yes! The east lounge was the women's lounge and the lounge at the west end was for the men. Both were beautifully furnished with grand pianos, elegant furnishings, and so forth. Incidentally, upstairs on the east end was another elegant lounge, the Auerbach Room, which was a gift to the university from the Auerbach family, a very handsome, beautifully furnished room. These rooms were large. They ran the whole width of the building. Then upstairs on the west end were some recreation rooms like billiards, and a little theater on the third floor and student offices.

Well, the men were not allowed in the women's lounge and vice versa. Just weren't allowed there.

But what about dances? No segregation there, but plenty of supervision?

Well, that was the exception. For dances, for which people dressed up, those two lounges were open and that's when the men got to sniff around in the women's lounge, walk in there with their partners and vice versa. It was a beautiful building and I can understand the desire to preserve it. Everything was kept in beautiful condition. In fact, it was kept in such good condition that they literally drove the students out of the building. There was just never anyone around.

So if you went into the lounge, you'd feel downright uncomfortable?

I'll say! And if you want a sample of how uncomfortable they made you feel, I had two experiences. Now I had been spoiled at UCLA, which had a very beautiful new union building, Kirkhoff Hall. It had a men's lounge, a women's lounge, and one where the two sexes could intermingle. Now in the men's lounge, it was very informal. It was common for some to stretch out on a sofa and go to sleep. Well, that may have been going too far. But at Utah on one occasion I was sitting up in a high-backed chair and dozed off. You can understand why. I was milking cows, getting up at 4:30 or 5:00 in the morning. Well, the woman in charge was watching and came over. "This is no place to sleep, young man," she said and asked me to leave. So I did. And the next time, I was sitting up in a straight-back chair reading in the men's lounge. The woman came over and said, "The place to read is in the library. Either put up the book or leave." So I left and never went back. Others had the same experience. Now, there was enough freedom that a fellow could come in and pound around on the piano or talk; but to be frank, I didn't have enough friends among the students to even go in and talk with anybody.

Sad that the students didn't feel welcome in their own building.

About the only indoor place you could talk with a woman, except for empty classrooms, was the reserved book room. And during warm weather, student social life centered on the front steps of the Park Building. In the good weather, those Park Building steps would be so solid with students that people couldn't walk up and down them. That's where the students would come to sit and talk, see and be seen. In cold weather, the social center moved inside the Park Building on the lower floor where the bookstore was located and on the stairways leading to the library. Now I didn't sit there because I wasn't involved in student life.

What about your studies? Your undergraduate degree was in philosophy and history?

No, actually it was in the history and political science department. By the summer of 1934, I'd decided that I didn't want to pursue the study of law but had decided to stick with philosophy and history. I didn't do as much work in history as I should have done. I've always regretted that I didn't concentrate on history, but I was quite taken with political science at that time. As graduation approached, I actually qualified for graduation either from the history and political science department or from the philosophy department. Professor Neff wanted me to get the degree from his department, and Ericksen thought it would be a good idea. By then it was obvious that I was going to go on for my M.A. in philosophy. So that's why I did it.

You wrote your master's thesis during the academic year 1936-37, Sterling. What was your topic?

Well, my subject was the theory of knowledge in St. Augustine, Anselm, and Aquinas. The university library was very short on a lot of things—didn't have all of Augustine's works. I had to get the complete works of Aquinas through Monsignor Duane G. Hunt, later bishop of the Utah diocese of the Catholic church. He had it in his personal library. He lived in Holy Cross Hospital and made arrangements for me to use his library any time of the day or night. I lived very near there. We became good friends and had some association after he became bishop and I returned to Utah. But when I'd worked on the university history, I ran into a complete set of St. Augustine's works at the LDS Church Historical Library. So I went back down to the library and told Alvin Smith that I would like to have the privilege of spending some time with the writings of St. Augustine. "Never heard of him," said the official librarian of the Mormon church. Well, I'm sure he hadn't! "Never heard of him. We don't have anything of his here," he said. "Well," I said, "Brother Smith, you do." "You show it to me," he said gruffly, so I took him back and there it was. So he gave me permission to use it.

Your lifelong affiliation with the University of Utah began with two degrees, an excellent education, and many strong friendships. Let's turn next to exploring those friendships and how they influenced you.

3.
Friend of Great Teachers

Sterling, you had a remarkable experience as an undergraduate through the quality of friendships you developed with your professors. It isn't just that they befriended you out of goodwill, but you genuinely became their colleague. Let's focus for the moment on two of your finest teachers, Waldemer Read and Milton Bennion.

Yes. Let me mention Milton Bennion first. He was dean of the School of Education at the University of Utah and Milton Bennion Hall is, of course, named for him. He was also professor of philosophy. Education was his main area, but he gave attention to ethics and religion. He offered a course on citizenship, which I didn't ever have occasion to take, but I taught it for him when he needed a substitute. I did, however, take Moral Teachings of the New Testament and the philosophy of religion from Milton Bennion. As far as I know, this was the university's first course in the philosophy of religion. It was probably 1935-36—not my first year. He used William Kelly Wright's text, a rather conservative but very good book.

How did the course come about and why was it so late in its arrival?

Ericksen, who was chair of the department, told me that he had been trying for a long time to get President Thomas to let them teach a course in the philosophy of religion. Now Thomas was a very wise man and had tremendous influence on the history of this university by working for its independence from the Mormon church, but he knew a thing like this had to be done carefully. And, of course, in those days the president was the boss. They didn't have as many committees and as much bureaucratic rigmarole as we're accustomed to now. Ericksen said he'd ask about that course every year, and every year Thomas would tell him, "No, you can't have such a course now. I'll tell you when you can." And this had gone on for several years before he finally said, "Well, now you can have that course in the philosophy of religion, but you can't teach it. You can have that course only if Dean Bennion teaches it." Bennion was a prominent Mormon, but also an able social critic and reformer.

President Thomas needed to avoid problems not only with the Mormon church but the Protestants and the Catholic church as well. They probably all worried about how such a course might be taught at the university.

Yes, Bennion was safer on a thing like that as far as the churches were concerned, so he taught it. Ericksen was too much of a skeptic for any of the local religious leaders to find comfort with him. Milton Bennion's office was in the northwest corner on the main floor of the Park Building, now the office of the president. He was looked upon with the greatest respect by everyone in the state and the university. The portrait of him that hangs in Bennion Hall was being painted when I was his student; on two occasions he invited me down to the artist's studio in the old Zion's First National Bank Building. I met him there twice to observe the painting—a very interesting process. He gave me a photograph of the painting. I had it framed and on my desk when I was sharing Ericksen's office.

The next year when I was teaching LDS seminary in Richfield, I still kept Dean Bennion's portrait on my desk. One day in walked Lynn Bennion, the church's seminary supervisor, and here was his father's portrait on my desk. It worries me right to this day that Lynn may have thought that I put that portrait on my desk because I knew he was going to show up.

Did your interest in moral philosophy stem from your association with Ericksen and Bennion?

Yes, although I have less interest in moral philosophy today than I did then, and my father was probably the most important influence on me in that area. Dean Bennion was quite conservative in his religious views—but very progressive in his political and social views. He and Ericksen and Read got along very well. They were less conservative than he was. Bennion was highly respected in the LDS church and became general superintendent of the Sunday schools after his retirement. When I came back to the University of Utah to teach, he phoned me on several occasions to ask my opinion about books they were considering for a Sunday school library they were creating.

Do you recall specific titles that you recommended?

Oh, I remember he asked about Ralph Tyler Flewelling, who was head of philosophy at Southern California. So Bennion was very active right up to the time of his death. I still regard him as a great man.

Who else shaped your thought and the intellectual climate of the university when you were an undergraduate? Was one of the major figures Ralph

Chamberlin, the professor of zoology, with whom you had some association?

Yes, he was one of the great figures in the university. As a matter of fact, Chamberlin was the university's most celebrated scientist, world famous in entomology. I think his specialty was spiders. Now, I mention Chamberlin not simply because he was important as a scientist, though he certainly was, but because he was tremendously important in the intellectual life of Utah. He was at the center of the 1911 hassle over evolution at the BYU, in many ways the most important dispute in the intellectual history of Utah. He left BYU, went to Harvard, and later returned to the University of Utah. He taught a course in evolution which was one of the most popular classes in the institution. I took that course and it was absolutely first rate.

After Chamberlin's retirement, he devoted considerable attention to writing the history of the university. He was working on that history when I joined the faculty here in 1948. An earlier and very influential book was *The Life and Philosophy of W. H. Chamberlin,* his biography of his brother who had died as a comparatively young man in the very early '20s.

William Henry Chamberlin was, with Ralph, at BYU in 1911 when all hell broke loose over the teaching of evolution, wasn't he?

That's right. He was a mathematician and philosopher who joined the BYU faculty in 1910 after a year at the University of Utah. Joseph and Henry Peterson, another set of brothers, also came under pressure from the BYU board of trustees for teaching evolution. They were all told they had to behave or be fired, but W. H. Chamberlin's major offense, apparently, had to do with higher criticism in biblical scholarship.

They saw it as an issue of academic freedom. The Petersons and Ralph Chamberlin resigned but, in effect, they were fired.

The interesting thing is that W. H. Chamberlin remained there, I believe, until 1916, taking a more moderate course. But he was gradually deprived of the courses in philosophy and the Bible that he went there to teach and was left only with mathematics. He was competent in that area, but he wasn't interested in teaching mathematics so he went back to Harvard in 1916, intending to complete a doctorate in philosophy. Josiah Royce, the great absolute idealist, had been his mentor when he had worked earlier at Harvard; but unfortunately, he died just before W. H. returned to Harvard. Chamberlin did biblical studies at the University of Chicago and philosophy at Berkeley under George Holmes Howison. Howison's philosophy appealed to him because, except for William

James among contemporary American philosophers, Howison's position was most like Mormonism—a pluralistic type of metaphysics.

W. H. produced a doctoral dissertation on evolution and idealist metaphysics, the thing that Royce was himself much interested in; but with Royce out of the picture, he failed to win the approval of his committee.

You must have read that dissertation. What did you think of it?

When I was a student in Ralph Chamberlin's course on evolution, he loaned me a copy of his brother's dissertation and two or three other things W. H. had published. I read them with a great deal of interest and received an hour of credit in biology for reading the dissertation. It was a great favor to me—I needed a little more credit in the sciences to graduate. But Ralph Chamberlin also knew that I was interested in his brother's philosophy.

Many years later, when I was on the Utah faculty, Ralph Chamberlin had retired but still had an office and I think a laboratory on campus. He was also working on his history of the university, which was published in 1960. I then became quite well acquainted with him. I was interested in writing an essay on W. H. Chamberlin's philosophy. I asked Ralph if I could borrow that material again, and he very graciously loaned it to me. It took me a long time to get around to writing the essay, in fact I haven't done it yet, but each time I went to return the material, he would say, "Oh, just keep it until you're through with it." Ralph's son, Elliot Chamberlin, approved my sending the W. H. Chamberlin dissertation to the Special Collections of the Marriott Library after his father's death.

What will be in this essay that you've been planning to do for forty years?

It was to be an essay in a volume entitled *Five Mormon Philosophers.* W. H. Chamberlin fully deserves a place in such a volume. In many ways he was Mormonism's foremost philosopher—treated very shabbily by the church. He is now virtually unknown.

Who will the other four essays be about?

Orson Pratt, B. H. Roberts, E. E. Ericksen and Waldemer P. Read. I now plan to add two more: P. A. Christensen, a major figure at BYU and for many years head of its English department. He was a rather strong idealist with inclinations along the line of the American transcendentalists, Jack. You would have liked him. The other essay will be about someone close to both of us, Obert Tanner, a genuine philosopher-statesman and a major figure in Mormon intellectual life.

I hope you will complete it. A very worthwhile undertaking. Where are you now with the project?

Well, I've written the essays on B. H. Roberts and Ericksen and Read, and I've done quite a bit on Tanner and some things on Orson Pratt. So actually, the thing is at least half done. I really intend to do it. If I weren't so lazy, it would have been done long ago.

It sounds as if both Chamberlin brothers were an intellectual influence on you, one directly and one indirectly?

When W. H. left the BYU in 1916, it was a sad thing. He had a hard time making a living. From 1917 to 1920 he taught for the Extension Division of the University of Utah. In 1920 he received an appointment in what is now Utah State University in Logan, but he died soon afterward. Chamberlin had great talent and ability and taught any number of the leading intellectual figures in the state, most of whom I knew rather well. Their testimonials to his memory appear at the end of Ralph Chamberlin's book on W. H.

Who were some of these people?

E. E. Ericksen, Arthur A. Beeley, P. A. Christensen, John C. Swenson, BYU's leading sociologist; Heber C. Snell, the church's leading Bible scholar; W. H. Hendersen, a person of very considerable influence in Logan; Thomas L. Martin, science dean at BYU; and BYU psychologist M. Wilford Poulson. At any rate, here you have in William Henry Chamberlin, a very devout Mormon, a man of tremendous potential influence on the intellectual life of the Mormon church, and the church simply turned its back on him. It's really a tragic story. He could have done great things for the church, and desperately wanted to. But some of his students became the great teachers in Utah during the '20s, '30s, and '40s.

So he died, prematurely and rather unappreciated. Makes you wonder if there was a connection between his spiritual struggles and his physical demise. It sounds as if his life and thought paralleled Ericksen's.

Exactly. W. H. Chamberlin was a more competent philosopher than Orson Pratt or B. H. Roberts. I wonder what would have happened to the philosophy department at the University of Utah if he had taught here for several years—Chamberlin and Ericksen together. What a combination! Ericksen was primarily a moral philosopher with an interest in ethics, while W. H. Chamberlin was very much interested in metaphysics. He was the best chance the Mormon church had for cultivating a philosopher who wanted desperately—I mean, *desperately*— to develop a meaningful philosophical position for the Mormon people.

Ralph Chamberlin, as a scientist, didn't have the same interests. How did he come to write his brother's biography?

Spiders *are* different from metaphysics, and I think Ralph was not such a devout Mormon. But after W. H.'s death, some of his students organized the W. H. Chamberlin Philosophical Society to honor him and commemorate his work. Their major project was getting Ralph to write *The Life and Philosophy of W. H. Chamberlin.* I'm not sure they did much beside that. The fact that the book adequately and persuasively presents W. H. Chamberlin's philosophic thought shows the philosophical competence of Ralph Chamberlin. I must confess that I sometimes wonder whether Ralph Chamberlin's description of W. H. Chamberlin's philosophical views is a full description of his brother's views or his own.

But W. H. Chamberlin's importance to you is that you're one of his students once removed—through people like Ericksen, Heber Snell, and others. Can you describe his philosophy?

He called it personal realism. I would call it personal idealism, though some idealists refer to their position by the term *realism.* W. H.'s views were more like the leading American idealists who taught me as a graduate student than they were like the views of Ericksen and others with whom I worked as an undergraduate. The difference is that, although there's a strong pragmatic element running through W. H. Chamberlin's philosophy, Chamberlin was not a pragmatist of the stripe of Ericksen and Read. One of the reasons I was attracted to studying philosophy with Ralph Tyler Flewelling, for instance, a leading figure in American idealism, was the strong attraction I felt for W. H. Chamberlin's idealism—which, you must remember, he called realism. I'm not so inclined toward that metaphysical position today—

You're not so much an idealist now as you were, and W. H. might have moved away from it if he had lived longer. Who knows? Is the Chamberlin biography still in print?

You're quite right, this book had a considerable impact on me, and I was more an idealist. I was younger then! The book was still in print in my student days, and I purchased my copy at the Deseret Book Store. It had been published by the Deseret News Press, a church-related publisher. I have recently been very much interested in attempting to get it republished. It deserves to be republished. Some of Orson Pratt's writing is being republished—some of B. H. Roberts's and some of Ericksen's work.

Now, you've mentioned Waldemer Read several times. What was his influence on your development?

Strange as it may seem, I had only one class from Waldemer; and that was after I had received my bachelor's degree. He was away part of the time that I was an undergraduate, finishing up his own graduate work for the Ph.D. at the University of Chicago. I actually met him in a French class! I was taking it as an undergraduate, and he was taking it to pass his Ph.D. exam in languages.

Fellow students then?

Yes, we sat by each other and that's how we got acquainted. Read's office was next to Ericksen's, both on the lower level of the present Cowles Building. We became very close friends during my last year at the university, when I was working on a master's degree and helping Ericksen with his volume on social ethics. Waldemer was working on the same project, so we spent many hours together, at the university and in his home with his family. After I left the university, I often returned to visit, always with Read and Ericksen.

As a student at the university, you had few friends among the students, but many among the faculty.

That's true. Read was an excellent critic of my master's thesis on medieval philosophy, and I learned a great deal from him about philosophical criticism. Of course, when I joined the Utah philosophy department in 1948, we were brought together as colleagues as well as friends. Read was a confirmed pragmatist, which I was not, but I learned a great deal from him in moral philosophy.

You've also mentioned Stephen Tornay on several occasions.

Yes, Tornay, now deceased, was an interesting person, a Hungarian. His name was actually Stephen Chaktornay, but he anglicized it when he came to this country. He made "Chak" his middle name and kept Tornay as his surname. He was a defrocked Catholic priest, not a member of any special order, as far as I'm aware. He had been a parish priest in Budapest and had liberal leanings that, as he told me, got him into some trouble with the Vatican. A cardinal who had taken very great interest in him arranged to have him transferred to America, where it was thought he would have less trouble with the church.

So they sent him to Utah?

No, to somewhere else in the United States; but it didn't help very much and he ended up being excommunicated. He then married a former nun and they had two boys and a girl. She died before he came to Utah. He had a doctorate in sacred theology from the University of Vienna and was a medieval specialist—concentrated on the work of

William of Occam.

Tornay was a man of many talents and absolutely self-confident, so he did all sorts of things. Tornay and I became very good friends, and he used to tell me in detail the story of his quite fascinating life. Following the First World War, when there were revolutionary activities in Hungary, he said everybody else was shooting so he got a couple of pistols, stood on the front steps of his parish church, and just shot into the air.

He wanted to be a part of the thing!

Yes, he didn't want to be left out, and he never was. After his excommunication, he worked as secretary to a wealthy American for a while, and then he became an ordained Presbyterian minister. Well, Tornay finally decided to turn his attention to teaching. He was a brilliant teacher, but I think I'm the only one at the university who fully appreciated his talents. Although he already had a doctorate in sacred theology, he went to the University of Chicago to get a Ph.D. in philosophy. He met Waldemer Read there when Read was at Chicago. Waldemer recommended Tornay to fill in for him at Utah while he was on leave for 1935-36. Ericksen hired Tornay for the one-year appointment, and he was so successful as a teacher and impressive as a scholar that he was kept on.

You wouldn't have known him long, though, since that was your senior year, yet he had a large influence on you and on the community, didn't he?

Yes, but I stayed on another year to get my master's. Tornay was eloquent and very interesting. He spoke English with a heavy Hungarian accent, and the ladies' clubs all thought he was great. He was a colorful speaker, very popular. President Thomas had a session with Tornay and told him that he was in competition with the university by going out and taking pay from all these women's clubs. He told him to do his lecturing through the University Extension Division. Tornay was also a very brilliant classroom lecturer. I took his classes in metaphysics, epistemology, and aesthetics.

Just having a former priest with three children would have been pretty racy in Salt Lake City in the 1930s. What eventually became of Tornay?

During the war, Tornay wrote manuals on gunnery for Hill Field. He would take on anything, anything. It used to annoy Ericksen terribly that Tornay thought he could do anything. He was never popular with Ericksen and Read and was more than a little careless in some decisions involving honesty. The plain facts are that he was dropped here after about a decade. After leaving Utah, he came to Los Angeles and got in touch with me. As a matter of fact, he married a Mormon woman—wanted me to perform the marriage—but that was out of the question. He and I remained really very good friends and were until his death a few years ago. He deserves to be remembered for the shot in the arm he gave the philosophy department. Nobody here knew much about medieval philosophy. Read had very little use for it, Ericksen had none, and here came Tornay with a great deal of talent in that field. I should write a book about Tornay because I think I was as good a friend as he had. He had a capacity for alienating his friends, but I liked him in spite of his foibles.

Well, I shouldn't go on talking about Tornay, but he's one of the more picturesque figures in my experience. He was quite well acquainted with Natalie; and one day as she left the two of us, he said to me, "Natalie has a transparent soul." I was never quite sure what a transparent soul is, but it is something wonderful and I agree Natalie certainly has one.

So your undergraduate years were filled with contacts with unusual people. Sterling, wasn't Levi Edgar Young on the faculty here in your student days?

Yes, he was and he certainly deserves mention. Levi Edgar Young was a member of the First Council of the Seventy of the LDS church . . .

Like B. H. Roberts and your grandfather . . .

Yes, and he was also a professor of western history at the university—a one-man department. His office was in the Park Building on the main floor. In those days, incidentally, before the university bureaucracy became bloated, as it now is, three professors not connected with the central administration had offices on the main floor of the Park Building—Young, Frederick J. Pack, chair of the Department of Geology, and Dean Milton Bennion. Levi Edgar—that's what everyone called him—was a very genteel, highly cultivated, very sensitive, aesthetically oriented person. He'd studied at Columbia University, had a master's in history and did considerable writing in western history. He was not a major scholar, but he was a great figure in the church, in my opinion—too liberal for some of the general authorities.

How did that work out, mixing high church position with the duties of a professor? That is a rare and ill-advised combination in my view.

He divided his time between the university on one hand and the church on the other hand. Some people in the university weren't happy about that even then, and it's obvious that some people in the church weren't either; but that's what he insisted on doing. From things he told me, I think he was under some pressure from the church to give up his university affiliation—certainly he was the only general authority who was at the university—but he didn't want to give it up and he had enough prestige and status that he stayed with the university until retirement age.

Levi Edgar was a major figure in the state. For many years he hosted important visitors because he knew the regional history so well and could explain it so persuasively. He entertained President Warren G. Harding on the president's last visit to the West—accompanied him on a trip through Zion National Park.

Well, as long as I'm at it, I think I'll tell you the story of the visit of Arthur Conan Doyle in the late 1920s that Levi Edgar himself told me. Doyle was coming here to address the Knife and Fork Club, a local lecture group, if I'm not mistaken; and his wife came with him. As usual, Levi Edgar was appointed to meet them at the station, accompany them to the hotel, and generally entertain them.

How was Conan Doyle received here? After all, he'd recently written that Sherlock Holmes mystery A Study in Scarlet. *It wasn't appreciated much by Mormons.*

Oh yes, all about girls being forced into polygamy and murderous Danites and so on. Blasted the living hell out of the Mormons. But what he knew about the Mormons he had simply learned from reading British newspapers, you know—all those editorials about the evils of Mormon missionaries coming over and seducing the English women.

Well, as Levi Edgar and the Doyles drove from the station, they passed the Tabernacle and the temple. Doyle asked, "Now, your name is Young?" "Yes." "There was a Brigham Young. Are you related to him?" Levi Edgar said, "I'm a grandson of his brother." Conan Doyle continued, "Well, now, all of this Mormon stuff—it's all a thing of the past, isn't it?" Levi Edgar explained to him that it was not a thing of the past, "that there were Mormons all over the place." Well, when he was saying goodbye to the Doyles at the Union Pacific Station, Conan Doyle was somewhat repentant. He said the Mormons didn't look quite so bad to him now and confessed to Levi Edgar that he had "written a scurrilous book about the Mormons." He said, "When I get back to England, I'm going to do some more writing and retract what I said about the Mormons."

Did he do it?

I think so. I'm quite sure that I read an essay by Conan Doyle in which he indicated that he regretted having written *A Study in Scarlet*. It was well known that Conan Doyle and his wife were heavily involved in psychic research. Levi Edgar said he had dinner with them in their Hotel Utah room, and the table was laid for four. The fourth place was for their son who had died.

Amazing story.

Well, Levi Edgar Young was a great character. He was a small man, kind of delicate in his make-up. As a general conference speaker in the Tabernacle, he didn't have the force and the power of some; but he emitted a kind of grace, love, and liberality that far exceeded most of the other general authorities. Some of them didn't like that very much.

You maintained some association with him right up until his death?

In 1936 or 1937 when I was a graduate student, my mother came to Salt Lake City; she had some piece of church business to take up with Levi Edgar. I accompanied her to the Church Administration Building to call on him. He wasn't there; but as we were leaving, we encountered J. Golden Kimball, who had succeeded B. H. Roberts as senior president of the First Council of the Seventy. He saw us through the door, got up, and came out in the hall. He knew my mother and asked if there was anything that he could do for us. Now, you know, J. Golden was tall and thin and Levi Edgar Young was quite short. I said we were looking for President Young, and J. Golden said, in that high-pitched monotone of his, "That little shrimp. He goes around here carrying water on both shoulders, and he's afraid to lean one way or the other for fear of spilling some of it."

An apt remark, given Levi Edgar's dual career as cleric and scholar!

Well, that was J. Golden Kimball for you. It was said in good humor. Levi Edgar Young was a marvelous person. In the 1950s when I was here on the faculty, I would encounter him downtown, usually on the corner of South Temple and State Street where he caught his bus. He would have just come out of meetings with other general authorities or from an afternoon of church business, and on more than one occasion, he said to me with a groan, "Oh, you have no idea, Sterling, you have *no* idea what I have to go through in that building."

Needed to unload his problems with a trusted friend. He envied your freedom, Sterling, I'm sure.

I imagine. And since my grandfather had gone through the same thing, he thought I had a pretty good idea of what he meant. I have to tell you, since we're being personal, of my first encounter with Levi Edgar, my first day at the University of Utah. I registered for his class; and I think there were fifteen people in it. We met in the L Building. When the bell rang, he came in, took a good look at us, shuffled through his registration cards, and said, "No one is supposed to register for my classes without my permission." I think he wanted to get rid of some of those students. Later he proceeded to cut the class down to about five students—I was one of those whom he kept—and then he moved the class into his office. I think I had three courses with Levi Edgar, and we always met in his office. These seminars were delightful. Some of our current faculty have greater expertise in western history, but he was just a marvelous human being. Everyone held him in high respect, even his critics.

What kind of a teacher was Levi Edgar?

I don't think the average Mormon ever fully appreciated him because, to be frank with you, they liked those who spoke dogmatically and knew the answers to all the questions. He wasn't that type of person. To give you a sample: he came into class the first day and said, "No one knows anything about the origin of the American Indians." Then he turned and pointed his finger at me—this was a characteristic of his, a bit dramatic—and said, "Did you hear what I said, McMurrin? I said no one, and I mean no one, knows anything about the origin of the American Indians." Well, I sat there astonished. I had no idea he knew who I was, and this was the first time I had ever seen him. From that day on, I sensed a feeling of friendship.

This rapport continued to grow?

Yes. In one of the later seminars, when he had just returned from a trip to San Francisco, he gave me a book and said, "I saw this in a bookstore, and I thought you would like it." It was *The Story of Religion* by Charles Francis Potter. It was a very good book and it included biographies of such leading religious figures as Jesus, Buddha, and Muhammad. One of the chapters was on Joseph Smith. Levi Edgar inscribed the book, and as he handed it to me, he said, "I want you to pay special attention to that opening paragraph on Joseph Smith."

And what did it say?

The first sentence said something like: "The remarkable thing about Mormonism is that such a reputable religion would spring from such a disreputable person."

That certainly reveals Levi Edgar's confident attitude toward his religion, doesn't it? And his robust attitude toward ideas.

Oh, yes, and you can see why some of the general authorities didn't take too easily to his brand of Mormonism.

Very different from the kind of attitude projected by, say, Joseph Fielding

Smith, who was his contemporary, wasn't he?

Couldn't have been more different. Let me just give you a quick illustration. Years later, in the early 1950s, I was involved with Heber C. Snell in a session with Joseph Fielding Smith, who was then president of the Quorum of the Twelve, and Apostle Harold B. Lee, about Snell's book on the Old Testament. Now, the church Commissioner of Education had officially asked him to write the book, but the church had decided not to publish it. Snell was naturally confused and wanted to know why. In the course of this session, Snell produced several letters from church authorities praising the book.

Those were the days.

We were meeting around Joseph Fielding's desk, and Heber handed over letters from Levi Edgar Young, Joseph F. Merrill, and John A. Widtsoe. Joseph Fielding Smith read through the letter from Levi Edgar Young praising Snell's book. He said, "Well, I'm not surprised."

Lets you know what he thought of Levi Edgar Young!

Well, he didn't think much of the others, either. When he read the letter from Apostle Merrill praising the book, he said, "Well, we shall have a few things to say to Apostle Merrill." And then he read the one from Widtsoe. He got right up out of his chair, walked across the room, turned and walked back, and said, "And we shall have a few things to say to Apostle Widtsoe."

You and Obert Tanner swapped a lot of Levi Edgar Young stories, didn't you?

Sure, and Obert, as you know, had a genius for impersonation. He did marvelous impersonations of Levi Edgar Young giving lectures on the history of the Mississippi River or the Southwest.

That was a rare treat. I've heard him do that too.

I should tell you one other thing before we leave Levi Edgar. He told me that he once called on William James—I assume while Levi Edgar was doing some work at Harvard (though he got his master's at Columbia). He may have had classes from William James. I'm not sure. Anyway, he told me that he had presented William James with a copy of the Book of Mormon, inscribed as a gift. I believe James told him he would eventually give the book to the Widener Library at Harvard. In any event, Levi Edgar visited the Widener years later and discovered James's presentation copy in the library. Of course, it would be a rather prized possession if it was given to them by William James.

Sterling, I have also heard you mention Gail Plummer and George Fellows.

What about their influence on your education?

Gail Plummer was a wonderful person and a very dear friend of mine. He was not very old when he died. It was an untimely death and a great loss to his friends and to the university. He was a professor of speech and manager of Kingsbury Hall. This was before the university had a theater, so he was responsible for all of the productions put on at Kingsbury Hall. He brought some wonderful things to the university. When I was dean in the 1950s, he used to come and see me about his work there. We had remained in close contact since my student days. Speech, ballet, and theater were in the College of Letters and Science when I was dean, so I was associated with him in that connection.

Kingsbury Hall had a major role in the city's cultural life during the 1950s and 1960s, didn't it?

You bet your life. That's where all of the major lectures took place, the operas, all of the dramatic productions. In the 1950s, Ballet West and the Utah Symphony performed there. Plummer was a close friend and associate of Willam Christensen in ballet, Maurice Abravanel at the Symphony, and Lowell Lees and his predecessors at the theater. Up until about 1961, theater and speech were in the same department. Ballet, too.

What I want to say about Gail Plummer is that he would bring excellent things to the university. He had a tie with various traveling companies. Did you ever hear of the San Carlo Opera Company?

No, I haven't.

Well, San Carlo Opera was made up of former professional Italian opera singers. They were good, you know. Not Metropolitan stuff, but they sure sounded good in Kingsbury Hall. It was a semi-commercial operation. Gail introduced me to its head—an Italian fellow. I had a couple of interesting conversations with him. This sort of thing was good for Salt Lake City in those days. They'd bring a few orchestra people and then pick up some locals—and they'd put on good stuff!

Meat and drink to an opera lover like you, Sterling.

You bet. And another of Plummer's great contributions to this community was the Salt Lake Public Library. He was chairman of the board when the present library on Fifth South between Second and Third East was built and the old public library was transformed into the Hansen Planetarium. Gail Plummer, more than any other person, was responsible for that whole project. The dedication of the library occurred after Gail died; I was asked to pay tribute to him at the ceremonies. I was very moved on that occasion. The chief speaker was John Kenneth

Galbraith, the lanky economist from Harvard, and he offered an excellent address.

Now, how had you met Plummer?

Well, in those days, every Mormon kid was supposed to be able to make a decent speech. I certainly felt that way. I don't have those feelings any more because you hear very few decent speeches these days, so there isn't the drive to achieve in that field. The church itself was heavily involved in offering its own speech classes for the youth. During my first quarter at the University of Utah, I registered for a course in speech which happened to be with Gail Plummer. He was a marvelous person and first-rate teacher. The main thing that I learned was that a speech should be an expanded conversation. More speeches would be worthwhile if that's what they actually were instead of the rambling, ranting, and raving that we hear these days.

A conversation? That suggests an intimate interaction with the audience.

That's quite right. Of course, if the audience is large you may have to raise your voice a bit. But more than a great teacher, Gail Plummer was a marvelous friend. We became very close in that first quarter and remained friends for the balance of his life. Even when I was living out of state, I'd always call on him when I was visiting. When I was discouraged and homesick as a student, Gail was very concerned about me. I'm not subject to depression; but I think I became somewhat depressed at one point and came close to leaving the university. He spent considerable time trying to talk me out of it. And of course, all it took was visiting California and having the breathing difficulty come back to clinch matters. Everyone in this university in those days held Gail in the highest regard. His is a name that should not be forgotten in the history of this university. Wonderful human being.

And how about George Emory Fellows?

Now that's a different kind of case but very interesting. As I mentioned before, I was interested in international law and diplomacy with the view in mind of entering the foreign service. So when I first looked at a catalog of the University of Utah, the thing that immediately caught my attention was two classes taught by George Emory Fellows, one in international law and the other on the history of American diplomacy.

Fellows was then chair of the Department of History and Political Science—in those days a single department—was he not?

Yes. I didn't, at that time, know anything about Professor Fellows, but I was soon to learn. He had been president of the University of

Maine before he came to Salt Lake City and joined the faculty of the
University of Utah, largely in an attempt to find a place where his wife's
health would improve. He was getting along in years, very impressive
in appearance and in the quality of his conversation and certainly in his
scholarship. He is one of the important figures in the history of this
university, and one whose memory has been virtually lost. His specialty
was the French Revolution, and I've always been sorry that I didn't take
his courses on French history. But I was more interested in political
thought then than I am now and less interested in history than I am now.

At any rate, his were upper division classes; and because I was a
sophomore, I had to get his approval to take one of them.

And that's how you met Fellows? You called on Fellows in his office?

Yes, and he very kindly said, "Oh, no, you can't register for my
class. You're not advanced enough." I was disappointed, but fortunately
he continued, "For instance, what would you say if I were to ask you a
question about Grotius?" And I said, "Do you have in mind Grotius the
Greek historian or Grotius the author of *De Jure Belli ac Pacis*?" I thought
I'd just spring a little Latin while I was at it, and he almost fell off his
chair. From then on he and I were good friends. Just a good streak of
luck that during the previous year when I spent so much of my time
sick in bed, I had read Grotius' great work on international law and I
knew a little Latin.

And that did the trick.

You bet. Fellows was one of these people who makes a university.
He was like Chamberlin in the sciences and Ericksen in philosophy. He
was a man of great stature and a good friend to me. He lived on U Street,
just beyond South Temple. He had a marvelous library; and before he
moved back East after his wife died, he invited me to come over and
take whatever books I would like to have.

*A marvelous invitation for a young scholar. I'm sure you made the most
of it.*

Yes, and I still have two or three things on international law that he
gave me that spring day. He had a very large library and gave a lot of his
books to the university library, then more things to me, some of them
quite rare. As a matter of fact, I put a couple of them in the philosophy
library at USC. One of them was a very early publication of Sir Isaac
Newton's work on eschatological elements in the Bible, *Newton on the
Apocalypse*. Newton liked to fool around with things he didn't know
anything about in biblical scholarship, but historically it was quite an
important work.

You also knew two university presidents when you were a student, George Thomas and Leroy Cowles. We've talked some about Thomas. How about Cowles?

Leroy Cowles was then dean of the Lower Division, which was later known as General Education and still later under you, Jack, as Liberal Education. He was very kind to me in countless ways. I'll just give you an example. During my second year here, I lived with my Uncle Ezra Moss in Woods Cross (West Bountiful) and milked cows for my room and board. He had inherited this farm when my Grandfather Moss died. My grandmother was still living, but she spent most of her time with her daughters in California and traveled a good deal.

Uncle Ez was my mother's youngest brother. He'd developed a very prosperous dairy farm of registered Guernseys and had already invited me to live with him. Guernsey milk sold for a higher price than the Jersey milk. Arden Dairy marketed it as "Golden Guernsey."

The second year at the university, I accepted his invitation because I thought I ought to be working for a living. Though this was an arrangement which I liked, it consumed a lot of my time. Cows have to be milked every morning and every night, weekends included. I had to get up before five, milk cows, ride into Salt Lake with someone who had a car, take the streetcar up to the university, and then return to Bountiful without fail every afternoon—either by bus or by the Bamberger, the electric interurban train.

How did things work out?

It was a very rough year. I didn't mind the work, but it was very, very cold and there was a lot of snow that winter. At times we'd go out to carry these ten-gallon milk cans; and if you didn't have gloves on, your hands would stick to the metal. It'd be so cold you couldn't let go of them without ripping the skin off your fingers unless you could get somebody to throw water on your hands.

Well, it was a rough year from the standpoint of work and time. President Cowles lived right across the street from what is now Gardner Hall; and he knew the struggle I was having with my schedule. He was so kind as to offer me a room in his home. He said, "We have a room in our basement, and you won't have to go clear out there to earn your board. Just come and live here with us. You'll have your own entrance to your room."

Rent-free?

Yes. Well, I was overwhelmed by his kindness; but I simply couldn't accept it. I just didn't think I should. But he was that kind of person, you know—very, very generous toward me. He hired me, however, to work on a couple of projects for his office. When he became president we continued our friendship. I wrote to him, reminding him that I had told him once I was sure someday he would be president of the university. He wrote a nice letter back and said, "I'm sure it was your faith in me that was the cause of my being made president." When I came back to the university as a faculty member, he had been retired for two years; but I occasionally saw him and Mrs. Cowles.

He was president during the war years from 1941 until the end of 1945. But the way Cowles became president of the university is especially interesting.

Yes, George Thomas stayed a year longer than he wanted to because there was a big hassle over his successor. The heir apparent was Adam S. Bennion, a man of very great talents and a civic leader. He became an apostle in the LDS church in 1953, when he was sixty-six, and died five years later. I was a pallbearer at his funeral.

Adam Bennion had been a professor of English, a man held in very high regard; and I knew him by reputation, of course; but he was a man of many talents and he left the university before I came here as a student to take an executive position with Utah Power & Light Company. As I recall, his work involved public relations; and he was the ideal man to do it because he was so highly respected.

At that time, some towns had their own power and light systems. I would pick up this inside stuff from Ericksen, Read, Cowles, Beeley, and others. Ericksen would always include me when he gave a luncheon or a dinner for some visiting person, so I'd sit there and keep my mouth shut and hear things that kids weren't supposed to hear.

Well, Adam Bennion represented the power company which was trying to consolidate its public; but there was a strong preference in university circles for independent civic companies. I don't know how much of that was in the background of the problem between Bennion and George Thomas; but Thomas was determined that Adam S. Bennion was not going to succeed him as president. The Board of Regents split right down the middle. As Cowles told me the story, the regents were up in the Park Building trying to decide on a president with this big split over Bennion—

Did Bennion want the job?

I think so. Cowles had gone to bed—it was late at night—but somebody came to the door and told him the regents wanted him to come up to the Park Building. So he got up, got dressed, and went to the meeting. He thought they just wanted to ask him some questions; but when he walked through the door, the chairman said, "Leroy, you're the new president." He hadn't thought of himself as a candidate at all. Told me it had never, never occurred to him.

He made a fine president, by all reports.

Well, Cowles was the kind of person whom everybody respected. I'm sure that he didn't have an enemy in the world, highly competent. He ran this university during World War II, a difficult time. I wasn't here at the time, but I'm sure he was very successful. You know he wrote a book, *The University of Utah and World War II,* which is a valuable piece of history, after he was replaced by A. Ray Olpin in 1946. Cowles was really a wonderful person and a great friend to me. He would go out of his way to do things for me when I was a student that simply took your breath away. For instance, the university had a scholarship to give—not very much money but anything was a lot in those days. It wasn't anything you applied for—I didn't even know about it. President Thomas sent me a check once, out of the clear blue sky, and said I had been awarded this small endowed scholarship. I had a feeling that Cowles suggested me for it.

What about your dealings with President Thomas?

He was always very friendly, but he didn't have the personal warmth of Cowles or Plummer. I became rather friendly with Thomas when I was one of the university's candidates for a Rhodes Scholarship. Thomas was chairman of Utah's Rhodes Scholarship committee and very encouraging.

I didn't realize you were ever a Rhodes candidate.

My bronchial condition eliminated me. I suppose I would have been eliminated anyway, but a person's general health and ability to live in England was part of the condition of the award.

Now you served as the first historian of the university under George Thomas, I believe. How did that happen to an undergraduate?

During my senior year, 1935–36, Thomas and Cowles had a session with me, told me there'd never been a history of the University of Utah, and hired me at twenty-five cents an hour to start accumulating materials. This was during the first Roosevelt administration, and I believe that these funds for student work came from the NYA, National Youth Administration.

Do you know why they selected you?

Well, possibly they had inflated ideas about my organizational ability and productivity. I'd already done another task for them. Cowles was chairman of a faculty committee that had made an extensive survey of American universities to determine degree requirements and length of service for appointments and promotions in terms of degrees. They'd sent out a questionnaire to numerous institutions and had received a great sheaf of replies. Dean Cowles and President Thomas asked me if I would take this stuff and put it in some kind of order. I worked on it for quite a while and drew up a rather complicated chart which tabulated the replies.

Do you remember any of the results?

Well, yes, and some of them were astonishing. They showed an amazing contrast between two great institutions. The University of California responded that it was its policy to not appoint a person to the faculty who didn't have a Ph.D. degree or equivalent. And Harvard said that a person's degrees just weren't a major consideration in making appointments. They had some faculty who had no degrees.

So they took opposite positions. But, let's see, weren't you already working for Ericksen?

Yes. Beginning in my junior year, I graded papers for some professors in history and philosophy. I read papers for Harold Dalgliesh, who was a new professor in political science and European government. I also read papers and did some research for Andrew Love Neff, who was later chair of the Department of History and Political Science.

So you weren't living with your aunt and uncle in Bountiful?

Yes, I was, but for my senior year I lived in Federal Heights close to the university for the first half year. I received room and board in a very fine home in return for chauffeuring R. T. Harris, who was president of the Gunnison Sugar Company. It was then owned by the Wrigley Company, the chewing gum manufacturers.

It's quite interesting. Mr. Harris had been working for the Bank of America but severed his association to go back East. He passed the Utah-Idaho Sugar Factory just south of Gunnison on Highway 89. It had been recently closed because the sugar beet industry was faltering, and that gave him an idea. In Chicago he met P. K. Wrigley, who had inherited the company, at a social gathering. Do you know what P.K.'s are?

Never heard of them.

They were little thick chunks, almost cubes, of chewing gum.

Like Chiclets?

Yes. Anyway, Wrigley complained to Harris about the price of sugar and fluctuations in the price, so Harris suggested to Wrigley that he ought to acquire his own sugar factory. The idea appealed to Wrigley, so he financed Harris to come back to Utah and buy the Gunnison Sugar Factory. There used to be a big Wrigley electrical sign on it, but the building is gone now.

And you were his chauffeur?

I certainly was. Their house in Federal Heights had a very awkward driveway that curved and went uphill. It was cemented on both sides with ledges, just barely wide enough for the car. They could drive into the garage, but they couldn't back out. So they sent over to the university looking for a student who knew how to back up a car; and Myrtle Austin, then dean of women, told me about the job.

That was very gracious of her.

I certainly thought so. She knew I was living out in Bountiful and getting up long before daylight to milk cows. It was certainly a change of work! Once in a great while I would drive Mr. Harris down to his office on Main Street or pick him up at the Alta Club, but as many times as not he would just call a cab. And often Mrs. Harris and her daughter would just leave the car out on the street rather than putting it back in the garage.

You lived with the Harrises?

I had a room and bath on the lower floor off the garage. Their cook, a young Swiss LDS convert, would turn out the most elaborate meals, so I was really living the life of royalty. She was a delightful person, very interested in discussing religion. Her brother headed up a sort of dissident sect—believed that everyone was supposed to kneel during the administration of the sacrament, so they'd meet in a separate group and have their own sacrament. They were ardent temple workers but would go all the way to the Canadian temple because the president there, they felt, was much more spiritual than the Salt Lake temple president. It was interesting for me to see this version of Mormonism.

You say you did this for the first half year?

Yes, then my younger brother, Harold, who was still in high school in Los Angeles, decided to finish up at East High School in Salt Lake City. My mother came with him, and the three of us set up housekeeping in an apartment in Federal Heights, again within walking distance of the campus. A cousin, then a freshman in college, joined us. He was B. H. Roberts's grandson, Vaughn Moss.

And during this same year, you kept on working for Professor Neff?

And Ericksen in the philosophy department. Neff was making a survey of the condition of records in various counties. I spent some time evaluating the records of Salt Lake and Davis counties. I kept on reading and grading papers during the next year, as well, when I was writing my master's thesis. At twenty-five cents an hour, that was pretty good money. I must say I don't know where I found the time to do all of these things. During my graduate year, I also worked on the history of the university for President Thomas and Dean Cowles.

Where did you live the next year as a graduate student?

My mother went back to California; but Harold, Vaughn, and I rented two different apartments during the year 1936-37 and batched. Nothing palatial, but we managed.

What about your summers?

Summers were kind of rough. I didn't want to go back to the ranch, even though my brothers and cousins were up there, because of the impact of my grandfather's death. So I spent my summers in Los Angeles. And every summer the bronchial asthma would come back. So I didn't work while I was in Los Angeles during the summers. I did a lot of reading. During one of those summers, I tried to teach myself to type; but I gave it up as a bad job and I haven't touched a typewriter since. I should mention that the last summer I was here, the summer of 1937, I stayed on after receiving my master's degree and did some additional graduate work.

Tell me more about your work on the university history for President Thomas.

Well, I'm the first university historian that I know about. I didn't come across any historical materials that had been written or compiled by an earlier historian. I had a number of sessions with President Thomas. One day he sent for me and said in his typical gruff, crusty way, "I just wanted to tell you, Sterling, that you'll have to have a session with old Kingsbury." Kingsbury was the third president of the university, after John R. Park and James E. Talmage. Kingsbury retired in 1915 but still had an office there in the Park Building, right next to Cowles's office. I used to see the old man. He was quite friendly and would greet students as they passed, so I knew who Kingsbury was. Then President Thomas said, "But I want to warn you that Kingsbury doesn't know that anything happened around here before he was president and he's not aware that anything has happened since." I had a couple of sessions with Kingsbury and they came off very well.

So you had an early experience doing oral history. What else did you do?

Well, I didn't have any particular skill and certainly no training in historical research methods, you know. And of course we had no recording equipment. I had to work things out myself, kind of making it up as I went along. I just put all of the information on note cards with complete citations, so that the whole batch could be turned over to someone else when I left.

What happened to your note cards?

I actually took the cards with me when I left the university and started teaching seminary for the LDS church. For some weeks I kept working on the stuff that I had and then turned it all over to Dean Cowles and President Thomas. I had hundreds of cards with dates and events from the university's history on them.

Did Chamberlin use them in his history?

I really don't know. I didn't ever ask Chamberlin about it, and we never discussed his history. I had some conversations with him about other matters, and I have a feeling that if he did have those notes, he might have mentioned it to me. I went through all the old catalogs and documents and all the newspapers that were in the library. Frankly, I don't know who was supposed to be taking care of the archives. I just rummaged around and found things. But I read every page of the *Salt Lake Tribune* and the *Deseret News*—quite an education to read about the battles between the *Tribune* and the church. I well remember, for instance, a *Tribune* article reporting on a general conference in the Tabernacle. The headline read: "Big Doings in Mormon Hippodrome."

This must have been about the time you read the story about Marshal Collin shooting your Grandfather McMurrin?

Yes, the university paid me to read that, I suppose. Then I shifted my attention down to the Church Historian's library, and I must tell you that was an experience.

Joseph Fielding Smith was then the Church Historian. His office was in the southwest corner of the top floor of the Church Administration Building at 47 East South Temple. And just off from his outer office was the church's historical library. It's much more expansive now, but it was a magnificent collection even then.

Well, I presented myself at the front counter and there was Alvin Smith, Joseph Fielding's brother, who was the librarian. He asked me what I wanted. I introduced myself and told him that the president of the university had assigned me the task of working on the history of the University of Utah and that I'd like very much to have access to library materials dealing with the University of Deseret in the early days before it became the University of Utah. He was very gruff, actually mean, in his reply. He wasn't about to let me use the library. He said, "There's nothing in this library that has anything to do with that university."

So with that statement alone, you knew there were some good things to be found there!

You bet your life. That was a preposterous thing for him to say. I think he was a very ignorant man, frankly; he knew little about history or his own collection; but he knew that he was lying to me. I tried to reason with him a little but made no headway at all. He didn't order me out of the place but he almost did—said very brusquely that there was nothing they could do for me and that was that. I wasn't about to take that kind of a reply, and I knew that Joseph Fielding Smith was over him.

You were going straight to the top, eh?

Yes. B. H. Roberts had died in 1933, and then Joseph Fielding Smith came into his period of greatest influence as the church's leading scholar, and of course he was Church Historian and over the library. So I simply went next door and asked Joseph Fielding's secretary if I could make an appointment to see Apostle Smith. She said, "He's here now," and ushered me right in.

And what was that experience like?

Well, I'll have to say it was the best I ever had with Joseph Fielding. He was very gracious, asked me to sit down, and wanted to know what he could do for me. I didn't tell him that I had been rebuffed by his younger brother. I simply started all over and told him what my research needs and interests were. He immediately reached over and pressed a button. In a matter of seconds, Alvin came in, I stood up, and Joseph Fielding introduced us. We shook hands—and this was a kind of ridiculous thing—we both pretended that we'd never seen each other before. Joseph Fielding said, "Now, Brother McMurrin is here to work on the history of the University of Deseret. You see that he is given every possible consideration and provide him with all the pertinent materials the library has in its possession." Alvin assured him that he would. I thanked Apostle Smith, and Alvin and I went out arm in arm, so to speak. He was obviously mad at me, but I certainly couldn't complain about lack of cooperation. I got decent treatment after that—cool, but decent. He didn't turn me loose with the collection, but he had someone locate stuff dealing with the university, so when I went down there, I always got a good deal of material. And there was a lot there.

Your time was somewhat limited at that point, but do you recall anything specific that you uncovered about the founding of the university in 1850?

One of the most interesting sources I worked in was the Journal History of the church. Fascinating. It was a kind of daily scrapbook, consisting of newspaper clippings pasted in and typewritten material—typed newspaper accounts, correspondence, minutes of meetings, and so forth. They were pasted in long volumes—maybe fourteen or eighteen inches tall. They would bring me various volumes with certain items marked that had to do with the university. I was supposed to read those and forbidden to read anything else, but it was all bound together.

And that posed a practical problem in ethics for you?

Oh, I didn't even try to resist that temptation. I wasn't any too honorable in such matters. They gave me a little cubicle, and I read a lot of the stuff that I wasn't supposed to read and it was obvious to me why I wasn't supposed to read it. I remember one item—a kind of epistle from Brigham Young to mission presidents. There had been some Indian depredations around Tooele, which, Brigham Young said, he solved—it was in first person, but he wasn't there, of course—by ambushing the Indians. "They killed off all the men and distributed the women and children among the Saints." Signed, "Yours in the bowels of Christ, B. Young." I believe those were the exact words.

Appalling. Your father had had you read Frederick J. Pack's book when you were young. Was he still here when you were a student?

Yes, he was and well deserving of mention. He was head of the Department of Geology and, like Levi Edgar Young, had his office on the main floor of the Park Building. I got very well acquainted with Frederick J. Pack. I had a paleontology course from him and a course in physiographic geology. He was an outstanding teacher, but he was also a personal friend of my mother's, so we had a mutual admiration for her in common. As you can guess, he took a strong stand in favor of evolution and still maintained high status in the church.

Now how did he do that?

Well, I don't know whether it can be done today or not, but in those days it could be done so long as you didn't teach at BYU. James E. Talmage took a strong stand in favor of evolution too, and so did B. H. Roberts, but he kind of garbled the thing by mixing it up with a lot of nonsense about pre-Adamites. The Mormon church, so far as I'm aware, has never taken a formal stand on evolution one way or the other; but Pack was all for evolution in his courses.

Do you think an undergraduate student today would have the opportunity to rub shoulders with as many fine scholars as you did?

I'm inclined to think that a typical student today would probably have a more specialized association, within a department or college. In my case, you see, I had association with faculty in philosophy, history, and political science, western history, and even the sciences. Not only Frederick J. Pack, but personal conversations with Angus Woodbury, the biologist, who was Ericksen's next-door neighbor. I had far more conversations, actually, with faculty than I ever had with students. My time was limited, and I was thrown into the company of faculty more than students. Actually, I was somewhat anti-social and had little in common with any but a very few students.

Well, you certainly got an extraordinary liberal education from this broad exposure to faculty.

I think so, and I learned far more from my personal conversations with faculty members than I ever did in classes.

4.
Love and Living

If we left your college years without introducing your partner of more than fifty years, Natalie Cotterel McMurrin, we would have only half the story. You met her at the University of Utah, did you not?

Actually, Jack, we met each other separately, in a manner of speaking. I first saw her on the stairway of the Cowles Building, then the L Building—L for Liberal Arts. I was going down the east staircase between classes, and she was coming up—narrow staircase. Now don't laugh. She looked right at me—though she has no recollection of it—and I looked at her and thought, "By damn, that's the girl I'm going to marry."

Electrifying . . .

That's the word for it. I had to catch my breath for a minute. Shortly after that, by some stroke of luck which I think must have been arranged in heaven, I was sitting at a table in the library's reserve book room when Natalie came and sat opposite me.

Wholly by accident, of course!

That's what she says. Mind you, I've always been of the opinion that she'd seen me on the stairs and was scheming for a chance to sit by me. At least, that's what I've always wanted to believe. It was March 1935, and I decided before I left that stairway I *was* going to marry her. Our first date was on June 8, 1935, and we were married exactly three years later on June 8, 1938, a whirlwind courtship for those days.

In 1988 you celebrated your golden wedding anniversary. Tell me about Natalie's background.

I'm a year older than Natalie; but because I had dropped out of UCLA for a year due to asthma, we were in the same graduating class. Her story actually starts in Idaho. Her paternal grandfather, Samuel Cotterel, was born in a Mormon pioneer family here in Utah. His mother, a plural wife, died; and young Samuel fell under the jurisdiction of a wife he didn't like. He ran away from home, and the family, for all practical purposes, disowned him—even gave his name to the next-born male child!

He had a romantic career—freighting from Corinne at the north end of the Great Salt Lake up into Idaho and Montana. He bought a ranch in the Raft River country where there's a mountain named for him. The first checking station across the border into Idaho is the Cotterell station.

So Natalie was born there?

Near there. Her parents were ranchers, too. Her mother, Mattie Alice Easley Cotterel, was a very devout Campbellite, a member of the Church of Christ. Her father, Clyde C. Cotterel, was reared as a Mormon but no longer practiced the religion. He was a rancher, and Natalie is the third of their seven children. Natalie was born in a log cabin at Yale, Idaho, at the junction of the Oregon Trail and the California Trail where the Raft River enters the Snake River.

Named "Yale" by someone with a sense of humor, no doubt, but an appropriate place for Natalie to enter this world—destined to spend her whole adult life among scholars.

It certainly was. Nothing there now but sagebrush. There's still a Yale exit on the freeway, but you can't find a thing there except a ranch home or two. Natalie and I took her mother over there once. She thought she might find the location of the cabin, but she couldn't identify anything.

Is the ranch near there?

Yes, Natalie's father ranched near Aberdeen. Natalie rode to school in a school wagon—like a bus, only pulled by horses. And no padded seats, either! There was no Campbellite church there, so they attended the Baptist church. Natalie didn't like the preaching, but she learned a great deal of Bible and had a good religious upbringing. She has always been very devout in a way that I like.

When did she first encounter the Mormon church in earnest?

She had lived among Mormons in Idaho and her parents sent her to Salt Lake City to attend high school. She lived with her great-aunt and her husband, Mattie and William Prosser.

What about Natalie's education? She is a highly cultured person.

Natalie graduated from East High School, where she was an excellent student. She was awarded a scholarship to Mills College in Oakland, California, a prestigious women's school, but she couldn't afford to go there. Her aunt was her grandmother's sister on her mother's side. The Prossers were highly cultivated, well-educated people from the Middle

West and the South. They were intensely anti-Mormon. They were staunch Masons—and in those days the Masons and the Mormons were certainly on the outs, especially with regard to matters pertaining to the schools.

Mr. and Mrs. Prosser were both school people. He was a school principal, and she had been a teacher. When Natalie and I had our first date they discovered that I was a Mormon. The next time that I called to take her out, she told me that her great-aunt and -uncle had decreed that she was never to see me again. All of this had to do with the fact that I was a Mormon, and Natalie was forbidden to have anything to do with Mormons.

This could make dating difficult. What happened?

Well, it's a long story, but actually very interesting and at times very exciting as to how Natalie and I managed to carry on in spite of this ban. As a matter of fact, her aunt hired a young man who was a family friend to spy on us at the university and to report to her if he found us together. It turned out that he was really a friend to Natalie. He had a car, and I didn't have a car. On more than one occasion, he actually furnished his car and took us to where we were going on our dates. At any rate, we kept things going without really being caught. But I suppose they may have suspected from time to time that we were seeing one another. It's a long story that would make an interesting book or a movie on how we eluded them—both here in Utah and once in California and Idaho.

Did Natalie's parents share the Prossers' biases about Mormons?

Natalie's father (who died before I became acquainted with her) was reared in a Mormon family, and her mother was a very devout Protestant, but they had no anti-Mormon attitudes whatsoever. The same was true of Natalie's brothers and her sisters. She had three brothers and three sisters. The religious issue was never a factor as far as they were concerned.

How did Natalie deal with all of this?

Well, a year before we were married, which was three years after the beginning of our courtship, Natalie joined the LDS church. When this happened, the Prossers, in effect, threw in the towel. They knew they were defeated, but they were very gracious about it. When Natalie and I were married, Mrs. Prosser had a lovely reception for us in her home. All in all, in my opinion, it was a great gain for Natalie to have lived with them.

So we both ended up at the University of Utah. It was obviously destined to be that way for both of us. Natalie majored in Spanish and

psychology as an undergraduate, then did graduate work in Spanish
literature at USC. She never completed her graduate degree, but she's
maintained a lifelong love of Spanish—the language, the literature,
Spanish-speaking countries.

*So you met in the spring of 1935 and graduated in the spring of 1936.
What then?*

I stayed here, worked on my thesis during 1936-37, and was awarded
my M.A. degree in the spring of '37. We were in the depths of the Great
Depression, and Idaho offered more money than Utah, so Natalie went
to Idaho to teach high school. She went to the University of Idaho
during the summer of 1936 to get Idaho certification. "Idaho school
law" was one of her courses, I recall. Then she taught in Dubois, Idaho,
for two years before we married. During the first of those years, I was
at the university, and the second year I was teaching seminary in
Richfield, Utah. To put it mildly, I was madly in love with her, and it
was rough on me to be so far from her. But we communicated regularly
by mail. In those days you didn't make a long-distance phone call except
in dire emergencies, but we managed to get together several times each
year and in the summers.

*I know Natalie felt rather conflicted about joining the Mormon church,
wondering whether she was doing it out of religious conviction or for you.
Didn't Ephraim Ericksen offer her some advice about this matter?*

Dr. Ericksen's advice was just right. "Now Natalie," he said, "there
is no better reason for joining a church than for love." That made it easy
for her. She has never looked back.

*David O. McKay, who was then a member of the First Presidency,
performed the ceremony in the Salt Lake temple. Was that a difficult decision
for you and Natalie, since her family could not attend?*

Yes, we were married in the Salt Lake temple. It was simply the
appropriate thing for a Mormon couple to do. And as far as I was
concerned, the Salt Lake temple was the only real temple in the church.
It looks and feels like one, inside and out.

Natalie had joined the church more than a year before we were
married, and it was a matter of much concern to her that her mother
could not be present for the ceremony, as my mother was. But her
great-aunt, Mrs. Prosser, as I said, gave her a lovely reception that
evening for all of our family and friends.

It was a double wedding, a beautiful ceremony, and my oldest
brother, Blaine, was married at the same time to Lillian Miller. We asked
David O. McKay to perform the ceremony as we all had greatly admired

him over the years. He was a man of great stature and was most gracious in every way. The four of us went on a trip through the southern Utah parks and Grand Canyon, and we all ended up in Los Angeles where Blaine and Lillian were to live and Natalie and I were to go to USC for the summer session.

Natalie is a lovely person, totally devoted to her family. I can say in all seriousness and all honesty that Natalie and I have never had a dispute of any consequence so far as I'm aware.

I'd say that's unusual in the extreme.

Perhaps it is. I hear marriage counselors talk about fighting fair in marriage and hear talk-show therapists hold forth on couples listening to each other, forgiving, expressing your anger appropriately—well, I hardly know what they're talking about. Natalie and I have never had a serious disagreement.

Now, Sterling, I'm prepared to believe that you've never had a fight, but I'm not prepared to believe that you've never had a serious disagreement.

It may very well be that we don't have anything beyond very trivial disagreements because Natalie is so genuinely sweet and eager to please that she just gives in to me on everything. We have differences of opinion, but there's no heat involved. Here's an example: Several years ago, I let a stockbroker talk me into selling a small piece of preferred stock in Utah Power & Light, trading it for something else. It wasn't much, so I authorized the sale, even though I said, "I really should consult with my wife about this." When I told Natalie, she said, "You know, I don't think that was wise." I said something like, "Well, it's done now," and the subject was dropped. Do you know, she was absolutely right? The stuff he got me to buy turned out to be worthless.

If you'd consulted with Natalie first and she'd told you it was unwise, what would you have done?

I wouldn't have sold. Absolutely not. I don't know how Natalie does it, but she has an intuition about things that I'd be very foolish to disregard. Now—you're making me think about this, Jack—I think it's true that there are many things that one of us cares about more than the other, but the one who cares less accommodates the other.

More than "accommodates," I'd say, Sterling. I've seen both of you put in a lot of effort so that something will work out the way the other one wants it.

Well, it's true that Natalie and I have been remarkably compatible. We discuss decisions—even trivial ones like a little weekend trip—a lot. We like the same kinds of things. The same things make us happy. We

want the same things for each other—the same things for our children.
I've never gone alone without Natalie without wishing she were with
me. I mean that very seriously. I've never stopped being in love with
Natalie. I guess we're old-fashioned soul mates, companions in the
highest sense of the word.

My Lord, I hear about people who've been married for thirty years
getting divorced, and it takes my breath away. I simply can't envisage a
life that doesn't include Natalie. It's probably old-fashioned. You and
Linda have been married for twenty-five years?

Thirty-two now.

And I think of you as having a modern marriage. Both of you are
highly involved with your work and both of you have been very
involved with your four children. I think of your marriage as ideal for
these times. It is a real partnership across the board.

*You and Natalie have an equally happy but much more traditional marriage.
I've heard Natalie say, however, that you have almost always done the
grocery shopping for the family.*

That's right, but it is a small thing. I'm really glad you're asking about
Natalie. I love to see her get some of the credit she deserves. She's a
beautiful, warm, affectionate person. She's as sensitive about things that
are negative or crude as any person I've ever known. She has genuinely
refined sensibilities—morally, artistically, and spiritually. She's a deeply
religious person. Not dogmatic at all, no rigid orthodoxies or conservative attitudes, but genuinely spiritual with a kind of natural piety.

*I'm glad you've mentioned spirituality. Was it difficult for Natalie when
you found your philosophy was diverging from that of the church?*

Not at all. Natalie's views are as heretical as my own—if it's religious
orthodoxy you're talking about—but she's much more devout than I
am. Her religion is a genuine goodness, not a set of observances and
practices. I've never heard her say a discouraging word to anyone. She's
completely loyal to her friends and her family.

*You've had a career that's demanded a lot of traveling and intensive periods
of work. Has that been hard on Natalie, and was it for the children?*

It's been hard because we've missed each other, but it hasn't been
hard on our marriage, and I have avoided protracted absences. The only
exception was in the late fifties when I went to Iran for the State
Department for five months. I was homesick the whole time. Later when
I first went to Washington, D.C., as Commissioner of Education, it was
in January, right after the inauguration of President Kennedy. Natalie
stayed here with the children until school let out in the spring. But I

came home fairly frequently that spring. During the '60s and '70s, I served on a variety of commissions for the university or the government, but those were comparatively short trips.

It sounds as if Natalie has been very supportive of your work.

Yes, and this might be an example of an area where we work for each other. Natalie doesn't have much interest in the finer technicalities of philosophy—not that she is indifferent to the great questions—but she knows that the pursuit of philosophical problems is the great intellectual love of my life. She's never felt that she needs to understand every detail to know that it's important for me, and she's always made every effort to accommodate my work hours and my travel schedule.

I know that you and Natalie enjoy traveling together.

Oh, yes! It's one of our favorite things. We've been to Israel two or three times. Everywhere in Europe except Bulgaria, Romania, and Albania. We've been to Russia, Egypt, Ethiopia, the Middle East, India, Japan, and, most recently, China. Natalie particularly enjoys Spain and Mexico. She's an extremely good traveler, remarkably well organized. We have lived for a short period in both Rome and Germany.

Did you ever take the children with you when they were young?

Of course. I came to BYU to teach during its summer session in '47. That was our first family trip. Trudy was three and Joe was two. The other three—Jim, Laurie, and Melanie—hadn't been born yet. When we left Utah, we went to Oregon and down the Columbia River, then down the California Coast. We've been taking the children on trips ever since. All of them except Laurie have traveled in Europe. Joe spent some time in Europe on his own; but Trudy, Melanie, and Jim have covered large parts of Europe with us separately. Laurie, our fourth child, was two when we went to live for a year in New York by way of Texas and Florida. We had a new car, so every weekend we were off somewhere—up into New England, all over New York, or down to Washington, and later home by way of Boston and Quebec.

So traveling was one of your family's main forms of recreation?

Absolutely. We were constantly piling into the car and going off to a drive-in theater when we wanted to see a movie. Here in Salt Lake City, we had a three-seated station wagon, which had ample room for five kids. I hear people saying how hard it is to travel with children. Well, it was about the easiest thing we ever did. In New York, our children saw more of the city than most native New Yorkers. We had them in all of the major museums when Joe was only a first grader and Jim, our third child, was younger. We took Joe and Trudy to the old

Metropolitan Opera to see *Aida*—first-rate box seats up near the front. It was a great spectacle for them.

An unforgettable experience for a kid, or for anyone!

Pretty unforgettable. In Milan, when Melanie, our youngest, was sixteen, we went to La Scala for *Rigoletto* and to the Vienna Opera for *Parsifal*. Now *Parsifal* lasts five hours, and that's one hell of a workout; but Melanie followed the libretto all the way. We were really rather proud of her.

How did you and Natalie work together as parents?

If you have a perfect mother like Natalie, the father can get away with quite a bit. I came home for the bedtime stories and hugs while she spent the day with the scraped knees and the runny noses. She's always been willing to sacrifice her time or her convenience if she can help one of the children—and she's still doing it, now that they're adults with children of their own. She gives them everything. If they could wear my clothes, she'd be handing out my coats and shoes. I don't think any mother could receive greater affection from all of her children and grandchildren than she does—or from her husband, I might say.

And when your children grew up, it sounds as if you and Natalie simply carried on as before and more. Do you have any favorite places to travel in the United States?

We used to go to New York a lot. When I was with the Committee for Economic Development, spouses were invited to social occasions at periodic intervals. For twenty years, during the '60s and into the '70s, I was a trustee of the Carnegie Foundation, which sponsors a very plush annual meeting with first-class travel, elegant accommodations, and a fine banquet. On one of my first visits, I facetiously asked the Carnegie secretary, "What would Andrew Carnegie think if he could see you spending his money on an elaborate affair like this and bringing our wives at considerable expense?" She answered seriously, "As a matter of fact, you're required to bring your wife. In his will, in which the foundation was established, Andrew Carnegie stipulated that the trustees shall attend an annual meeting in New York City to which they are to bring their wives or daughters." Then she smiled a little and said, "Now, you know what *that* was for. That was to keep you out of mischief while you were in New York. So he'd think this is great, you see!" She said that Carnegie was a phonetics crank and spelled daughters "dotters."

What if the two of you have a free evening?

We've had season tickets to the university's Pioneer Memorial Theatre ever since it opened, and for Ballet West, the Utah Symphony, and the Utah Opera Company. But it is the opera first for us. Sometimes it gets a bit too much, and we'll give our tickets to friends. But we go to almost everything.

Movies? Television?

We rarely go to movies anymore. As for TV, we watch PBS and newscasts, mostly. We don't have cable. I'm a news-aholic, so I watch McNeil-Lehrer regularly, and *Nightline* and the Sunday news shows.

Sounds pretty respectable, Sterling. Now what else?

Oh, let me confess my secret vice, Jack. I listen to the TV evangelists on Sunday mornings. The wilder they are, the better I like them. They're pretty tame around here, you know; but down in Texas you can see the real thing. Of course, the best ones are now off the air—some in the doghouse or in jail.

Does Natalie share this vice?

Oh, no. She won't even be in the room with one of my preachers. I guess this is our most serious difference. Sunday morning for her is the Tabernacle Choir. She never misses it. We have several TV's so we can watch separate programs if we want to. But on a typical evening at home, I'll read or write, Natalie will read or sew, and we'll listen to music. We have a very good stereophonic system.

You were the first people we knew who bought a compact disc system. What do you read?

Natalie reads biography and history. I read mainly philosophical stuff and the history of religion and philosophy. And we read together quite a lot. If we're driving somewhere, Natalie will often read out loud to me. She read *Conversations with Wallace Stegner* while we were going to southern Utah. Very interesting stuff. Recently she read aloud to me the biography of Father Theodore Hesburgh, the president of Notre Dame. Father Hesburgh is a very dear friend of ours.

Do you spend much time with your children?

Oh yes. Two of our daughters, Laurie and Melanie, are here in Salt Lake City. Trudy, the oldest, recently moved to Las Vegas where she is an editor for the University of Nevada Press. Our oldest son, Joe, is in Honolulu, and Jim—Sterling James—is in Vermont. Some of our grandchildren are old enough to come visiting on their own, too. There's a great deal of affection and informal visiting; but when we do family gatherings, Natalie will fix dinner or we'll take everyone out to a restaurant.

And let someone else wash the dishes?

That's right. It just makes for less confusion. Even after Natalie and I were married, it was quite an event to eat in a restaurant, but teenagers these days would just as soon go to a restaurant and squander their money as eat a piece of bread and peanut butter at home.

Well, wouldn't you?

You've got me there.

Tell me a little bit more about Natalie's sewing. That's a side to her we don't see.

Natalie still uses a portable Singer sewing machine that she purchased after a repossession the first year we were married. It fits into a wooden folding table and she's used it almost every day for over fifty years.

No upgrading to a newer model?

She won't touch another one. She's a remarkably gifted seamstress—suits, drapes, quilts, clothes for the kids, costumes—you name it. She and the Singer can whip it up. Sometimes I'll take her shopping and nag her until she buys something, but she always says, "Oh, I would rather make that than buy it."

What are some other hobbies you share?

We don't exactly share this one, but Natalie enjoys gardening. She loves flowers and really works with them. I don't do much around the place except run the snowblower.

As you know, we have a mountain cabin on Kolob Plateau at 8,000 feet elevation, overlooking Zion National Park from the north. We built it well over twenty years ago as a family project. Natalie loves the place and we always enjoy being there. We keep horses, and I'll ride some; but Natalie doesn't ride any more, even though she's very fond of horses. In California we occasionally went to horse races. Not to bet—we just enjoy seeing these majestic creatures run.

Then there is our condominium in St. George, Utah, a great place for the winter. Our kids enjoy visiting us there, as the place is a kind of resort. We stable our horses in St. George in the winter and pasture them on Kolob Mountain in the summer. With my nephew, Bill McMurrin, who is an architect in St. George, we have a horse set-up—barns, corrals, etc. We are in the business of raising Tennessee Walking Horses, the world's best riding horses.

Could you describe your work patterns when the children were growing up?

Except when we were in Washington, I didn't often stay late at the office, but I quite commonly took work home. Unless I was reading papers or grading those damn bluebooks, though, I was mostly reading or writing. I did most of my writing at home.

Including your correspondence?

No, until I retired from the university I always dictated correspondence at the office, except for personal letters.

What are your work habits, Sterling?

Well, to start with, I can't use a typewriter. I wouldn't even know how to put a piece of paper in these new fancy typewriters. I'm fascinated by computers. I have an excellent computer but really don't know how to use it. I can be hypnotized watching printers turning out the stuff. But I compose almost everything in longhand.

When do you do your best serious work?

I found years ago that I can read and write better at night than in the daytime. I break into my work frequently by listening to music or just raiding the refrigerator.

Now where are your children today? What are their passions in life?

I'm of the opinion that they are quite an unusual group. They were about the prettiest set of little children that I've ever seen, the five of them. They were all born in Catholic hospitals, incidentally. The first three in St. Vincent's in Los Angeles, and the last two in the Holy Cross Hospital in Salt Lake.

Trudy has a degree in history from the University of Utah. She has remarkable linguistic skills and does a great deal with books as an editor. She is very much in demand and has done freelance work in Salt Lake City. Trudy is now acquisitions editor for the University of Nevada Press in Las Vegas and previously was director of the Southern Methodist University Press in Dallas and editor-in-chief of the University of Utah Press. She has an unusual capability for making books, sometimes almost out of things that hardly seem to be interrelated, and she has done some teaching at Westminster College on editing and publishing. Trudy is a person of many talents. When she was fourteen one of the leading producers of Paramount Pictures, Sam Jaffe, wanted to put her in the movies, but we didn't go along with him. She did do some things on the stage here at the University of Utah in Kingsbury Hall and the Pioneer Memorial Theatre. For several years she was a student of Willam Christensen in ballet and danced in the University Ballet—which became Ballet West. Trudy is the very soul of cheerfulness. When she enters a room it comes alive.

Was your second child, Joe, named for your father?

Yes, just as Trudy was named for my mother, Gertrude. Joe has unusual capabilities in mathematics and science. He went to several universities—the University of Utah, the University of Maryland, and the California State University at Northridge. He earned a degree in engineering at UCLA and a master's at UCLA in engineering.

What does he do now?

He did a little teaching after he got his degree. Didn't like it. Then he worked at the Jet Propulsion Laboratory in Pasadena for some time but was bothered a great deal by the smog in California. He eventually moved north in California, on the coast, and then to Salt Lake City. He became involved in doing a good deal of computer work and now is in Hawaii, where he contracts with an engineering firm that deals with environmental problems. Joe has quite a fine bibliography and has been primarily interested in environmental issues and especially the development of solar energy. His master's thesis was in the field of solar energy.

Was Joe drafted during the Vietnam War?

No, he enlisted in the Army in military intelligence. Though he selected Vietnamese as his first choice for language school in Monterey, Japanese as his second choice, and Russian as his third, they put him in Spanish. During much of the Vietnam War, he was located in Panama where he was doing intelligence work. He has never been able to tell us just what it was because it was secret. But I think it had to do largely with Cuba.

How about your third child, Sterling James?

Jim was interested in building from a very early time. When he was in junior high school, for instance, in Virginia, he won first prize in the State Science Fair for some architectural things that he did. Jim favored art and architecture and eventually went to the School of Architecture at the University of Utah. I think he put in at least one year—maybe two. He did work in the architectural office of the university itself—but he got interested also in sculpture. He had earlier graduated from the University of Washington with a bachelor's degree in sculpture and architecture.

What has Jim done since graduating?

He is very competent as a builder but has always been more interested in design than anything else. He went on to MIT, spent three years in its School of Architecture, and received his master's degree. He has stuck with design ever since. Today he's involved with one of his teachers at MIT who is a world-class sculptor, Michael Singer. Jim and he, with two or three others, work together on contracts in Europe and all over America. They are very successful and have done some remarkable things. Jim was involved for some time in the development of a large water park in Stuttgart, Germany, and recently they completed a major art project for the new Denver airport. They develop their plans and designs in Vermont where Jim and Singer live. Then Jim carries through on the construction end of things. He owns a farm, raises horses, and helps his wife, Karen, with their lovely baby Sadie.

Jim must have been caught in the Vietnam War, too.

Yes, Jim enlisted in the naval reserve. After a short time, he was called into action and given a choice of several things. Because of his interest in building construction, he chose to be in the SEABEES, the construction arm of the Marines. We saw him off to Danang from the air base in San Bernardino, but when the plane stopped for refueling in Okinawa, they took Jim off and assigned him work there. He remained in Okinawa with the Navy until they ordered the base closed.

Joe had several excellent opportunities for positions as an engineer in defense industries—both in California and here. But he simply refused to take a job that had anything to do with the manufacture of war materials. Joe and Jim both, as I have indicated, voluntarily enlisted in the military during the Vietnam War, but neither of them had any inclinations to favor war or any kind of military activity.

Now, your fourth child, Laurie?

Her full name is Natalie Laurie. She is a person who from her very earliest years showed a great deal of curiosity about everything. She was taken with mythology and legends and with matters pertaining to religion. At an early age she was concerned with such things as death and immortality. She is a very sensitive person. Laurie also showed from a very early age a good deal of organizational talent. At the University of Utah she received her degree in anthropology—and then worked as an anthropologist for the state of Utah's historical division. Laurie later went into personnel work—directing personnel for one or two firms—and that led her into the world of finance, where she was connected for a number of years with a leading brokerage firm. She enjoyed that work very much, had a great deal of aptitude for it, and passed the examinations to become a licensed broker in the state of Utah.

And now?

She has moved up the ladder to manage an office for a financial firm that deals with brokerage houses. She enjoys that very much, and Natalie and I have a great deal of confidence in her. Whenever we have a little money to invest, we simply turn it over to Laurie, and she takes care of things. Laurie is very stylish in her dress and her appearance and very professional in every way. She has a twelve-year-old boy, Scott, as bright as they come, who has joined the Boy Scouts and is active in athletics. She is completely devoted to him.

Now, Melanie, your fifth child?

Melanie was born here in Salt Lake City and has always had a mind of her own. Now all of our kids have had minds of their own from the time they were born, and certainly at the present time, but this independence of mind, I think, showed up earlier in Melanie than in the others. And it's very evident at the present time. She's so good natured and is a delightful person to be around. In college she had a little difficulty deciding what to study. Very early on she decided she wanted to be in forestry. She was in some tree-planting expeditions and things of that kind up in the mountains and later left the University of Utah and went to Utah State University to study forestry. I don't think that lasted for more than a year, and when she came back, it looked like she was going into biology, but she ended up in geography for her degree. Her interests seem to have been mainly in art. Melanie is the most cosmopolitan of our children. She was with Natalie and me in Rome and has traveled widely in Europe. Before settling in Utah, she lived in Paris and Toronto. She has two children, Mira, a beautiful teenager, and Lyra Zöe who sets her grade school on fire. They both shine like the stars they are named for, and Melanie is passionately devoted to them. She is studying art at the University of Utah again and will probably become an art teacher.

Do your older children have children too?

Joe has a daughter, Kivalani Grace, a beautiful child—very bright for a preschooler. Trudy's daughter, Robbie (Natalie Howard), is grown up and lives outside of Portland. She has a great deal of talent in the field of visual arts and with her partner Kerry Haladae has founded a beautiful art shop. Robbie has a fine stepbrother, too, Jeof McAllister, an accomplished young aerospace scientist.

You and Natalie must be very proud of your progeny.

Yes, our offspring are all very cultivated. They all have university degrees, and they engage in high-level conversation. I frankly doubt that there is a family anywhere in which there is more mutual affection and concern for one another and interest in what the others are doing. A very strong bond of family ties, and this has always been the case. I know of no alienation whatsoever of our children from Natalie and me. I have difficulty understanding why in so many families today there is so much distance between parents and children.

5.
Teacher of Religion

By the age of twenty-three, Sterling, you had received your master's degree and had a job teaching for the Mormon church. Natalie continued teaching school in Idaho, and the two of you were hoping to save enough to marry soon. Is that right?

That's correct, Jack, and the date tells it all. Being in Utah in 1937 meant being where money was very scarce. My parents had helped some with expenses, but Natalie and I were each pretty much self-supporting at this point. We were both just squeaking by, the way most students did in those days.

Even so, I considered going straight for my doctorate. Ephraim Ericksen and Waldemer Read both believed that the only respectable place for me to study philosophy was the University of Chicago. I applied for a fellowship there, with strong support from them and President Thomas. In the middle of the Great Depression, however, there were simply no fellowships or scholarships available for me there or anywhere else. So Ericksen and Read urged me to apply for a position teaching high school seminary for the LDS church. Read had taught seminary for a number of years before he turned to the study of philosophy at the University of Chicago and then joined the University of Utah faculty.

What was your initial reaction to their advice?

To be frank with you, I hardly knew what a seminary was. They didn't have such things in California. But I was willing, so Read drove me downtown to see Dr. Lynn Bennion, who was the supervisor of LDS seminaries. I'd never met him before. Lynn told me their faculty positions were all filled but they might add one more teacher.

Lynn then introduced me to Dr. Franklin L. West, the church Commissioner of Education. When they learned that I was engaged to be married, they wanted to meet Natalie. They asked about my tastes in music and literature and my attitudes toward religion and the church, but never raised questions regarding my religious orthodoxy. I thought they were great. A couple of days after meeting Natalie, Lynn called me up and offered me the position of second teacher in Richfield, Utah. Richfield had always had a one-man seminary, Moroni W. Smith, but it had grown enough to need another teacher. I accepted right away, but I think they hired me with the hope of getting Natalie!

What kind of salary did they offer you?

The pay was $1,300 a year, which shocked Read. He thought it would be more like $1,800. I think they had been paying more before the Depression. At any rate, $1,300 sounded like a lot of money to me! And it was better than the average salary for new high school teachers in Utah at that time.

Why would that be?

Well, as I understand it, seminary teachers averaged more education than high school teachers. Quite a few had masters' degrees then, although I was the first to show up with a master's in philosophy. That appealed to both Dr. Bennion and Dr. West. I must tell you, though, that I didn't stay long at $1,300. At the end of my first year, I told Lynn Bennion that I was going to get married. He asked, "Are you marrying the woman you introduced me to last year?" When I said, "Yes, Natalie Cotterel," he replied, "You marry her and we will raise your salary fifty dollars next year!"

Looking back, would you still have been a seminary teacher?

In many ways, I'm sorry I did it. It was an impediment, I think, to my progress in education, even though I didn't see many other financial alternatives at the time. But in other ways, it was a good experience and very rewarding. The main rewards were the people who became our friends, especially Lynn Bennion and Frank West. It was also through this experience that I became lifelong friends with Lowell Bennion, Obert Tanner, George Boyd, Boyer Jarvis, Stewart Udall, and others. Those friendships were a wonderful benefit of my seminary years.

You went to Richfield a single man and married Natalie the following summer?

Natalie and I were married in June 1938, so she was with me during the second year in Richfield. During 1939-40 I taught in Montpelier, Idaho, then transferred to Mesa and Tempe, Arizona, for two years— 1940-42. I contracted to teach half-time at the seminary and half-time at the Religious Conference of Arizona State College, now Arizona State University.

Then in the spring of 1942 you were granted a year's leave of absence without pay to work on your doctorate?

Yes, but not without pay; I received $15 a month from the church. Natalie and I had been going to the University of Southern California every summer since 1938. So with the summer of 1942, the academic school year of 1942-43 and the summer of 1943 I was able to finish my course work. Then in 1943 I became director of the LDS Institute of Religion at the University of Arizona in Tucson and served there for two and a half years—till the winter of 1945. It was during this time that I wrote my doctoral dissertation.

The University of Southern California offered me a position on its philosophy faculty beginning in the fall of 1945, but I'd already agreed to remain as director of the institute for a third year. So we compromised. I went back to Tucson for the first semester, until they could find someone else, and then in January of 1946 we moved to Los Angeles.

So your seven-and-a-half-year career as an LDS religion teacher came to a close. How did you like teaching seminary and institute?

I was very interested in the subject matter I was teaching, but I really wasn't much good as a teacher for high school kids. To be frank with you, I had a very difficult time putting my stuff on a high-school level. I liked college-level teaching better.

What about your relation with local church leaders and students' parents?

Well, in Richfield, it was very pleasant. I got along well with all three members of the stake presidency, and one became a particularly good friend. Smith—he didn't care much for "Moroni" as a name, so he went by M. W.—was in charge of the seminary. They may have been glad when I moved on, but I don't think there was any effort to get rid of me; and Smith seemed quite unhappy when I left. Except for a few real collisions over my religious liberalism, he and I got along very well.

Sterling, you must have been seen as reasonably orthodox at the start or they wouldn't have hired you in the first place.

I guess it depends on what you mean by "reasonably." I can say this: my attitudes then and now are very positive toward religion. I've always felt that I am a genuinely religious person. So my attitude was as positive as the most orthodox, but my beliefs simply were not orthodox even in 1937. Ericksen and Read knew I wasn't orthodox, but they were of the opinion that it wouldn't cause me any serious problems in working for the church.

Those were different times.

Yes. After my first meeting with Lynn, I went down a second time and had a very pleasant conversation with him and Dr. West. They didn't

examine my orthodoxy, and I didn't volunteer any information—
though I would certainly have been candid about my heresies if they'd
asked.

This is what I'm getting at. Were you a heretic then?

Oh yes, I was already becoming a good, well-rounded heretic. I
didn't believe that Joseph Smith had seen the Father and the Son in the
first vision. I didn't believe the Book of Mormon was an authentic
ancient document. I thought Adam and Eve were cultural myths, and I
didn't accept the divinity of Christ. Shall I go on?

*That's quite a collection of statements for a Mormon of any stripe. Why
don't you comment on the evolution of your religious ideas through the
college years.*

It's fair to say, Jack, that I'm intellectually and emotionally con-
structed with a rather strong religious disposition. I see religion as a
profound, important sentiment, not a theological formula or something
one finds at the end of a syllogism.

It's more a set of values than a set of beliefs?

Religion is a matter of feeling, of disposition. I'm of the opinion
that religion, to be entirely acceptable, must be supportable by rational
argument; but the rational argument is not the religion. Theology is an
attempt to be reasonable about religion, and it's important. Otherwise,
religion would become a matter of emotion and affective enthusiasm.
Of course, to some that's what religion is, but this to me is a very bad
form of religion.

So theology provides boundaries for the expression of religious sentiment?

Exactly. There couldn't be any genuine religion independent of
emotion and passion, but reason and theology set some bounds around
these passions. Well, my point is that I have what I honestly believe is a
constitutional makeup which is congenial to religion. During my
adolescence, my religious feelings probably got the better of my reason
quite regularly. I was religious as a child, probably due to family
upbringing and community environment, but also by personal temperament. I became very attached to the church during my high school years
in Los Angeles. We weren't one of those families who ran down to the
church every time the lights were on; but we were very active, and I
was very much involved in ward activities.

And when you came to the University of Utah?

I had a solid foundation in readings about the church's theology and
attended church regularly during my freshman year while living with

my aunt and uncle. They were in the Yale Ward, near your home on Harvard Avenue, Jack. It was very pleasant for me. During my second year, however, the cows interfered with Sunday schedule and I saw the inside of a church only two or three times. During my remaining years in college, I was somewhat indifferent to religious attendance. I don't mean that I became indifferent to religion or developed negative attitudes about Mormonism or ceased to be interested in its theology. I simply didn't show up at church very often.

That's a fairly typical experience for a college student.

I suppose so. And of course, the LDS church didn't have college wards at the university; although the University Ward, adjacent to the campus, roughly served that function. Lowell Bennion was teaching his institute of religion classes in that building at that time. I didn't attend his classes and I'm sorry about that. He would have been a very good influence on me. We became very good friends, though; and we had many long conversations about religion. We're still close friends.

There's a tendency for Latter-day Saints in this area to sharply differentiate between active and "inactive" members. Was that true in your undergraduate days?

Well, there were certainly insiders and outsiders; but the outsiders were members of other churches. No, a person in those days could be more or less inactive and still be accepted as a full-fledged member. I think the LDS church goes in for Chamber of Commerce figures. If you haven't been kicked out or taken to the cemetery, you get counted. They keep track of you. I was not a churchgoer when I was hired, although I attended church regularly while I was teaching. I had nothing against attending church. My "falling away," if that's what they call it, during my undergraduate days, was sheer laziness. I'd rather sleep in on Sunday mornings than get up and go to church. I was not irreligious or disillusioned with the church in any way.

Did you find the nature of your faith changing during these years?

I think that my approach to religion became more intellectual, if I can put it like that. I had the same positive feelings about the church; but my main religious activity was conversations with professors Ericksen, Read, Tornay, and other members of the university faculty. Professor Louis Zucker and I would have long conversations on Judaism, Christianity, and Mormonism. Ericksen was radical in his theology but devoted to the church's purposes, especially its work with young people. These were serious religious discussions. Nobody was flippant or disrespectful toward religion, even at their most critical moments.

These were very fruitful years for the development of your religious thought.

Oh, yes, and it had nothing to do with showing up in church. Have I told you that Ericksen assigned me the project of writing text materials for him during my graduate year for a class he taught on the history of moral thought? Well, that was quite an interesting experience. Ericksen was not a scholar of competence in the Old Testament, but he had the feel of it and a scholarly approach to it. He understood the moral substance of prophetic religion. He couldn't find a textbook he was willing to use, so he enlisted me. He'd indicate the kinds of things he liked—largely the works of ethicists and some of the more liberal biblical scholars in Old Testament studies. He'd sketch out an idea or two in conversation, then tell me to write up a chapter with accompanying readings. It kept me busy trying to stay ahead of his class. The stuff was mimeographed for his students.

I didn't keep a full set of the chapters I had written, but when I came back to the University of Utah in 1948, Waldemer Read, who was chair of the department at the time, gave me his entire set of copies.

Working through these Old Testament materials—really coming to terms with these various scholarly approaches—must have been tremendously important for the development of your own religious thought. What specifically did you conclude was most important?

The Old Testament interests me much more than the New Testament to this very day, even though I recently wrote and published *Toward Understanding the New Testament* (1990) with Obert Tanner and Max Rogers. The historical sweep of the Old Testament is very impressive, with the variety of religious ideas and experiences in it and the fundamental contrast between priests and prophets. The prophets with their religiously grounded morality often stood in sharp judgment of the priests with their institutionalized, ceremonial, rule-following religion.

The prophet-priest distinction is so evident in Ezekiel's writing as he plays these two themes off each other.

Yes, and Deuteronomy is a prophet-priestly work—one of history's most important socio-religious documents. But Amos and Jeremiah were my favorite prophets. They modeled an approach to religious writing that was simultaneously positive and critical. Liberal in the old-fashioned sense of liberal religion.

Sterling, it seems to me that many people come to know religion primarily as a social phenomenon—they enjoy the religious culture and their church friends—and then develop their moral and ethical commitments out of that

*experience. But I hear you saying that your commitment arose more from
the theology, the philosophy, and the history. Is that right?*

Well, I'm not sure. That certainly is a proper characterization of my
approach over the last several decades, in which I've focused primarily
on religious ideas. But as I think back into adolescence and childhood,
I remember experiencing feelings of worship and awe connected directly
to nature. I remember terrifying thunderstorms in the wild that produced
a sense of awe, fear, even mystery. It's the quality that Rudolf Otto
identified as the *numinous* in his book *The Idea of the Holy*—the sense of
being overwhelmed by awful majesty. I sometimes wonder whether I
could have become a mystic, if I had let myself go. I don't want to
exaggerate this, of course; and, mind you, I'm not sorry that I didn't
follow my mystic tendencies.have a more mystical nature than you and,
believe me, it isn't something one works at!

*How would you characterize those experiences that made you wonder a
little?*

I was always alone when I felt these things. Wasn't it Alfred North
Whitehead who said, "Religion is what one does with his solitude"?
That was the case for me. I usually wanted to be alone—until I met
Natalie. Then I just wanted to be with her. But as an adolescent, I used
to seek opportunities to be alone. In my solitude, I sometimes had what
I believe were genuine religious experiences.

*Are these feelings similar to moments of artistic or moral ecstasy—when a
magnificent symphony performance or witnessing a selfless act of generosity
causes the boundary between yourself and the world around you to blur or
temporarily seem to disappear?*

I'd say that there's a real connection, yes, although I'm inclined to
agree with Otto that religion, art, and morals, though intimately related,
are autonomous and that it's an error to reduce religion to morals or
religion to art. The mainstream liberal development in modern religion
has, I think, been guilty of that error—reducing religion to morals.

*What about extending it to personal contact? How do you respond to people
whose religious experiences are tied up with seeing a divine personage or
hearing the voice of God?*

I've never had the inclination to associate my experience with persons. This doesn't mean that I don't think in terms of a relationship with
God, but such a thing as encountering Christ has never had any real
meaning for me—not in the sense that it does for many Christians. I'm
not making fun of these people; but whenever I hear that popular song
you hear at funerals and in church, "In the Garden"—do you know it?

I think the chorus goes: "And He walks with me and He talks with me, and He tells me I am His own"?

That's it. It always makes me think of hearing Reinhold Niebuhr lecture on religion and sex, in which he stated that many women fall in love erotically with Christ. In relation to that song, he used the phrase "peripatetic eroticism." Well, I'm afraid that there are a great many things associated with religious experience that are not particularly admirable, and a fixation on persons may be one of them. And now that I've just picked on this song, I should hasten to add that music has had a tremendous effect on me—much more of an effect than most of the things I have read. And I certainly know what you mean, Jack, when I consider the selflessness some people exhibit in their moral lives—and the effects their actions have on me.

We've come to a simple truth for me. I virtually never have a religious experience in an institutional setting.

Oh, church is no place to go to get a religious experience! Unless you go in when no one else is there.

But some people do. We can't deny their experiences, which I know are genuine to the core for many of our friends in different faiths, including Mormonism.

I guess they do have religious experiences. I won't say they don't. But here, now, a friend told me that she had a very profound religious experience during the University of Utah Tanner Lecture of 1983, when former Chancellor Helmut Schmidt was discussing German and American politics.

I have had such an experience myself, about that same year, listening to Barry Lopez talk about writing Arctic Dreams. *He spoke of things I too have seen and felt alone in wilderness that have quickened my spirit—my sense of what matters ultimately. I rejoice at being alive when I reflect on those moments. My spine tingles.*

To get us back on the subject, I've always felt that one of the major strengths in Mormon theology is its concern for reasonableness in religion. I see John A. Widtsoe as making a major contribution to this facet of Mormonism through his book *Rational Theology.* So did James E. Talmage and B. H. Roberts.

I'm sitting here savoring a transcendent experience, and you're trying to talk Mormon theology again! Well, how do you explain Widtsoe's theology in light of the church's early history?

Let's take the moment of Mormonism's greatest outburst of religious enthusiasm, in Kirtland, Ohio. People were having visions, hearing angelic choirs singing at the temple dedication, receiving revelations, planning to build a new Jerusalem, and so forth. It seems pretty clear to me in reading it that there was a fair amount of delusion; and when they got through cleaning the place up, there were only half the members left. Now I think this set a rather good example that was generally followed later by the church. Religion should be reasonable, not just an outburst of emotion.

Can you expand on that? It sounds to me ominously like the church's crackdown on liberals, feminists, working mothers, and homosexuals.

Yes, for instance during the Mormon Reformation of 1857-58, when Jedediah Grant was hustling around the Salt Lake Valley calling people to repentance and having people rebaptized for playing cards or swearing, it was a very intense period, but it didn't last very long. It was like a burst of emotion that reason soon dispelled. As another example, it's still in the LDS Articles of Faith that we believe in the gift of tongues. There are many reported examples of such manifestations in early church history. Well, I've never heard anyone speak in tongues in the Mormon church. My father told me that he'd never encountered it. My mother remembers one example, a woman in the ward she lived in; but there was no one to interpret it, so it wasn't taken as an authentic manifestation. My point is that the church gives lip service to some things that it's not really willing to accept in practice at the present time. There's a kind of rationality that tends to pervade Mormonism and keep down excessive enthusiasm—sooner or later. The purge that is going on now will pass, too, but I hope it doesn't take too long. It is too often a purge in the wrong direction—against those who are attempting to be reasonable and face the facts.

The church excommunicates people for being too enthusiastic, or too liberal. You and I tend to know the latter, but what about the too enthusiastic? And what about Joseph Smith? Was he a mystic?

I've certainly known Mormons who were involved in spiritual excesses of various kinds, but none of them have been the type of people whom you would take very seriously. William James gave some attention to Joseph Smith in his *The Varieties of Religious Experience*, but he doesn't make a real mystic of Joseph Smith. Paul M. Edwards, the chief philosopher of the Reorganized LDS church, did some very competent work on Joseph Smith's mysticism, but an equally competent critique has been made of that position by Max Nolan, who is in the Education Ministry in Western Australia. It seems clear to me that there's not a good case for Joseph Smith being a true mystic. He was certainly charismatic, but not a mystic.

What are your views on the Book of Mormon?

I've never read the entire Book of Mormon, Jack. Brig Madsen and I were having lunch a while ago with Ernest Poulson, former head of personnel at the University of Utah, when the subject of the Book of Mormon came up. "Oh, I've read every word of it," said Ernest. We were surprised and asked, "When did you do that?" It turned out that when he was in a World War II POW camp in Romania he read the whole thing. It was the only book he had to read.

Why haven't you felt a need to read it, Sterling, if only to make an informed decision? Aren't you like anyone else who condemns a book without reading it or pans a film without seeing it?

I simply haven't been able to take the Book of Mormon seriously as an authentic record, considering the claims of its coming from an angel and being translated by a miracle. But I have read enough of it to know that it has a confused theology and is a mixture of good and bad religion.

Given, then, your feelings about Joseph Smith, the social role of the church, and the other issues we've discussed here, did you feel any conflict in going to work for the church?

Yes and no. No in the sense that I had a genuine love for the church as an institution and its people. My attitude was entirely positive in spite of the fact that I was in various ways as critical of the church as I am now. I consider this to be in-house criticism.

Loyal opposition?

Loyal opposition. I was devoted to the church, really was, and am right now. I've always considered myself as Mormon as these orthodox Mormons, though I have been a confirmed heretic. You have to realize, too, that in those days there was much greater liberality in matters of this kind, especially among the general authorities. The same was true of Brigham Young University under President Franklin S. Harris. He was a man of real breadth and depth. He's the person who made the BYU into a university.

When did this spirit of liberality begin to flag at BYU?

It certainly flagged when Ernest L. Wilkinson became president in 1951. He was an extremely conservative president in everything except building expansion, but the atmosphere in the church had already changed, thanks to the influence of J. Reuben Clark, Jr. He became a member of the First Presidency in 1933 and remained a power to be reckoned with through the 1950s—until his death in 1961. As he gained in power, the leadership of the church began to clamp down in matters of doctrine. Authoritarianism took over.

Did you have any encounters with J. Reuben Clark?

Well, not directly, but I certainly felt the impact of his views. During the summer of 1938, when Natalie and I were newly married and I had a contract to teach a second year at Richfield, we attended the BYU Aspen Grove program held for seminary and religion teachers. It lasted six weeks, and they expected us to be there. Because Natalie and I were both attending summer school at the University of Southern California, we got permission to show up a week late.

What was it like?

We camped out, really. The Wests and the Bennions had cabins, but here were the seminary, institute, and BYU religion teachers from all over the West living in tents. We divided ourselves up pretty quickly into liberal and conservative camps, and I landed among the liberals. Guest speakers came in every week for the Sunday morning service. Among the speakers were John A. Widtsoe, J. Reuben Clark, and myself. Recently appointed to the First Presidency of the church, Clark gave his notorious address which was printed immediately in the *Improvement Era* (Summer 1938). It continues to be cited even today.

This was President Clark's clarion call for orthodoxy and obedience in the ranks of church educators. The former U.S. Ambassador to Mexico's retreat from the larger world of ideas?

Yes, and church leaders still bring it up whenever they're inaugurating a president at BYU or Ricks. It quite clearly lays down the law on matters of academic freedom in church institutions: there is to be no freedom in matters pertaining to religion and morals. Clark laid it out very firmly, and there was considerable discussion about it around our campfires. Natalie and I were included in the campfire discussion presided over by Newell K. Young, a grand old polygamist who had two wives and many children. He had decided that polygamy was wrong; but he was devoted to his wives and children. That evening by the campfire, Newell got up—white beard, majestic bearing, he really reminded me of an Old Testament prophet—and said, "I don't know about the rest of you; but before I go to bed, I'm going over to see Lynn Bennion and resign." He did, too.

But Lynn refused to accept his resignation?

Yes, Newell apparently did this quite often. Lynn later told me that when he left the seminaries to take his position as superintendent of Salt Lake City schools, he called Newell into his office and said, "Now,

Newell, I'm leaving this job. You can't resign any more, because the next time you do, they'll probably accept your resignation!"

I think that underscores the shift away from liberality in the church during those years.

No question about it. I always thought of President Clark as a conservative reactionary; but I tell you, Jack, if he were living today, he'd look as if he were right down the center, if not a little to the left.

When did you speak and what did you say?

Well, I spoke the very next Sunday, and Apostle John A. Widtsoe spoke the week after me. I addressed distinguishing characteristics of Mormon theology, especially our conception of a non-absolutistic God. Just the sort of thing I would say today. I didn't respond to Clark's remarks in any way. The following week Widtsoe really laid down the law, again, but not as a response to me. After that meeting was over, however, Natalie and I were walking back to our tent behind three or four seminary teachers who were more than a shade on the conservative side. The path was too narrow for us to pass, and they didn't know we were with them. One of them announced, "Well, that was certainly better stuff than we heard last week." Just then we reached a clearing where Natalie and I could walk past them. One man, seeing us, suddenly added, "Of course, there's room for all kinds of opinions!"

Were any strictures placed on you that next year in Richfield as a result of President Clark's call for strict orthodoxy among church educators?

Well, despite the changing atmosphere, I was determined to be absolutely honest. When I was invited to speak at the Third Ward's sacrament meeting, I talked about the meaning of prayer and communion and commented how it could involve silent meditation. As an example, I said, "We run into this problem very often in fast meeting after someone has borne his or her testimony and it's very quiet. If somebody doesn't immediately get up to talk, the bishop will sometimes say, 'Now, brothers and sisters, let's not let this time go to waste.'"

Yes, I've heard that myself.

"Well," I told these people, "the time wasn't going to waste at all. That was the best part of the meeting—when everyone was being quiet." I turned to the bishop and said, "Of course this couldn't happen in your ward." It was in the nature of a joke, but I could see the expression on his face, and by damn, he didn't like it one bit. The next week was fast meeting, and the bishop got up and said—one of my students told me this—"We want you to ignore what a certain speaker had to say here last week. We don't want any of this time to go to waste."

One of my students came in the next day and told me very seriously, "I just want to tell you to stay on the west side of Main Street; if you go on the east side"—Third Ward was on the east side—"you're gonna be in trouble."

So you were persona non grata in at least one ward.

I taught Sunday school briefly in the ward where I lived. I never lasted very long in these jobs. One Sunday I was walking back to Mrs. Hansen's large house where I lived that first year with the coach and the music teacher from the high school—all of us unmarried. I heard footsteps running behind me, and here came a man from my class. He said, "Brother McMurrin, I want you to know that I tell these people they don't understand you." I said, "Now look, that's not the problem. The problem is they *do* understand me."

Your youthful candor was splitting the community down the middle.

Exactly. There was a lot of animosity developing against me, even though some people were very much on my side. The next year when Natalie and I were married, a wonderful old couple, the Dastrups, invited us to dinner. She was as bright as they come, the local theologian, and she really grilled me on theology. Well, I answered her questions honestly, and one of them was, "Brother McMurrin, there are people here who suspect that you don't believe in the divinity of Christ." "Sister Dastrup," I said, "I don't." And she almost collapsed.

Not what the local theologian expects to hear from the local seminary teacher.

She got that testimony look in her eye and that testimony sound in her voice and said, very earnestly, "I want you to know that I know as I live that Jesus is the Son of God, that he is a divine being . . . " Really laid it out effectively. This was probably not a proper thing for me to do, but I was young and didn't have good sense, so I got that testimony look in *my* eye and that testimony tone in *my* voice and said, "I want to testify to you that I know as I live that he was not divine and he was not the son of God." She gasped and said, "I never thought I'd ever hear anyone say that." Well, she was shocked but she took it in her stride and didn't judge me an enemy.

You have to hand it to that woman. That was an audacious response to her and she handled it gracefully.

Oh, much more gracefully than I did. And there's certainly nothing unique about that kind of testimonial fervor. George Boyd and I used to frequent some evangelical spots in Los Angeles during the summers when he was working on his philosophy degree at USC. I remember once with Lynn Bennion we visited Father Divine's, the black man whose followers accepted him as God. They would all sit down together and share a holy meal. Well, there was no room at the table for the three of us, but lots of people were milling around, so we circulated and talked with quite a few of them. Before we left, we became conscious that an older black fellow had had his eye on us the whole time. He followed us back to the car, and we nodded to him while I was unlocking the car doors. Then he said, "Well, boys, I suppose this looks like a lot of nonsense to you," and we politely protested, "Oh, no, no," and he got that Mormon missionary glint in his eye and that Mormon testimony tone in his voice and said, "Yes, it looks very foolish to you, but I want to tell you boys that this man is Almighty God." Man, he laid it out! He was as impressive as any prophet I've ever listened to.

And probably just as sincere. How did your boss in Richfield, Moroni Smith, respond to the controversy surrounding you?

He told me that he'd been a liberal in his day. As a matter of fact, I read his master's thesis, which he'd written at BYU. It was on primitivisms in the Old Testament and was a good treatment of the subject. But he took offense at my liberality from time to time. I remember I cut out a verse by Edwin Arlington Robinson and stuck it on my bulletin board. It said: "Peace on Earth. We sing it/ We pay ten thousand priests to bring it./ After nineteen hundred years at Mass/ We've got as far as poison gas." Made Smith mad as the devil. Oddly enough, he didn't want me to leave. When Lynn Bennion asked me if I'd go head up a seminary elsewhere, and I agreed, Smith was quite unhappy.

What about ecclesiastical leaders in Richfield—except for the bishop of the Third Ward?

The stake president, a dentist, didn't take to my stuff. But one of the counselors, a Dr. Gledhill, was very friendly. I did some home teaching with another M.D., Dr. Ostler, a wonderful person liberal in his interpretations of Mormonism. The principal of the high school, Angus Maughan, was absolutely first-rate too. I had a close friendship with him. No, Richfield was nothing like what I encountered in Montpelier the next year.

Well, let's hear about that, Sterling!

I really locked horns with the stake president in Montpelier the next year, even though his two counselors were very much for me, which made the thing interesting.

What were the details of that episode?

The stake president, Silas Wright, lived in Bennington, a little farming community outside Montpelier, and he apparently heard from the father of one of my students that I'd taught that not everything in the Old Testament was true—specifically, that God had ordered the Israelites to kill off all of the women and children of the conquered cities during the invasion of Canaan. I said to the boy's father when he came to see me about it, "Now, I want you to face this question. Would you rather have me teach your son that God ordered these atrocities—that God could be immoral   or teach him that whoever put that item in the Bible was probably mistaken?" I might say that, in the course of our conversation, he asked me which came first, the New Testament or the Old Testament.

Not exactly a student of the scriptures. What did he say?

He thought this over very carefully, very seriously, and I waited for his reply. At last he said, "I'd rather have you teach that God ordered murder than have you teach that there's anything in the Bible that is in error." This rather shocked me. It was not a view characteristic of Mormons.

I can see why.

What the hell can you do in a case like that? And then one of my students told me, "I thought you'd be interested in knowing that you're the subject of our ward teaching lesson this month. The ward teachers are warning the parents to be sure that their kids don't take seminary from you next year."

It sounds as if there was some personal conflict as well?

Not from me, but it was pretty clear that President Wright had no use for me and was anxious to use any excuse to get me out. Now the summer prior to my going there, when Natalie and I were in Los Angeles, the dean of the School of Religion at USC called me in and said that the Hollywood Methodist church had contacted him and wanted someone to come and teach their adult Sunday class. This church is a famous place just north of Hollywood Boulevard on Highland, a beautiful church often photographed because that's where a lot of the movie stars get married and buried. Well, I taught the adult class there every week until it was time to leave. They wanted me to stay permanently, but of course I couldn't do that.

Anyway, I didn't tell anybody about it; but one Sunday I was asked to speak to the high priests class in the Montpelier Third Ward. Some of them liked what I had to say—

And some didn't?

A friend of mine ran the drugstore, which was open on Sunday. Several men had come in after my class, he said, and one of them exclaimed, "Well, I don't know why in the world they let him teach our young people, because he's not even a member of the church. He's a damned Methodist minister!"

Back to Idaho . . .

That was 1939, the year Vardis Fisher's great novel *The Children of God* came out and the county library in Montpelier invited me to review the book. It wasn't a big place, and it was absolutely jammed. People were standing in the halls and sitting in the windows. I took the position that Fisher's stuff basically had good historical merits, and I read them his impressive description of Joseph Smith's first vision. Once again people were divided on whether they agreed with me or not.

I think the only thing that really offended me was something the stake president Silas Wright did. Natalie's mother, who lived in American Falls, Idaho, wasn't very well; and we went to take care of her the weekend of stake conference. I had no duties at the conference; but when President Wright noticed that I wasn't in the audience, he seized the chance to get at me. Still, we ended the year in pretty good shape, partly because his two counselors were very fair-minded.

Did he complain about you to Lynn Bennion or Frank West?

As a matter of fact, he did. Late in the year Lynn Bennion came up to iron things out in a meeting with me and the stake presidency. He managed to smooth things over, but he told me, "You and Heber Snell"—Heber C. Snell was a fine biblical scholar and then head of the LDS institute at Idaho State—"are both in trouble. I had to flip with Frank West to see which one we got, and I got you." I would have just quit at the end of the year, but Lynn worked out a proposal with Frank West. Arizona State wanted to establish a program of religious studies, and the church agreed to furnish an instructor half time to teach these college courses. Lynn offered me the job of heading the LDS seminary in Mesa half-time and teaching in the college at Tempe half-time.

A much more compatible situation for you.

Yes, it was a definite inducement. I don't know why they wanted me to stay in church education at all. President Heber J. Grant had given them explicit instructions to fire me.

Over the problems in Montpelier?

Oh, no. It was because of an article I had published. In those days the Church Education Department published *Weekday Religious Education,* a nice professional journal for religion teachers. In the early summer of 1939, Dr. West, the Commissioner of Education, asked me to write an article on the philosophy of religion that would be appropriate for a graduate seminar in philosophy. I dealt with absolutism and non–absolutism in theology and their implications for religious-based ethics. Dr. West liked it, and *Weekday* published it in December 1939. There was not a word of heresy in the piece. On the contrary, it was an argument for the LDS conception of God. One of the apostles, whom I shall not name but who was anxious to make trouble for the Department of Education, showed it to President Grant.

President Grant called Dr. West in—I got this story directly from him and also from Lynn Bennion—and there was the article laid out on the president's desk. He said to West, "I have given this article to seven lawyers, *seven lawyers,* and every one of them agrees with me that this article is a lot of damn tommyrot. I want that man fired; you get rid of him. And this magazine is to be discontinued." It was stopped, too.

And they sent you into exile in southern Arizona!

I suppose they thought President Grant would never find me down there. Same as Siberia, except for the weather. But on one of his trips President Grant eventually found me in Mesa and we had a most cordial conversation.

At this time, Arizona State was developing an interdenominational religious studies program, in cooperation with the Jews, Catholics, Protestants, and Mormons, and you got involved?

Yes, the president of the college was very enthusiastic about it. I think it was his idea. We had regular faculty meetings. I represented the Mormon church and the secretary of the group was a Mormon professor at the college. There was a Catholic priest, two Protestant ministers, and a Jewish rabbi. I taught half the classes and the other four split the other half among them.

Did you become close as a group?

I became very close friends with Abraham Lincoln Krone, the rabbi of the Reform congregation in Phoenix. He had moved to Phoenix from New York for his wife's health. A marvelous human being, brilliant. He had a regular book review program on the radio. A few months earlier, he'd reviewed Vardis Fisher's *The Children of God.* In the review he had some very favorable things to say about the Mormons; and at the next meeting of the Ministerial Society, one of the leading Protestant ministers said, "Krone, what we can't understand is why you have such a positive attitude toward a bastard religion like Mormonism," and as Krone told me, he replied, "If you Christian churches hadn't been so illegitimate in your relations with one another, Mormonism wouldn't be a bastard religion."

After your problems in Richfield and Montpelier, how did you get along with Arizona Mormons?

The stake presidency was 100 percent for me, and it made a big difference. Of course, some people were quite critical, but by that time I had become accustomed to it.

Did you hold leadership positions in the church in this period of your life?

As a matter of fact I did, especially in Arizona. I served in the Sunday school presidency of the Maricopa Stake for some time, and then on the stake high council in Tucson, the governing board of the diocese, so to speak. I was quite involved at that level, and some hoped I would go higher.

But that was plenty for you. Even so, you had some memorable experiences, didn't you?

The one that really stands out was a visit from Dr. John A. Widtsoe. He was the one who had raised the devil about that *Weekday* article, the one President Grant said they should fire me for writing. He came down to Tucson and we spent two or three hours talking very pleasantly together in my office while it was raining cats and dogs outside. It was the last conversation I had with Widtsoe. When a man came to take him to the train, I walked out on the veranda with him, we shook hands, and his parting words of advice to me were, "Well, preach the gospel; sugar-coat it where necessary." He was a master sugar-coater.

Widtsoe had earlier served as president of the University of Utah. How did his academic values bear on his relationship with you?

Well, he had a spy on me in Los Angeles! Did I ever tell you that? It was while I was teaching the high priests in the Wilshire Ward. Byron Done, a close friend of mine, was a very intimate friend of John and Leah Widtsoe's only son, who had died at an early age. Byron never came to Salt Lake City without calling on them. I used to see him around USC because he taught a class on Mormonism in the Department of Religion for the university. Done took me aside one day and said, "I hate to say this, but I had a long talk with Dr. Widtsoe recently and it's clear to me that he's got someone spying on you in that high priests' class." "Oh, really?" I said with surprise, "Who is it?" "I don't know," Byron said, "but it could be Barry Harris." He may have known for sure but just wanted to put me on guard rather than exposing Harris.

Did you know Harris?

Yes, he was an older man whom I'd known ever since I was a high school kid. Sure enough, Barry Harris was there every week and I noticed that he was taking notes very carefully. And perhaps two or three weeks later he said, "I want to be sure and get exactly straight what you said about such and such," so I told him and he wrote it down. Then he had another question and wrote down the answer. He'd asked me questions before, but I hadn't paid much attention to them. After he was all through, I said, "Brother Harris, I think I should tell you that I'm aware you're spying on me for Dr. Widtsoe." "Oh, no, no," he said, very shocked and somewhat shaken. I said, "There's no need of you telling me 'no' because I'm well aware that you're keeping Dr. Widtsoe informed of what I'm saying. I don't mind your telling him. If he were in the class, I'd say the same thing." He caved in and said, "Well, I'm just doing what I was instructed to do." Frankly, by this time these things didn't bother me in the least, even though they're quite disgusting from a moral point of view.

I'm amazed you had such a good conversation with Widtsoe during his Arizona visit. Was that the only incident involving church authorities during that period?

Well, now that I think of it, there was one other experience. Harold B. Lee, who was then an apostle, came to Tucson and stayed a couple of nights in the institute apartment with Natalie and me. The university had invited him down to give an evening lecture for their annual Religion Week. It was the Mormons' turn that year. He did a beautiful job—all extemporaneous, very appropriate, one of the best statements by a Mormon I'd ever heard. The president of the university told me it was the best annual lecture on religion they'd ever had and by far the largest audience. Of course, Mormons came from far and near.

Apostle Harold Lee and I got along beautifully. He was very generous, most pleasant, but he was very critical of my predecessor, Daryl Chase. I defended Chase right up to the hilt, but I had the feeling that President Lee was really criticizing me because I was guilty of the same things he was criticizing in Chase and he knew it. Daryl went on to distinguish himself as president of Utah State University, and Apostle Lee went on to become president of the church.

You also got to know Spencer W. Kimball in Arizona, shortly after he became an LDS apostle.

Yes, Spencer Kimball was from Arizona and he came back on what I would call his maiden apostolic voyage just after I went to teach in Tucson, succeeding Lowell Bennion and Daryl Chase. He visited the stake I was in, and we became rather well acquainted. He was a delightful person. I invited him to the institute to meet with the students and to speak at our Sunday services. I enjoyed very much my contacts with him while he was in southern Arizona. We were on a program together for the LDS stake conference.

Later on a young man whose parents were friends of Apostle and Mrs. Kimball was studying in the university. He was as cantankerous as hell. The other Mormon students didn't want anything to do with him. I intervened in his behalf and was as friendly toward him as I could be. Well, his mother came down to the institute to visit him and check things out. She proceeded to write a letter to Apostle Kimball about me and my evil doings. She said when I was speaking in the Sunday service in the chapel she felt the presence of the devil. I don't know whether she considered me to be the devil or simply that the devil came through the place because of his association with me.

Apostle Kimball probably turned the letter over to Dr. West.

And Dr. West simply sent the letter on to me. The young man came into the institute building for an evening affair shortly after I received this letter, and I showed it to him. Oh, he was upset. He said that he had lied about me to his mother and broke down in tears. He got on the telephone and called his mother in Globe, close to a hundred miles from Tucson. His mother wanted to talk to me and said she was coming right down to Tucson that evening. I told her that wasn't necessary, but she insisted on coming. She got on a bus and came to Tucson that same night and met me at the institute. Her son had confessed that he had lied to her about things I had said—and he certainly had. She shed tears and was there until very late. I sent for a cab, and she stayed with a friend. In Arizona the Mormons have friends in every town.

Did you continue to enjoy her friendship over the years?

No, but the interesting thing is that Spencer Kimball never mentioned this incident to me and was always very gracious in his attitude toward me. I continued to have contact with him when he was president of the church. I was honored to write and read the citation when he was awarded an honorary degree at the University of Utah in 1981. I think he was a man of genuine decency and compassion and very great integrity. Well, that's the story, Jack.

I believe you learned a lot of Mormon folklore during those years in Arizona.

I learned a great deal in Arizona that I had not known before. In Mesa, for instance, I learned that one of the common trees in that area dropped some kind of edible stem and nut. It was well-known in church in those parts that this was the stuff that Moses and the children of Israel lived on for forty years in the wilderness. This was the manna that fell from heaven. If so, it was a rather boring diet.

I also learned in Mesa that the devil smelled like a wet dog. Now, as a matter of fact, maybe the devil does smell like a wet dog, but the evidence that was given by those who held this view was not particularly persuasive. Now to give you another example of folk religion, I discovered that quite a few people believed that the Gulf of Mexico was made by the city of Enoch being taken up into heaven! Now I'd say that was a pretty good sized city—as big as the Gulf of Mexico. When I pointed this out to a man who was arguing for this explanation, he simply said, "Well, look at the map. What else do you think could have created that gulf? Besides, they had big towns in those days."

All in all, you and Natalie found life in Arizona most pleasant, didn't you?

We made some lasting friends in Arizona—Beth and Jim Fillmore, Harry Rickel and his wife, and the stake president of the Maricopa Stake, Lorenzo Wright, and his sons. Arizona was a delightful place to live—especially because of the people. This is where we became close friends with Stewart Udall, Boyer Jarvis, and others I have already mentioned.

Now my work in the institute was very pleasant too. I had close affiliation with the University of Arizona. The university gave full academic credit for my courses on the history of religion, comparative religion, and the philosophy of religion. On several occasions I substituted for people in the department of philosophy when they had to be out, and several people on the faculty of the University of Arizona attended my courses on comparative religion.

By this time the United States was fighting in World War II, casting a dark shadow over everyday life. How did it affect you and Natalie?

I had very strong feelings and so did she. I was of an age that qualified me to be in the service. When the draft came out—this was actually before Pearl Harbor—we were living in Mesa and I went through the medical examination. In the middle of it, when I was standing stark naked with many men of varying colors, I was suddenly jerked out of the line by one of the physicians, Dr. Kent. He knew that I had suffered from asthma severely, though I was more or less clear of it when I was there in Mesa. He said, "You're not qualified." They ran down my medical records and classified me as 4F—unqualified for military service because of my physical condition.

But it didn't end there. What happened next?

During the next year when I was on leave and studying full-time at the University of Southern California, I undertook to find some kind of work in support of the war effort—both through the university and then at the Federal Building in Los Angeles. I also wrote to agencies in

Washington that advertised things you could do to support the war
effort. But I had no success. So I turned to the ads in the papers in Los
Angeles. The big thing down there, of course, was the manufacture of
aircraft. There were several big outfits there, particularly the Douglas
Aircraft Company and North American. It's almost laughable the
experiences that I had. I became quite disgusted. Douglas couldn't take
me because of the fact that I had asthma. North American wouldn't take
me either because they discovered I had injured my back.

*You've had severe back trouble on and off throughout your life. Was it
severe then?*

Yes, ever since I lived in Montpelier, Idaho. This has been one of
the chief pains of my life. North American's physician said they couldn't
take me and I was out. He said, however, "You know, if you go out to
the North American plant and apply there, they won't pay any attention
to your medical record." So the very next morning I was out at the plant
lined up with other people. The aircraft companies were putting out
full-page ads in the newspapers saying that they needed workers. They
were desperate for people and hiring on the spot. Well, when they sat
down with me to discuss things after I had filled out the application
forms, they said, "We don't have anything that you can do."

I said, "What do you mean you don't have anything?"

"Well," they said, "you've got too much education."

I said, "What's that got to do with it?"

"Well, we don't have anything that you can do."

I said, "Look, I can take a broom and sweep the floors in these
factories. Things like that. I can do that as well as these other people
you're hiring."

"No, no, no. We don't have any place for a person like you."

Well, this was disgusting to me, but I finally gave up on it.

Was that the end of it?

No, back in Tucson the next year—over a period of the next two
years—I worked through the Surgeon General's office of the Sixth Army
headquartered at Fort Douglas in Salt Lake City to see if there was any
possibility of my getting an Army position even though I had asthma.
They told me there might be some chance that their regulations would
change and I could be accepted for a post in the Army. But that never
came off.

How about the Navy?

I undertook to enlist in the Navy too, but they rudely rejected me.
Well, I figured if I didn't make it in one of those, I'd never make it in

the Air Force, so I gave it up. I did manage to do some things for the military in the form of counseling and meeting with groups at Davis-Monthan Field outside of Tucson and another air base to the north. There were a good many military people who came to the institute. Very often these men needed some counseling and somebody to talk to and so on, so I tried to make myself as useful as possible. But my whole point in mentioning this is that I was not in the service and felt that I should be. It created a real sense of guilt on my part. The war ended in Europe while we were still in Tucson. Later, in August 1945, of course, it came to an end in the Pacific with the atomic bomb.

How did your life in Tucson end? Those were eventful years in every sense for you and Natalie.

The University of Arizona offered me a position on its philosophy faculty during the last year that I was there. I had to tell them that I had already accepted a position at the University of Southern California and was going to leave in the middle of the year. As it turned out, I was also offered a position on the philosophy faculty at the University of Utah just about the same time—after I had accepted the position at USC. I would rather have had the USC position, but if it hadn't been offered to me I would have been happy to have taken either the Arizona or the Utah offer. Natalie liked Tucson very much. She hated to leave. I was not as attracted to life in Arizona as she was.

But it was time for you to move on—both from church employment and to your academic career.

Yes, I must confess that leaving church employment and settling into a great university lifted a great burden from me. I felt like a free man for the first time in years.

6.
Student of Philosophy

When you began doctoral work, why did you choose the University of Southern California rather than your undergraduate school, UCLA? It also had a fine philosophy department.

That was a tough decision, but I chose USC for two reasons. First, it had a highly competent School of Religion, and it would be possible for me to take a degree in philosophy with a minor in religion. Second, Edgar Sheffield Brightman was a visiting professor for the summer of 1938. I'd never met him, but I'd read a little of his stuff. He was a leading philosopher in personalistic idealism and the head of philosophy at Boston University.

These were still Depression years at first, then war years. Was your choice of a Los Angeles university made for economic reasons?

Yes. We couldn't have done it without my parents. We lived with them in Los Angeles, at their invitation. My fellowship paid some of my university expenses. Natalie studied for a master's degree in Spanish and worked as a nursing assistant at a hospital. After a while she got a good job at a Sears Roebuck store within walking distance of my parents' home. Natalie really financed my Ph.D.—or, better, "our" Ph.D.

To put your entire doctoral program in focus at once, let's place a bookend at the conclusion too. When did you pass your exams, and when did you defend your dissertation?

I finished my course work in the summer of 1943, passed my qualifying examinations in December that year, and defended my dissertation in the spring of 1946. I was awarded the Ph.D. at commencement exercises in June that year.

Ten years after your B.A. at Utah.

That's right. Now Ph.D. candidates sometimes whiz through in three or four years and think there's something the matter with them if they don't. But this ten years was an excellent arrangement for me. I must confess that I matured very slowly in my thinking—perhaps I haven't entirely matured yet. This pattern gave me a chance to do a great deal of study in the field and it gave things a chance to soak in. I have encountered many of these fast-degree scholars, you know. Unquestionably, they're bright and excellent technicians but they don't seem to be very wise. I don't know, of course, how wise I seemed to my professors, or my students. Maturity in philosophy calls for wisdom as well as knowledge.

Another advantage of this drawn-out arrangement was that USC's philosophy school brought in top-flight people every summer from around the country and from Europe.

Yes. This made it possible for me to have contacts with a number of major figures who were at the university only during the summer. The subject that had interested me most aside from the history of philosophy and the philosophy of religion had always been the philosophy of history. I pursued that line of study as far as possible at USC with highly competent professors, including Heinrich Gomperz, Walter Muelder, and Ralph Tyler Flewelling.

Professor Heinrich Gomperz, who was originally at the University of Vienna, once remarked of another German philosopher, Johann Gottlieb Fichte, that he philosophized "with his fist on the table." I've always thought that description applied to Flewelling as well. He made a profound impression on me. He could be dogmatic as hell yet, at the same time, rational. He was a real philosopher, a man of wisdom and intellectual stature who took philosophy seriously. He wasn't playing around. His main interest was the development of a personalistically oriented philosophy of history. He was the founder and editor of *The Personalist,* a journal that stresses the metaphysical centrality of the person in defining reality.

Flewelling and you became very close friends too?

We certainly did. A remarkable man, Flewelling had raised the money for the philosophy building and his own son was the architect, so he pretty much had things his own way. It's too small now, but that building was ideal then and won several architectural prizes. It was built on the model of a medieval Italian monastery and was an artistic triumph.

So Flewelling became something of a mentor to you?

To be frank with you, Flewelling was very unhappy about my leaving the faculty when I joined the University of Utah faculty in 1948. When I first became a USC faculty member, he asked me to serve as managing editor of *The Personalist.* But Paul Helsel, who had been managing editor for a number of years, warned me: "It's an awful lot of work, and I'd advise you against it."

That put you in something of a bind, didn't it? He put a lot of pressure on you.

Yes, it was very hard for me, but I told Flewelling no. I simply wanted to concentrate on my academic work at that point. He didn't give up, though, and later when I left for Utah he asked me to have the journal transferred to the University of Utah. I'm sorry to say that Flewelling was a person who liked to have disciples, and I'm afraid I disappointed him. He let me know that he looked on me as his successor in advancing personalistic idealism. After he retired and I moved to Utah, I gravitated away from his philosophy.

Personalism was primarily an American and French manifestation of idealism, wasn't it?

Yes. Idealism is a term in both metaphysics—the theory of reality—and epistemology—the theory of knowledge. A more accurate term would probably be "idea-ism," but that's hard to say.

The point is that idealism is a philosophical system that deals with ideas, not with ideals as we usually think of them.

That's right. In metaphysics, idealism means that reality is of the nature of mind or the product of mind. And in epistemology, or the theory of knowledge, idealism has to do with the relationship between the subject—the mind which knows—and the object—whatever it is that is known. What is known may be a sensory object, such as a stone, or a universal or concept, such as love or justice. The idealist position is that the object that is known is, either partially or entirely, a product of its being known. In idealistic philosophy, the mind is creative. It partially constructs what it knows.

That's classical idealism. What about personalism?

Well, American idealism sometimes took the form of personalism. The leading American idealist, Josiah Royce, was an absolute idealist of the Hegelian school who had done his graduate work in Germany. In his metaphysics, set forth in his *The World and the Individual,* Royce made an effort, as a good American, to preserve the reality of the individual while still accepting the position of much Hegelian idealism that reality is ultimately an absolute. Royce's chief opposition came from his friend and colleague William James, whose philosophy was thoroughly pluralistic. James was allergic to the Absolute, insisting that reality resides in the individual. The chief personalistic idealist was Borden Parker Bowne, a contemporary of Royce and William James. Flewelling and Brightman were his students. Bowne's position was that, ultimately, reality must be seen in terms of the concept of the person because some of the paradoxes that are fundamental to our experience of reality cannot be explained except through personalistic categories.

What are the paradoxes in human experience that submit to personalistic idealism?

One is the problem of change and identity. The pre-Socratic Greek philosophers asked how a thing can continue to be itself if it is changing. The problem is based on the logical principles of identity and non-contradiction—that a thing is what it is and is not what it is not. Then how can something change, because to change it has to become what it is not? It becomes a question of whether to believe the evidence of the senses or the dictates of reason. The personalistic argument is that some of the basic metaphysical, epistemological, ethical, and even logical problems such as this cannot be resolved apart from personalistic categories.

What do you mean by personalistic categories?

According to the personalists, there is no possibility of rationally explaining the appearance of change in the world unless you think of it as having basically a personal foundation, which Bowne called the World Ground—the equivalent of God in his system. The world could not be the kind of thing that it appears to be without this grounding in a reality that is both identical with itself and in process. The point is simple: individuals maintain their identity while they are constantly changing. Personal identity is not an identity of substance but rather of thought, memory, and self-awareness or consciousness. For the personalist, personality is the foundation or world ground of our reality. Otherwise, the world of our experience could not be what it obviously is.

To take another example—the question of unity and plurality, another problem in metaphysics dating from the pre-Socratics. The world considered rationally seems to be a unity, but the experience of our senses tells us it is a plurality, made up of many particular things. Parmenides, the most thoroughgoing rationalist, denied the testimony of the senses and held that the world is a unity without plurality and a unity in which there is only a changeless identity. He held that the plurality of the world, the diversity of phenomena, change, and process are really a kind of illusion. He held that the world must rationally be seen as a single, processless entity.

But the opposite could also be logically true, couldn't it?

That was the position of some pre-Socratics. They had a pluralistic metaphysics which held that the unity of the world is the illusion and that multiplicity and process are real. This position appears, for instance, in the atomism of Leucippus and Democritus.

Now, back to the contemporary personalistic idealists!

Well, the position of the personalists is that if you want to be faithful to both reason and sensory experience—or what we would simply call the empirical claim on knowledge—you can reconcile the two by recognizing that your personal experience provides evidence of both unity and plurality. If the ground of the world is personal, reality is both one and many, as well as identical and changing. Personality is an organic unity of conscious states, but it is also a plurality as a collection of conscious states. Everything that exists, Jack, is either this chair I'm sitting on or it's not this particular chair—there's nothing in between. So it's a logical principle, you see.

The law of the excluded middle.

Yes. Another name for it is identity and contradiction. The thing is what it is—that's its identity.

And the contradiction is, "a thing is not what it is not."

Yes. Terrifically important, because this principle was the ground of logic right down into the nineteenth century. But of course, as I have said, the problem is how can there be any change, process, or movement if a thing is what it is and is not what it is not, because, presumably, in any kind of change it becomes something else.

This coherence theory of truth, based on a small set of universal principles, is a logical system that appears to defy reality.

That's the problem. We can observe change, even though, by a strict rationalistic logic, change is impossible. Well, that's been a basic problem in metaphysics along with the issue of unity and plurality right down to the present. The development of Hegelian logic and metaphysics was an attempt to handle it through the dialectic. Friedrich Hegel saw the universe fundamentally as a process, an ongoing process of dialogue between thesis and antithesis, which produced a synthesis, which in turn became the new thesis and generated a new antithesis, and so on. He denied the traditional logic and held that a thing is what it is *and* what it is not, which accounts for all change and process.

So it's possible to argue that Hegel has been the chief philosophical influence on the world since his time because he was the first to postulate a system that countered Aristotelian logic?

Yes. Thinking of fundamental reality in terms of process is a remarkably productive idea. I've always thought the tremendous upsurge in great historical research and writing among nineteenth-century Germans was due in a very considerable degree to Hegel's influence, because reality, for him, is the history of the Absolute—and the Absolute is the logical unfolding of the world.

Change superseded the static Absolute and became the basic description of reality. And today neo-Marxists and post-modernists embrace relativism with the same fanatic zeal as the fundamentalist religionists embrace their absolutes.

Not only that but Karl Marx was a Hegelian philosopher who used the Hegelian dialectic and identified logic with metaphysics. So even though Marx was a materialist where Hegel was an idealist, you can see how far Hegelian influence went with this double impetus. Hegel's philosophy was religious in character but had a pantheistic quality to it. Personalism is not pantheistic. The personalists have made an effort to distinguish God from the multiplicity of the world. Hegelianism had a tremendous influence on the rise of British idealism, then American idealism. And—I'll bet you didn't know this—the center of American idealism after the Civil War was St. Louis, Missouri.

There on the banks of the timeless Mississippi River, which is constantly changing its course?

It's also because of the German colonies near there. A lot of Germans immigrated to the United States after the Civil War, and the Germans who had a philosophical interest were most likely to be Hegelians during the 1860s. There was the problem of making some kind of sense of the Civil War, finding historical meaning in it; and the Hegelian dialectic seemed to provide that meaning. And to prove my point, the first philosophical periodical published in English appeared in St. Louis in 1864 or 1865—*The Journal of Speculative Philosophy*. Josiah Royce and many leading philosophers contributed articles to it. W. T. Harris, the first editor of the *Journal*, later became the United States Commissioner of Education.

Do you mean to say that no philosophical journal had been published in England before that date?

That's right, as far as I know. Astonishing, isn't it? Idealism had become a very strong movement in America. It was a powerful reaction against the growing nineteenth-century materialism. If you adopt the notion that reality, taken as a whole, is compatible with mind, you can see that it has a sort of compatibility with religion. So it gave great support to the philosophically minded who were religious.

So personalism, being an offshoot of idealism, was also congenial to religion?

Oh, very much so. In fact, personalism can be partially explained as an attempt to overcome both materialism and the pantheistic tendencies of idealism in favor of a more traditional form of theism that preserves the identity and freedom of the individual.

Sterling, do you find personalism personally congenial?

Well, not entirely. In my youth as a student at the University of Utah under the tutelage of Ericksen and Read, I was a rather faithful pragmatist. Royce was long gone and the great British idealists such as Francis Herbert Bradley and Bernard Bosanquet had died in the 1920s. But when I went to USC, I found that personalistic idealism was very much alive. I found personalism appealing to my philosophical interests and religious sensibilities. Personalists define person primarily in terms of the capacity for thought and will. That's how the traditional theologians defined person, including the divine Person, so the World Ground or foundation of reality is personal in the sense that it is thought and will. Of course, there is also feeling or passion, which theologians haven't liked but which the personalists were more amenable to.

So in speaking of the World Ground, it's a problem of whether you're talking about a being in the sense that most people think of God as a being or something which is simply the substructure of reality.

Yes. Paul Tillich held that God is not a being but rather is the ground of being. Tillich was one of my teachers at Union Theological Seminary in New York. Once when I was in conversation with him, I asked Tillich if he regarded himself as an existential philosopher, and he said, "No, I don't," which shocked me—because he's clearly an existentialist. Then he added, "I'm an existential theologian," and I was unshocked.

But my point is that Tillich said that if God were a being, he would be an idol, a thing alongside other things. You shouldn't call God a thing, even though the word "thing" is the most general in our language. Everything is a thing and "nothing" is a thing. D. C. Williams, a logician at Harvard University some years ago, claimed quite seriously that nothing is something, because, if it weren't so, Old Mother Hubbard couldn't have gone to the cupboard and found nothing there. The German existentialist Martin Heidegger dealt with the ontological status of nothingness. It's sort of a philosophical counterpart of the physicist's black hole theory.

Well, the personalists have a religious form of idealistic philosophy. Idealism has always appealed to the religious temperament. That's why Platonism has always been so strong in Christianity, because of its emphasis on the mental, the human mind, and ideas.

How about you personally, Sterling?

Idealism, when I began to seriously encounter it, made a very strong appeal to me, and I wanted in the worst way to be a convert and a good convert to Flewelling's idea that the moral and religious personality is the key to understanding reality. Interestingly enough, when I was first in Russia in 1958, I had a long session with three professors of philosophy at the University of Moscow who regarded Flewelling as their chief enemy because he represented religiously oriented idealism as opposed to Marxism's atheistic materialism. This pleased Flewelling when I reported it to him.

Are there other philosophers or teachers who were influential on your development during this period?

I should certainly mention Walter Muelder, later dean of the School of Religion at Boston University. He was professor of theology in the religion school at USC. A brilliant scholar, a brilliant teacher. If I were to line up the six or seven teachers who had the greatest influence on me, Muelder would certainly be one of them. I studied Hegelian and Marxist philosophy with him, particularly their impact on the philosophy of history.

I studied German philosophy and the philosophy of history with Heinrich Gomperz, who also gave considerable attention to Hegelianism and Marxism. Gomperz was a scholar of phenomenal proportions. He was a son of Theodor Gomperz, regarded by many as the foremost scholar in ancient Greek philosophy; and Heinrich Gomperz was regarded by many to be even superior to his father. He was professor of philosophy at the University of Vienna, where he led the movement against Hitler. Fortunately, he was teaching at Oxford University when Hitler invaded Austria and came to USC from there. He was in his seventies then and died while I was his student.

Gomperz was a man of remarkable intellectual capacity.

They used to say that if the entire corpus of Plato and Aristotle were lost, Gomperz could reproduce it from memory in Greek and give you the English translation as he went along. He never brought books or notes to a seminar, a man of amazing erudition. He always learned the language of a country before he went there, even on a vacation. When Gomperz would come into the seminar, the students would all stand— I've never seen this before or since—and someone would hold a chair for him while he sat down at the seminar table.

At his last session with students, Gomperz came into the room but couldn't make it to the table; so he just sat down in a chair near the door. We all just moved over and sat by him. We'd known he was ill but hadn't realized it was serious. After talking with us, he went to the hospital and died a short time later. I gave him blood when he needed transfusions, and I have always been pleased that I did.

Mrs. Gomperz was an interesting character. She smoked cigars and took quite a liking to Natalie and me. Gomperz and his wife put me in their wills for two or three of his own books and a classical Greek typewriter. The typewriter was to be mine if one of Gomperz's students from Vienna, who was a professor at Claremont College, didn't want it. I'm sorry to say that he did. Gomperz had a magnificent private library in Vienna, widely known as the largest and most important private philosophical library in Europe and—no doubt—in the world.

The story of his library and its surviving the Second World War is remarkable.

It was based on a collection he had inherited from his own father. Theodor Gomperz was a close friend of John Stuart Mill. Between the father and son, they had created a magnificent collection of some 40,000 volumes of the most important philosophical writings, many of them first editions, autographed, and so on. I asked Mrs. Gomperz once, "Did Professor Gomperz have all of those books at home?" and she said, "Mr. McMurrin, we did not have a home. We lived in a library." It was literally true. Theodor Gomperz had built a separate library in Vienna for his books; when Professor and Mrs. Gomperz married, they moved into the library—just added a bed in one room of the library, remodeled one section into a kitchen, and so forth.

When Gomperz came to the United States to avoid Hitler, he left this tremendously valuable library in Vienna under the control of his librarian, an extremely resourceful woman. As soon as the Germans occupied Vienna, they came for the Gomperz library, to ship the books to Germany. The librarian claimed that Gomperz had sold the library to an American university and that it was no longer Austrian property. This was before the United States had entered the war against Germany, so the Germans left the library alone. Then she had the books crated and hid them someplace in Vienna at great personal risk. She watched over them faithfully until the war ended. After the war Gomperz sold about 30,000 of his most important volumes to the University of Southern California. While I was on the faculty at USC, dozens of enormous crates were delivered to the Philosophy Building. It was a long process, and Gomperz died before they all reached USC. Flewelling raised as much money as he could to buy the library, but it was worth many times what the university actually paid for it. Fortunately, in the basement of the Philosophy Building below the library, there was a big room with safes where various incunabula and rare books were kept. Gomperz's student from Claremont—the one who got the Greek typewriter—worked for a long time with the collection, cataloging and setting it up as a separate Gomperz library.

Gomperz was affiliated loosely with the Vienna Circle during the 1920s and 1930s, wasn't he?

Under the leadership of Moritz Schlick, a group of philosophically minded physicists and mathematicians made Vienna the chief center for the development of logical positivism. But despite his connections with the Vienna Circle, Gomperz did not regard himself as a positivist. His largest influence on me was simply as a philosophical scholar. His immense knowledge was a great inspiration.

You also studied with a number of remarkable visiting professors at USC, didn't you?

Yes, F. C. S. Schiller was the leading figure in British pragmatism, a professor at Oxford, and H. Wildon Carr, a leading British idealist, both ended their careers there. This was before my time. Even though I was at USC, I took a seminar at UCLA with William Pepperell Montague, professor of philosophy at Columbia University, who was one of the creators of the New Realism.

His work The Ways of Knowing *is a philosophical classic.*

It certainly is. Montague was a delightful person with an astounding sense of humor, tremendously interesting. Another of his books, written with others, *The New Realism,* was a historic volume, in part a response to pragmatism by those who could not go along with the Peirce/James/Dewey pragmatic philosophy. It was also a response to the strong development of absolute idealism and the idealistic epistemology that was then taking place in England and America. Montague and I became friends, in a way. He had a strong influence on me. My inclinations, you see, had been toward pragmatism and then toward idealism, but I always had strong realistic inclinations, and Gomperz and Montague pretty well finalized that for me.

Let me see if I've got your philosophical journey straight, Sterling. You started out as a pragmatist, thanks largely to the influence of Ericksen and Read, then went on to idealism, when you were a student of Flewelling, Brightman, and Muelder. Third came realism, where you were influenced by Gomperz and Montague; and, fourth, came positivism. Were any teachers especially influential in your reaching this last stage?

No, not really in the same way that I had strongly identifiable mentors in the three earlier stages.

Well, let's go back. I think we may have slighted realism in our discussion to this point.

Realism has the general, commonplace meaning that we all use a great deal, but it also has technical meanings in epistemology and metaphysics. It has flourished primarily in England and the United States since the beginning of this century. Metaphysically, realism is the view that the objects of our knowledge, whether they are universals which we think or objects which we actually experience through the senses, have a genuine reality independent of their being thought or sensed. Now here you have a combination of metaphysics and epistemology because epistemology is fundamentally the theory of the relationship between the knowing subject and the known object, and metaphysics is the theory of the nature of reality.

In the branch of realism that has developed, especially in America since early in this century, there is the commonsense idea that what we know is not dependent on our knowing it.

That is epistemological realism; and since the objects of knowledge are real in themselves, they have ontological status in the very nature of being, and that's metaphysical realism. The interesting thing is that if you consider Plato, for instance, from whom many of the problems of philosophy have stemmed, you have a person who is both an idealist and a realist.

Plato can be considered in some senses an idealist in metaphysics because of his emphasis on mind and mental realities, but he is a realist in epistemology because he holds that the objects of knowledge, even abstract universals, have reality independently of their being known.

One of the main creators of idealism in modern thought is the philosopher George Berkeley. In his great essay "The Principles of Human Knowledge," he argued that "to be is to be perceived," but he didn't hold that the being of the things we perceive depends on our perception. Though he was of the opinion that things were not real independently of their being perceived, his argument was intended to defend the existence of God—because the reality of the objects of our knowledge depends not on our perception but rather on a cosmic divine perception. The American realists hold that even if things did not depend for their reality on being perceived, they still could not be known to be real independently of our process of knowing. So the process of knowing them is not in itself a proof that they depend upon perception. What most people believe, of course, is a kind of commonsense realism, sometimes referred to as naive realism.

Berkeley's proof for God derived from his idealism, and there is a pair of limericks about him that has always helped me define idealism and realism in graphic clarity.
    The first limerick developed at Oxford goes like this:

> There was a young man who said, "God
> must think it exceedingly odd
>   That this tree
>   Which we see
>   Continues to be
> When there's no one about in the quad."

Well, that expresses the idealist's position. Then another character wrote a response to it which goes:

> Dear Sir, your astonishment's odd,
> For I'm always about in the quad.
>   And that's why this tree
>   Will continue to be
> Since observed by yours faithfully, God.

    Berkeley's argument is that if this table and these books depend for their being upon their being perceived, and if you and I go out of the room—along with all the ants, bookworms, and other sentient creatures that can see or smell—and if we believe the books and table are still here, as Berkeley did, then some mind must still perceive them. And that someone can only be God.

What influence did Montague have on your thinking?
    Montague and John Dewey were good friends as well as colleagues at Columbia, but Dewey was a pragmatist, of course, and Montague was a realist. He didn't care at all for Dewey's educational philosophy. In fact, he once told me, "My great and good friend John Dewey has deprived my granddaughter of her intellectual birthright." That's an exact quote. It struck me very deeply at the time.
    Well, Montague was one of the first to hold the Flint Professorship at UCLA, and he gave me permission to attend his seminar on the theory of knowledge. Montague was a chain smoker, and smoking was not allowed in the seminar room, so he moved the class to his office. There was also a young faculty member in the seminar from UCLA, Richard Hocking, the son of Harvard's great idealist philoso-

pher, William Ernest Hocking.

How was the seminar? And did your relationship continue outside it?

The seminar was absolutely brilliant. Epistemology was Montague's specialty, along with methodology. He invited me to have lunch with him at the Beverly Wilshire Hotel in Beverly Hills one day and two cocktails immediately appeared on our table. Montague said, "Mr. McMurrin, am I correctly informed that you Mormons are not supposed to drink alcoholic beverages?" I said, "That's right." He said, "I thought so," and reached over and took mine. Montague was well known for his taste for strong drink.

Did he seem to know much else about Mormonism?

Yes. In that seminar one day he said, "Mr. McMurrin, all I know about Mormons is what I have learned from my great and good friend and colleague Professor John Dewey, who informs me that when you Mormons die, you don't go to heaven and play on harps. Now is that true?" He had a real twinkle in his eye, and I answered, "That's true. Professor Dewey is absolutely right." "And as I understand it," he said, "you get yourself a job and continue to work, maybe along the lines that you were following in this world?" I said again, "That's right." Then he said, "That's wonderful. I like that. I was never partial to string music." I'm sure Montague was gracious to everyone, but I certainly enjoyed our association. I attended several faculty evenings with him that were part social events and part discussions, we drove around town on two or three occasions, and we corresponded afterward. I later wrote an article on Montague's finitistic philosophical viewpoint which was published in *The Personalist*. It pleased him very much. The last time I saw Montague was in 1953 in the faculty club of Columbia University.

Did you consult him while you were writing the paper on his philosophy?

No, but I'd studied his stuff carefully and it was a pretty good essay. Montague laid a good deal of stress on the possibility of intuitive knowledge. He was neither an extreme rationalist nor an extreme empiricist. I recall that one of his essays related an experience he'd had walking across the campus at Berkeley where he was teaching in his early days. He was crossing a stream and paused to look into the water when he had a strange mystic experience—that's his word. He seemed to have immediate access to the whole problem of the relation of the mind and body, and it had a great effect on his conception of the mind.

Such a mystical experience is rarely acknowledged by twentieth-century philosophers. Have you ever felt anything like that, Sterling?

No I haven't, but as I said, Montague was a very interesting man.

He gave an Ingersoll lecture at Yale published under the title *The Chances of Surviving Death*. He'd worked out the chances that your soul survives death, and they're higher than you might think. He was a student of William James, and James's finitism shows up in Montague as a very temperate and cautious theism.

Another of my teachers, John Elof Boodin, was also a student of James. I had classes with him at UCLA but got better acquainted with him when I was on the faculty at USC. He had retired by then. Boodin made the interesting claim that he was probably more responsible than any other person for James's writing his famous essay, "The Will to Believe." Boodin was a graduate student, involved in some kind of philosophical club at Harvard. They invited James to come and address them; the paper he wrote for that meeting eventually turned into "The Will to Believe." James was sorry in later years that he had taken such an extreme position and said he didn't even like the expression "will to believe."

You had quite a few once-removed contacts with James through mutual friends.

Montague told me some good stories about James. When Montague was an undergraduate at Harvard, he was taking a psychology course from James. James took the students on a field trip to a nearby mental hospital, giving them an orientation lecture first. He cautioned them not to create any problems, to be sociable and agreeable with the inmates, and not to argue, no matter how strange the patients' ideas seemed. Well, while Montague was there, a man suddenly came over and said to him, "I'm Julius Caesar." Montague, anxious to be agreeable, asked him how things were in Rome and they had a pleasant conversation. Later, just as they were about to leave, this same man came over again and said, "You know, I'm Napoleon." Now Montague wasn't anxious to start an argument, but he couldn't resist commenting, "You know, you told me earlier today that you were Julius Caesar. How can you be Julius Caesar and also Napoleon?" "That's the point," said this fellow. "Not by the same mother."

Sounds as if Montague had an engaging sense of humor.

Oh, he did. He used unforgettable examples in his teaching. For instance, in dealing with the status of the objects of knowledge—and the extent to which they were genuinely real or somewhat subjective—I recall him saying, "You wake up in the morning and you can see serpents twining around your bedpost. What kind of an experience is that?" Or when he talked about the tendency in our culture to give priority to the physical over the mental, he'd use the Missouri "show-me" motto as an example of giving priority to the sense of sight. He insisted that we should actually give the tactile sense priority. "Those ghosts you can see but can't touch," he said, "don't frighten you half as much as those you can touch but can't see." This made the point in a very unmistakable way.

Want to say something else about William James?

William James for me is a great philosophical saint—not that he was terribly saintly. He was not the main creator of pragmatism, but he was its chief luminary. James was somewhat loose and got himself into difficulties because of his ambiguities. For example, he said, "If you analyze *verify,* it comes from the two Latin words—*truth* and *make.* To verify," said James, "doesn't mean to find out whether something is true. It means to make it come true." Well that was a rather extreme position which I think he regretted in his later years. Montague formulated a simple maxim to express the adventurous nature of philosophers: "Philosophy proposes, science disposes."

Montague also said that of the great Harvard philosophy faculty at the turn of the century, Palmer and Santayana were both better lecturers than James, who was actually rather jerky in his presentation. But the students loved James because of his wonderful generosity. He was always giving students credit for his own ideas. If a student asked a question or made a comment, in a few minutes James would suddenly say, "Mr. Jones, the very profound truth of the statement you made a few minutes ago has just occurred to me—that what you meant was such and such—" and he would weave it into his own lecture in ways that Mr. Jones had not, of course, intended or imagined. But the other students were always pleased because their turn would come.

That's a good strategy for any fine teacher, to encourage students to think for themselves and become full partners in the creative process. To do this, a teacher must be both profoundly committed and brashly irreverent.

It's probably one of the reasons I was so drawn to Montague, besides the realism for which I have a natural affinity. He was a kind of agnostic believer, if there could be such a thing—that is, he hoped there is a God but suspected that there isn't. He didn't believe that you can prove the existence of God, but he hoped that theism is true.

He was very anti-church, I understand, but a brilliant theologian in his own right?

Yes. He was born and reared in New England and rebelled violently against the puritanical nature of the religion he encountered there. He told me once, "A church is just an organized effort to deny human beings the pleasures of life." Contempt isn't too strong a word for his feelings about churches and traditional absolutistic theology. T. V. Smith included him in his book Creative Skeptics. Montague was attracted to William James's finitism because he felt that any theology must come to terms with the problem of suffering and evil, and the only basis upon which you can come to such terms within the framework of theism is through a finitistic conception of God in which there are realities external to God which he or she does not fully control. In this connection he produced one of the most delightful books that I have ever read, *Belief Unbound*.

In *Belief Unbound* he deals primarily with the problem of evil within the framework of finitistic theism. It's extremely readable, a first-rate piece of work, beautifully done. I'll have to confess that one of the reasons I like Montague's stuff so much is that he agrees with me on a position I held before I ever had any contact with his work, partly because I'm a Mormon and partly because of James's influence.

The idea of a finite God certainly is compatible with Mormon thought and theology, but most Mormon writers use the language of absolutism and confuse the issue.

Let me give you an example, Jack. In 1951 I was involved in a long conversation, two or three hours, with Heber C. Snell, Joseph Fielding Smith, and Harold B. Lee. They were grilling Snell on his book on the Old Testament. Snell raised a very fine question with Elder Smith, in essence, how could he argue that God was totally omnipotent, totally omniscient, and so forth, yet simultaneously hold that God used to be a man or was like a man. Joseph Fielding Smith's reply was very clear but completely ridiculous. He said, "God was a finite being until he became God. When he became God, from then on he was absolute." I remember thinking, "Now, how can you argue with a man who thinks like that?" I mean, there's no possibility of any common ground upon which an exchange of ideas can occur.

Well, perhaps that's enough about Montague and his ideas. He was a very remarkable person and had considerable influence on me.

What about your dissertation, Sterling? When did you choose logical positivism as your topic?

I came by the topic late during 1942-43, when I was at USC. I had been very interested in epistemology since my undergraduate days. My master's thesis dealt with the relation of knowledge and faith in medieval philosophy, which is historically a very important problem in the theory of knowledge. During 1942-43 I became very interested in the positivistic critique of metaphysics.

The positivist position, as held by the logical positivists or logical empiricists, can be defined as the view that scientific knowledge exhausts the totality of knowledge.

That's the positive definition of positivism. The negative definition is that metaphysics is meaningless, that any knowledge claim that is not empirically based, or is not in principle logic or mathematics, is cognitively meaningless. That is, the statement does not communicate knowledge. I remember Montague, who was intensely opposed to logical positivism, referring to "this negativism called positivism."

I was reading vast quantities of things on the problem of knowledge, cognitive meaning, and meaningfulness. You see, the Nazi pressures had brought to America philosophers who were associated with logical positivism, whether they were strictly in that school or not. Gomperz's famous essay "The Meanings of Meaning" fascinated me. Logical positivists were very concerned with the problem of meaning, primarily the distinction between formal and factual meaning. A. J. Ayer at Oxford did more than any other person to put logical positivism in terms accessible to the lay person in his book *Language, Truth, and Logic.*

So this was a very exciting movement precisely at the moment you were looking for a dissertation topic?

It certainly was. I became much involved in the whole question. If the logical positivists were correct, then the propositions of metaphysics—including those of theology—were cognitively meaningless—also the sentences of normative ethics.

I can see why a young Mormon philosopher would want to sink his teeth into that topic. Who was your adviser?

Herbert Searles was the person with whom I had the most involvement. He was on the USC philosophy faculty and very interested in my subject. I took seminars with Searles and wrote several papers for him. Walter Muelder, who was on my committee, was also interested in logical positivism, but he was quite negative about it while Searles was more or less neutral. I didn't really have associates who were, strictly speaking, logical positivists until after I had my degree.

Most of those contacts came during 1952-53 when you were in New York on leave from the University of Utah?

Yes. A seminar at Princeton with Carl Hempel from the University of Berlin, a major figure among positivists, on the nature of scientific theory, was very useful, but this was long after I had written my dissertation. I also visited with Rudolf Carnap at the Institute for Advanced Study and discussed some positivist problems with him. He was flat on his back with back trouble, but he had me come to his cottage. He was very generous with his time. He was the chief positivist whom I had dealt with in the dissertation, so I was very interested in what he had to say.

Who constituted your committee?

Searles chaired it. Gomperz might have, but he died before I got that far. Flewelling, Wilbur Long, brilliant in ethics and the history of philosophy, and Paul Helsel, a scholar in Greek philosophy and a defender of metaphysics, were on the committee. Also Matilla Ghyka, a Romanian logician. I had a minor in religion, so Walter Muelder and Floyd Ross represented the School of Religion. Ross was a specialist in oriental religion. None of them was a logical positivist. Flewelling retired and Muelder left for Boston University.

After I began writing my dissertation, I had no contact at all with members of my committee. I wrote it *in absentia* over a period of more than two years when I was at the LDS Institute of Religion at the University of Arizona. I finished it two or three months before I was to join the USC faculty and sent the draft to Searles. I heard nothing from him until I encountered him the first day I began teaching at USC. He then told me that everyone had approved it. They accepted it without suggesting the change of a single word. Helsel told me that Mrs. Helsel had read it and hoped that I would get rid of my split infinitives, but I like split infinitives, so I let them stand.

But there was a hitch . . .

When I received the draft of the dissertation, I discovered a new name on the committee, Whitchurch. And Whitchurch insisted that I junk the entire affair and write on a different subject. I had never heard of the man before. While I was away, he was brought in as dean of the School of Religion. He simply put himself on the committee. When the dean of the Graduate School learned of this, he raised ten kinds of hell. Before the end of the year, his first year, the university fired Whitchurch by buying up his contract. He had been a menace from the day he hit the campus.

All that for criticizing your dissertation, I'll bet! You dealt with the problem of normative value judgments—"ought/ought not" sentences?

The title was "Positivism and the Logical Meaning of Normative Value Judgments." From the standpoint of positivism, sentences in metaphysics are cognitively meaningless because they are neither true nor false. Such sentences look like genuine propositions because of their syntax and symbolism, but they lack a semantic reference and are not genuine propositions. Now normative value judgments of "ought/ought not" are also meaningless. The usual position of positivists is that such sentences, being noncognitive, function simply as expressions of emotion or as directives.

Take the sentence, "Killing is evil."

This looks like a meaningful proposition, but it can't be discussed as either true or false. What it really conveys, according to the positivists, is your emotional reaction to killing or a directive, which could be expressed as "don't kill." It's not true, it's not false, it's just a sentence that appears, because of its syntactical structure, to be a genuine factual proposition, true or false.

I started out to establish that the positivists were wrong, and I think I came up with some pretty good arguments. But in the process, I was almost converted to positivism and still have a strong positivistic streak in my thinking. For example, I have concluded that most metaphysics is nonsense, just as the positivists hold. But I don't agree that it's impossible to construct a cognitively meaningful metaphysical or theological sentence. I'd like to remain open on that question, and here I take a position which is closer to that of the realists like Bertrand Russell. Russell was pretty hard on most theologies, but he certainly didn't take the position that metaphysics is meaningless. The key sentences of theology, of course, are metaphysical sentences.

During the fifties, when I participated frequently in philosophical society meetings of one kind or another, I often defended the positivistic position, sometimes for the purposes of argument, sometimes with the clear intention of agreeing with the positivists. My colleagues generally regarded me as a logical positivist, although I've never actually felt that I belonged with that crowd.

You know, Sterling, you communicate a real sense of pleasure when you talk about your dissertation. The problem still absorbs you. It seems that you got right to the heart of your own philosophical interests while you were still a graduate student. How do you explain your forty-year love affair with the idea that "the conduct of people and nations should be brought under the dominion of a moral ideal"?

I think I had a twofold interest then, and I still do today. I wondered whether there was any possibility of reliable religious knowledge, and I wondered whether the propositions of morality might be put on a genuinely scientific basis so that it might be possible to establish normative values on a factual foundation. My dissertation was a logical extension of the question of normative judgments of a moral and aesthetic nature. I still have considerable interest in these problems; but I must say, I don't lose any sleep over them.

What conclusions did you reach about religious knowledge and value judgments?

I'm essentially agnostic when it comes to religious knowledge. I think that with very careful definition, the sentence, "There is a God," can be made cognitively meaningful. But I am of the opinion that there is no way of establishing whether it is true or false. On the question of normative value judgments, I simply hold that they must be distinguished from factual propositions. Statements of fact such as "This table is round" are fundamentally different from normative judgments such as "Brotherly love is good" or "You ought to love your neighbor."

Have recent developments and controversies in the field of philosophy, which have tended to place less importance on logical positivism, or challenged it, had an influence on your own thinking?

Well, I certainly hold the very definite view at present that there cannot be any genuine normative moral, aesthetic, or artistic science, for the reasons I've already indicated. But I've also been very interested in the work being done by the Scandinavian logicians in the logic of imperatives, the most important of whom was probably Jøergen Jøergensen. But a logic of imperatives still isn't a ground for a genuine moral science.

John Dewey, as a pragmatist, developed what may be regarded as a hypothetical moral science or, to use his terms, an instrumental moral science.

But his position isn't genuinely normative. His field was social psychology, of course, and he was analyzing what must happen to achieve certain moral ends. Well, no one questions the fact that you can have this hypothetical type of moral science, that is, certain things must be done to achieve certain ends. So a sentence like "killing produces disharmony in society" is a meaningful sentence and can be translated as "don't kill if you want harmony." But the big issue is how we can determine moral ends—intrinsic values. What are the goals we should seek?

Certainly the whole question of individual morality is one of great concern to our society as a whole.

And certainly the fact that normative statements are fundamentally different from factual statements—except for the illusion created by the fact that they can be cast in the same syntax—doesn't mean that normative value judgments have no relevance to facts. That's a different matter. We should and do make our normative judgments on the basis of facts, scientific knowledge, the results of activities we label good or bad—but that doesn't make the judgments factual. They're still normative. The best morality obviously is the morality which has a profound respect for the facts and for scientific knowledge relating to values and conduct.

What we actually got in the more extreme form of positivism back in the heyday of the whole movement was physicalism, largely developed by refugees from Hitler's Germany. How would you define physicalism?

Physicalism asserts that in order for a sentence to be factual, it has to designate a space-time location in the predicate of whatever is indicated by the subject. Physicalists tend to hold that there is only one science—physics, which has a relationship with biology through biophysics or organic chemistry, while biology has a relationship to sociology, and so forth because the fundamental propositions are propositions having to do with the physical world.

Carnap, Dewey, and Gomperz were all focusing on this idea that science is a single body of knowledge . . .

Carnap and Otto Neurath were the chief physicalists. Another of their tenets was the sharp distinction between formal and factual propositions. Formal propositions are those of logic and mathematics; factual propositions are those of physics and other sciences that are in principle reducible to physics. The propositions of logic and mathematics are statements of formal relationships and have nothing to do with matters of fact. In contrast, John Stuart Mill held that arithmetic was empirical while most logicians today would regard all branches of mathematics as being formal and nonempirical. In Whitehead and Russell's great three-volume work, *Principia Mathematica,* done way back in 1910-13, the content of mathematics in all its branches is reduced to a few propositions in logic.

But again these have nothing to do with matters of fact.

Not at all. You have basically one formal science, logic—or mathematics, if you prefer—and one factual science for the more extreme positivists—or four if you're not so extreme: physics, biology, psychology, and sociology.

Now, if I read your dissertation correctly, you were concerned that our moral reasoning had not kept pace with the power conferred upon us by our technology. It seems to me that you're asking a fundamental question here:

Are we morally capable of controlling our science, our new-found power?

This, of course, is the major problem. There's no question that morally we haven't been able to keep up with our technology. The positivists would not disagree with that. They'd say, "Well, get busy and get up-to-date morally." The positivist position, despite their popular image, isn't at all anti-moral or amoral. It's just that they don't regard moral attitudes and sentiments as yielding factual knowledge. I think it's interesting but not at all anomalous that Moritz Schlick, head of the Vienna Circle, wrote an important book on problems of ethics, while John Dewey, whom I'd be inclined to regard as the greatest moral philosopher of our era, wrote one of his last treatises on ethics with a strong positivist flavor. His *Theory of Valuation* appeared in the *International Encyclopedia of Unified Science.*

There's no question that the relationship between knowledge and ethics is a crucial area of inquiry.

I should say so. I think one of Dewey's greatest contributions is his position that you can't divorce ends from means. This is fundamental to both his moral philosophy and his education theory, as you know—the ends, or the normative judgments of what is good or bad, right or wrong, have to be tied to the means for reaching or avoiding those ends; you can't entirely divorce them. In one of Dewey's greatest works, his Gifford Lectures, *Quest for Certainty,* he argues persuasively that the root of much of society's ills stems from our tendency to divorce ends from means and absolutize the ends. I think that may be the most important idea in Dewey's whole philosophy.

Dewey held that "If something is to be achieved, certain things must be done." This ties morality to the factual sciences.

Yes. Ericksen was a Deweyite. So was Read. Not that either one had been a student of Dewey's—he'd gone to Columbia in 1905, I believe, which was before Ericksen ever went to Chicago—but they were much influenced by the Dewey school. William M. Stewart, the educator for whom the old lab school at the University of Utah was named, was, I believe, a friend of Dewey. Dewey was the guest of some people in Logan Canyon during the summer of 1937, as I recall, and he delivered a lecture in the Greek amphitheater on the Utah State campus. Ericksen invited me to go with him and Mrs. Ericksen to Logan for Dewey's lecture. That was the only time I ever met Dewey.

How was the lecture?

It was brilliant. All extemporaneous. There was a very good crowd—mainly school teachers interested in the subject, but even more in Dewey. He dealt with the positive relationship between the cultural achievement of a species and the length of time the maturing individual of the species is dependent on its parent or parents. I recall Dewey describing birds in Africa that would pause and lay their eggs on the ground—not even stopping to build a nest—and then just keep going. When the young hatched, they'd just get up and run along like the parents. No dependence, no culture. From there, of course, he worked up to human beings, who have the longest period of dependency on their parents and the most advanced culture.

Here's something rather comical. The young man who had escorted Dewey to the lecture was standing off to the side. I think he was the son of the people who were hosting Dewey in Logan Canyon—a wealthy family named Budge, if I'm not mistaken. He stepped over to me after I'd had a conversation with Dewey and asked, "Who is this man? What has he done?" Well, the first time I ever heard of Dewey in a class, I thought they were referring to Admiral George Dewey, who captured Manila. Now this guy had been Dewey's host for a week without knowing who he was, except that his parents had arranged for Dewey to vacation at their place in Logan Canyon!

As an early convert to pragmatism, though one who has partially abandoned it, what aspects of it do you carry with you today?

I'm not sure that there's a personal impact as much as a cultural impact. Many historians regard pragmatism as an expression of the practical nature of American culture. In its academic development, of course, it's the American philosophy par excellence even today. Pragmatism has never made much headway in Europe except with such people as F. C. S. Schiller of Oxford, who ended his academic career as professor at the University of Southern California. He called his philosophy humanism and tried to convince James to use that term—emphasizing human beings, human experience, human effort—instead of pragmatism, which refers to practice.

That's something of a digression. The point I want to make is that pragmatism is not only an outgrowth of the basic characteristics of American culture, but it has, in turn, influenced American thought. The key concept, developed loosely by James but tightly by Dewey, is that truth has to do with practical consequences. According to Dewey's concept of truth as "warranted assertibility," you're warranted in making an assertion only if it functions effectively in the symbolic structure of the development of a scientific theory.

Dewey asserted that we must abandon the traditional ideas of truth, the so-called coherence concept of truth—that a proposition is true if it logically coheres with the accepted body of propositions—and the correspondence concept that statements correspond with observable facts.

But you obviously can have two or more systems of propositions that are internally consistent but contradictory to each other. That's the problem with the coherence concept of truth.

Two sets of truth that contradict each other.

The concept that a proposition is true if it corresponds with the facts is intriguing because it seems to make good sense. It is the commonsense idea of truth and falsity that most of us take for granted, at least until we are corrupted by philosophy.

The *correspondence* theory of truth is often referred to as the *semantic* theory of truth. Semantics is a term that gets misused mercilessly in settings having anything to do with language, but its technical meaning has to do with the relationship of the sign or symbol to what is signified or symbolized.

The *coherence* theory, on the other hand, is often referred to as the *syntactic* theory of truth because syntax refers to the relation of symbols to each other, rather than to what they symbolize. One of my students at the University of Southern California, George Watson, wrote a dissertation on Carnap under my chairmanship. He wrote Carnap and showed me the letter in which he demanded, "How could you be so dogmatic as you were earlier in saying that truth is a matter of coherence, and now in your *Introduction to Semantics* you talk about correspondence?" Carnap wrote back a wonderful one-sentence response: "Dear Mr. Watson: I write after the manner of philosophers—in the indicative mood. Rudolf Carnap."

You mentioned that Eph Ericksen was disappointed to discover when you joined the faculty at the University of Utah that you had abandoned at least part of your earlier pragmatic philosophy?

Yes, and that's an interesting story. Ericksen published *Social Ethics,* as I've already mentioned, giving considerable attention to the philosophy of religion. Waldemer Read and I were both involved with Ericksen in the later stages of his writing that book. In it he defined religion as being, on its inner or spiritual side, faith in the purposive control of life. On its external or moral side, he defined it as active participation in the cultivation of human values. I'd quoted this definition in my 1946 commencement address at Utah State University. Ericksen had come to Logan for the occasion and was pleased that I quoted him on this—although I would have quoted him whether he had been there or not.

But a few years later I remember that some of us who were Ericksen's former students and our wives were having a potluck dinner at Ericksen's, and we had a warm discussion of my Reynolds Lecture. In that lecture I dealt with what religion is about and I not only didn't use Ericksen's definition but I also didn't follow Ericksen's pragmatic line. He kind of gritted his teeth and said, "Sterling, it seems to me you have gone off on some questionable tangent."

How did you take that?

Well, I had to laugh, of course, but I could tell that he was a bit disappointed. Ericksen was a genuine philosopher, and I don't think a philosopher should have disciples. It's all right for religious leaders, I guess, but a philosopher should not have disciples. He would have liked to have seen "his boys"—that's how he saw us—go out and disseminate his word. Actually all of us were much influenced by him. I think Ericksen's definition of religion neglects the mystical element in it. He used to say, "Religion is a crusade, not a consolation." But I regard religion as a sentiment that may give consolation. To me religion is the faith that the things that matter most are not ultimately at the mercy of the things that matter least. You can see the influence of Montague on my thinking.

Ericksen and Read were very staunch advocates of pragmatism, and they gave their students the impression that it was the only respectable philosophy.

Yes. I remember a Baptist minister I knew in New York, who said, "I'm from Tennessee. And if you meet someone in Tennessee who isn't a Baptist, you know he's been tampered with." Well, Ericksen and Read felt that if you weren't a pragmatist, you'd been tampered with. I think it was especially hard on Ericksen because it was his retirement that created the vacancy I was appointed to fill. I think he had a dream of how the department would be. Actually he had decided that I had become an idealist because of my involvements at Southern California.

We've slighted one of the major philosophical movements of the twentieth century—existentialism.

Well, existentialism is a kind of strange philosophy that approaches the problems of philosophy quite differently from any of the others we've mentioned. It tries to get at things from the standpoint of the living human being. Existentialism is really a modern philosophy, although the existentialists find existential facets in St. Augustine, even the Bible, and they also claim Pascal. And of course the nineteenth-century Danish theologian Søren Kierkegaard, the German philosophical poet Friedrich

Nietzsche, and then, in more recent times, German philosophers like Martin Heidegger and Karl Jaspers, the philosophical theologian Paul Tillich, the Catholic philosopher Gabriel Marcel, and the French humanist Jean-Paul Sartre are all representatives of existentialism. Existentialism has had some influence in this country but has not been strong here. The main thing about existentialism is that you get at things in terms of genuine existence.

For an existentialist, the only things that exist are things that are aware of their existence, and this means they are the things that know they're going to die—only human beings.

Yes. Heidegger, for instance, said, "Man is the animal that knows he is going to die," and it is in facing death that one finds the key to the meaning of existence. Nothing else genuinely exists. The other things are real, but they don't exist. It's only human beings that exist.

Existentialists can be seen in two camps: Christian existentialists like Marcel or Tillich, and secular existentialists like Sartre and perhaps Karl Jaspers.

The most important thing about existentialism, I think, is that it lays a tremendous emphasis upon freedom.

That is its main contribution. Because of that freedom, a human being creates himself. Existence is ontologically prior to essence. The individual human creates his or her own moral standards—so you get a considerable reaction against traditional morality with its social grounding.

Existentialism ties itself to free will in the same way that idealism ties itself to idea. Another of its impacts is its pessimistic quality, a kind of sadness that almost verges on morbidity because of its emphasis on decline and death. An existentialist can say to a typical theist, "You say that things are moving upward and onward. That's because you're thinking of society or mankind as a universal; but society doesn't exist and the universal man in the platonic sense doesn't exist. The only thing that exists is the individual, and the individual isn't moving onward and upward. The individual doesn't have a bright future. The individual is the animal that suffers, bleeds, and dies.

Existentialism's emphasis on the individual is both its weakness and its strength.

Yes. Its weakness is that in its constant emphasis on the creative individual, it doesn't recognize the fundamental importance of the social foundations of personality and what you might call moral solidarity. As you know, existentialism has been expressed probably most effectively through literature, through fiction, drama, and poetry. Its strength is that same individualism and its insistent concern with freedom.

Doesn't existentialism, then, take us full circle back to idealism—that the ideas we hold in our minds create the reality of ourselves?

Well, it does have an idealistic character about it. None of these philosophical schools, if you want to call them that, are capable of standing by themselves. I mean, there's always interlacing and overlapping. They all connect, so much so that today it's not uncommon for philosophers to adhere to two or more schools simultaneously or refuse to be identified with any philosophical school whatsoever. The three Marxist philosophers at the University of Moscow I mentioned earlier were just appalled that in an American university we would tolerate more than one school of thought. I suspect that the only place you can find one school of thought trying to stand on its own feet without involvement with others is in the Marxist institutions of North Korea and maybe China. The Soviet men acted very shocked when I told them that a really good university philosophy department would try to have the various schools of thought represented, including Marxism. They thought that was terrible.

Now having been around this circle, which of these schools of thought do you identify with most yourself?

Well, if you get down to fundamental problems in metaphysics and epistemology, my identification is with some form of realism. But I also have strong positivist leanings, strong pragmatic leanings, strong idealist leanings . . .

And strong existentialist leanings?

Yes, existentialist leanings too. I don't want to be catalogued in a philosophical school. I have studied the history of philosophy and religion, and the unfettered quest for understanding remains the important thing to me.

7.
Professor of Philosophy

Your first professorial appointment was in the philosophy department at the University of Southern California, Sterling. How did that come about?

After I had passed my written and oral examinations at USC, Professor Flewelling dropped into my office and said they wanted me to accept a position as an instructor in philosophy beginning that fall 1945. I told him I'd like that very much but I was already committed to a third year with the LDS institute at Tucson. He proposed that I see if I could gracefully leave the church position at the end of the first semester. Commissioner West was agreeable, and both schools were on a semester system, so there was no difficulty. The appointment when it came was actually as assistant professor. Later that summer and fall I was also offered positions on the philosophy faculties of the University of Utah and the University of Arizona. If either of them had come first, I would have taken it; but I was greatly pleased to be joining the USC faculty.

So you began teaching at USC in January 1946?

Yes. We moved to Los Angeles; and because there was no housing available, we lived with my parents again until we were able to rent a home. By then Trudy and Joe had been born so Natalie had her hands full. Los Angeles was a good place to live in those days, and I was very happy in every way at USC. We'd probably be there yet—unless they'd fired me—but my breathing difficulties in that climate gradually became worse. I tried to control my bronchial asthma with various medications, but it didn't work. In 1948 USC offered me an associate professorship in philosophy. After much soul searching, however, I accepted instead the offer of a full professorship at the University of Utah. I didn't want to leave USC, but it had become clear that I couldn't keep on breathing in Southern California. It was that simple.

What was your teaching experience at USC?

It seemed much longer than two and a half years—from 1946

through the summer of 1948—because so much was going on. In addition to advanced seminars, I taught a general education course, "Human Values." For the first semester I was one of four faculty members from the Philosophy School teaching it—former teachers of mine, who were now my colleagues.

I've taught a humanities core course on human values at the University of Utah for twenty years now. You urged me to start, as I recall. What was the content of yours?

It was primarily a course on the historical development of moral practices and ethical theory. We used a book of readings and commentaries that Flewelling had edited called *The Things That Matter Most.* Usually I don't like survey courses, but this was a good one, even though I wasn't in on designing it. It covered moral systems from the very early period—Plato, Aristotle, Epicureanism, and Stoicism—right up to modern thought.

If it was a general education course, you were dealing with large classes?

Oh, yes. It was a big lecture operation. We lectured in an auditorium twice a week, then the students would meet in discussion groups twice a week with the teaching assistants. The understanding was that each of the instructors would attend all of the lectures given by the other three instructors as well. My colleagues—all of them my former teachers—would get up on the platform with a folder of notes. I was up against a very serious problem. I don't have any use for notes, but how could I as a new faculty member look serious without notes? I finally solved the problem by going to the podium with a folder of blank yellow pages. I'd stand up there and, from time to time, turn a page and glance down. It was a rather effective deception and no one was any the wiser.

You weren't going to run the risk of losing credibility as a newly appointed professor!

You bet your life I wasn't. But some years later I encountered a problem here at the University of Utah. I had a student from the Law School, older than the average, who came to my office the second week of class and said, "Do you want my criticism of your course now or at the end?" I'd never had quite so blunt an introduction, but of course I invited him to give me the works on the spot.

"You're not prepared," he said, "and you apparently don't know your subject."

"What are your evidences of that?" I asked.

"You don't have any notes," he said.

Well, he dropped the class. I got quite a kick out of that.

But to return to this course in human values.

At the end of the first semester, the academic vice-president, Albert Raubenheimer, called me in and said, "I am releasing the other people from that large course and you are to do the whole thing yourself." Raubenheimer was a real powerhouse in the university. People were scared of him. Well, this gave me four lectures a week, two classes of about four or five hundred students each. I did that for the next two years with a staff of teaching assistants. It operated like a separate department with its own budget. I had some excellent teaching assistants, two of them with Ph.D.s.

Did this let you design it more the way you wanted to teach it?

Yes, but I liked the basic design of the course and the materials that had been prepared for it were excellent. So I carried on and had quite a good time with the course.

I have a theory that those large multi-section courses that we are often asked to teach when starting out—in my case Western Civilization at Clemson University—lay a broad pedagogical foundation that nourishes our whole careers. What else did you teach?

Mostly graduate courses. My students were not only philosophy majors but from other disciplines as well, especially religion. Students in the Graduate School of Religion who were working on professional degrees like doctor of theology and academic degrees like Ph.D.s very often minored in philosophy. There were a lot of good, mature students there. My courses and seminars were in such fields as realism, idealism, and pragmatism—the emphasis being on epistemology and metaphysics.

You started out teaching high school students in seminary, then high school and college simultaneously, then undergraduate and graduate students. Where did you find the greatest challenge and satisfaction?

I definitely prefer college students. But I wouldn't draw a line between undergraduates and graduates. I take great satisfaction in teaching good students. Before I retired, I taught courses in both the Department of History and the Department of Philosophy. Most of my students here, unlike USC, have not been advanced—they're often mature in their thinking but they have very little academic preparation. That doesn't bother me, as long as they have real intellectual competence and a genuine interest in the subject or a desire to learn.

I think we can find those qualities in students at any stage. Also I think you attract good students, Sterling.

Maybe I attract serious students. A course in intellectual history that I taught for you in liberal education during your years as dean usually started out so full that students were sitting on the floor, and there often was a waiting list. But after a short shakedown period, when they looked at how much reading I required and the research papers, the classes always shrank. Faculty members used to attend my advanced classes.

I must say, as long as we're on this topic, that I've never particularly liked teaching courses in ethics.

Why is that?

I don't know, perhaps it's because I'm unethical! I've liked courses in the history of ethical theory or the analysis of ethical theory, but I've never had any interest in doing the kind of thing that both Ericksen and Read did superbly—courses in ethics where you dealt with what's right and what's wrong. As important as that is, it has never interested me as an academic pursuit.

And yet so much of your work has had to do with causing other people to consider what is right and wrong.

Well, yes. I've been interested in what goes into the making of an ethical theory, rather than in the issue of what's right or wrong. I like analyzing the logical meaning of a proposition. If I had it to do all over again, I'd study far more logic and mathematics than I did as a student.

You're overlooking the power of your example, Sterling. I think it's fair to say that you've been, in many respects, the conscience of the university with regard to most of its central values. I think it springs from the fact that you have thought so much about underlying ethical issues.

The underlying issues are really very crucial and always will be; but the big issue is the one we've already talked about—the tremendous disparity between technological advancement and moral progress. I think there's no question that we've made significant moral progress since the end of World War II—in human rights, environmental ethics, and public health for instance. When I was young, nobody gave a damn about the environment. I didn't even know the word. I've had to learn environmental morality from my children.

Even more significant is the fact that we're dealing with moral issues that haven't even come up before. There has been major concern about human rights for several hundred years, but more people seem to think about human dignity now, all around the world, and more people act on moral ideas with regard to human rights. There is, of course, a frightening backlash too.

You're absolutely right. No question about it. When it comes to personal morality, though, you have a different kind of problem on your hands. I'd say here there's been no great advance. Are people more honest today than they were three hundred years ago? Do we have a stronger and finer sense of community now than we had two generations ago? I'm very old-fashioned when it comes to sexual morality, and I'm pretty sure we've here seen disastrous retrogression. The idea of progress is a modern one, and so is the question about whether there's such a thing as real progress.

We always tout technological advances, of course, but if they result in the destruction of the world's life-sustaining environment, because our individual and social morality is at such a low ebb, then it's hard to argue that we have "progressed."

The irony about what we're saying, of course, Jack, is that I'd argue from now till Tuesday against any theoretical absolutes, even in sexual morality. It's simply that in actual practice I've gone in for moral absolutes.

I'm inclined to think that your moral instincts are pretty conservative, Sterling, and they have contributed to an unusually happy life. But what have been the effects of the scientific method on social morality? Our analysis of problems has become more rational, but are we making better decisions? What about the responsibility of Robert Oppenheimer and the others who worked on the atom bomb during World War II?

Well, I have to remind you, Jack, that you're speaking as a university professor when you talk about the scientific method. Most people never give a thought to such methods and give little attention to science. But I know what you mean, and I very much agree that we should cultivate good sense, authentic experience, and verifiable knowledge as the foundation for moral judgment. Since the most reliable form of knowledge is scientific knowledge, we should pursue the sciences seriously if we want a moral society. But we should not be taken in by the idea that the sciences are the last word in everything. In matters of morals, they're not—though they are of immeasurable importance.

There isn't any last word. But what's the best word?

Well, it's the cultivation of good judgment.

Isn't that begging the question?

Guilty! But we're caught in that kind of predicament. Our moral judgments must be based squarely on knowledge and experience. Without this foundation we cannot arrive at acceptable norms for morality.

Don't mystical experiences have the potential to yield moral insight, if not knowledge?

I'm inclined to think that they do not. Most mystics have described their experiences as ineffable and indescribable, except by analogy. But

I respect W. T. Stace, a British civil servant who spent a great deal of time studying mysticism in India and the Far East and then became professor of philosophy at Princeton University. He has been one of the best contemporary authorities on mysticism. Stace takes the position that the mystic experience can yield knowledge; and partly out of respect for him—he produces very good stuff—I've become a little more hesitant in the last few decades in asserting that mysticism can never yield knowledge.

Is this a change from your earlier stance?

It is. I used to be far more dogmatic about the position that mysticism does not yield genuine propositional knowledge. But let me tell you a story about Stace. I was living in New York in 1953 and attended a three-cornered debate among Stace, Paul Tillich, the theologian, and Ernest Nagel, one of America's leading logicians, professor of philosophy at Columbia. It was quite an exciting debate. When I went to Princeton a few days later, I called on Stace, who was already acquainted with Obert Tanner.

Obert had studied with Stace when he was teaching at Stanford. We talked, of course, about the debate, and Stace thought he and Nagel agreed pretty well, but that Tillich's theology was just a lot of nonsense. Then he said, "I know this can't be true, but I'd swear that Tanner told me that the Mormons believe that God actually has a body like a human being, like a man."

I said, "Yes, that's what he told you."

Stace stared, "You mean Mormons really believe that God is a person who has a body and looks like a man?"

I nodded. "That's what they believe."

Then Stace, a big rawboned Englishman, slammed his enormous hand down on the table and said, "God *damn!* It's nice to find a religion that makes some sense." Stace was great.

Mystics are not immune to the lure of the concrete! Didn't William James toy around with parapsychology?

He certainly did. I think James would have liked to have been a mystic, but he couldn't quite make it. You know, we all have strange insights that come just when we're halfway between waking and sleeping, intimations that time is standing still, that space is infinite, and so on. I'd be hesitant to rule out the remote possibility of some kind of knowledge through mystical experience but also very hesitant to rule it in.

We don't have a good taxonomy to deal with these things, even now, but another place along this continuum is intuition. Where does it fit among our ways of knowing?

I don't really distinguish between intuition and the mystical experience. From the standpoint of knowledge claims, I think they should be regarded as the same thing. Montague, in his *Ways of Knowing*, presented six different methods, beginning with skepticism, which is the position that knowledge is an impossibility. Next comes authority, which is not a way of knowing but at best a way of transmitting knowledge, and pragmatism, which is a way of testing knowledge, not of getting it. So that leaves us with the claim to three ways of knowing: reason, experience (usually sensory), and mysticism, the extra-sensory apprehension of something other. That is the meaning of intuition, the immediate (non-mediated) grasp of the object by the mind.

What else have you concluded about the relationship among intellectual, physical, and spiritual methods of knowing, Sterling?

I must say that I'm very much of an empiricist. I'm completely converted to the notion that factual knowledge has to have an empirical foundation. Obviously, we're justified in making claims to certain kinds of factual knowledge that can't actually be verified directly through the senses—the existence of an electron, for instance.

But here there is a joining of reason and sensory data.

Yes. It deals with rational inferences from propositions based on facts. Rationalism is not necessarily nonempirical. The sciences embrace as a method both observation and experimentation, or empirical method, and the processes of reasoning, or rational method. The more advanced a discipline's mathematical processes, the more rational it becomes. The important thing is to recognize the limits of knowledge. Bertrand Russell, who has my vote as the foremost philosopher of the twentieth century, wrote a very profound essay entitled "The Limits of Empiricism," in which he made clear that the empirical method is not the whole of scientific method.

It's obvious that philosophy has been a lifelong passion of yours. Would you reflect a bit on the meaning of philosophy?

Now that's a deceptively simple-sounding question. Of course, we have to start with its etymology—it's the love of wisdom. And ordinarily you think of a philosopher as being a person of wisdom and learning. I'm always amused when young people in philosophy departments refer to themselves as philosophers. It doesn't seem to me that the meaning of "philosopher" can be equated with "professor of philosophy," even though I have no objection when professors of mathematics call them-

selves mathematicians or professors of sociology call themselves sociolo-
gists.

So you want a broader definition for philosopher?

Yes. You can find a philosopher anywhere—in a cave in the
Himalayas, on the waterfront like Eric Hoffer—although I don't think
of Hoffer as being a very good philosopher. It isn't necessary to look
within university philosophy departments to find philosophers. You may
find some there, of course, if you're lucky.

But to define philosophy—

Of course you can do it by divisions, which is the way it typically
happens in American universities: metaphysics, epistemology, logic, and
axiology, which includes ethics and aesthetics. Or you can define it by
function—analytic philosophy, where you're doing linguistic and logical
analyses of meaning, or substantive philosophy, which looks at the basic
assumptions and arguments of metaphysics, epistemology, axiology, and
so forth.

But you?

I tend to take the position that Aristotle did—that "philosophy is
the science of the principles"—the basics. I was intrigued by a taxi driver
in New York who asked what I did for a living. When I told him, he
said, "Oh, I have a philosophy of cab driving." Well, that's amusing, but
it gets at some of the very things Aristotle had in mind when he said
philosophy is the science of the principles.

*Sure. You can have a philosophy of history, a philosophy of law. Why not
a philosophy of cab driving? It gets at the essence of the activity.*

I'm not sure that's a very good answer to your question. When I was
a student, analytical philosophy with its emphasis on logic and language
was on the rise. It began in the thirties and was very strong through the
fifties. But I think that metaphysics, which deals with the nature of the
real, has been making something of a comeback in the last decade or so.
In recent years I have taught two courses in the philosophy of history:
one is listed in the catalogue as analytical and the other as substantive.

What different emphases do you stress in teaching these two courses?

In the analytical course I dealt with the meaning of historical
sentences, the problem of the nature of historical explanations—that sort
of thing. In the substantive course I dealt with specific philosophies of
history: the ideas of Isaiah in the Bible, of St. Augustine, Marx, Sorokin,
and so on. My feeling is that we really ought to preserve both approaches
in studying history—and tie them together.

Would you agree that axiology is making a comeback?

Oh, yes, like metaphysics, now that positivism has declined in influence. Value philosophy never did suffer a decline comparable to that of traditional metaphysics, but it was affected by that decline. Both ethics and aesthetics suffered. I think the revival of metaphysics is breathing new life into value philosophy.

The term "axiology" derives from the Greek term meaning "value," but it includes aesthetic value or artistic value as well as moral value. Often there's a tendency to downplay the aesthetic side of the picture. I personally think the tie between morality and art is very, very strong. We regard many things as immoral because they are repugnant to our artistic sensibilities.

What do you make of the current interest in practical ethics—medical ethics, legal ethics, administrative ethics, and so on?

Oh, it's tremendously important. I'm very pleased that in academic circles increasing attention is being given to practical ethics. As a matter of fact, that was the main focus of the philosophy department here at the University of Utah even after the Second World War. Milton Bennion's course on citizenship, which I mentioned earlier, for instance, was very practical. Philosophy I, which was titled "Social Ethics," was always bulging at the seams, partly because it was required for teacher certification.

Would Ericksen ever have used the term "practical ethics"?

Oh yes. Ethics for Ericksen was practical. He taught courses in ethical theory, but his main interest was in practical, moral problems. He introduced a course in courtship and marriage which he taught during the 1920s and 1930s. It received national attention. Now you expect this sort of thing in sociology, but here it was in the philosophy department.

Well, we've started out with your first professorial appointment and ranged broadly over your whole philosophy. Do you have other comments on your experience as a faculty member at USC? You said there was a lot going on.

Not just with me, with the whole university. I'd only been there a short time when the president was made chancellor and a new president came in. No sooner was he on campus than he appointed me chair of a faculty committee on religion on the campus—not for academic courses but for student religious life and services.

To meet students' religious interests, there was a Methodist church on the edge of campus, and no doubt a Newman Center, Hillel Foundation, and others, but of course they were not part of the university. As a junior member of the faculty, I felt a little out of place as chair of the committee. The dean of women and dean of men were both on the committee. The dean of women was very active in her denomination, and I think she wasn't very happy with a Mormon chairing the committee. We did a few things before I left—decided to have a university chaplain, which they hadn't had, and laid the groundwork for constructing a small interdenominational campus chapel, and that sort of thing.

You have described two experiences where you were given uncommon responsibility as a junior faculty member. Was it difficult for you, making the switch from student to colleague as far as the other faculty members went?

In some ways, yes. Raubenheimer gave me quite a little lecture on that when he first discussed with me my faculty appointment. He said, "Now there's one thing you're going to have to forget. These men who are now your colleagues—you must forget that they were ever your teachers." That's good advice, but it's a hard thing to do.

Do you think you and they succeeded?

I think so. We always got along famously. No problems. I always had great respect for them. They're all dead now except one; without exception, I maintained friendships with them right up till their deaths. The last one is Wilbur Long, now in his advanced years.

Who was the university president?

When I was appointed it was Rufus B. Von Klein Schmid, whom I already knew slightly. When I was at the Institute of Religion at Tucson, he came to Arizona to give the commencement address. I was asked to give the invocation, and we were teamed up for the procession to the stadium. He was very cordial during that long, slow walk—told me he knew and greatly respected Heber J. Grant, president of the LDS church. He also commented on his great admiration for the Mormon system of tithing. "A wonderful thing," he said. I replied as diplomatically as I could, "Well, I guess there are certain things to be said for it, but there are also some things to be said against it. It can become very mechanical, and it's not very democratic." He listened to me very thoughtfully and then had the final word. "Young man," he said, "if you were an administrator, you'd have higher regard for that tithing system."

There's a lot of truth in that. Those in power rarely relinquish an advantage voluntarily. How did you feel about making the move from USC to the University of Utah in the summer of 1948?

I was very sorry to leave USC, and they made a strong effort to keep me—offered a promotion to associate professor and a salary increase from $4,800 to $5,600, which was not bad for those days, strange as it now seems. There were some real losses, particularly the administrative status of the philosophy department, the number and maturity of graduate students, and the great philosophical library. The philosophy library at the University of Utah is not bad now, but it wasn't very good when I came; and USC had a magnificent library. But in addition to being able to breathe more freely, the plus of coming to Utah, aside from the fact that we were in a sense returning home, was the noticeable enthusiasm of students here for the study of philosophy and the very pleasant association with both old and new friends.

Your medical condition has pretty well assured that you stayed in Utah after you got here?

That's been the result, although I should say that USC made two really valiant efforts to get me back as director of the School of Philosophy, first during the winter of 1952-53 and again in the middle 1960s. The first time, I didn't even entertain the idea seriously because I felt that I simply couldn't live down there. But when the second invitation came, President Norman Hubbard of USC, who was an M.D., checked into the medical problem very closely and assured me that the Medical School could take care of my breathing problem. They pressed me pretty persuasively, and I was very close to leaving Utah in 1965. I even went down to Los Angeles and met with the president, some trustees, and the philosophy faculty to discuss the matter. They offered me everything—a high salary, excellent budget for the School of Philosophy, freedom from the directorship if I preferred simply to teach, and no teaching unless I wanted to teach.

They handed you a blank check!

Yes, but Waldemer Read tattled to the academic vice-president, Jack Adamson, and he hauled me into a meeting with President Fletcher. Those two guys just beat me until I was bloody, so I had no choice.

They made a counteroffer you couldn't refuse! Any regrets?

There was no counteroffer except assurance that the department of philosophy would be strengthened. I did have some regrets about leaving USC, and about moving away from family in Los Angeles. But even spending a couple of days in Southern California brought back suggestions of the old trouble, so I'm sure it was wise for me to stay in Utah.

Was this condition a problem in the other places you've lived?

I had a tough several weeks in New York when I was living there in 1952, but then it left and didn't come back. I had no problem in

Washington, D.C., when I was living there during the early sixties, and I have never had trouble anywhere else in the world.

Let's talk about other transitions, Sterling. What conclusions did you reach as a young man about the nature of human beings, the nature of God—where do you stand, for instance, on free will and determinism?

I must say that I am 100 percent a believer in the freedom of the will. Now there are certain problems with that because I also believe in universal causation—that everything occurs as a result of a cause. The thoroughgoing determinists quite commonly base their determinism on the notion of universal causation. The problem is whether you can be a "free willer" and also believe in causation. Now there are a good many problems connected with this, as you know. In quantum mechanics . . .

The Heisenberg uncertainty principle? You can't predict the path of an electron because you have to know both location and velocity, and they can't be determined simultaneously.

Yes, uncertainty in knowledge is apparently built into the very structure of the situation. Many physicists, philosophers, and theologians have therefore concluded that, on the subatomic level, the world is indeterminate. Professor Henry Eyring of our university, a really great man in theoretical chemistry who taught quantum mechanics for years, held that view—that the world ultimately is indeterminate. He and I used to disagree with one another on this issue as on many others. I put forth the fairly standard argument that the impossibility of prediction doesn't necessarily mean that the course of the electron is not caused, while Eyring argued for a breakdown in the causal structure of things at the subatomic level. The classical position of Newtonian mechanics is that everything functions according to causation on essentially a mechanical level. The indeterminists hold, of course, that determinism is found only on the macroscopic level dealt with by the Newtonians prior to this century.

The problem is where you try to apply the indeterminate model to free will.

Maybe the world is indeterminate. Maybe it's not a case of universal causation, but no one has been able to show that the human will is a subatomic particle, so I don't think that this is a satisfactory way to handle the question of free will. Einstein, for instance, was very much opposed to indeterminacy based on the Heisenberg principle of uncertainty.

My book *Religion, Reason, and Truth* contains a long essay on the freedom of the will. Two highly competent people have challenged me on it, but I'm not sure either one read the last pages where I came out solidly on the side of free will. One was the American philosopher

Charles Hartshorne who, in my opinion, is the most important philosopher of religion today. He wrote that he didn't agree with my denial of
the freedom of the will. I didn't deny the freedom of the will. I hold
that free will is compatible with causation. What I attempted to do was
to develop a theory that accounts for freedom and still allows universal
causation. What Hartshorne should have said instead, in my opinion is,
"You have made a very bad argument." The evidences for free will are
simply that we behave freely and we have the experience of being free.
For example, you will walk out the door to this room when you decide
it's time to go, but still there are causes. You may look at the clock, you
may recall that you have another appointment, you may be sick of this
conversation—but you still decide to go. Now the problem is: How do
you reconcile the fact that you are caused to do something with the fact
that you do it freely?

You presumably choose to do it.

Yes. Well what I've attempted to do is to develop a theory which
I believe, frankly, has a certain amount of originality, at least I've never
seen it handled in this way by others, though the reconciliation of
freedom and causation is not uncommon. When you say, "I am free,"
what do you mean by *I*? Well, the I, among other things, is a combination of countless causes—genetic, biological, environmental—and that's
what we are.

Typical arguments for freedom of the will tend to center on moral
decisions. For example, a friend says to you, "I know that my son will
make the right decision." You say, "How do you know that?" "Well,
he has free agency, and he will make the right decision." "But how do
you know?" "Well, I taught him from the ground up. He went to
Sunday school; he read the scriptures and all the right literature." Well,
the kid may indeed make his father's predicted decision, but it is because
these various factors have caused him to make that decision. There
would be no meaning to moral education if moral decisions and actions
were not subject to causes. But are you going to say that the decision
was not made freely? Without causes for moral action, there would be
moral anarchy. Chaos.

Now I have attempted to produce a reconciliation of freedom with
causation. The way in which the problem is often stated is that to be
free is not to be subject to coercion, rather than not to be subject to
cause. Who makes our decisions? We make our decisions, or we choose
to let someone else make the decision for us. In either case, we are free.

Take the case of Harry Truman firing Douglas MacArthur in 1953. We generally regard that as a courageous moral decision where a controversial president fires a revered general. I might argue that Truman's background—specifically his distaste for the powerful and their arrogant use of power—made that decision inevitable. But the source of his courage was his determination not to let power run unchecked.

Absolutely, he made that decision. But you see, when you say everything in his experience up to that time made the decision inevitable, you put your finger right on the problem. *Did* those factors make it inevitable? The determinists would say, "Well, if it was inevitable, there was no freedom."

The very nature of human psychological and physiological processes is so utterly complex that you cannot say that it is inevitable in such a way that the person was not involved in the decision.

If you put it in a religious context, some of the most competent logicians have shown that even divine foreknowledge does not destroy freedom of the will.

St. Augustine, for example, held that God is a timeless being, so our future is in his present just as our past is in his present. Augustine had two kinds of arguments: One, God is timeless. For God there is no past and no future, so God's knowing what you're going to do tomorrow does not mean that you will not act freely any more than his remembering what you did yesterday means that you were not free. But his other argument is a very simple one. He said, "Yes, God knows that you're going to make this decision tomorrow. He knows that you're going to make it freely."

You see, if you get rid of the notion of causation the whole structure of morality collapses. Without causes for moral decisions, morality would be an aimless confusion and moral education would be impossible. In moral education, you attempt to cause the student or child to think and act in certain ways.

Another point I'd make is that you treat people differently if you believe they're free agents. And they're likely to respond differently as a result.

Yes, as you know that's also the ethical principle at the foundation of Immanuel Kant's moral philosophy. You should always treat another human being as an end and never as a means only. When you emphasize freedom, you are treating a person as an end. Determinism is more likely to lead to treating an individual as a means, as part of a mechanism you're manipulating. Now you may be doing a little manipulating when you try to get this person to be intellectually honest. That's a very real problem. But I must confess that I think there is a sense in which the problem of free will may be meaningless.

When my positivistic temperament gets the best of me, I'm inclined to think that this is the case, that the question of free will may be cognitively meaningless. Most of the time, however, I think it's a meaningful problem. And when it comes right down to it, free willers and determinists both tend to behave as if they have freedom.

Some people assume that human nature is basically good but vulnerable to temptation, while others think it's basically bad but the individual can be redeemed. How have you unraveled that dichotomy?

Well, in the first place I'm not sure that I even go along with the notion that there is any such thing as human nature. But leaving that aside, if we find a human being in a natural condition—a newborn, say—what we have here is moral neutrality—able to be influenced but neutral in itself.

So human beings are good or bad but not human nature?

Yes, that would be my view.

What about the concept of human corruptibility or original sin?

I'm inclined to think that human beings are more good than bad, but certainly all are vulnerable to corruption. The Christian idea of original sin is probably the worst idea that the mind of man ever concocted, and it's basic to most of Christianity, both Catholic and Protestant, though it's moderate in Catholicism and has been pretty much abandoned in the liberal forms of Protestantism. I think it's not just nonsense but evil nonsense—the idea that human nature is fundamentally corrupt from its origins.

What about Mormon thought on this topic?

I've always been quite pleased that Mormonism rejects original sin. The term is used occasionally by Mormon writers, but what they usually mean by it is simply "the sin of Adam," the cultural myth.

If you believe people are basically good, though corruptible, then you have a democratic temperament because you think people are not only free to make their own decisions but also likely to make decent decisions. But if you don't believe people are free, then you might as well go ahead and make their decisions for them. Or if you believe they're free but instinctively bad, then you can't afford to let them make their own decisions.

So we only have one chance in four! Well, Jack, let's believe that people aren't basically bad and also that they're free. It always pays to be on the side of truth and righteousness.

The Marxist view sees our behavior as so determined by economic and social institutions that the only way we can redeem society and the individuals in it is to change our environment—to totally eradicate all the ills of competition, greed, and exploitation that come with a capitalist system. Create a perfect economic system and produce perfectly cooperative human beings.

Yes, of course. But I think you would find on close examination that Karl Marx believed in the freedom of the will, too, despite his strong element of historical determinism. And then it's complicated by whether you're dealing with the Leninist, Stalinist, or Marx-Engels form of Marxism. But your point is certainly an excellent one. What you're getting at, it seems to me, is the problem of freedom in connection with democracy, or the problem of the individual versus society. And that's a problem determinists and free willers both face.

I had an interesting experience a few years ago when I helped organize an international philosophers' conference held at the East-West Center on the University of Hawaii campus. Fifteen or twenty philosophers from Asia, Europe, and the Americas gathered to discuss fundamental philosophical problems in a session that lasted six weeks. It was quite an exclusive group—a few observers were admitted, and there were a couple of public lectures; but most of the time it was a more or less private conversation. "The World and the Individual" was our subject. The Asians tended to put community first, emphasizing obligations and responsibilities associated with corporate and public life. The Americans and British held that individual rights are more original than responsibilities. You recognize your moral responsibilities because the other person has rights.

Now does this distinction predate Locke and Rousseau?

No, I think it's primarily a modern emphasis. If you go back into the Middle Ages, the social structure clearly takes precedence over the individual in Europe. Catholicism certainly fit this pattern.

But Luther's concept of the "priesthood of all believers" involved a strong shift toward individualism, though he didn't go as far as Locke.

I think Luther was influenced by the nominalism of William of Occam, a late medieval philosopher at Oxford University. Occam opposed the Platonic approach to reality and asserted that universals like justice, truth, beauty, blueness, and so forth are just names—hence the term nominalism. If only particulars are real, then the nation or the church is not a reality, only the individual person is real.

Where does Occam's famous razor fit into his nominalism?

Its literal translation from Latin is: "You should not multiply entities beyond necessity." Stop with what you can see, hear, taste, touch, and smell. Not that he didn't believe in other things. He believed in the reality of God, for instance, and that the good is good because God wills it. Occam would say that if God changed his mind, then killing would be good. Makes all the difference in the world.

And you think he had an influence on Luther and Calvin?

Oh, absolutely. You get Calvin laying tremendous stress on the inscrutable but sovereign will of God. If God wills that you go to heaven and I go to hell, then we have no grounds for complaint because we can't question the will of God. Both of us glorify God equally; I can glorify his justice just as well from hell as you can glorify it from heaven.

As your philosophy developed, Sterling, so did your career. When did you decide to join the University of Utah faculty?

Meredith Wilson, the dean of the College of Arts and Science, and President A. Ray Olpin both got in touch with me and asked me if I would come to the university. I've never known, to be frank with you, whether the philosophy department, in which I was appointed, was ever consulted. I rather think the chairman was, but I've never known for sure. Waldemer Read was department chair, and he wrote to me asking what I would like to teach. I told him anything but aesthetics.

When President Olpin, who had just assumed office in 1946, visited me in Los Angeles in the spring of 1948 to persuade me to come to the University of Utah, he apparently didn't know that I had already agreed with Dean Meredith Wilson to come. So I didn't tell him. I listened with a great deal of interest as he made a very persuasive case. We sat in the lobby of the Biltmore Hotel downtown in Los Angeles while he described his plans for the university, especially in research. Frankly, I was impressed.

Although many seem to have forgotten now, he boosted the reputation of the university across the board. But what were his plans when he began?

Olpin, who had had extensive experience in scientific research, came to the University of Utah from Ohio State, where he had spearheaded their movement toward research. He had a vision of the University of Utah becoming a major research center. One of his first acts as president was to attract world-class chemist Henry Eyring here from Princeton University. Himself a physicist, Olpin did as much to promote excellence in the arts as he did for the sciences at the university. He and George Thomas were our most influential presidents. Thomas vouchsafed our intellectual independence in the twenties and thirties; Olpin transformed us into a major research university and cultural center after World War II.

You had been here for only about a year and a half when the university celebrated its centennial on February 28, 1950. Was that something of a marker in the university's history, a turning point of any kind?

It was certainly a milepost. I don't think you could regard it as a turning point. The turning point was the post–World War II combination of circumstances that hit all of the schools in the country: the flood of veterans into the schools, the increase of federal funds for research, and increased private money for research and development as well. The University of Utah was lucky because it was ready for this and it got first-rate leadership just at the right time. A. Ray Olpin as president and Henry Eyring as dean of the graduate school transformed us quickly and effectively into a research university.

Olpin and Eyring were a great combination, but who else contributed centrally to this institution-building process?

It's difficult to start naming them, because a great many people were involved in making this a real university. Meredith Wilson was a major factor and Maxwell Wintrobe and Louis Goodman in the Medical School were certainly two of the most important.

Did Olpin and Eyring jump on a moving train and hit the throttle or did they switch to another track and then pour on the coal?

I think the university was moving on that track already. Olpin was remarkably effective in getting things done, but he had a very firm foundation to build on. The University of Utah was a competent institution before he came here.

But it had been primarily a teaching institution rather than one distinguished for its scholarship.

Certainly there was research going on before, but I think there was more at Utah State University because of the agricultural experiment station with its federal funding.

I've heard you say over the years that you know of no institution that defends academic freedom more fully than the University of Utah. Why do you say that?

Yes, the University of Utah has genuine intellectual freedom. It's partly because there has always been a powerful interest group, the Mormon church, right on the university's doorstep. Olpin used to tell me in the 1950s of complaints from Mormon officials—and others, of course—about what professor so-and-so was saying in the classroom, what questionable plays were performed by the theater, and so on. Without exception, Olpin was a stalwart defender of the freedom of his faculty. He was almost bullheaded about it. And, for the most part, the faculty exercised its academic freedom responsibly—speaking and writing honestly but without malice toward local institutions and interests.

I'm sure you've got an example or two in mind.

One such event occurred in 1949, or possibly 1950. There was a great deal of concern over the loyalty oath that California initiated, a concern which was spreading across the country. There was some agitation in Utah for requiring loyalty oaths from university professors. The faculty met in Kingsbury Hall to discuss the matter and President Olpin said very firmly, "There will be no loyalty oaths in this university while I am president," and that settled that. Thereafter loyalty oaths were a dead issue at the university and, generally, in the Utah community.

I would occasionally run into people—who were not Utahns, incidentally—who would ask, "When are you going to get rid of the communists in the university?"

It was a common assumption in the 1950s that universities were full of communists.

Absolutely. I said, "I don't know that we have any communists." "Oh, don't talk like that," they'd snap back. "You know very well that place is full of communists." Well, as a matter of fact, we did have at least one card-carrying communist at the Medical School; but he wasn't thrown out. At the end of the year he simply left.

Were faculty salaries an issue with the public at that time, as they seem to be now? What was your salary when you came here in the fall of 1948?

This issue is a perennial one, of course, and it never gets much better or goes away. I was appointed a full professor and my salary was $5,600, quite respectable then.

During the academic year 1952-53, you were a Ford Fellow and spent some time in New York. How did that come about?

That was quite a delightful year in many ways. Ford Faculty Fellowships paid your salary, moving, and travel expenses. In the application you told them what you wanted to do; if they agreed with you and appointed you, you were on your own. My education had all been in the West and I thought I should have some experience in the East; so when I received the appointment, I took the family and drove through the South and down into Florida before going up the east coast to New York. It was a great experience for us. I hadn't been east of Denver before. We had four of our children at that time. Trudy, the oldest, was in the third grade. We managed to rent a house in Queens—looked just like the Sugarhouse-type bungalow that Archie Bunker lived in and just the same kind of neighborhood. That was a stroke of luck; we rented it for the same price that we rented our house here to some people who were coming to Salt Lake in connection with the Medical

School. It worked out nicely.

Back up just a bit, Sterling. What were you doing? Where were you studying?

I wanted to study philosophy, of course; and I chose New York because I felt that it was the center of the universe and that you could get to other places from there. I was doing postdoctoral work at Columbia, Princeton, and Union Theological Seminary. I was appointed visiting scholar at Columbia and the Union Theological Seminary and a Ford Fellow in philosophy at Princeton. And as if that weren't enough, I was appointed as some kind of fellow at Yale.

This sounds like four part-time jobs, not a leisurely year of study! What was the heart of the experience?

Well, I did go up to Yale quite a bit to spend time with their people in philosophy. I also went to Harvard several times. Mainly, however, I concentrated on Columbia and Union Theological Seminary. Union was, and may still be, the best place in America for the scholarly study of religion, and, of course, it is right by Columbia so this was very convenient. I could attend lectures at both places with no difficulty. This was a great experience for me because I made contact with many leaders in the field of philosophy and religion. The most celebrated of them was Protestant theologian Paul Tillich. For that entire year I attended his classes—four of them: one on the history of Christianity, one on Luther, one on Calvin, and a seminar on Tillich's own systematic theology. Later he and I participated in a week-long seminar at the College of Wooster in Ohio on the problem of the self.

Were there other people at Columbia and Union Theological Seminary that you especially remember from that year?

At Columbia I was especially attracted to Ernest Nagel's lectures on logic. At Union I got to know John T. McNeill, one of the leading historians of Protestantism. A major figure at Yale with whom I had contact was Richard Niebuhr, a brother of Reinhold Niebuhr and a man of great distinction in Christian ethics. Reinhold had just retired from Union Seminary because of a heart attack. I was fortunate to hear him lecture a time or two in later years, but I regretted missing the chance to take a seminar with Reinhold that year, since he was probably the leading American theologian at the time.

You made contact with philosophers at Princeton that year, too?

Yes. Rudolf Carnap, the leading figure among the logical positivists, was at the Institute for Advanced Study at Princeton, and I spent some time with him at his home at the institute. I also had a marvelous seminar on the logical structure of scientific theory with Carl Hempel, a German who had been in this country for some time and was one of the leading logical positivists. He had been a professor at the University of Berlin and left during the Nazi regime, went to Queen's College in New York, and then to Yale and finally Princeton. I'd studied his stuff and very much enjoyed it. I joined his seminar on the structure of scientific theory.

Years later I was appointed a member of the visiting committee for the Department of Philosophy at Princeton—you know, we would snoop around to see whether they were doing good things or bad in the philosophy department. It was a very pleasant occasion to renew old acquaintances there.

At Harvard you had some very interesting sessions with the Russian-American sociologist and philosopher Pitirim Sorokin, who invited you to his home. Now that is the way to get to know a scholar!

Yes, you can see what kinds of books they have in their bookcases and whether they pick up after themselves, and so on. Sorokin had been at Harvard for some years and produced a multivolume social approach to the philosophy of history entitled *Social and Cultural Dynamics.* I was pleased to spend the afternoon with him, because he had advanced a conception of history based on three types of culture—ideational, idealistic, and sensate—that move in cycles. When a culture dies, it may be reborn as one of the other types.

I suppose classical Greece was an ideational culture and medieval Christian was idealistic.

And our own time is sensate, or, a roughly equivalent term, materialistic. These three aren't in any kind of progressive form. You don't necessarily start with the ideational and go to the idealistic. Both Oswald Spengler and Sorokin held that our culture is nearing its end, and I'm inclined to think they were right. Well, during this fascinating time with Sorokin—it was about 1953—I asked him if he still held to the view set forth in his major work on the cyclical movement of cultures. He didn't say yes or no. He just smiled and said, "I doubt if any other philosopher has wasted as much paper as I have." Well, his work wasn't as extensive as Arnold Toynbee's.

Did you ever meet Professor Toynbee?

As a matter of fact, we had Toynbee out here in Utah. Cal Taylor in our psychology department invited me to read a paper for one of his projects on multiple talents; Toynbee was another of the lecturers. I got acquainted with him then. Later, during the Vietnam War, we had

Toynbee as commencement speaker. He sure blasted the hell out of us.

It sounds as if your year in New York led to a lot of good things later on. It was a fast-paced year. Did you have time to taste the culture of New York City?

Oh, we were serious about pleasure, too, Jack. Lowell Durham, Sr., professor of music and later fine arts dean at the University of Utah, was also at Columbia University that year on a Ford Fellowship. We went to the Metropolitan Opera together on a number of occasions. Sometimes we stood up, sometimes we sat down; but I must say we didn't miss anything in New York.

I notice you said "we." This experience must have been wonderful for Natalie and your children as well?

Our family did more in one year than most New Yorkers would ever think of doing in ten. We made the most of it—museums, concerts, parks, monuments, bridges—you name it. Then on the way home we drove up through New England and Quebec, before heading west across country. I think the children enjoyed the whole year a great deal. But that was the first time Trudy had encountered written homework, and she was quite upset about it. So I settled down to see if I could give her some help. The first question was, "What is the home field of the Brooklyn Dodgers?"

That's a geographically and culturally loaded question, and it didn't favor a Utah child!

No it didn't, and she deserved a little help with it.

Shortly after your return home, you began to get a number of tempting offers. The Aspen Institute called on you to lead its seminars in 1954, Reed College wooed you for its presidency in 1956, Columbia pursued you for a philosophy professorship in its Graduate School of Business in 1958, and later you received a most attractive offer from the Ford Foundation. How did you respond to these enticing possibilities?

Well, I'm simply attached to Utah and attached to the university. It's true that I received numerous offers, some of them exceedingly attractive, but I was never seriously tempted by any of them. I have accepted many visiting assignments in other parts of the nation and the world, but coming home—to Utah and to the classroom—was always a pleasure for me. I am a Utahn and a teacher at heart.

8.
Heresies and Criticism

When you returned to Utah as a professor in 1948, Sterling, were you already known as a Mormon heretic?

If I wasn't, it didn't take long. During my first year I was invited to address a returned missionary fraternity in the old Union Building—now Gardner Hall. At that time there was a lot of hullabaloo over labor problems, and some Mormon general authorities were making outspoken anti-labor statements.

They supported the Taft-Hartley Act and the movement to trim the power of unions and require anti-communist loyalty oaths of all labor leaders.

That's it, and I talked about religion and society and brought up the matter of the church's position on labor. Everything was fairly moderate—at least for me—but at the end one young man got up, pointed his finger at me, and announced that I should be excommunicated from the church because I was in opposition to the Brethren. It broke the meeting up into a general argument.

So that marked you as a rabble-rouser?

No, by damn, even before I started teaching at the University of Utah, I was in trouble. I taught two classes at BYU's summer session in 1947, one on contemporary philosophy and the other on types of religious philosophies. I had some excellent students, many of them quite advanced. But Sydney Sperry, who held a doctorate from the University of Chicago and directed Old Testament studies at BYU, had become an apologist for the church. I quickly discovered that he had had two spies enroll in my classes. The spies were both graduate students, and I think I gave them both A's. Well, about two-thirds of the way along in the term, they met with me after class and quizzed me about what I did and did not believe.

Knowing they were spies, you must have had some fun.

One of the first questions was: "Do you believe the devil is a real person?" I said, "No, but, come to think of it, every devil I know is a

179

real person." I answered all their questions, taking things slow and easy so they could write down my answers. When they were through I said, "I think I should tell you that I'm well aware that you two are in my classes to spy for Professor Sperry." "Oh, no, no," they protested. I said, "There is no use denying it, because I know you are. Even the other students know that you are spies." They looked a little abashed and said, "Well, we're just doing our duty, just doing our duty."

The BYU administration must have known they were only going to get one crack at you, so they decided to get their money's worth that summer.

Maybe so. In addition to teaching my classes, they assigned me to give a sermon every Sunday morning at the devotional meetings in the chapel of the Joseph Smith Building. I did, too, and I spoke mostly on Mormon philosophy. That created some problems. Every Thursday afternoon I also gave a public lecture on Mormonism and society. These sessions attracted a lot of people and stirred up a lot of controversy. One of the spies would stand against the back wall and periodically slip down the hall to Sperry's office and tell him what I was saying. It is beyond belief that this kind of thing could take place in an institution of higher learning. I think they had first-rate students, and still do, but they were deprived of a first-rate education—and that's a crime.

This whole affair ended with a bang, did it not?

The last session was so crowded that people brought in chairs and some stood along the walls. I was talking about the church and social problems when a young man—in his twenties—stepped forward, raised his fist, and said, "I say if we're going to fight the church, we've got to strike now." I was flabbergasted, and Wiley Sessions, who was the head of religion, was utterly shocked. He got up and shushed everyone down again. Ray Canning told me that Wiley was fired for having me there. I hope it's not true. But Wiley was near retirement age. He had started building houses and, as it turned out, had a more lucrative career ahead of him.

I understand your old friend Eugene Roberts ran into Sidney Sperry later that summer and said, "I'd like to know when Sterling McMurrin will be invited back to BYU."

Yes, and Sperry said, "That man will never again be allowed to speak on this campus."

A rather accurate prophecy, I'd say. Even so, you have known and respected most of the presidents of the LDS church over the last half century.

For the most part, my relations with church leaders have been both pleasant and rewarding. I have had personal contact with a number of the general authorities, from James E. Talmage and B. H. Roberts in the late 1920s and thirties to the present.

Differences among them in philosophy and style have been sharper than most people realize. I understand, for example, that Joseph Fielding Smith's book **Man, His Origin and Destiny** *wasn't embraced by President David O. McKay?*

No, but I don't think President McKay ever mentioned it in a conversation with me. However, his second son, Llewellyn, who was professor of German at the University of Utah for many years, would often drop in my office to visit with me, and he let me know of his father's strong opposition to that book. President McKay took the position that Joseph Fielding Smith was free to say or write whatever he pleased, but that his book should not be taken as representing the official position of the church or of the general authorities collectively. It was not to be used as a text in any church class.

McKay seemed more than fair in this instance, as in many others.

I thought so. Well, we had a study group here at the university around 1950. We used to get together to discuss religious issues with invited guests who had made special studies or written books of interest to us, usually but not always relating to Mormonism. We were known as the Swearing Elders.

Why the "swearing" elders? Who was doing the swearing and what about?

We weren't a tame bunch, you know, and we included a few professors from BYU, such as P. A. Christensen from the English department, Wilford Poulson from psychology, George Hansen from geology, John Swenson from sociology, and others. There were people from the institute of religion here at the University of Utah—Lowell Bennion, Ed Lyon, and George Boyd. Heber Snell, the Bible scholar, and Joseph Geddes, a leading sociologist, usually came down from Utah State, and Jennings Olsen from Weber College. Once three undergraduates from BYU hitchhiked up to Salt Lake to join us, but we didn't let them in. The BYU faculty simply served notice that they wouldn't be able to talk freely if those students were present.

Sounds as if the BYU contingent regarded this as risky business. How did the Swearing Elders get started?

Several graduate students and young faculty members at the University of Utah organized the group in the spring of 1949. Their leader graduated a few months later, however, and that nearly ended it. But Lowell Bennion at the LDS Institute of Religion got hold of Bill Mulder in our English department and me and said, "Look, this thing is very important for us but we can't very well hold it at the institute of religion, so why don't you two take it over?" After some persuasion, Bill and I agreed to do it. As a matter of fact, we did have a couple of sessions in the institute and we were entirely open about our activities. At one of these, Apostle Adam S. Bennion addressed the group.

I understand you didn't have a regular meeting schedule; but when you got someone who had done an important piece of research or writing on Mormonism, you'd send out notices to the faithful and have a meeting?

Oh, yes, and usually twenty would attend. Rarely more. We met in a pretty good-sized room in the old Union Building. Usually we met about 4:00 or 4:30 in the afternoon in the east room of the basement. There was a cafeteria there and we'd sit at tables and have milkshakes and sundaes during the session. It was always pleasant.

Back to the Swearing Elders. Where did that name come from?

Lowry Nelson, a leading sociologist at the University of Minnesota, was at the University of Utah during the early months of the group's meetings. He attended and called it the "Swearing Elders." The name stuck. Most of those who met were Mormons, as he was, but we invited a variety of other people to the sessions when we thought they would be interested—Louis Zucker, the region's leading Jewish scholar, Henry Frost, a sociologist, and others. For speakers we sought a variety of viewpoints—both Mormon and non-Mormon—always persons whose research and writing deserved attention. BYU's scholar of ancient languages, Hugh Nibley, University of Utah anthropologist Charles Dibble, Whitney Cross, author of the *Burned-Over District,* and others. It was always an excellent affair for those who wanted to talk freely and listen to others who spoke freely.

The Swearing Elders went on for several years, as I recall, encountering resistance from various church authorities. I understand BYU's president Ernest Wilkinson tried with little success to prevent members of his faculty from participating. So why did the thing fizzle out?

Well, Bill Mulder and I finally got tired of making the arrangements. Our final session was a semi-formal debate over Joseph Fielding Smith's infamous anti-science book, which had been out a year or two by then. On one side was Jennings Olsen, a professor of philosophy at Weber College who also taught anthropology and psychology. Olsen was a man of great talent, certainly the leading luminary of Weber College in those days, and a regular member of the Swearing Elders. He was so incensed by Apostle Smith's book that he wanted to make a public statement on it. I wasn't sure it was even worth discussing, but Olsen was determined.

Somehow I don't see Joseph Fielding Smith agreeing to debate his views with a bunch of skeptics.

Nor did he! But I did get Melvin Cook, who wrote the book's introduction, to defend the work against Olsen's attack. Cook was a world-class authority on explosives, a professor of engineering and metallurgy here. In religion, though, he was a conservative Mormon—very traditional and exceedingly orthodox. He was, in a sense, President Smith's scientific adviser for this book, which contained a remarkable amount of bad science, if you could call it science at all. Cook had a very high opinion of the book and wrote that if they gave Nobel prizes in theology, Joseph Fielding Smith would have received one.

This adds up to an interesting evening!

Oh, it was. Word got out, you know. We didn't advertise the affair, but a number of people asked to come, including Lee Stokes, head of our geology department, and Llewellyn McKay, professor of languages and a son of President McKay. We were happy to have them, of course. Several LDS general authorities also showed up. Bruce R. McConkie came and was quite active in the discussion—he was President Smith's son-in-law—and Milton Hunter, another Seventy, and, as I recall, Apostle Mark E. Petersen.

It's remarkable that general authorities would attend. They certainly wouldn't do such a thing today. Can you summarize the arguments?

Well, Cook argued for a very young earth, insisting that geological antiquities and the processes known to create sedimentary rock were pure nonsense. After Cook and Olsen had equal time for their statement and rebuttal, discussion broke open. Lee Stokes summarized the typical geological view of the development of the earth's crust and said, "Now, Dr. Cook, apparently you don't believe this?" I had a feeling that it was a little rough on Stokes to think he had such a naive colleague. And Cook answered, "Oh, no. That would take a long time." I thought it was fairly comical—that he could have God hustling around creating the earth in short order but he couldn't think of God as having enough time to let natural processes take their course.

A Mormon God has many worlds to look after, and no time to waste! Did Bruce McConkie really play a role?

He got into the act defending Cook—defending Joseph Fielding Smith, of course, being as dogmatic as ever. He and I were both in our early thirties when we had had an encounter several years earlier in a church meeting in the Los Angeles Stake. He was a newly appointed member of the First Council of Seventy, and I blasted him in the meeting

for insulting those who could not answer his questions the way he
wanted. He would call out a name, have the man stand, ask him a
question, then say, "You're wrong. You sit down." If the victim
protested at all, he'd say, "I told you to sit down!" His behavior was
disgraceful, and I couldn't sit still for any more of it. I interrupted the
meeting to tell him we were not going to tolerate any more of this
humiliation. So there we were years later, and McConkie was holding
forth again. It was getting quite late and the custodian came in and said
he had to lock the building. I was chairing the meeting, so I said, "How
much time can we have?" He said, "I'll give you ten minutes." Everyone
heard him.

So I said, "Any further comments must be limited to two minutes."
Well, McConkie was on his feet and he kept talking. When his time
was up, I pointed to my watch. He kept talking, so I stood up. He said,
"Now just a minute, Sterling . . ." I shot back, "Now, *you* wait a minute,
Bruce, your time is up, so you sit down." He did sit down, too. I don't
often talk like that, of course, but I'd been waiting for years to tell
McConkie to sit down!

I'd guess a majority of the people in the room were amused by the exchange.
Were most of them also critical of the book?

Yes, you'd expect that from an academic crowd. I don't recall
Apostle Petersen saying anything, but Llewellyn McKay stood up and
said, "I've talked to my father about this book, and he doesn't like it.
He doesn't agree with it. He would like it to be known that this book
doesn't represent the church's position and that it must not be used for
teaching any religion classes." Then he added that President McKay said
Joseph Fielding Smith was free to say or write what he wanted to, so
long as he didn't claim it was church doctrine.

None of this apparently discouraged Mel Cook, the father of Merrill Cook,
our persistent third-party candidate for Utah public office in the 1980s and
nineties. Didn't the elder Cook go on to publish some of his views?

Oh, yes. He blasted our world-class chemist Henry Eyring for his
scientific views on the age of the earth, and he gave me hell in several
passages. I will say for Cook, however, that he sent over proofs of those
critical paragraphs about me and asked if I had any objections. I wrote
back that I had no objections whatever, but that he hadn't cited sources
for my statements in at least a couple of places. I gave him the sources,
and they showed up in the published version.

I have a personal connection with this story, Sterling. In 1963-64 I was a
recent convert to the LDS church and a new faculty member at Clemson

*University in South Carolina. Several local members told me that I couldn't
be a Mormon in good standing if I accepted the theory of evolution. Well,
I wrote Joseph Fielding Smith a letter, explained that I was wrestling with
this issue, and asked what he thought about the matter. He scrawled across
the bottom of my letter, "See my book,* **Man, His Origin and Destiny,**"
*and mailed it back to me. I ordered a copy from Deseret Book, read it, and
just about left the church right then.*

A very logical decision, given the circumstances. Why didn't you?

As it turned out, the church's **Improvement Era** *magazine published an
article by none other than Lee Stokes shortly after that. His point was that
evolution is perfectly logical, that the scriptures don't proscribe it—they're
simply silent on it—and members are free to make up their own minds.
Given the background you've provided here, I'll bet President McKay wanted
Lee Stokes's views aired in order to counter Smith's book.*

Yes! I hope Stokes also made the point that the LDS church has
never officially taken a stand against evolution. Even so, I think things
have slipped quite a bit since those days. Bruce McConkie made a speech
against evolution at BYU shortly before he died, and Boyd Packer
continues to attack it periodically. I miss the old days when Fred Pack,
James E. Talmage, and B. H. Roberts actually took science seriously. I
remember Talmage commenting on the popular view that the six-day
creation period was actually six thousand years because of some scripture
that a thousand years is as a day with the Lord. Talmage's comment was,
"This is like saying, 'If you can't dam the Mississippi with a teaspoon,
use a tablespoon.'"

*There always seem to be one or two LDS apostles who think a young earth
is better than an old one, and they preach as though their salvation—and
everyone else's faith—depends on it.*

I think the evolution hassle is strange considering that the Mormon
church lays so much stress on development—even eternal progression.
You would think it would try to come to terms with evolution sooner
or later. Even the Catholic church has managed to do this quite
effectively, and its theology doesn't have anywhere near the pro-evolu-
tion possibilities of Mormon theology.

*Isn't this part of a larger problem with Mormon theology? There are not
any good theologians or philosophers among the leadership. When members
try to work seriously on a theological problem, they get slapped down.*

No wonder they say to hell with it. The Mormon church is always
vulnerable to ultra-conservatives, biblical literalists, and scientific illiter-
ates. Henry Eyring, the foremost Mormon scientist, was attacked for his

views on evolution from podiums at the LDS institute across the way from his office. That's shocking. Henry was as devout a Mormon as one could find, a person of genuine piety.

President McKay was a charismatic leader during his early years as president. He seemed to soar above these battles, didn't he?

He certainly did. I had occasion to take Walter Reuther, the great labor leader, to meet President McKay in the 1950s. We had a long and pleasant discussion with him in the president's conference room. As we left the building, Walter said to me, "I have met with major leaders all over the world, including kings and presidents; but I have never in my life met a person who made such an impression on me as this man has."

I understand that you have one great regret in relation to President McKay?

Back in the sixties Pope John XXIII issued the famous document *Pacem in terris* that received attention all over the world. I was invited to participate in an affair relating to it at the United Nations in New York. This gave me the idea that it would be a wonderful thing if President McKay were to make an extended statement on personal and social values that could also be widely disseminated and discussed. I met with his sons, Lawrence, Llewellyn, and Edward, and suggested that they take this proposal to their father. Word came back that he wanted to go ahead with it and would like me to write the document. It had never occurred to me that I would become involved in this way, but I agreed to do it. Unfortunately, I was so involved in work with the university and the federal government at that time that I simply couldn't find time for the writing. I should have put other things aside and gone ahead with it. I'll always regret this.

Indeed, you missed an opportunity that might have benefitted the church for years! President McKay was a remarkable speaker, as I recall, who spoke to the essential values of Christianity and did so with style.

He had uncommon talent for communicating with individuals or congregations. I know a good story that Alexander Schreiner told me that will amuse you, Jack. In 1948 or 1949, when the Tabernacle organ was being reconstructed, Schreiner wanted to develop a first-rate antiphonal organ in the back of the Tabernacle. There's an organ there, but it's in the basement and its sound is muffled. Alex wanted to bring it up into the east end of the balcony and enlarge it to match the style of the case of the main organ. President McKay, then a counselor to President George Albert Smith, presided over church music. When Schreiner talked to him about the antiphonal organ idea, President McKay said, "I don't want an organ in the balcony, interrupting the sweep and flow of faces in that great assemblage. When I speak at conference, I want nothing breaking my view of the people." Alex said, "President McKay, the trouble is you just don't want to face the music."

I think that story also illustrates the intimate relationship with the audience that existed before the introduction of television and those awful teleprompters.

There was a spontaneity, an aliveness. You weren't sure what was going to happen next. You know J. Golden Kimball used to swear in his sermons, an occasional "hell" or "damn"—just ordinary swear words—and the people loved it. When it was announced that he was going to be the speaker, you could hear the audience shuffling their feet, sitting up a little straighter, getting on the edge of their seats.

Well, at one conference in 1933, B. H. Roberts, who was suffering from diabetes, gave a farewell address, a final conference sermon. It was very moving. People were weeping. Then J. Golden Kimball, Roberts's colleague in the presidency of the Seventy, stood up next—you know that high-pitched monotone he talked in—and said, "I should worry about B. H. When he dies, I'll get his job." This gave B. H. and everyone else a good laugh. President Grant stood up, had the KSL radio microphone cut off, and dressed Kimball down, right from the stand. It was so humiliating for Kimball that he actually became ill. The first speech he gave after he recovered was in the University Ward. I was present and his first words were, "Well, I had it coming. I might have known that if I stuck my head in that lion's mouth and twisted his tail, he'd bite me."

Didn't President Grant also serve notice on J. Golden that from then on he would have to write his speeches in advance?

Yes, and at the next conference session I was sitting in the balcony near the front on the south side, because I didn't want to miss anything. When J. Golden stood up to speak, he took a folded manuscript out of his pocket and spread out the pages. The microphone carried the rattling sound all over the Tabernacle—and this really meant something in those days when no one wrote out his sermon. They wouldn't think of it, of course, because it would be a sign that they weren't inspired. Well, J. Golden started: "The president and some of the other Brethren thought it would be a good idea if I would write my sermon out and submit it to them before I delivered it. So I'm going to have to read this sermon today." There was an air of expectancy, and everyone was trying to keep a straight face as J. Golden began to read aloud. He started having trouble right away—stumbling over the words and fumbling with the pages.

Finally he turned around to President Grant, who was sitting just behind him, and said, "Hell, Heber, I can't read this damn thing."

A truly irrepressible spirit! What did President Grant do?

He laughed as hard as anybody. I was sitting close enough to see him. His attempt to censor J. Golden Kimball's sermons ended with that one effort. I know there are a lot of apocryphal J. Golden Kimball stories around, but this one is true. Let me tell you just one more. A very tall and thin man, he spoke at Obert Tanner's Sunday school class in the University Ward, telling about a time in the Southern States Mission when he had only one dime. "I was saving this dime to buy stamps to write to my dear old mother, but if I did that, then I'd have to fast. I was never built for fasting, and I never fasted either if I had a dime for a cup of coffee." He was a remarkable combination of humor and wisdom.

Well, Sterling, you've occasionally uttered heretical statements, and this brings to mind the move to excommunicate you. What started it?

When I came here in 1948, Heber C. Snell was publishing *Ancient Israel: Its Story and Meaning*. The church Commissioner of Education had commissioned him to do it as a textbook for the institutes and BYU. Snell had asked me to read the manuscript and make recommendations, which I did. I regarded it as a first-rate book. Snell was a fine scholar with a doctorate from the Divinity School of the University of Chicago, and he had worked for the church all his life. He was mildly heretical in his views but genuinely pious, deeply religious, very devoted to the church. This is an important part of the picture.

Well, before the manuscript was published, Franklin West, the Commissioner of Education, took it before the church education board, of which Joseph Fielding Smith was the executive officer. Apostle Smith didn't like it and made a motion, which passed, to reject the book. The church would not publish it and it could not be used in any classroom, although it could be used as a reference work in church libraries. I got this from Dr. West himself.

Snell was devastated, of course. He had to have it published privately, but it sold very well. Later, I proposed to the University of Utah Press that they take it on, and they published a second edition.

What was your involvement in the Snell case?

Dr. West was very unhappy and greatly disappointed by this decision. Snell was what I would call the last of the Mormon liberals.

What do you mean by that?

I mean a Mormon in the liberal tradition—one who banks on the potential of human reason and believes that people and institutions can and will act reasonably. So, you see, Snell wanted to get together with Joseph Fielding Smith and resolve the matter. He said in his slow drawl, "Now Brother Joseph is a reasonable man; and if I can just get together with him so we can go over some of these things, he'll see what I'm driving at. He won't have this negative attitude toward my work." Well, more than once I said, "Look, Heber, he is *not* a reasonable man, and there's no sense in your getting together with him because the two of you simply don't live intellectually in the same world."

That's exactly what we ran into when my wife Linda and I made an appointment to talk with apostles Dallin Oaks and Neal Maxwell about Linda and Val Avery's biography of Emma Smith, Mormon Enigma. *We assumed that we could reason together and dispatch our disagreements . . .*

. . . and then found out that you couldn't.

That's right. They listened respectfully, but they did not budge. They couldn't. The church leadership had already made up its mind about sanctioning the book and proscribing the authors. That was that. Principles of due process simply didn't apply, as they saw it.

That's what I mean. In Heber Snell's case, he wrote to Apostle Smith proposing the kind of debate that they had in the early days of the church. He said, "It seems to me that it might be a good thing if you and I were to enter into that kind of discussion. If you were to state your objections to what I have written, then I could reply to you, and the correspondence could be published." Well, that was naive of Snell, I think. Joseph Fielding Smith wrote back and said he would have to have the Brethren's permission to engage in an epistolary give and take, and he certainly had no authority to get anything like this published.

A little later he wrote to Snell that the Brethren—I don't know who—had advised him that no good would come of this, but he would be happy to meet with Snell in person to discuss these matters. Joseph Fielding then wrote to Snell and said, "I trust that you will not object if I have a witness present, Apostle Harold B. Lee." Snell wrote back, "By all means, and I trust that you won't mind my having a witness as well, Sterling McMurrin."

So this is where you came in?

Joseph Fielding wrote back and said, "I think you should have a witness and I propose Sterling McMurrin." By this time, 1952, Snell had published the book privately.

We met in Joseph Fielding Smith's office, and Snell's wife, Phoebe, was also present. Apostle Smith sat behind his desk, I sat directly opposite him, Snell was at one end of the desk, and Harold B. Lee was at the other. Now Joseph Fielding didn't have the slightest inclination to take Snell seriously on anything he had to say, although he was very polite.

At one point he said, "Now, Dr. Snell, we know that your book is a good book in the eyes of the scholars of the world, a great book, but what you don't seem to understand is that we care not one whit for the opinions of the scholars of the world." It devastated Snell, who couldn't believe what he had heard.

One of the things Joseph Fielding objected to was that Snell described the concept of God as developing over the course of the Old Testament. He wanted Snell to know that God didn't develop. He couldn't get the point that Snell was dealing not with God but with the concept of God held by the Hebrew people. He just kept harping on the fact that God is absolute. No change, no development. Snell said, "Well, Brother Smith, in some of your writings you've made it clear that God was once like we are and had to learn things and go through the processes of moral and intellectual development. So how can you say God is an absolute without the slightest change?" And Joseph Fielding said, "Well, that's the point. He wasn't absolute until he became God. From that point on, he was absolute." Well, you can't beat an argument like that, you know. When I asked Apostle Smith just what it was that he objected to in Snell's book, he replied that "He never once mentions the Book of Mormon."

That's asking a lot from a book about the Old Testament! Well, I take it the discussion ended with pleasantries that masked underlying disagreements?

Disillusionment, too. It was a terribly destructive experience for Snell, who had worked faithfully in the church, obtained all of the learning he possibly could in the interest of the church, and was a scholar of genuine humility and piety. Snell was about seventy but in good health. Phoebe was very upset, too, but the two of us had to support Snell between us and walk him over to the Hotel Utah to get some food into him. He was simply speechless. It wasn't just that they were rejecting his book; he had believed all along that there was a kind of fundamental rationality in the church leadership, and here he'd finally discovered that there was nothing of the sort.

Well, as we were going into the Hotel Utah, we encountered Charlie Redd and John C. Swenson, close friends, just up from Provo for the day. Swenson said, "Heber, you don't look so good." Heber *didn't* look very well either, and he tried to say something and couldn't. I explained, "We've just come from a long session with Joseph Fielding

Smith." Swenson understood the whole thing at once and said, "Now, Heber, you've been in this church a long time—as long as I have—and you ought to know better than to get into a poker game with Brother Joseph when he holds all the aces."

That captures the situation perfectly. But how did this lead to your problems with the church, Sterling? Was it your participation in the meeting?

Yes and no. When we were leaving the meeting, Apostle Lee said to me, "President Smith and I would like very much to meet with you in the future, if you're willing to meet with us." I said, "I'll be very happy to."

A few weeks afterward, Apostle Lee sent me a letter reminding me that I'd agreed to meet with him and Apostle Smith, and he suggested a time. But something came up and the matter was delayed for several months. Then Apostle Lee wrote again—

Why did you two write each other when you had phones on your desks and were only two miles apart?

Just to put it on the record, I suppose. He said, "We're interested in discussing a number of things with you, including the meetings being held at the University of Utah for the purpose of criticizing us."

He meant the Swearing Elders?

Yes. So we arranged another session in Joseph Fielding's office. This occurred during the summer of 1952 and our session probably lasted three hours. In the course of the discussion, referring to the Swearing Elders' sessions, Apostle Lee said, "I'm interested in knowing what criticisms you have of President Smith," and Apostle Smith added, "And I'm interested in knowing what criticisms you have of Apostle Lee." I was a little brutal in my reply, but I had to be honest. I said, "To be frank, Elder Lee, I don't remember your name ever being mentioned." Then I said, "Now President Smith"—he was president of the Quorum of the Twelve—"you're the leading theologian of the church and the Church Historian, and you speak and write a great deal. You know very well that when people get together to discuss Mormonism, you're going to be mentioned frequently and criticized a great deal. I'll be happy to give you examples, but first let me say that these same people who criticize you have a great admiration for your moral and intellectual courage and your independence of mind. You say what you think, and you don't care what anyone else thinks when you say it."

What was his response?

He smiled and said, "Thank you. I appreciate that." So I continued, "Just as an example, I attended a recent commencement convocation at the University of Utah institute where you were the speaker, and you were there, too, Apostle Lee." Joseph Fielding interrupted and asked, "Were you there? I didn't see you." I said, "Yes, I was there. I came especially because you were the speaker. You discussed the Negroes and you said that in your opinion—" and he cut me off right there, interrupted me. He had said at the institute, "In my opinion, the Negroes are getting just what they deserve." But now he went on to say: "As far as we're concerned, Negroes are entitled to full civil rights, employment benefits, and educational opportunities."

He skirted the priesthood issue—the denial of priesthood ordination and temple privileges to African American Mormons?

Apostle Smith called critics who raised such questions, or met with the Swearing Elders, "the educated people of the church" and Harold B. Lee called them the "intellectuals of the church." Both of these terms grated on me, but I must say that Joseph Fielding was more open and generous than you might expect. For instance, I said, "I'd like to know for sure what you're getting at. Do you mean that you think we shouldn't be meeting together to discuss issues in Mormonism?" He said, "Oh, no, we wouldn't for a moment suggest that you discontinue your meetings. You educated men of the church have just as much right to get together and discuss these things as any of the rest of us."

Then Harold B. Lee broke in, "But Sterling—" he was my second cousin and always addressed me by name—"you know what the church teaches. Wouldn't it be possible at the end of every session for you to summarize the position of the church and simply remind everyone what the beliefs of the church are?"

In other words, keep them on the strait and narrow?

That's it exactly. I said, "That would be an utter impossibility. In the first place these people all know what the position of the church is. They don't have to be told. Furthermore, most of them are BYU professors and half of them are old enough to be my father. It would be ludicrous for me to do such a thing." They didn't press me any further. I gave them a rather comprehensive picture of our Swearing Elders sessions, the speakers, subjects, etc., without mentioning the names of those who attended, and at no time did they ask me to identify anyone. But as we parted, they said, "We'd like to carry on further discussion with respect to your own personal beliefs, if you're willing." I said that I'd be very happy to meet again.

You did meet with them, too, and talked about your personal religious beliefs?

Yes, we met again in the summer of 1952. I just laid my heresies out from start to finish. They didn't have to ask me many questions, because I said, "Well, we might as well start at the beginning with Adam and Eve. I don't believe they existed. I don't believe there was such a place as the Garden of Eden. I think the whole story is a cultural myth. I don't believe in the fall of man and man's estrangement from God." They just sat there, obviously shocked, and waited to see what would come next. So I went on until I got to the divinity of Christ. I didn't believe in that either, which must have been a major shock to them. But I pointed out, if you don't believe in the Fall, then there's no point in believing in a savior. But I did say, "I don't want you to think that I regard Jesus as just a great teacher. He was a man of enormous spiritual insight." I laid it out so there was no mistaking what I meant.

Then Joseph Fielding asked, "Well, what about Joseph Smith? What about the first vision?" Well, I was coming to that, you know. I said, "President Smith, my views are essentially naturalistic." He wanted to know what I meant by naturalistic. I said, "Well, some people believe in evil spirits." "I do," he said. "I know you do," I said, "and that's why I'm taking this example. Let's assume that someone comes into your outer office and is behaving very strangely. You might go out there and say, 'He's possessed of an evil spirit. Let's lay our hands on him and cast out the devil.' But I might look at the same man and say, 'He's out of his mind. Let's get him to a hospital.' The first explanation is supernaturalistic and the second one is naturalistic."

Let's go back to the origins of the Mormon church. Joseph Smith's first vision was the anchor for the whole movement. You were treading on the most sacred ground.

Yes, and I said, "President Smith, we have to face the fact that your great-grandmother, Lucy Mack Smith, made it pretty clear in her book about Joseph Smith that everything Joseph saw in the first vision was already believed by members of the family—and I'm not referring to the uncensored original version but to the censored version of the book that the church itself published in 1902, the one that has your father's picture in the front. It has a foreword assuring members of the church that the old version was taken out of print and that this version was correct. Most of the members of the censoring committee were your relatives—at least, most of their names were Smith. Your father's statement was that the book had been examined by members of the family and was true."

That was about as close to home as you could get, Sterling. Did mercy begin to cross your mind?

Well, not yet. I told them, as well, that I didn't believe Joseph Smith had actually seen God. I raised a question with them about the matter of seeing with your spiritual eyes, rather than your physical eyes, but they didn't want to discuss it.

Well, we went from there to the Book of Mormon, and I assured them that I didn't believe it was authentic. They didn't ask any specific questions, just went on to other things, asking me to tell them more about what I believed and didn't believe.

How did you feel about this examination? People react to such experiences in very different ways.

It was a very profound experience for me. It enabled me to explain my heresies to two men who were future presidents of the church and let them know exactly what I thought about matters basic to our faith. Afterward I felt as if a great burden had been lifted from me and I had become a genuinely free person.

Had you ever felt that way before?

Yes, on two occasions—when I left church employment and when I passed my doctoral examinations. But the third and most memorable time was when I walked out of Joseph Fielding Smith's office that afternoon.

Joseph Fielding was most gracious to you when you left his office, which must have added to your sense of satisfaction.

Both of them were gracious. Joseph Fielding said, "Dr. McMurrin (he always addressed me as Doctor), in spite of your telling us of your disbeliefs and heresies, we want you to know that you have the Holy Ghost." Those were his exact words.

That's a remarkable story and, I must say, a high tribute to you both.

I thought that was very generous of him. You'd hardly expect that today. I liked him, you know. Always liked Joseph Fielding Smith, as much as I differed with him. Then he went on, "You know things about the views and opinions of the educated people of the church that we need to know." He pointed to his door and said, "My door is always open to you, if you would be willing to come in and talk to us about these things, because we need to know more about them."

This image is not the one most people have of Joseph Fielding Smith.

Not at all. Well, as I left, Harold B. Lee walked out to the top of the stairs with me. He was very pleasant, but he said in rather ominous tones, "Sterling, you could do great things for this church, or you can be a very, very dangerous man in the church." "Well," I said, "I have no desire to do the church any harm. I don't want to be a danger to anyone." They had asked if I would meet with them again, and I told them that I would. But we didn't get together again.

Never did?

Oh, I had many conversations with each of them after that, but never as a threesome. An amusing incident occurred a night or two after Joseph Fielding was named president of the church. We received a phone call from his wife, Jesse Evans Smith, who said: "Sterling, Joseph wanted me to tell you that he doesn't want you and Natalie to take us off your list." I said, "You tell President Smith that as long as you keep us on your list, we'll keep you on ours." This was one of many pleasant encounters we had with both of them in those years.

Now, would you say more about your emotional reaction to your unburdening with apostles Smith and Lee. Why did you feel so free?

I had similar feelings when I heard that President Spencer Kimball had reversed the church's prohibition on granting the priesthood to African Americans. That action lifted a moral burden off the soul of the entire church. I think you've probably had the same feelings, Jack. Haven't there been occasions when you have felt a great weight lifted from you and you suddenly became free?

Whenever I've taken time to write and publish my beliefs about the essential things in life, I have felt liberated. It started with a paper I read at the Sunstone Symposium in 1979, published in Dialogue *in 1980, called "Personal Conscience and Priesthood Authority." That process of sorting out my philosophical and religious bearings by writing about them is something I have needed to do periodically as my life has continued to unfold.*

I can understand that. There's something liberating about letting it be known, not just to yourself but in a sense publicly, what you think. When I left the session with apostles Smith and Lee, I actually felt a kind of physical buoyancy. It was a very strange feeling. It shows the close involvement of the mind with the body. I thought, "Here I am, really as free as the birds." I wasn't about to fly away, but it had a very profound effect on me. Having told them very honestly what I did not believe, I felt that there was no need to be concerned about this matter any longer. God already knew the level of my heresy. I had dealt with that matter earlier.

In that conversation with apostles Lee and Smith, you also said a great deal about what you do believe and hold sacred, including personal integrity, freedom, and respect for the truth as you see it. That had as much—or more—to do with your exhilaration as did the casting off of your disbeliefs.

Well, what happened next?

After returning from my Ford Fellowship in New York in the summer of 1953, I began to hear from a variety of sources that I was in trouble with the church. No one in any position of authority ever called my attention to it, but people who were friendly toward me told me that they had word that I was going to be excommunicated. These were people in my Salt Lake City ward and they encouraged me to look into it. So in the spring of 1954 I made an appointment with my bishop. He was in the employ of the church at a rather high level, something to do with the welfare system. He didn't like me and didn't take to any of my stuff, but he hadn't previously made an issue of it. I initiated the session with him, but he began in a very formal way: "It is my ecclesiastical duty to investigate you to determine whether you should be brought to trial for excommunication." Later he said, "We haven't been able to find anyone who is willing to testify against you so I'm wondering if you could give us the names of some people we could use as witnesses." Now, Jack, I'm telling you the truth.

I have never heard of anything like that, anywhere!

That didn't seem to be the proper way to go about it, but I said, "Well, I've taught hundreds of students at the university in philosophy courses that have some bearing on religion, and I've taught Sunday school in this ward. Surely you can find someone!" He shook his head and said, "No, we haven't been able to get anyone who will testify against you." "Well," I said, "I'll give you the names of two members who are thoroughly acquainted with the depth of my heresies. President Joseph Fielding Smith and Apostle Harold B. Lee." He said, "Now, you know we can't use them." "Well," I said, "I think they'd be good witnesses and they are the best I can think of."

He could hardly argue with that.

It was clear to me from what others had told me that this movement originated with President Smith. I told the bishop that President Smith was engineering the whole thing, but he denied it. How could he have admitted it? He was clearly operating under instructions—instructions which he thoroughly enjoyed, I might say.

Sterling, what was your involvement in the church at that time? Were you still teaching Sunday school?

No, a couple of years earlier, before this man became bishop, I had taught the adult Sunday school class. He attended, but I could tell he didn't like my stuff. I taught it for six weeks, and somebody complained, so the stake president visited my class along with one of his counselors,

Gordon B. Hinckley, who is now president of the church. Hinckley was very pleasant. It was a large class and I didn't know the stake president, so at the end of the class, I stepped over to shake hands with him. He said, "Now, Brother McMurrin, we don't want you here confusing these people like this." I said, "Well, I certainly don't want to confuse these people, so I won't be here anymore." He said, "Now, I'm not asking you to quit." I said, "I know you're not, but I'm quitting. You just get yourself someone else to teach this class." That was the end of that. It created quite a hassle in the ward, I might say, and the bishop, a very decent person, was entirely on my side.

Do you have any idea what the stake president objected to?

No idea whatsoever. It could have been almost anything, but no one ever told me what my crimes against the church were.

Concern began to spread among your friends by this time?

Prior to my session with the new bishop, I hadn't mentioned this development to anyone except perhaps George Boyd, who lived in the same ward. Obert Tanner and I shared an office at the university and had been close friends for years, so I knew he'd want to know what was going on. I didn't make much of it, but Obert was very concerned; and as nearly as I can piece it together, Obert told his great and good friend Apostle Adam S. Bennion, and Bennion told David O. McKay, who had been president of the church since 1951. To make a very long story short, Obert told me that President McKay wanted me to write a statement about what was going on, which I did.

Meanwhile you met with the bishop a second time?

He was still trying to find something on me. He said I wasn't paying a full tithe. "Well," I said, "are you going to put everybody on trial who's not paying a full tithe?" That was the end of that, but he asked, "Sterling, this matter has gotten all the way up to the general authorities. Have you been talking to them?" I said, "No, I haven't." And I hadn't—not since that 1952 meeting. He concluded this conversation with, "Now, you know, I haven't guaranteed that we're going to put you on trial. All I said is that I'm supposed to investigate you to see if you should be put on trial." That was the last session with the bishop.

So it never escalated to the point of a church court? The stories, you know, have entered the realm of folklore!

I've heard and read accounts that a date was actually set for the trial and then got called off, but I've never been aware that any date was set. There was never any trial, although it was perfectly obvious that there was going to be one. I have heard many reports over the years that I had been excommunicated. I still hear such rumors from time to time!

Well, sooner or later, it may be true. But there is more to the story, isn't there? Why was the trial called off?

I was at home for lunch just a few days later when I got a call from William Kent, a member of our philosophy faculty. He was rather excited and said, "Someone just called here for you—said he's David O. McKay. It may just be a practical joke, but I gave him your home phone number." Well, within a couple of minutes I received a call from President McKay himself, who said, "I want to come and see you, and I'd like to come now." "Well, President McKay," I said, "I can't let you do that. I just read in the newspaper that you're home sick." He said, "I am home, but I'm not that sick." "I'll come to your home," I said. "I'll come and see you. Shall I come to your home or to your office?" He said, "No, you're not to come to see me. I am coming to see you." He was adamant. President McKay was over eighty years old then, but he still did his own driving. So I said, "How would it be if we met on neutral ground?" He laughed.

How well did you know him personally at this time?

He had performed the wedding ceremony for Natalie and me, and we'd stayed fairly close across the sixteen years since then. I proposed the old Union Building, now Gardner Hall, which was not far from his home on South Temple. I beat him there by about five minutes and arranged to get the Auerbach Room unlocked. President McKay showed up promptly, and we spent much of the afternoon together. He did most of the talking.

How did he open the conversation?

He took out of his pocket that statement I'd written, which Obert had given to Adam S. Bennion. In the last sentence or two I said something like this, "I realize that a person of my beliefs does not have any claim on membership in the church." President McKay said, "Now, just what is it that a person is not permitted to believe without being asked to leave this church? Just what is it? Is it evolution? I hope not, because I believe in evolution."

Did he have a twinkle in his eye as he said these things?

Perhaps, but he was angry. There's no question about that. I've never felt such warm support. He said, "They can't do this to you. They can't *do* this to you!" I kind of smiled and said, "Well now, President McKay, you know more than I about what they can do, but it looks like this is what they are going to do." He said, "They *cannot* do this to you!" There was a pause, then he said, "All I will say is that if they put you on trial

for excommunication, I will be there as the first witness in your behalf."
I said, "Well, now, I can't imagine anyone having a better witness for
such an occasion."

Did President Smith's name come up?

No, not explicitly, but there was no question that we both knew
who was involved.

What did you discuss?

The evolution issue, for one thing. And whenever he said "they,"
he pointed up. President Smith's office was above and opposite his in
the Church Administration Building. It was obvious that he knew about
the meetings with President Smith and Apostle Lee, for he said, "I'm
going to give you a piece of advice. If those men—and he pointed up
again toward Joseph Smith's office—try to get you in a corner again and
badger you with questions about your religious beliefs and your faith,
you just refuse to answer them because what you believe is none of their
business."

Finally, he said, "I have only one piece of advice to give you. It's
the advice that an uncle of mine gave me at the railroad station when I
left for my mission to Scotland. He shook my hand and said, 'David,
you just think and believe as you please.' Now that's my advice to you,
Sterling. You just think and believe as you please." Well, he was so
positive that I was beginning to feel a bit guilty. I wasn't half as clean as
he seemed to be making me out to be.

*You'd gone from sinner to saint mighty fast here. It's mainly in the eye of
the beholder.*

Very fast, very, very fast. He wanted to know about the situation
out in my ward. "Kind of rigid people, are they?" he asked, meaning
the bishop and the stake president. I guess he'd heard this from his son
Edward, who lived in my ward. But I said, "Now, President McKay, I
think I should tell you that I've probably contributed to the problem.
In Sunday school class a year ago, the teacher kept talking about our
belief that the Negroes are under a divine curse and I finally raised my
hand and said, 'Now I want you to know that I don't believe Negroes
are under any kind of curse. I'm not interested in arguing about it, but
I want it known that I don't believe that.' I think that irritated some of
the locals."

*Did President McKay's reply lead to a discussion of the situation of blacks
in the church?*

Yes. He said, "I'm glad you said that because I don't believe it either.
As far as I am concerned, it is not now nor has it ever been a doctrine

of this church that the Negroes are under a divine curse. We believe that we have scriptural precedent"—by which he meant a passage in the Pearl of Great Price—"for withholding the priesthood from Negroes, but they will eventually receive it. This is not a matter of doctrine. It is simply a practice and it is going to change." Well, I thought that was a historic statement.

It was, indeed. I wish he had broadcast it!

I said, "Well, now, President McKay, you're well aware that large numbers of people in the church believe that there is an established doctrine that the Negroes are cursed by God. Wouldn't it be possible for you to make an official statement on this matter so the people will understand? This is something that needs to be done."

I'm on the edge of my chair, Sterling, what did he say?

I was on the edge *my* chair because I was in hopes, you know, for such a statement. He was silent for what seemed to be a long moment, then he said, "All I will say is that there is no such doctrine in this church. It is simply a practice, and that's all there is to it."

What constraint do you suppose caused him to pause? And why do you think he failed to change the practice?

Well, this is only speculation, but I think it was resistance from other general authorities. Hugh B. Brown was a brand new general authority—an assistant to the Quorum of the Twelve—in the fall of 1953. He became an apostle in the spring of 1958 and wrote to me at that time expressing unusually liberal views for a high church official. He wanted to extend the priesthood to blacks. But his position soon precipitated serious opposition from other apostles.

President Brown was very frank in stating his views, too.

Yes, and he strongly favored the priesthood for blacks. But he let me know in no uncertain terms that there was strong opposition within the quorum. If there hadn't been, I'm confident that because of his genuine liberality and compassion, President McKay would have taken steps to give blacks full fellowship in the church while he was president.

So that remarkable pause, there in the Auerbach Room in the spring of '54, may have been prompted by President McKay pondering whether he could make a statement on the "divine curse" issue—and get the quorum to endorse it.

Speculation, of course, but maybe so. Now later on, in the 1960s, I became involved as a liaison between the church and the NAACP, when the NAACP was putting pressure on the church for its failure to actively pursue the cause of civil rights. It planned a large-scale demonstration against the church at the October 1964 general conference. I arranged for the NAACP leaders to meet with Nathan Eldon Tanner and Hugh B. Brown, President McKay's two counselors, and their discussion went well. At Tanner's and Brown's request, I wrote a statement which, with President McKay's approval, President Brown read in opening the Sunday morning session of general conference. It affirmed the church's support of full civil rights for blacks and everyone else.

As I recall, however, full religious fellowship for blacks wasn't part of that statement.

That's right, it dealt entirely with civil rights. Even so, as a result of President Brown's reading the statement, the NAACP called off the planned demonstration. The *Salt Lake Tribune* featured the story, as did the national news media. Later there were editorials, even in the *Deseret News*, describing President Brown's statement as church policy. Not until 1978, after President McKay and his two successors Joseph Fielding Smith and Harold B. Lee were all three dead, did President Spencer W. Kimball extend priesthood privileges to all faithful males. It was a dramatic fourteen-year episode.

With a welcome outcome. Now I want to go back to the Auerbach Room in the spring of '54. What other issues did you and President McKay talk about?

Evolution, civil rights, and priesthood for blacks were the substantive issues. We spent the rest of the time discussing the freedom of individuals to say and think as they please. President McKay believed very strongly in individual rights, while at the same time being absolutely loyal to the institutional church. I saw some conflict—or at least some potential conflict—between those two positions. I honestly think that he didn't. President McKay was a man of great and genuine love for others, a man of extraordinary compassion and love for humanity.

I think I sensed that as a young outsider investigating Mormonism at about the same time. He certainly inspired me, as did Hugh B. Brown. They are the reason I took the church seriously and eventually joined it.

President McKay functioned in a matrix of interpersonal relationships. I don't think he approached things primarily on an institutional basis. He was a great leader for the institutional church, but he didn't seem to be an organization type. Now his counselor J. Reuben Clark *was* an organization leader. I don't mean this as a criticism of him, but he thought in terms of the institution. I don't see President Clark, for instance, driving out to some dissident's house to discuss his heretical views in a friendly, positive way. Instead I see him as appraising the political and social effect on the church of a given move and deciding on that basis what action to take. I suspect that he was one source of the negative policy on the blacks, although I'm not absolutely sure. This much I am sure of: that without President McKay in leadership over a long period of time, the change of policy that came under President Kimball could not have had the immediate transforming effect which it had on the Mormon people.

And by that you mean the immediate and widespread acceptance?

Absolutely. President McKay could have achieved the same wide-spread acceptance, but I think he paved the way. Now to get back to the issue of individual freedom, he was a teacher, you know, and at one time head of the church academy in Ogden—which has become Weber State University. By personality, too, he was very much inclined to give his colleagues and other individuals complete freedom to write and say what they thought.

It seems that President Kimball, among the presidents in recent decades, was much more like McKay in spirit and style than any of the others.

What you say about President Kimball is absolutely true. I think he was more like President McKay in temperament, disposition, and personal style than either Joseph Fielding Smith or Harold B. Lee. Joseph Fielding Smith was, of course, a theologian and historian, and he concentrated on those things. I don't know very much about his administration—it wasn't very long—but Harold B. Lee told me that "In matters having to do with theology, I look to Apostle Joseph Fielding Smith; and in matters having to do with church affairs and government, I look to J. Reuben Clark."

Now back to President McKay. He said that you didn't need to explain your views to anyone. Yet when you had been so forthcoming with apostles Smith and Lee a year or two earlier, you described a great sense of freedom. How did you play that issue thereafter?

I didn't take his advice. I appreciated what he said very much, of course; but I told him, "I have never objected to questions about my religious beliefs if they're within a decent context." Sometimes you get somebody who is just being nasty, but these two apostles were very generous.

How do you look back on this brush with excommunication now?

It was just an interesting episode except for the session with President McKay. As you can see, however, that was an important experience for me. But there is an aspect of the story that I didn't know about until much later. A half dozen years after this incident, while I was still harboring the friendliest of feelings toward President Smith, a former student of mine wrote to President Smith to complain that I was a dangerous apostate. He asked President Smith why I was ever permitted to teach in the church, and why I hadn't been properly excommunicated. Well, if I'd known this man had those views, I could have given his name to my bishop when he was looking for witnesses! President Smith wrote back to him on Quorum of the Twelve letterhead and said, "Sterling McMurrin is a betrayer of the church and its teachings. No one knows this better than I. But there is nothing I can do about it. . . . Why not present your case to the First Presidency?"*

It appears that higher authority, namely President David McKay, had the situation well in hand.

He did. But I knew nothing of this correspondence until several years later when my friend George Boyd mentioned it to me. It must have been obvious from my reaction to the news that I hadn't known anything about it, so George sent me a copy of both letters. He said everybody in the LDS institutes of religion seemed to have copies of the correspondence, so I deserved copies too!

I always marvel at the efficiency of underground communications in large organizations. There are no secrets, no matter how hard a bureaucracy tries to find and seal the leaks. But what if your case had come to an excommunication trial, Sterling?

Oh, I would have attended the trial, by all means. I wouldn't want to stay away and get kicked out *in absentia*. I'd want to be in on the thing. I would want a witness there to observe what went on, but I would not want anyone to testify in my behalf, nor would I make any argument. I would simply say, "Now, look, you people running the church have the authority. If you don't want people like me in the church, you should excommunicate me. It's your decision to make." I mean that very sincerely.

But you must feel that the church should make room for people like you? Why wouldn't you argue on your own behalf?

That may seem strange, but I no longer think the church should necessarily make room for people like me. I did when I was young and

---

* A photocopy of this August 29, 1960, letter from Fred W. Morrison to President Joseph Fielding Smith is in Sterling McMurrin's personal files.

idealistic. I thought the church belonged to everyone, that it was as much the church of the unorthodox as the church of the orthodox; but I no longer think that. The church is an institution which is owned and operated by the people who pay the tithing and who do the believing; if they think dissidents like me don't belong in it, I wouldn't argue with them. I wouldn't be silent, of course, if they wanted to ask questions I'd give them honest answers.

Okay, but I also know you have a very deep, heartfelt spirituality, although you're doctrinally unorthodox. Would you not want to express that side of yourself to them as well?

Well, if it didn't come up in the course of the conversation, I might be inclined to say, "You haven't asked me whether I love the church or my fellow men or whether I believe in God." I should mention that, during my conversation with apostles Smith and Lee, I started by saying, "Now I must tell you that there are many of the teachings of the church which I do not believe." Joseph Fielding interrupted me at that point and said, "Dr. McMurrin, let me explain that in this church a person has the freedom to believe whatever he wants to as long as he accepts certain fundamentals." But I answered, "President Smith, I know what the fundamentals are, and they are the things I don't believe."

His fundamentals were not your fundamentals.

That's a good way of putting it.

Adam S. Bennion has the reputation of being a liberal apostle, and I'm assuming some kind of compatibility with President McKay or President McKay wouldn't have ordained him an apostle in 1953.

I don't know anything about that, of course; but I recall one experience with Adam S. Bennion that makes me chuckle a little. It would have been during the middle 1950s—he died in 1958—but he wanted me to come down and see him at the Church Administration Building. I can't even remember what it was all about, but at one point, he said, "I'd like to have us talk to President McKay about this." So he phoned President McKay and then told me, "President McKay would like us to come down to his office. Now we don't want to be seen, so we won't go down the main stairway."

Meaning he didn't want to be seen with you?"

That's my assumption. We went down a rear stairway and through a couple of offices. Some secretaries saw us, but we got in there without any general authorities seeing us.

What did you talk about with President McKay?
Damned if I can remember. I just remember a lot of laughter.

How active were you in church after these events?
Not very active for some time. But early in the summer of 1959
I was asked again to teach a Sunday school class. Natalie and I had
moved and we were in a different ward. The bishop was an acquaintance from college and he came by to ask me if I'd teach the adult
course. I told him that this assignment was not even a possibility. We
had a long discussion, and he was very persuasive—said his request
had all been cleared higher up. Now just who he had to clear it with,
I'm not sure. I told him that if I were to teach I wouldn't follow a
manual—that if I'd written the manual myself I would never pay any
attention to it as a teacher, and the only thing I would be interested
in teaching was the Mormon philosophy of religion. He said that was
perfectly all right.

It sounds like a softening-up exercise.
It certainly was. Within a few minutes the three members of the
Sunday school superintendency called on me. They insisted and were
very persuasive. So, finally, against my better judgment, I agreed to do
it for six weeks. After that time I would be moderating seminars and
lecturing for the Aspen Institute in Colorado. "That's fine," they said.
"We'll just get a substitute for you while you're gone, and you can pick
up where you left off when you get back."

And how did it work out?
The teaching was a very pleasant experience. It was in the chapel
and the bishop attended at times. Carl Christensen, who was head of
research at the university and was on the Sunday school general board,
attended. The bishop told me that people came from as far away as Davis
County to attend the class. So when I went to Aspen, they got a
substitute; and when I returned I called the Sunday school superintendent, an FBI man, to tell him I was back and ready to return to class. He
said, "Well, we liked the interim teacher, and we have asked him to stay,
so we won't need you to teach anymore."

As bluntly as that?
Yes, just as bluntly as that. He was a little flustered by my call and
just blurted it out. Anyway, I said, "Well, now, let's understand that I'm
not resigning. I'm being fired. Just why am I being thrown out?" You're
not going to believe this, Jack.

Try me.

"Well," he said, "this class was not doing well until you took it, and then attendance increased until it was very large. But when you left, it collapsed. We don't want that to happen again. If you take the class back, it'll build up again, and then you'll go off somewhere and it'll collapse again."

That's astonishing! Did he expect you to believe that was a reason to void your teaching?

I told him that I was well aware that somebody had told them to get rid of me, and he protested that it wasn't so, but he wasn't convincing. I just let the matter drop, but I made up my mind, firmly, never again to take on any kind of teaching position in the church. I've occasionally given talks for special occasions but under no circumstances would I take on a teaching position—and of course, no one asks me to any more.

Wasn't it in 1957 and 1958 that you gave the lectures at Ohio State, USU, the University of Utah, and BYU that were published by the University of Utah Press as **The Philosophical Foundations of the Mormon Religion?**

Yes, the presidents of these three Utah universities were involved in a cooperative venture—all of them were attending a meeting of the National Council of Christians and Jews in Salt Lake City. The question came up about what might be done to further understanding among the various religions. Ernest L. Wilkinson, then president of BYU, proposed a cooperative lecture series to be sponsored by the three Utah universities. President Olpin tossed our end of the project over to me, and I handled it for several years.

Your lecture at Ohio State was a little different?

Yes. Harold B. Lee informed me that the church had been invited to present a lecture on the Mormon religion at some special conference at Ohio State. He asked if I'd be willing to prepare and give it. He didn't lay down any ground rules—just asked me if I'd go. So I gave pretty much the same address that I had given in the Utah series.

If I understand your situation in the late 1950s, then, Apostle Lee was inviting you to represent the church at a prestigious national forum, President McKay was assuring you of your right as a church member to think and speak as you pleased, and, all the while, President Smith was trying to get you kicked out altogether! What finally happened, at least with the Utah lecture series?

Oh, it came to an end, as all good things do—although you might be interested in one detail from its last days. The lecturers went to each institution in turn; some of them were imported and some were our own people. There were some failures; but on the whole, I think it was a very successful series on world religions. Now at one of the planning meetings, I complained to the BYU representative that BYU wasn't giving us their best people. I named two or three very strong BYU people in religion who I thought ought to be included in the lecture program. He said, "The people you want simply could not be approved for this series. Not only must the president of the university approve the lecturer, it has to be approved by the board of trustees. The people you want are simply not approvable."

Not quite what you were used to dealing with in a university.

I should say not. As much as I was aware that BYU controlled its faculty and managed intellectual issues, I was still shocked. The president of the University of Utah used to come to most of these lectures and enjoy them, but he wouldn't have dreamed of suggesting who should be on the program. We had full autonomy. I arranged for people from outside the university who had expertise on Judaism, Catholicism, and Protestantism, and so forth, not only for this series but for other occasions. We also sponsored a TV program on Sundays over a commercial station on the great issues in religion, which I moderated.

One more question, Sterling, about these events during the 1950s. Was it public knowledge that you had these differences with President Smith and Elder Lee?

I mentioned the meetings only to a very few of my most intimate friends, but word always gets around. For instance, just at the time that the rumors about excommunication were rolling around, Homer Durham, then vice-president, and A. Ray Olpin, asked me to become dean of University College. (We later renamed this the College of Letters and Science. It included the colleges of science, behavioral science, humanities, and three ROTC units—about half the university.) President Olpin was a very active Mormon. After we'd had our conversation and I'd agreed to take the position, he said, "By the way, is it true that you have been excommunicated?" He'd heard this in a barber shop downtown. "The last time I got my hair cut there," he said, "someone said they were making you an apostle. Then someone else said, 'No, he's been excommunicated.'"

You wouldn't have relished either fate, Sterling. What about the attitude of ward members?

We were living in a ward of young married people at the time, and I'll have to admit that some of them looked askance at me. Young people are far more bigoted than elderly people, you know.

I have certainly found this to be true in my neighborhood ward.

Yes, my children, even up into high school, felt various kinds of discrimination from the other kids and some of their teachers; but I've had the finest of relationships with people in our present neighborhood. Most of them are aware that I'm a thoroughgoing heretic, but it doesn't seem to bother them. I go to church occasionally, but I never volunteer to say anything in class or make comments, other than pleasantries. Occasionally a teacher will call on me to say something, but I just shake my head and say, "Well, I don't know anything about it," and let it go at that. Natalie and I enjoy the people in our ward and stake, including the officials.

For years you were the most frequently quoted Latter-day Saint by the national media when issues like the ordination of blacks came up, but I've never noticed any malice toward the church, even when you've been most critical. I'm sure that has something to do with the good relationships you've enjoyed.

Well, I *don't* feel any malice toward the church or anyone in it. I do love the church. People sometimes find that hard to believe. Here I am, a person who doesn't fully approve of much that the church does, and strongly disapproves of some things, and who thinks that a fair number of its fundamental teachings are sheer nonsense. It's hard for them to believe that I can have good will toward the church, but I do. My ancestors chose the church. I was born in it and reared in it. It's just part of my make-up. But of course, I don't think of churches as being true or false. Churches are good or bad or better or worse, but not true or false. Being a Mormon is simply being part of a family, and you know even the stray sheep in the family can love the family and even defend it.

And is often loved by the family.

The church is a culture, a community, and for me it is my territory. Its people are my crowd. These mountains and our history—the whole works—I just feel a part of it all.

You are a part of it all. What changes in members' attitudes toward authority have you noticed over the last thirty years?

From the standpoint of intellectual openness and the freedom of the people to be candid and honest, there's no question that things are getting worse.

Frankly, I think the intellectual life of the church—in terms of openness and free discussion—has been going downhill since the deaths of B. H. Roberts and James E. Talmage in 1933. On the other hand, the intellectual achievements of Mormons and faithful members of the church have been going uphill. That's part of the problem. There are now many well-trained and really competent young scholars, mainly historians, who are coming up with things that seem to frighten the general authorities. That may be one of the reasons why this authoritarian censorship is developing. I know you've given this considerable thought, Jack. Your wife Linda is one of those historians, one of the best. What are your views about these trends, Jack?

When I came into the church in 1962, David O. McKay was president and Hugh B. Brown was making clarion calls for intellectual honesty and free inquiry. I'm aware now, but I wasn't then, that this was hardly representative of Mormon culture! I see two factors contributing to the current anti-intellectualism: First, the sheer size of the church means that the hierarchy is more removed from members. General authorities don't deal with ordinary people; they deal with their chosen subordinates (other general authorities and stake presidents) and with career bureaucrats who manage the massive system. Second, again because of the size, the general authorities are overwhelmed with official duties. They have no time to read and think. They are also cut off from real people, real give-and-take, fresh ideas. Power and deference are crippling. The more power, the greater the danger . . . and the loss. The person with power is the last one to see this.

You are quite right, Jack. The point you make about the size of the church is very important, because one consequence of growth has been the enormous proliferation of the bureaucracy. When I was in seminary and institute work, one man oversaw each branch. Each one had a secretary, there was an accountant or bookkeeper, and one person, maybe two, who did some research and arranged for publications. Well, about 1982, the Commissioner of Education, Hal Eyring, now an apostle, wanted to get together with me. There he was in that tall office building—in which the Church Education System occupied two whole floors!

One consequence of the small size when you were involved would have been the quality of personal contacts you had.

There's no question about it. It was very personal. The Commissioner of Education and the Director of Seminaries and their wives became our very close friends. Dr. Franklin West and I spent many hours talking about church affairs. Lynn Bennion and I spent a great deal of time together, too. He knew I wasn't orthodox, but he seemed to know *me* in a way that transcended my beliefs. What they knew *about* me would get a person thrown out today.

*I'm concerned about the attempts of the church leaders to maintain the
mythology of the early church period; but I wonder if all this emphasis on
orthodoxy and obedience isn't causing a reaction as dangerous as the
mythology in the first place.*

I think you're absolutely right. And it's so unnecessary. The church
can weather any danger now. It's a going concern. It rolls on and on,
and nothing is going to slow it down. It can be seriously injured only
by its own authoritarianism. Things are going to seriously injure many
individuals in it, but the institution will roll on. I have to tell you
something our mutual friend Bill Mulder told me back in the early 1950s.
He was walking from the Church Administration Building at 47 East
South Temple to the Hotel Utah when he passed one of the elder
statesmen of the church, who then worked in the Church Historian's
office. Without even glancing at him, the older man said, "Isn't it
amazing the way the money just keeps rolling in?"

Well, it *is* amazing, the solidarity of the Mormon people, their
devotion to one another and to the institution, and the sacrifices they
make for the church. It's quite remarkable and gives the church great
strength. On the other hand, countless individuals are being hurt,
morally, spiritually, and intellectually, by some of the things that are
going on to stifle their intellectual freedom.

What is your view of the received version of church history, Sterling?

I've felt for a long time that the church has made a very serious error
in tying itself to all kinds of historical claims instead of focusing its claims
on the quality of life it can engender, the happiness it can bring to people,
and the spiritual and moral strength it can build in its members. It has
always insisted that if X, Y, and Z historical events did not occur, then
the church is not true. That's a lot of nonsense. No church looks very
good under a close inspection of its own history. The Catholics don't,
the Protestants don't, and the Mormons don't. There's no need to
pretend that our history is free of unsavory episodes—Joseph Smith's
involvement in magic and all that damned nonsense—to say nothing of
polygamy. There's no point in trying to cover them up. It makes more
sense to focus the case for the church on something other than its
historical origins. But it's not an easy thing to do. We are so steeped in
historical consciousness—often historical error.

*For example, Joseph Smith's first vision is highly questionable, in part
because he told about it in very different terms as he grew older. It got
increasingly miraculous in telling and retelling.*

The Book of Mormon is entirely questionable too; there is no evidence that it is historically authentic. Yet the church has tied itself so completely to these claims. You can't argue over someone else's claim of a vision, but when you've got a book that you can pick up and carry around and read, then it is important to face the internal and external evidence for and against it. The people down at BYU who are spending their time trying to prove the authenticity of the Book of Mormon are just making fools of themselves. The church simply doesn't need to live or die on such things. The church needs to live or die on the quality of the moral life it can produce in its people, and there it looks very, very good.

My observation is that most members aren't concerned about the authenticity of our history. Their attachment to the church is to its moral life, to its community life. It's baffling to find leaders panicky over a situation that most members are simply taking in stride.

I like that word "panicky." It's almost a frenzy with some. I could name general authorities who are as sensible and decent about these things as any human being could be, but the frenzied ones are very vocal and very powerful. Linda and Val Avery's book on Emma Smith, for instance, is a brilliant biography and an honest attempt to correct some of the serious errors made by the church in reference to its own history. The kind of censorship they've met is not only disgusting; it's disgraceful for a church to not have better judgment than that.

That, of course, is a view that's not very popular downtown.

Probably not. That reminds me of an amusing story. You'd mentioned earlier that a number of journalists and authors have asked for my views on the Mormon religion. Two different writers looked me up because the church public relations staff had told them to avoid me, not to talk to me. Neither of the two had ever heard of me before; but after getting this advice, they thought they'd better get acquainted with me!

And did they learn what they needed?

Well, in one case, Desmond Clayton, a German television producer, was planning to do a documentary on the church to be shown in Germany and France. This was in 1975. He had received so little historical and doctrinal information from the church public relations people that he and I were both shocked. So I drove him over the route of the pioneers entering the valley and even gave him some technical advice. It was a magnificent day on Big Mountain, so I said, "Here's the way to begin your film: some shots from the mountains here with the Tabernacle Choir singing 'High on a Mountain Top' in the background." And that's what he did! Before he brought his crew back to do the filming—he called me and said his superiors wanted him to do a program on me as well. He did, too: thirty minutes on the church and forty minutes on me!

Amusing. And how did it turn out?

I thought the one on me was very well done. I haven't seen the one on the church. It was actually a moving picture film with the sound track on a separate film, in the German style. I thought the reason he wanted the interview with me was because I had been U.S. Commissioner of Education. It turned out that he was very surprised to discover that about me. It was all news to him. Anyway, we shot some of the film on the patio of our home, some at the university dealing with problems in education, and then another section on Temple Square dealing with the church. I made the church look as good as I could.

The only criticism I've ever heard of my book *The Theological Foundations of the Mormon Religion* is that I make the Mormon religion look better than it is. Sidney Angleman, a sophisticated Mormon-watcher and for years director of general education at the University of Utah, made that observation. I replied, "I'm aware of that. I attempted to make it look as good as I possibly could because the church's leaders make it look so bad. The church doesn't do justice to its own theology."

What was the reaction within the church to this book?

I think the Mormon educators and most general authorities didn't care much for it. I left out polygamy, Mormon polytheism, and the nonsense that human beings could become gods. I guess that's why the church didn't like my commentary.

In 1978, when you and Natalie were in Moscow, you received a telephone call from the head of the Moscow Bureau of Time *magazine. The revelation on blacks and priesthood had just been announced?*

Yes, the *Time* editor had told him to look me up and get a statement. When he came in to our hotel room, he put his finger to his lips and pointed to several places in the room, indicating that it was bugged; so we confined our conversation to the Mormon church. He showed me the telex with his instructions on it. They had described me as the leader of Mormon intellectual dissidents and listed a full page of questions which he was to ask me. I answered them all for him.

What's your general impression of reporters and writers who want to do stories, either on the church or on your views?

Very mixed. Some had researched the subject extensively and were responsible people, so they produced very competent stuff; but others have just been looking for sensational elements. I've tried to call their attention to the more solid substance of Mormonism and the best features of the church—but such efforts usually don't succeed. They know what they want.

Sterling, tell me what your reaction has been over the years as you've been described by some Mormon fanatics as an anti-Christ.

For so many years now I've found the whole thing so humorous that it doesn't bother me in the least. I just have to laugh, because I've been described as a "son of perdition," a "latter-day Korihor," and the anti-Christ . . .

Which caused some pain for your children, when they were growing up?

I don't think they pay any attention to it now, but yes, when they were little kids, it was a problem. I don't know whether parents actually told their children not to play with our children because I was an apostate, but they picked it up from somewhere. In two or three cases, some of our kids' teachers caused some problems because of strong prejudices.

I am appalled when I see children take the rap for their parents' beliefs or even behavior, although I know such prejudice springs from irrational fears of "contamination." But to be criticized for an opinion you hold or a position you take yourself is just part of life. Having your integrity impugned or your ethics maligned, however, is a sting of a different type. How have you reacted to this sort of thing over the years?

I wasn't ever happy about it, but at the same time I was able to live with it and so was Natalie. There was always gossip about things I reputedly said that weren't true, but there was enough that *was* true to send me to hell in the eyes of the orthodox. I never suffered criticism for my behavior, however, just my beliefs. While I readily confess to being a heretic—one who doesn't believe—I frankly resent being called an apostate—one who turns against the church. I am critical of the church, but I'm for it, not against it.

9.
Academic Leader

Sterling, you assumed the deanship of University College at the University of Utah in the summer of 1954. What do you remember about your appointment? Did you apply for the position?

No, I didn't seek the job. When the academic vice-president, G. Homer Durham, approached me about it, I said, "Hell, Homer, I don't have any desire to do this kind of thing. I want to do research and write." Homer's reply was, "You take this job for a few years, and you'll write a better book." Well, I think he was right. It shows you a little more what the world is like than sitting in a library. You have to dirty your hands with the actual processes of institutional life. Not as dirty as being a department head. I was never a department head—thank the Lord for that—but being a dean, that wasn't so bad.

Deans are to be regarded with suspicion, you know.

Oh, absolutely. Did I ever tell you the story that George Beadle, president of the University of Chicago and a Nobel Prize winner in biology, told me about deans? A senior faculty member came to the president and said, "You know, I'm getting a little bored with teaching. I'd like a position in the administration." And the president said, "Well, there's certainly no question about your talents and your service to the university, but we don't have any administrative positions open." The faculty member said, "You don't?" "No, I can't think of a thing." "You mean in an institution of this size, with our high rate of turnover among administrators, that not one post is available?" "No, I can't think of one." And the professor said, "Well, I'll be a son of a bitch." And President Beadle said, "Oh, why didn't you say so, we do have a deanship open!"

Well, we've both earned the right to laugh at that one, Sterling. What sort of a college did you inherit?

Well, my deanship covered about half the university when I took over. It was called University College then because of Meredith Wilson's fondness for the British term. But I found that as a name it was widely misunderstood. Institutions all over the country were using it as the name for their downtown campuses and evening schools. I got a lot of mail that should have gone to the extension division. So in 1957 I proposed and the regents agreed to change the name to the College of Letters and Science.

What did it include?

Under both names it had all of the departments that we now find in the colleges of humanities, science, social and behavioral science, and the ROTC units. It also included theater and ballet, now in the College of Fine Arts. So we had about half the students, half the faculty, and half the work of the university. The general education program was also under Letters and Science.

If you were picking some landmarks in the university's history from that era . . .

I'm afraid some of them were peripheral to my work in the college; like the creation of KUED, the university television station. I had no official connection with it, but President Olpin was involved personally and used to consult with me about it. That was an important development for the university and for this whole region. Another thing was the creation of the Middle East Center, which was first under President Olpin's direct jurisdiction and then shifted to Letters and Science. The General Education Program, later called Liberal Education under you, Jack, was my responsibility, but Sydney Angleman directed it competently as my associate dean. I just tried to keep out of his way.

Perhaps the biggest factor influencing higher education in that era was the enormous expansion of the student population due to the passage in 1946 of the GI Bill of Rights, which provided significant educational benefits for World War II veterans. What was it like on this campus in the 1950s?

You've described the situation properly. The University of Utah grew rapidly from a small institution to a rather large one. I think we had grown to about 13,000 students by the middle of the 1950s. Money was scarce for most things, but the development of research in the university was spectacular. The arts also flourished—especially ballet and music. Space and buildings were scarce, but the federal government gave the university a large tract of land from Fort Douglas, everything east of the bookstore—and a great many frame buildings on it, which we used to good advantage.

And still do. They've been "temporary buildings" for over a half-century now.

Our challenge, of course, was not simply to accommodate the

students but also to build a strong faculty. During the nationwide expansion, acquiring people of real stature and quality as scholars, research scientists, and teachers was difficult. The demand for mathematicians was growing rapidly during that era of expanding technology, and mathematicians were as scarce as hen's teeth. It's a great compliment to our mathematics faculty that they were able to attract as many good mathematicians as we added to the department at that time. The same can be said of chemistry and physics and many other departments. Much of my effort was going toward building a strong faculty during those years.

The year the college was renamed, 1957, was also the year the Soviet Union shocked the world by launching their Sputnik satellite into orbit. Did that event shift the university's balance between the arts and the sciences during the succeeding decade?

It generated a great deal of new federal money for engineering and the basic sciences; but we didn't see much in the humanities. More and more competent young scholars were going into the sciences, which created a problem for maintaining the strength and balance of the liberal arts and sciences as a whole.

You also got very involved in relations with high schools, did you not?

I worked on early admissions for honors-level students and arranging advanced placement so that seniors who were doing advanced work could get college credit. I was influenced by a good publication from the American Philosophical Association describing experiments across the nation with introductory philosophy courses being taught in high schools. Waldemer Read, the head of the philosophy department, and I proposed to the Salt Lake City School District that they offer an experimental course in philosophy that would be on the level of a freshman university course. He and I both offered to go free to any high school to teach such a class. All they had to do was furnish the students and the classroom.

You found some of your best philosophy students through the School of Education, didn't you?

That's right. Prior to World War II, under Dean Milton Bennion, all education majors were required to take a course in ethics. His grandson, John Bennion, until recently superintendent of schools in Salt Lake City, was a philosophy major here as an undergraduate.

It's rare to find a serious interest in philosophy among educational administrators today. We need it. John's leadership has a rare resonance and perspective, as evidenced by his recently taking leave for a term from the superintendency to teach philosophy to high school seniors in his district. I'm delighted that he is now teaching full time in our school of education and directing a new project on inner-city school problems. He is driven by his ideal of social justice.

That's why this whole topic is so relevant right now.

What became of the proposal that you and Waldemer made?

Well, Lynn Bennion, John's father, who was then superintendent of schools in Salt Lake, invited me to come over to East High to meet and discuss the idea with some of his principals. There was a good-sized group there, and I made my pitch about upgrading education. I said a lot of introductory college courses should be taught in the high schools and some high school courses should be taught in junior high. Then I made our offer to teach a philosophy course whenever they wanted—a full professor of philosophy at no cost to them.

Did they take you up on this bargain or feel insulted?

Hell, I had no takers at all. Most of them just sat there and frowned. One fellow, Lynn's assistant superintendent, got boiling mad. He said, "Look, if you want to come here"—well, I'd been invited, so I thought that was a little rude of him—"and tell us we should be doing a better job, all right; but don't come here and tell us we should be teaching what *you're* teaching." When I later explained the national advanced placement program to all of the superintendents in Utah, I got one taker for that project; and that was the Granite School District. Other districts joined the program later.

Homer Durham was vice-president of the university during some of the years Olpin was president. What were his contributions?

Durham came to the University of Utah just before I did—about 1946—as professor of political science and head of the political science department. We didn't have vice-presidents at that time. As a matter of fact, when Olpin was describing the ambitious plans he had for the University of Utah to me early in 1948, I mentioned that it looked to me as if he would eventually need a business vice-president and an academic vice-president. That kind of arrangement was fairly innovative in American universities at that time; they had established it at the University of Southern California and a few other places. He said, "Oh no, I don't want any vice-presidents around." Olpin liked to keep his own hands on new things. He didn't want somebody between him and their actual operation. After he got something going, however, he would turn it over to someone else to run.

How did Olpin end up with the vice-presidential structure then?

The regents insisted on a thorough examination of the university structure by a competent management firm. In 1951-52 Booz, Allen, and Hamilton conducted an extensive study and made recommendations for an academic vice-president and business vice-president. While I was in New York during my leave of absence in 1952-53, I learned that Homer Durham had been made academic vice-president and Elmo Morgan, then research coordinator, business vice-president. Meredith Wilson, until the fall of 1952 dean of University College, had functioned very much like an academic vice-president, so to some extent the reform simply offered a new name for a job he had previously defined.

What were Homer's vice-presidential duties and what kind of working relationship did he enjoy with President Olpin?

They were highly compatible. The college deans, the library and museum directors, and others reported to the academic vice-president. Olpin recognized Durham's talent for organization, and he used him as a kind of consultant to the administration even before he assumed the duties of the vice-presidency.

As acting chair of the Faculty Council and as vice-president, Homer took the lead in developing the faculty code and the regents' code—both of them great contributions to the university. He had fine capabilities for delegating responsibility, although he was inclined to be quite impersonal, almost mechanical. On the whole, he was a first-rate administrator and highly respected. When he left the headship of political science to become vice-president, that department lapsed into confusion. He got me involved as dean very early in his administration—dumping his old department in my lap.

I can see that he had a talent for delegation, all right. I understand that during this period the deans met with the administration every Thursday afternoon. What happened at those meetings?

All of the deans met with the president and the two vice-presidents to discuss university goals and programs. At times all of us felt that Olpin was keeping too short a rein on Homer about academic policy.

As academic vice-president, was Homer Durham a powerful defender of academic freedom? Nothing is more central to the emergence of a great university.

Oh yes. There was no better defender of academic freedom than Homer Durham or A. Ray Olpin.

Years later Homer became a member of the First Council of the Seventy in the LDS church and spearheaded the dismantling in 1977 of Leonard

Arrington's bright young group of professional scholars in the Church History Division. He also closed many important archival collections of the church. This seems like a strange and ironic twist in Homer's values.

Well, he was almost certainly acting on orders, but I think that was a different Homer Durham. That's about all I can say. As you know, he left here in the summer of 1960 to be president of Arizona State University when it was expanding very rapidly. His problems down there were mainly with extreme right-wingers; and he staunchly protected his faculty from their attacks. I think he was a real defender of academic freedom then—at least, that's the opinion of people in Arizona who reported to me on it, and I think the same can be said of him when he returned to Utah as Commissioner of Higher Education in 1969.

As far as I know that's true, but it makes his change all the more mystifying.

Well, as you know, when a man takes one of those high-level positions in the Mormon church—and they are all men—it can change him. I don't like to say this of Homer, but I would be willing to say it of some: When they take one of those jobs, they simply sell their souls to the church and become instruments of sometimes ultraconservative and even repressive policies. After he became a general authority, we exchanged cordial greetings on formal occasions, but we never had a real conversation.

You had served on more than one national committee with Homer in earlier years.

Yes, I remember working with him on a committee on the future of higher education for the American Council on Education. He was a leader, there's no question about it. It seems to me that he had much to contribute toward the end of his life that the LDS church did not want from him. I guess for some reason he decided to give them what they wanted.

Throughout your professional career, Sterling, including this era, you've maintained a steady scholarly output. How did you blend research and writing with your teaching and administrative duties?

Well, in the first place, I disciplined myself more deliberately when I became dean. I wasted far less time as dean, so I managed to do about as much scholarly work as I had been doing earlier. I also gained a very definite advantage—a full-time secretary. When I was a professor, it was hard to get anything typed. As a result, I usually spoke extemporaneously. Knowing I could quickly have a beautifully typed text, however, tempted me to write up what I said—sometimes before I said it, sometimes afterwards.

What's your work style, Sterling? When do you write best?

Definitely after dark. It has to be dark when I write. Nor do I do much reading in the daytime. While I was dean, of course, I was doing administrative work all day. Now I spend hours a day in correspondence—responding to questions relating to philosophy and religion, the Mormon church, the university, the federal government, or the United Nations. I've always tried to answer unless I think they're crackpots. When I came back from Washington, though, I had to share the departmental secretary, and there were dozens and dozens of letters that I simply couldn't answer. I felt bad about that, but there was nothing I could do about it.

Writing at night is a preference rather than a necessity?

I'd say so. I don't go to bed early, anyway; and if I'm writing, I might stay up till two or three o'clock. Writing is not easy for me, but the first paragraph is usually the most difficult.

It always is.

Yes, I guess that's right. I devote a lot of time to thinking, partly in my sleep and partly when I'm awake, of what I'm going to say, so that once I get started, the stuff comes a little easier and very often when I start writing I have virtually everything in my mind even down to the grammatical structure of a paragraph or argument. I do most everything in longhand, although when I had a secretary I often dictated the first draft of a long paper and then messed around with the typescript making revisions. Most of my stuff I write in longhand. I have never touched a typewriter or used a computer. When my drafts are typed, I revise them by hand. Editing is the pleasant part of writing for me, not the original draft. And, oddly enough, I can revise in daylight. I just can't write in daylight.

Writing until two or three o'clock in the morning must mean that you require less sleep than most people?

Not at all, Jack! I think I require more sleep than most, but I just can't get it. I've suffered from insomnia for years. I must have a guilty conscience.

What do you do when you can't sleep?

It happens frequently, and I usually just lie there and try to sleep; but one of the things that keeps me awake is the thought of something I ought to be working on. I worry a lot at night and I can always use the time thinking up something good to worry about. I've got a reading light by the bed, and I'll often just flip the light on and read for awhile. Of course, I can always get up, go in the other room, and turn on the

TV. That often puts me to sleep. Very occasionally I'll take some across-the-counter stuff, but I don't like to do that.

I remember, when I was Roald Campbell's doctoral student, praising Andrew Halpin's essays or journal articles in education. I always thought he expressed himself extremely well. Roald said, "Would you like to write like that?" I said, "Sure, I would." "Fine," he said. "It takes Andrew about ten drafts before he's willing to release a manuscript for publication."
    Ten drafts! Is that right?

Yes, and I think I may have done six on occasion, but never ten. I believe my record of six was on my "Liberal Spirituality" article for Dialogue *recently, and it needed one more! Now you are known for a felicitous but complex style, Sterling. Do your final drafts come relatively easily? Are you a two-draft writer, or a six- or ten-draft person?*

I'd say I'm a three-draft man on papers. I fiddle around with the manuscript in my mind for a long time, then I write out one draft in longhand, then have it typed, and then work it over again. Well, maybe four times. I usually have some additional ideas before I read or publish it, so I write in more revisions. On the other hand, a book or chapter might involve many, many drafts.

When you go to your cabin on Kolob Plateau, or take a vacation trip with Natalie and the family, do you haul your work along or leave it behind?

I always take some—not a whole lot. If I'm going to a conference, I'll take along something to work on during the flight and in the hotel; but when I go to Kolob, with no phone or electricity, I usually take less. We just indulge ourselves in the quiet and in family and friends.

When you and Natalie steered us to the cabin nearby, you helped us realize a two decades' dream. What do you read when you have free and uninterrupted time?

I never read novels and I despise short stories, but I like history for recreational reading—intellectual history, the history of Rome and Greece, the history of Egypt, sometimes Oriental stuff. My main reading is intellectual history, but I read a lot of philosophical material—epistemology and metaphysics.

You seem to have a distinctive pattern for writing. What about for reading? Every room in your Salt Lake home, your Kolob cabin, and your St. George condominium is filled with books!

Most of my books are in my study at home, but I rarely carry a book from one place to another. I have certain books in the kitchen, certain books in the living room, others by my bed, and so on. If I'm in the living room, I'll pull a volume of Gibbon's *Decline and Fall of the Roman*

Empire off the shelf and just read wherever it falls open. I greatly admire his style and use of the language.

Do you usually march right through a book or dip into it at random?

No, I usually dip in only when I know the book well. Quite frequently I read the notes first, though. In fact, I will often read the last notes first, and then work toward the beginning notes. The notes are frequently more interesting than the text. I guess I am a browser. I open up a book and absorb it somehow. I read the final pages first.

Sterling, I have here **The History of Philosophy,** *the third edition in two volumes by B. A. G. Fuller, professor emeritus of philosophy at USC, revised with additions by Sterling M. McMurrin, professor of philosophy, University of Utah, published by Henry Holt and Company, as it then was. You inscribed the book "To my darling Mother, Sterling," June 1955. Tell me how you got involved with Fuller. Who was he?*

Well, Fuller was a very brilliant man in the history of philosophy, especially in Greek philosophy. He had taught at Harvard and came to USC back in the late twenties; but when I was doing my work there as a student, he was retired from active teaching and rarely came in. I was given his office to use when he wasn't there. He lived down in Mexico when he was away from Los Angeles, so he didn't come in often; but that's how I became acquainted with him. It was a very casual acquaintance, though I knew quite a lot about him. This book came out in 1938 with a revised edition in 1945, and it was very widely used. I had a lot of admiration for his work as a scholar, and he was an intensely interesting person.

So how did you become involved in revising his book?

I was living in New York in 1952-53 and I got a letter from the Henry Holt Company asking me if I would revise and update Fuller's history. Fuller concurred with the request. I agreed and plunged in, but I didn't ever team up with him. In fact, I really wasn't well acquainted with Fuller. I met him several times, but I never saw him after I joined the USC faculty in 1945.

Apparently it was the publisher's idea; Fuller did not propose that I redo the book. But he wrote and told me he was pleased that I had accepted the contract. He kept his hands off completely and made no suggestions of any kind, except one. He wrote, "Living here in Mexico, I've been giving quite a lot of attention to Latin American philosophy; and if you would like—" he put it that way "—if you would like to include a chapter on Latin American philosophy I would be very happy to write one for you." Well, the plain facts are that books on the history of philosophy had completely ignored Latin American philosophy, so of course I took Fuller up on his offer. He wrote a long chapter and I divided it into two.

How much work did you do on your revision, Sterling?

Well, the publisher had said not to make any unnecessary changes; and I certainly didn't see any point in doing much with his Greek sections, since that was Fuller's forte. I made some revisions in the Roman and medieval sections, but my revisions and additions are mainly in the modern period, the second volume. There was little or nothing on neo-scholasticism, phenomenology, or pragmatism. I added sections on those, and then I wrote chapters on such things as scholastic philosophy, logical empiricism, and existentialism.

I spent a couple of hours with the book last night, and I thought it's an unusually good reference work. Very well organized.

It is a good book, and at one time was the most widely used history of philosophy text in American universities. I'm sorry that it was taken out of print by the publishers. When they told me it was going to be discontinued, they asked if I would write another history of philosophy for them. In fact, I signed a contract to do it. I had already signed a contract to produce a couple of volumes of readings that would be companion volumes to the two-volume history of philosophy.

What happened?

I was an administrator by then, and it just used up my time. I wish I had done the writing. I wish I'd been doing that instead of hassling over faculty problems.

What was your arrangement with the publisher on Fuller's book?

The publisher offered me either a flat fee or part of the royalties. Fuller had indicated that he wanted to split the royalties with me. My own inclination was to take the flat fee because it was a sizable sum; but the administrator in the publisher's college books department advised me to take the royalties, and it paid off rather generously over a number of years. I believe after his death Fuller's heirs received 60 percent and I received 40, which was certainly fair as far as I was concerned. Holt asked if I had any objection to their authorizing a Polish translation. They later published an Oxford edition, too, which was sold only in India, Ceylon, and Burma.

Fuller died shortly after the revised edition of the history came out?

Yes, and I became the sole owner of the work. There were never any royalties from the Polish edition, but I recall receiving some from the Oxford edition.

Let me ask you about the Henry Holt book of philosophical readings that you did with Jim Jarrett in 1954.

Jarrett and I both taught contemporary philosophy at the University of Utah, and there wasn't a good collection of up-to-date contemporary stuff that you could put in the hands of the students. We wanted something that would include phenomenology, existentialism, and positivism, the three more recent developments along with the traditional stuff on pragmatism, idealism, realism, and so on. So along about 1951 we decided to put together a volume of readings. We were working on it while I was redoing the Fuller book, so after I'd settled a contract with Holt on that, I said, "Well, what would you think of doing a volume of readings on contemporary philosophy?" They liked the idea, so Jarrett and I finished it up and sent it in. It was published as *Contemporary Philosophy* just about the same time as *A History of Philosophy*.

You were busy with many projects and responsibilities in the 1950s. What about physical recreation, then and now? What do you do for fun, and to stay fit?

I don't jog, if that's what you mean. I have back trouble and jogging would kill me off. Natalie and I take walks in our neighborhood and in the mountains—not long or steep ones, but walking. I'd say that horses have been my main recreation, and I own some Tennessee Walkers. As you know, people who have horses not only ride them but like to lean on the corral rails and look at them. That's an important part of owning horses. They're magnificent animals. We have always liked driving trips, too; we have crossed the country many times by car. If there's time, we still drive to California or the Northwest. But I've always been a special fan of trains.

Traveling by rail is a lovely experience.

Natalie and I always get a bedroom so we've got some privacy where we can read, spread things out, and so forth. We're quite addicted to trains.

How many horses do you have now?

We are partners in raising Tennessee Walkers with my nephew, Bill McMurrin, who, as you know, is an architect who lives in St. George. We own some property together and keep about ten horses there. It's only a couple of acres but we call it a ranch. You know, Jack, in my next incarnation I plan to be a Tennessee Walking horse, live in Utah's southern canyons in the winters and on Kolob in the summers. If you're a horse, you can't get anything better than that.

Not only that, but they seldom suffer from insomnia and hardly worry at all about writing.

That's right. They're not hurting one damn bit.

In 1960, however, your appointment as academic vice-president meant less time for good things like riding horses and taking leisurely trips with the family. How did this happen?

President Olpin used to walk down to my office from time to time, just to pass the time of day and do a little gossiping. One summer day he walked in and said, "Homer Durham is leaving to take the presidency of Arizona State and I'd like you to take his place as vice-president." I was surprised but I agreed. I began my duties as soon as I got back from Aspen, Colorado, with Natalie and the kids that summer.

What kind of appeal did that new administrative post have for you? Did you accept Olpin's invitation out of duty to the university, out of respect for Olpin? Or was it something you were genuinely attracted to?

Well, to be very honest with you, I never enjoyed administrative work. But I discovered that I was able to do it. I kept getting asked to do it. I was pleased of course that Olpin and the regents wanted me for the position. But if you're asking whether I would have sought the job, the answer is no.

Did you consider saying no?

No, I didn't consider saying no. I just told him yes, partly because I felt I owed it to the president to do anything I felt I honestly could do—and partly because I didn't think being vice-president was any worse than being dean of Letters and Science. Except for doing the budget! That was definitely the worst part of the vice-president's job. In fact, when the offer came to go to Washington as U.S. Commissioner of Education, my first thought was, "Oh, boy! This is a chance to get out of doing next year's budget!" Dealing with many hundreds of millions of dollars in Washington is a lot simpler than dealing with a few million in the university.

Who succeeded you as the dean?

Boyer Jarvis was made acting dean; then when he went to Washington, Jack Adamson became dean.

And who became vice-president?

Daniel Dykstra, who had been dean of the Law School. He was vice-president for several years, very competent, absolutely first rate. He eventually left to take the deanship of the Law School at the University of California at Davis.

You were academic vice-president less than a year, but I believe you did quite a few interesting things.

Mainly, they had to do with faculty regulations, regents' regulations, routines for appointing faculty, and due process. I simply picked up in a sense where Homer had left off. This was a period in the university's history when we were paying more and more attention to how you go about settling on a person for the faculty and how you go about getting rid of people from the faculty. The whole question of due process was drawing attention from the courts. I worked on that quite a bit. And then there were internal things, for instance, the Middle East Center had been established and Olpin wanted to have it right under him. Well, when I became vice-president, he wanted me to take on the Middle East Center, too, and I did.

On promotions and appointments, you had discovered as dean that in more than one department there was not just looseness but some skulduggery.

Yes, for instance, a department head had to get faculty signatures on recommendations for tenure, promotion, and appointment. One department head, I discovered, would go to a faculty person and say, "If you will sign this, then so-and-so will sign it," and then use the first signature as leverage to get the second signature—playing faculty off against one another without any substantive discussion of the candidate's merits. Really, it was outrageous.

And how did you solve that problem?

The previous form had required a person to sign and also record how he or she had voted on a given appointment. I designed and implemented a form requiring faculty to sign their names—but not recording their vote—attesting that the faculty met on such and such a date, who was present, who was absent, and what the total vote was for and against. Now that, you see, seems like a trivial thing; but before we had it, some department heads were fine and others were pulling all kinds of shenanigans.

Sterling, could you comment on changes in the hiring and firing of faculty from your appointment here until you retired in 1988.

Well, at first there certainly wasn't much of an explicit routine laid out for governing either hiring or firing. When I became dean of the college in 1954, I implemented a procedure that was fairly standard in other universities and which governed hiring at the University of Southern California. The understanding was that there was a three-year period of mutual probation. It wasn't formal or spelled out in a contract or a regulation, but we'd explain this clearly during the hiring process.

If a new professor was not satisfactory, we'd give him or her at least a year's notice—enough time to find another position—but for three years they were on a trial basis. The department heads in the college went along with this, and there was no objection from the faculty.

What about firing someone?

If the department decided by majority vote that it didn't want a non-tenured professor anymore, we'd give the person adequate notice and that would be it. They always left—not always cheerfully—but they left.

So there was no litigation in those days?

No, no litigation and a minimum of committee activity. I don't mean that we dropped people arbitrarily, not by any means. I can best report on this for the Department of Philosophy. We would have very serious discussions; but we dropped several people between 1954 and 1961.

That sounds like a large number from one department.

A couple of them resigned, so I shouldn't count them; but we dropped others because they were not satisfactory teachers. We dropped one because he wasn't responsible. He would sit up half the night with his students drinking beer and then sleep the next day and miss his classes. I might say, he went to Japan and sent us back a postcard from San Francisco with a photograph of Alcatraz on it. He wrote: "Dear Former Colleagues, wish you were here."

Today, of course, AAUP guidelines specify a maximum seven-year probationary period; it is "up-or-out" at the end of six years—you either get promoted and tenure or get fired. If you aren't fired formally, you get tenure by default.

We did have tenure rules, but the up-or-out policy came later. When I came to the university, there was a length of time specified for achieving tenure if a person was an assistant professor, a little less time if he came as associate professor. I came as a full professor and I'm not sure how long was required—three years, I believe. The idea of early tenure didn't occur to any of us. I received no credit on tenure for the time I taught at the University of Southern California. But the same two-way rule applied. If you were not notified that you were unsatisfactory before the time was up, you got tenure automatically. I remember one or two cases during the 1950s where unsatisfactory people were notified a little late and they were able to keep their jobs. These became battles—not in court, but within the university. In one case, the situation was laid before the regents and they supported the faculty member.

Wasn't there an instructor dismissed without adequate notice back in the 1950s, and the case went all the way to the regents?

Yes. The result was what we called for many years the Bamberger Amendment. Clarence Bamberger, a member of the regents, took an interest in this case and insisted that, as I recall, people be given not less than three months' notice. Well, in the College of Letters and Science, our typical practice, as I've already said, was to give a year's notice unless there was some strong nonacademic reason like criminal activity for dropping them.

Today the process is more elaborate. Department students evaluate teaching and advising and provide a written report. Then the departmental faculty committee, made up of those at or above the rank to which the person would be promoted, convenes, reviews the whole record of achievement, and votes. The case moves next to the department chair, then to the College Faculty Advisory Committee, then to the college dean, then to the University Promotion and Tenure Advisory Committee, and finally to the vice-president, president, and trustees. All these steps, plus an appeals loop! How many of those steps were in place when you were dean?

Not many of them. It was rather easy then to drop a person. I think, however, the university was very well behaved in the way it did drop people. But the decision was made primarily in the department. The department would notify the dean. If a person wanted to appeal the decision, of course, that's a different matter. He could appeal it all the way up to the regents. That was taken for granted, and I can tell you of one rather interesting case in an appeal. This was in the sciences. The division head told me that they had a man who had been there for a short time who was a good scientist and a good teacher, but the faculty couldn't stand him, the students didn't like him, and they simply were rebelling against having this man around.

It didn't have to do with the quality of his work as a scientist?

No, the faculty had decided they wanted to drop him for other reasons. This was a unanimous decision of the departmental faculties and the head of the division, who, with the several department heads, were an executive committee. When they reported their recommendation to me, I said, "Go ahead. Let him know that he's to be terminated, but tell him that he has a right to appeal up the line to me and beyond. A short time later he came to see me. I had never met him before, except when he was first appointed. I interviewed all of the people before they were appointed in my college. Anyway, he asked, "Do I have a right to appeal?" and I said, "Yes, by all means."

I got all the department heads together—the head of the division

and the department heads—and we met with the professor around the
table. As chair of the affair, I asked him what he had to say. "Well," he
said, "I simply want to know why I'm being fired. I haven't been given
a reason for it." "Well," I said, "we'll ask these people right now just
what their reason is for dropping you." So I went around the table asking
these five people, one at a time, to explain to Professor X why they
wanted to get rid of him. Believe it or not, every one of them refused
to say a thing. Each one shook his head in the negative and passed.

*This wouldn't be tolerated today. It's outrages like this that have brought
all the procedures that ensnare us today.*

That's right. That's absolutely right. So when all of them refused to
give him a reason, I said, "Well, I know why they're dropping you, so
I guess I'll have to tell you why. They don't want you around here
anymore because they regard you as an ornery son of a bitch."

You would not get by with that today either!

Not at all. Nowadays, everything calls for litigation. It may be more
just, but it is also more mechanical and less human. There is no good
will or humor left in our system. Well, the professor laughed. He
laughed! I greatly admired him. He got up and said, "That's all I wanted
to know." Then he went around the table and shook hands with
everybody. That was the end of it.

That is remarkable.

And it's absolutely true. We were much involved during that decade
in sorting out these things, but you know it takes time. It really takes
time. Now in telling you stories like this I don't want you to get the
impression that the university was unfair with people, or cavalier or
arbitrary. It's just that if there were people whom we didn't want around
for good reason, we got rid of them. But I believe the university was
very decent and generous.

*You may be aware that we have very complex procedures now, even for
revising our promotion, tenure, and retention policy. The system has become
so unwieldy that nobody can understand it and any change seems to take
forever—it takes a solid year for the vice-president's office to review revisions
in departmental policies.*

I agree with you. It is too complex and there's too much inclination
to appeal this and appeal that, and yet I've seen cases in recent years
where it was very important for us to have these broad avenues of appeal.
The appeal side of it is tremendously important.

*It is, and my idea is not to trim the opportunity for appeal or reduce the
fairness in the system. It's to make it simpler and clearer so that fairness*

can be more easily identified when the issues surface and action can be more timely. Earning tenure and promotion to associate professor is tantamount to securing your foothold in the profession. The assumption used to be that, if you were reasonably competent but didn't receive tenure at the University of Utah, you'd simply go somewhere else and earn it there. Now, however, the job market is so competitive that if you don't make tenure where you start out, you'll likely not become a college professor anywhere else. Do you know now what happened to those half dozen who were not retained in the philosophy department in your early years here on the faculty? Perhaps one reason for the increasing formality and legalism of terminations today is that people's whole professional careers are on the line.

Yes, these people I've mentioned, and others in the 1950s and sixties, could get other positions. I don't think any of them had any real difficulty getting other positions. They were people who had good degrees from fine institutions; American education was still growing rapidly, money in education was generally improving, and there was a shortage of people for university teaching positions. So I don't think any of them were severely handicapped, except of course the one who was blatantly irresponsible. That is another matter.

These conditions changed around 1970, however, when an immense surplus of people qualified for university positions in history and languages appeared—when student enrollments leveled off but Ph.D. production didn't. That spread to other fields rather quickly, too.

Yes, if we could find somebody who knew the times tables, we'd give him a position in mathematics. Let me give you an example. We sent one or two of our mathematics professors to a meeting of the American Mathematical Association in Texas to recruit people for our mathematics faculty. What they discovered was that recruiters from other universities were getting onto airplanes that were flying into Austin and offering mathematicians jobs before they got to the convention! Competition was fierce. So a mathematician fired from one job could easily find another. But our way of handling the hiring and firing of all faculty was altogether too loose. But now, I think, it is far too complicated.

Maybe we can oscillate back to a happy medium.

In the late 1970s President David Gardner asked me to chair a committee to hear an appeal from a person who had been denied tenure and was to be dropped from a departmental faculty. It had gone right up through the normal process to the vice-president's office and the faculty person had lost. There was still the possibility of appealing to a special ad hoc committee which the president could create, and this was the committee I chaired. We had legal advice from Vice-president Arvo Van Alstyne, who had a fine legal mind, and the person involved had a very competent lawyer. We had several hearings with a considerable number of people testifying from the relevant department and the college. The thing was handled very rigorously.

What was your decision?

We found substantial procedural errors and recommended that the tenure review process start afresh. The president took a look at my report and said, "We're not going to start the review process over again. We'll simply give the person tenure." That person is still on the faculty. Here's a case that illustrates the importance of having strict regulations and following them closely. I think I learned about as much from that case as any other about the importance of due process.

You mentioned procedural matters having to do with students?

Yes, very soon after I took over as vice-president—a matter of days, as I recall—Olpin came in with a stack of papers on canceling the out-of-state fees for graduate students. He said, "Dean Eyring is in favor of canceling out-of-state fees for virtually all graduate students and Homer goes along with him, but I don't think we ought to do it quite that way. Can you give it some thought?" I set up a committee to examine the merits of such cases and the number of exceptions to the fee was greatly reduced. Well, there were a lot of things like that, and I certainly don't say these things in criticism of Homer. He had done a great deal to bring order out of considerable disorder, and Meredith Wilson had done the same thing.

Did you feel you left any major unfinished projects when you accepted the appointment in Washington?

Oh, of course I did. I think one that I should have done more on had to do with college councils. We didn't have regulations requiring them in those days; but in the College of Letters and Science, I created an informal council—meaning that it wasn't provided for in the faculty regulations. This council was made up of the heads of the twenty-three departments—

Twenty-three departments!

Oh yes, counting the three ROTCs. So I would have quite regular meetings with department heads to transact business. Well, when I became vice-president, I could see the benefit of having college councils university-wide and was working at it when I left. I was pleased that they were later made a matter of policy.

Lillian Ence worked with you over a long period of years as your assistant. Was she with you when you were vice-president?

I'm glad you asked, because I want to say a few things about her. I had known Lillian and her husband, Don, when I was a student. They were a little older than I. Lillian was typing Ericksen's book on social ethics during the spring of 1937. She was working mostly in Ericksen's home, and I was there quite often. Well, I was also writing my master's thesis, and Lillian volunteered to type it. Don was also a capable typist; and between the two of them, they typed my master's thesis and they wouldn't take a cent for doing it.

So your ties go way back.

When we moved back to Salt Lake, we'd run into them downtown, and Natalie became aware that Lillian was a secretary for General Motors at their offices here. I desperately needed an able assistant, and I had had two of them who stayed only a short time. I was at my wits' end when Natalie said, "I'm going to call up Lillian Ence." I said, "Look, Lillian's making much more money where she is. She's not going to take this job."

But Natalie went right ahead and called her.

Called her, interviewed her, and I hired her! And Lillian took a salary cut in coming. She was not only absolutely first-rate, she was phenomenal. She was everything that one could ask for in an assistant from the standpoint of executive ability, administrative talents, ability to get along with other people, and first-rate stenographic talents. She had been a student at the university, and then, as an administrator, she learned everything about the institution and its people—becoming an inexhaustible source of information and advice about every problem that came up.

Did you take her with you to the vice-president's office in 1960? I remember that she was in the president's office when I came in '74.

Yes, she went with me to the vice-president's office, but I'm not sure when she moved on to the president's office. It was sometime during Jim Fletcher's administration. She stayed on there during the administrations of presidents Fred Emery and David Gardner. I've already told you how I agreed to be provost of the university only if I could talk Lillian into being my secretary, but Fred Emery, who was then vice-president, wouldn't give her up! Everyone wanted Lillian's assistance, you see, she was an institution.

Indeed, her portrait by Al Gittins hangs in the Winder Board Room with yours and a few others. Pursuing now your collegial connections with Boyer

Jarvis, when did you and he first work together?

In Tucson, when I was director of the LDS Institute of Religion there and Boyer was a student. I'd taken the position at the end of a school year but I wouldn't be moving to Tucson until fall. Somebody had to look after the institute building and grounds during the summer. I was replacing Daryl Chase, and he and I conferred about who could do the job. We both knew Boyer. He had a summer job in the Valley National Bank and also worked as a radio broadcaster. So we went down to the bank, found Boyer, and said, "How would you like to live in the institute"—it had a beautiful apartment in it—"and just look after the place?" Boyer accepted and we have had a great deal of contact ever since.

But then you left Arizona?

Yes, and when Natalie and I were in New York on the Ford Fellowship, Boyer was working on his doctorate at Northwestern University in Evanston, Illinois. We drove through Chicago on our way back just to call on Boyer.

When did Boyer come to the University of Utah?

Boyer did his doctoral dissertation on nineteenth-century Mormon oratory. Ah, those pre-microphone days in the Tabernacle. They were all orators. I was in my first year as dean of Letters and Science when Boyer came to town to work in the Church Historian's Office to examine old Mormon speeches he was working on for his dissertation. Of course, he needed some kind of work. Boyer was not married and he had taught at the University of Arizona, Northwestern, and a year at Dartmouth—very fine experience, you see. Hal Bentley was director of the Extension Division and he needed an assistant in the worst way, had funding for an assistant, and was actually looking for an assistant. I knew Boyer Jarvis's unusual talents and argued for him until I was blue in the face. Here was Hal's chance to get an assistant who wouldn't let things fall through the cracks. He'd say, "What if he doesn't pan out?" I said, "Hell, Hal, if he doesn't then fire him. That's the way we do with faculty."

But nothing doing?

Nope, Hal wouldn't budge. Well, just when I was giving up on Hal, Homer Durham came through with some funds for an assistant for me. So I gave that job to Boyer. As soon as I did that, Hal changed his mind. He came around saying, "Why didn't you tell me that Boyer Jarvis was Joe Jarvis's son? I've known Joe Jarvis ever since my Mexico days." "Well," I said, "what's that got to do with it?" Later Boyer worked for

Hal and for me simultaneously. Then both of us wanted him full time and both of us had the funds. It became a kind of a tug of war.

That put Boyer in a good but difficult position.

It certainly did. He could have had either job. If Hal had taken him first, I wouldn't have had much to bargain with; but he'd been working with me for some time. So we just put it up to Boyer—both offers—and Boyer took my offer.

Well, you did a marvelous thing when you got Boyer Jarvis anchored to the University of Utah. I don't know anyone who's done more for this place than Boyer in the last twenty-five years. He was the conscience of the institution until he retired in 1989.

That's right, and everybody says the same thing, you know. Two of the people who became vice-presidents in recent years told me that they took the job only with the understanding that Boyer would stay there and work with them as associate vice-president. He's a remarkable person in more ways than one. Just virtually works himself to death. On weekends, for instance, or any time till about seven at night, if I needed to call Boyer, I'd always try his office first. And he does many, many things in community service—United Nations, NAACP, Committee for Russian-American Relations, and organizations of that kind.

Another of your lifelong friends, Obert Tanner, was a remarkable faculty colleague and university teacher, although most people in this community know him for other achievements. What were your experiences with him when he taught at the university?

Obert had a very distinguished career as a teacher that has nearly been lost from the public consciousness. I'm very pleased that in 1986 the plaza and fountain between the Student Union and the new Student Services Building—both of which he donated—were named in his honor. He's been a civic benefactor of the most impressive kind. He joined the faculty, I believe, in 1946, just before I got here in 1948. Ericksen was still dean of the College of Arts and Sciences and head of the philosophy department.

Where was Obert educated?

He had a master's and most of a Ph.D. from Stanford, but he started out with undergraduate and law degrees from the University of Utah. He was admitted to the bar but wasn't interested in practicing law.

Obert's mind ran naturally toward what ought to be, not with precedents or toward the past.

Yes it did. He'd taken work in philosophy with Ericksen when he was a student—he was about ten years older than I am—and with

Waldemer Read. He went to study the philosophy of law at Harvard, which suited him well, and later at Stanford he became good friends with Charles Hartshorne and especially C. I. Lewis—Clarence Irving Lewis—a leading philosopher of this nation in his later years. Obert always called on Mrs. Lewis when he visited Boston or Cambridge, and the Tanner Lectures at Harvard are given in honor of C. I. Lewis.

Did you know Lewis?

I was familiar with his works, of course, and I had a brief but very pleasant association with him at Harvard. We were chatting one day in his office, and he said, "I'm due for a lecture, and I wonder if you'd like to join me?" As we were walking toward the lecture room, he added, "This is my last lecture. I'm retiring." Well, at Harvard, last lectures are quite ceremonial events. Many people from around the university came to hear him and I joined heartily in the applause at the end. But that was nothing like the association Obert had with him at Stanford.

Obert once told me an amusing story that involved the American philosopher Morris Cohen, who was then on the Harvard faculty. Obert liked to argue, so he got into a wrangle with Cohen in a philosophy of law course and wound up by saying, "Your position is contrary to everything I've learned in theology." Cohen responded, "Well, young man, my advice to you is to stick with theology."

So at that point Obert went to Stanford?

That's right. I don't think he finished his degree at Harvard. He and Grace and Natalie and I became fast friends in the early fall of 1938. I remember that it was the fall of 1939 when he told me Stanford had invited him to join the faculty of the Department of Religion, which was then being organized, even while he was still a graduate student.

Quite an honor! Did it interfere with his graduate work?

Of course, as it always does. He was acting chaplain the next year when the chaplain went on leave. When he decided to move back to Utah, they tried to get him to stay and accept the regular chaplain's appointment. It kept him busy! He performed marriages for the students in that magnificent chapel at Stanford, and then the alumni would come back and have their babies baptized. He had regular Sunday services, too. Obert and Grace's oldest son died of polio at age twelve while they were in Palo Alto, and I think that made them want to come home to Utah. So he and Grace moved back, and Obert took the position in our philosophy department.

Was his jewelry business, the O. C. Tanner Company, already booming then?

Absolutely. Obert started that business in his mother's basement when he was an undergraduate and ran it until he died in 1993. That's nearly seventy years. And yet he also went to school or served as a full-time professor right up until he retired from the philosophy department at the University of Utah in the early 1970s, keeping the growing business going with the help of his sister, who managed it while he was at Harvard, and his nephew, Norman Tanner, who had a big hand in the operation for a long time.

And at the university . . .

He and I shared an office from 1948 until I was made dean in 1954. Obert functioned just like any other faculty member—engaging in extended conversations, taking part in examinations, teaching full-time, becoming involved in recreational affairs, coming to evening events and lectures—and we had many of them. He taught at the university for a quarter of a century. It was astounding that he was able to do all this and develop the business into a global operation at the same time.

He must have had a remarkable business sense; and he certainly had inexhaustible energy.

Oh, there's no question about that. And he himself gave most of the credit to the excellent people he had working with him. He used to talk with me about the business. Besides that, we had one phone and it was on my desk, so I overheard most of his telephone conversations. He had a sense of when to take a chance on things, and he could make decisions very rapidly. Somehow he usually made good decisions. But he never talked about making money. He liked to talk about creating high-quality jobs and, later, about gifts that would make our community better or stronger.

Obert's book, Christ's Ideals for Living, *is a remarkably broad-gauge religious text that sets Jesus' life and teachings in the larger history of ideas globally.*

That was during the 1950s. He wouldn't have done it, but church president David O. McKay pressed him personally, knew what Obert could bring to the task. Waldemer Read and I strongly urged him to do it too. We thought it would be a good thing for the church if Obert would write that book, and of course it *was* a good thing. The book is widely read even today. Well, these things interfered with his finishing his doctorate; but when it became evident that Obert was not going to get the degree, there was no point in not making him a full professor.

So this was done. Obert was a marvelous teacher, as I'm sure you know. He had an unusual facility for getting students to think and to think carefully about matters pertaining to philosophical, religious, and moral ideas. Really a teacher of great talents. When he was in his late sixties, he wanted to retire and spend more time traveling, but we urged him to just retire part-time—teach one quarter a year and have the other two quarters off.

Although Obert's business struggled in the early years, I understand he was as generous at heart then as he was later when his resources were enormous.

Yes, and he always seemed quite indifferent to compensation from the university! He taught, I think, for almost a year and never got a paycheck, until someone called it to the administration's attention. Obert would typically let all his third- and fourth-class mail accumulate on his desk, then put a wastebasket at the end of the desk and just push everything off. More than once I had to salvage his salary check. I'd say, "Now, Obert, this pile has a check in it." He'd say, "Check? What do you mean 'check'?" I said, "Obert, the university pays you for professing and this has your paycheck in it." He was truly indifferent about it.

Did Obert write in the field of philosophy?

Only locally, but what he did was important. We established in the very early 1950s a philosophical lecture series. We called it the Great Issues Forum and it lasted for fifteen years or more. Each of us on the philosophy faculty would write and deliver a lecture at least once each year that could be published. Obert always participated in those forums and in this connection he wrote quite a bit of stuff, some of which was published. Obert wrote and read a number of lectures having to do with educational and social issues. He was very much in demand to lecture on major civic issues as well as philosophical, religious, and educational subjects. Most of this was not intended for publication at the time, but he brought much of it together at the end of his life, and the University of Utah Press published the edited collection in 1989 as *One Man's Search: Addresses by Obert C. Tanner*. This book was a source of great satisfaction for him.

Tell me more about his teaching. What did he do in a classroom that made him so effective in pushing students and colleagues to think?

The students liked him partly because his technique of teaching was to challenge them in their views. A Socratic method. He would raise questions that were quite central to their interests and their thinking. While Obert had an excellent reputation as a teacher among faculty members too, he had something of a negative reputation among some people in the community, especially in the church, as you might expect. They didn't want their sons and daughters to be required to do any independent thinking, so Obert had his critics like all true scholars have; but, aside from that, he had an excellent reputation. He was quite dramatic. He wasn't a dull lecturer like some of us. He could at one and the same time entertain and inspire the kids. He could really do it.

Did faculty ever resent Obert for having made himself such a success in business, while gaining such recognition here on the campus?

I had a feeling that there was some resentment against Obert. On the other hand, as Obert became more prominent in the state and made public statements which would get into the press and so on, the faculty became more and more aware that he was one of higher education's chief assets in this state. There's no question about that. He took on people like the ultraconservative anti-communist Cleon Skousen, for instance, in a big debate at BYU. Obert did many things that showed on the one hand that he was completely committed to intellectual honesty and academic freedom and on the other hand that he wasn't scared of anybody—that he said what he thought. As this became more widely known, he became an object of very considerable admiration, not only at the University of Utah but increasingly regionally and nationally.

Obert's application of ideas to real situations seems to be a theme throughout his life. It characterized his teaching, and it was manifest in the O. C. Tanner Company. His was both a moral and a practical philosophy.

That's quite right. Obert was very pragmatic in his views, very practical in his behavior. He didn't approach the problems of philosophy, so far as I could see, in a purely academic manner. It was his life philosophy, his moral beliefs, and his attitudes toward the big questions we all ask that set him apart.

Give me an example.

Obert would come back from a class trailing several students who were arguing with him. I remember one student saying, as he entered the office behind Obert, "Apostle So-and-So said . . ." And Obert turned around and said, "Now, I want you to get one thing straight—that So-and-So and I are diametrically opposed on any subject that you want to name." That way of dealing with the students, you know, was a source of delight to them and also consternation in some cases—in cases, for instance, where the So-and-So was one of the LDS apostles and the student was Mormon.

Obert's teaching illustrated the importance of intellectual freedom, one of the basic values that defines the higher learning. Let's talk about the university's first public battle over intellectual freedom. I'm talking about the American Association of University Professors' 1915 investigation of the University of Utah on charges of violating academic freedom. At that time the AAUP was just cutting its eyeteeth as a national force—this was the first of hundreds of cases the organization has tackled in its quest to define and protect free inquiry in higher education.

It all started here in the spring of 1915 when President Kingsbury told some young, popular professors who had come from outside the state that they wouldn't be needed for the next year and that there would be no hearing on the matter. They had been outspoken about what they viewed as Kingsbury's narrow views and autocratic manner. The board of regents backed the president, but many alumni and students were up in arms and some from the community joined in protest. Seventeen faculty members resigned, led by Ansel Knowlton and George Wise. Kingsbury happily accepted all the resignations. The American Association of University Professors (AAUP), Committee A, came out to investigate the case. Arthur O. Lovejoy of Johns Hopkins University headed the visiting team, and John Dewey was one of three distinguished scholars who were involved in judging the evidence and formulating the conclusions, though he did not come to Utah.

The AAUP filed a very critical report on Kingsbury's actions, and therefore on the university as well, disapproving the dismissal of the professors for expressing their views, finding that reasonable due process had been ignored, and concluding that "the Board denied the limits of freedom of speech in the university in such a way as to justify any member of the Faculty in resigning forthwith." They didn't mince words.

Yes, and the issue was further inflamed by what was seen as Mormon church interference, although the committee did not concur with this charge. Chamberlin, in writing the history of the university which was published in 1960, deemed evidence of church interference "wholly circumstantial." E. E. Ericksen, for one, would talk to me about it. I'm not sure how much students in general knew about it in my student years, but it was still a lively subject of discussion among the older faculty in the late 1940s.

This was the first academic freedom case investigated by the AAUP, which had just been organized. I guess they wanted to do it right.

Walter Metzger, the historian at Columbia who was later the chair of Committee A—AAUP's academic freedom committee—made a thorough study of the Utah case some years later and wrote an article on it for the AAUP journal.

I've talked with Metzger about it. I brought him here about 1980 to give a Liberal Education Lecture on academic freedom.

I must have been away, or I certainly would have attended, Jack. Metzger and I had a day together in 1965, at a conference in the Pocono Mountains of Pennsylvania. We discussed the Utah case at length, and I tried to convince him that he should come to the University of Utah, take another look, and write an article entitled, "The University of Utah Fifty Years Later."

In 1965 you were provost of the university. Putting two and two together now, this 1915 embroglio over firing faculty members without due process must have inspired you and others to clarify and codify faculty personnel policies when you were in a position to do so?

Yes it did, no doubt about it. In fact, I described for Metzger our new policies and procedures in dealing with faculty and the discharge of faculty, especially in matters relating to due process. I was really candid with him, and Metzger said—I'm not exaggerating this—"Well, if that's the case, you're in better shape at the University of Utah than we are at Columbia." In fact, he said he only had one criticism. "Your policy is to give people an appeal hearing before you actually take the action. I'd fire them and then let them appeal." Now I regarded Metzger then as the leading authority on the subject of academic freedom in the country, absolutely first-rate.

And that was his only criticism. He was tougher than we were.

As you see it, Sterling, what are some of the limits of academic freedom? Have you seen it abused?

In the sixties, when there was a lot of student trouble and some faculty discontent in connection with the Vietnam War, I was one of those who felt that some elements in the faculty were really attempting to politicize the institution. I suggested to James Fletcher, who was then president, that we invite Metzger to come out here then to give some lectures on academic freedom and let the faculty have at the issue.

In other words, you don't believe that the university, this one or any other, should take a stand on public issues because that would encroach on the right of individual scholars to think or speak freely? In the early 1990s we had a new manifestation of this issue in the so-called political correctness or "PC" movement to ban particular words or ideas from campuses—politically or socially unpopular terms or notions. This is why free expression for scholars is not a right, but a duty, in Jefferson's terms. I find his idea compelling, even though it preceded the modern definition of academic freedom.

You are absolutely right, Jack.

Now I'm sure the university felt like a free and exciting place in the thirties and fifties; but as you look back, how would you compare the degree of academic freedom of faculty and students then to now, here at Utah, or at other major universities?

I have to say that as far as I was aware we had as much academic freedom then as we have now; but I can give you a single example illustrating that things weren't as open as they now are. The years 1933 through 1937 were crucial years for academic freedom in Utah, in my opinion. But I think the person most responsible for fighting and winning the battles to create an atmosphere of academic freedom here was George Thomas. The result of the 1915 fiasco was that Kingsbury left as president in 1916, and John A. Widtsoe became president. Widtsoe was president for five years—until 1921; then he left to become an LDS apostle. Thomas then became president.

And he remained president for twenty years.

Yes. He had some time to get things done. I think Thomas was pretty tough-minded, the two-fisted variety. A Mormon, but a Mormon of great independence of mind and behavior. And that's certainly the reputation he had among the faculty. Even as a student, I was in his office a number of times and had several conversations with him. He was, I think, a man of very great integrity. He was the kind of person who could stand up to anybody—the church, the government, you name it.

What kind of support did he have?

I'd say it was substantial. The faculty had great confidence in him. He was very involved, for example, in the timing of the philosophy of religion course and his decision that Dean Bennion had to be the one to teach it. After its successful introduction, however, Dean Bennion had a completely free hand in teaching what he wanted to, and in later years others like Obert Tanner and Eph Ericksen joined in offering the course. I once asked Waldemer Read, who'd joined the philosophy faculty about 1928, if he had ever heard of the philosophy department experiencing strictures or even serious administrative criticisms in matters having to do with academic freedom. He said, "From the time I came here, I have never known of anyone in the department experiencing any pressure from the university administration of any kind." I believe, Jack, that this university has for some time been, and is now, as free as any in the world. Perhaps we're lucky that in the Brigham Young University the church has its own university to kick around!

10.
Windows on the World

From 1954 into the 1960s you went to Aspen, Colorado, every summer to moderate executive seminars and lecture at the Aspen Institute for Humanistic Studies. How did you get involved in the Aspen Institute?

You know, I'm not absolutely sure. In early 1955 I was eating lunch at the Fort Douglas Club and got a call from Walter Paepcke, the man whose vision created and developed Aspen as a cultural center and also as a ski resort. He had a great interest in the arts, in architecture, and in great ideas. Paepcke was a remarkable person. A Chicagoan, he built the Container Corporation of America, served as a trustee of the University of Chicago, and then became the brains and money behind the Aspen Institute. On the phone that day he described his plan for the executive seminars at Aspen. Each seminar lasted two weeks and they were the academic core of the Aspen experience. He asked if I would be willing to moderate a seminar that coming summer. I agreed. I took my family and we just kept on going, year after year. I went every summer for some years, but I haven't been involved with the seminars since the sixties.

Did you know Paepcke before this time?

No, I had never met him. I suppose my friend Met [Meredith] Wilson was the connection, because Wilson was helping Paepcke develop his program in what was then a sleepy high mountain town whose mines had all closed down. Wilson had been on the faculty at the University of Chicago while Paepcke was a trustee. Met was a friend of Mortimer Adler at Chicago, and both of them became involved with Paepcke at Aspen. I've never asked Wilson whether or not this was how I got involved with Aspen, but I suspect that it was.

The Aspen Seminars have become known far and wide. They are now held at several other locations in this country and abroad. I participated in the Justice and Society Seminar at Aspen in 1994 and it is a high-powered operation. But, frankly, I was offended by the pandering to elites that goes on there. I formally proposed in writing that they hold at least one session

243

*of every seminar across Independence Pass in spartan Leadville, just for a dose of reality.**

How did they respond?

Politely in the extreme, but they obviously didn't comprehend what I was saying.

In moderating the seminars and giving occasional lectures at Aspen, I came in contact with people of great talents, great ability. We'd meet—eighteen people around a hexagonal table in a building fashioned to fit the table. Participants would include people from government, the arts, labor, education, usually a foreign diplomat, and then the paying patrons, so to speak, executives who were usually very highly placed in business and industry.

I became friends with an amazing group of people. Three Supreme Court justices—William Brennan, Byron White, and Potter Stewart—were in seminars that I moderated. With Brennan and White, Natalie and I continued our friendships after Aspen. Several prominent labor leaders, including Walter Reuther, two or three ambassadors to the United States from other countries, and high-level people in the arts, people such as Norman Corwin, the famous playwright.

You and Natalie also became close friends of Walter and Mae Reuther, didn't you?

With their children they came to visit us in Salt Lake. We had a great time—a luncheon with President Olpin and the regents of the university, a long meeting with David O. McKay, president of the Mormon church, and a private organ recital by Alexander Schreiner in the Tabernacle. One evening Walter gave us the details of his remarkable battle against organized crime in the unions and in some industries. Natalie and I were greatly saddened by the deaths in 1970 of the Reuthers in a plane crash. We had also been with him on several occasions in San Francisco and Washington.

In one seminar at Aspen we had nothing but the presidents or board chairs of several leading businesses, including two Standard Oil companies, two major U.S. banks, Kraft Cheese, Montgomery Ward, and Sears Roebuck. Meredith Wilson and I moderated that seminar together. Ted Hauser, the head of Sears Roebuck, was one of the most impressive people I ever met.

---

* "From Aspen to Leadville: Can the Institute Surmount Independence Pass?" Unpublished essay by L. Jackson Newell, sent to Aspen Institute directors, August 30, 1994.

Another memorable Aspen experience was a seminar arranged by Robert F. Kennedy when he was Attorney General. He was concerned about the anti-American attitude of foreign students in American colleges and universities, and he wanted to get to the bottom of it. He organized a roundtable for three or four days at Aspen. Bobby Kennedy asked if I'd join him and four or five others for that session. Eric Sevareid and Thurgood Marshall were in the group. Half the table was occupied by us old folks, and the other half by the leaders of foreign student organizations in the United States. The ringleader was the head of the national association of Iranian students in America. He was, in my opinion, a son of a bitch.

What did you think of Bobby Kennedy? This was an imaginative and gutsy initiative on his part.

Well, there was no question about his ability and political talent, but I didn't ever take to him very much, to be frank with you. I felt that he was quite arrogant and a little on the pushy side. Quite different from my feelings about President Kennedy. I've never met Ted Kennedy. I can't overlook that Chappaquiddick business; but when I hear him on television and read his stuff, he impresses me more favorably than Bobby Kennedy did.

Of the three Kennedy brothers, I respected Bobby the most in the end. So your view interests me. Go on.

Well, a couple of trivial items might interest you. Everything at Aspen was informal, but I still had a feeling that Bobby Kennedy was a little too informal. He'd take off his sandals and sit through the sessions barefoot, and, frankly, I didn't think that was appropriate for the Attorney General of the United States. He was also annoyed because I wouldn't play touch football with his crowd—you know all the Kennedys seemed to be touch football freaks. Hell, I never played touch football in my life, and I wasn't about to play with Bobby and his friends and make a fool of myself.

You turned him down? You missed a memorable opportunity!

You mean the touch football was a memorable opportunity? Not for me. But the conversations I had with him were very pleasant. Bobby's assassination was a great tragedy in our history. He probably would have become president, and the entire history of that awful era might have been different.

Do you ever regret giving up Aspen?

Yes and no. It was a great experience, especially when our kids were young and we went there as a family. But it's a lot of work and I had other things I preferred to do.

Would you believe that Mortimer Adler visited the Aspen Institute when I was there in 1994. He was in his nineties and still in the fray.

Remarkable. He's brilliant, but I have never been an admirer of his philosophical position. He, Meredith Wilson, and I edited three volumes of readings for the institute.

You turned down the presidency of a proposed liberal arts college in Aspen; whose idea was that and what became of it?

It was Walter Paepcke's idea, of course. Mrs. Paepcke, a remarkable woman, seemed relieved that the college never materialized, and I was apparently responsible for that. After I turned down Mr. Paepcke's invitation to head a new college at Aspen, he asked if I would meet that evening in New York at the Sherry Netherlands Hotel with several people who were involved in planning the college. We had dinner and then a long discussion. It was a very impressive group of people. It included the president of New York University and the liberal arts deans from Yale and Princeton, Columbia, Oberlin College, and Trinity College in Hartford, Connecticut. Mr. Paepcke had involved all of them in the project, and they forged an understanding that these institutions would support the new Aspen College and guarantee the high quality of its liberal arts program. Among other things, they would release faculty to teach at Aspen for short periods of time and would recognize the credential of Aspen immediately when it began. The University of Chicago was involved, and arrangements were being made for interlibrary loans and other connections.

That's an enviable foundation for a new college. I would jump at the chance to lead such an effort!

It was really quite remarkable. Princeton University had already approved this proposal, and so had one or two of the others. My main role—and I've never been too happy about this—was that, after the session in New York, the Ford Foundation Fund for Higher Education and Mr. Paepcke asked me to study the advisability of establishing this college at Aspen.

What were you supposed to ascertain?

I was asked to consult with highly placed educators who had some acquaintance with Aspen on whether it was a good idea to have a college in Aspen. I had sessions with the president of Goucher College, who had been brought into discussions on Aspen and with other personnel at Yale, Princeton, NYU, Columbia, and Oberlin. For the most part, they were negative on the matter. In the end I submitted a report that was essentially negative. Aspen had a resort character and was developing strongly along those lines, especially in the winter. It seemed to me that it was hardly the location for a college. In the summer Aspen was a cultural center with outstanding music, lectures, and impressive study seminars.

Aspen's isolation is nothing compared with that of Deep Springs College, my alma mater and soon-to-be home again! And Aspen has continued to be quite a hub for leaders and intellectuals.

Yes, some of the summer things now extend through the winter—for instance, the executive seminars and scientific seminars. At any rate, my report was negative, which was quite a disappointment to Mr. Paepcke, but he took it well.

Was your report the death blow?

I'm afraid it was, Jack. The Ford people were apparently ready to put money into it and Paepcke was going to put his own money in it. He had already arranged for the purchase and rental of various buildings where students could be housed, and he had already acquired a magnificent old mansion to house the president. Natalie and I and the children had stayed there on more than one occasion when I was moderating seminars.

I wish Paepcke and the Ford Foundation had considered another plan for their college. I can see your point about mixing the ski resort culture with a serious new college, but I also wonder if they couldn't have turned the academic year upside down and held classes spring, summer, and fall quarters with the winter off. You can see that I'm getting into Paepcke's hopes for this college, Sterling!

Too bad you weren't around then, Jack!

You spent five months during the winter of 1958-59 in Iran. Was that an outgrowth of your work at Aspen?

It may have been. I had had no previous connections with the U.S. government, but the Aspen Institute permits a few observers to sit in the background during their seminars. Occasionally there were people from the State Department. That must have been the connection, because the invitation came from the State Department.

The Department of State in those days attracted many idealistic people and was viewed as a major form of public service. A number of students who preceded me at Deep Springs College pursued careers in the State Department, but they seem quite disillusioned today. What was your view of it in the 1950s?

I think you're quite right. When I was in Washington later, during the Kennedy administration, I associated with quite a few people from the State Department. Many of the people in the U.S. embassies and in other government positions were of a very high level of ability. Their commitment and idealistic temperament is very much as you've described it; but I hear many negative things at present. On the other hand, I knew George Schultz, President Ronald Reagan's Secretary of State during the middle and late seventies, and I have had a most favorable impression of his talents and integrity. I worked with Schultz in connection with the Committee for Economic Development. But the Washington bureaucracy often has a deadening effect upon people, there's no question about that.

What were your impressions of Iran when you were approached about the assignment there?

My very first impressions were those that anyone would have from general reading, but I got an insider's perspective quite quickly. It's a complicated story; but Courtney Brown, a marvelous friend who was vice-president of Columbia and dean of its Graduate School of Business, had asked me to come back to meet with the faculty of the School of Business for three days. I talked to them about what could be done in philosophy within the school. They were setting up an endowed chair for a professor of philosophy, and they wanted to discuss this whole matter with me. I met with the whole business faculty more than once, with many students, and I think with every member of the faculty individually. They were very enthusiastic about the idea.

Then the whole matter got personal . . .

Yes, Dean Brown asked me to take the professorship. Well, even though it was a great honor, I wasn't enthusiastic about it. I didn't want to live in New York and raise our children there, and I didn't think that being a professor of philosophy in a school of business was quite what I wanted to do. It wasn't to teach business ethics or anything like that. They wanted a regular program in philosophical studies. I tried to convince them to send their students one hundred yards away to the philosophy department, but I made no headway on that. They were going to have an endowed professorship in philosophy all their own.

How was this related to your Iranian experience?

When I refused the professorship, Courtney asked me to come just for a year. I didn't have to teach—just come and design some courses. He thought I'd be converted if I did that. I told him I couldn't do that. Well, then, would I come for half a year? No, I couldn't do that either, because I was going to be in Iran at the very time he wanted me in New

York. Well, that interested him a great deal.

How so?

He'd been given an Eisenhower Fellowship to travel around the world and report back to President Eisenhower his personal observations on the countries he visited. Iran was one of those countries. He later sent me a copy of his report to the president. He described Iran as the most corrupt nation of all the developing nations he'd visited. He tried to convince me that it was a big mistake to go to Iran, that I'd waste my time. So, aside from just general reading, that's the first impression I had from someone who knew a few things firsthand. He said, "Don't do it. Don't do it. The country doesn't have any future." Well, in a pathetic and terrible way, he turned out to be right.

You ended up feeling the same way?

I ended up feeling that I shouldn't have gone, but it was for more personal reasons. I left Natalie at home with our five little kids and went away for five months. I should have had my head examined, but Natalie wanted me to go and it seemed like the thing to do. All went well, however, both at home and in Iran.

Why did you go? Were you curious about the country?

Not irresistibly. I really went because I felt I should respond to the call of public service. I didn't want to go—I mean, I had no desire to do that sort of thing, but, well, I felt it was the proper thing to do.

What exactly were you supposed to do?

That's the strange thing. I really didn't know what I was supposed to do until I got there. I was told that I was to be an adviser to the chancellor of the University of Tehran, to assist him on educational and administrative problems, especially in faculty-student relations. Well, following instructions, I checked in at the Iranian Desk of the Department of State in Washington and they sent me to two or three places for briefings, as they called them; but they didn't tell me a damn thing. One of these guys said, "Well, it's a nice time to be in Iran. The Shah will be coming back, and it'll be the social season."

You went early so you could learn something about the region by visiting Russia, Egypt, Israel, Turkey, and Lebanon on the way.

I did, and when I arrived in Tehran I lived in a small hotel right across from the gate to the U.S. embassy. It gave me a peculiar feeling years later to see the anti-American demonstrations on television there, night after night, during the hostage crisis. I took my breakfast and lunch in the embassy coffee shop, got my hair cut in the embassy, and picked up my mail there. I remember that when I'd get my *Time* magazine anything negative about Iran had been cut out with a pair of scissors.

Did you have a formal relationship with the embassy staff?

I was associated especially with the staff of the cultural attaché. They gave me an office, helped all they could, and assigned a delightful Iranian educator, Ali Kani, who had an American education and was a professor in the University of Tehran, to be my counterpart.

What did that mean?

He made my appointments, drove me around in his car, interpreted for me where needed, briefed me on Iranian affairs, and so forth. I became very attached to him. Now it turned out that communist ideology was spreading rapidly among the students. The Shah's regime was trying to prevent a revolution from starting at the University of Tehran. There had been a great deal of trouble there. My job, I learned, was to do something about the communist unrest and head off any student revolts. I wasn't what you'd call an expert in these matters, but I became expert very rapidly. I never stopped being amazed that the university could even survive with such alienation of students and faculty from one another. The Tudeh Party, the communist movement, was quite well organized and functional as an underground affair.

This was prior to the Vietnam and civil rights protests on U.S. campuses. What kinds of things did you do at the University of Tehran?

I met regularly with the deans and with the chancellor and with one or two student organizations—but more with the administration. The students were in a hell of a situation there. For them it was a police state. They saw the faculty as simply lining up with the Shah and against them. There was little respect for traditional religious leaders; they were under fire both from the Marxist students and their leaders, and from the westernizing government regime. Women students weren't allowed to wear the chador on the campus—Shah's orders.

I thought there was an inadequate effort being made to preserve Iranian traditions and arts. The Shah was pushing his westernization program far too hard and too fast. This was a source of some of his trouble with the conservatives, especially the religious leaders. For example, the finest restaurant in Tehran was in the new airport terminal, a handsome place on which they'd lavished a great deal of money so travelers coming through the airport would be impressed. But the travelers' one chance of getting a taste of Persian culture and art was totally lost. The restaurant's orchestra was a British group that played American and Western music; the floors were covered wall-to-wall with carpeting from Great Britain, and, except for some blue tile, there was nothing in the restaurant suggestive of Persia. You'd think they might have had a few Persian rugs around, wouldn't you?

Did you agree with any of the Shah's reform ideas?

Yes. He was serious about improving education, improving the economy, liberating women, distributing land to the peasants, and so forth. Bill Hatch, the agricultural attaché of the American embassy, was a prosperous farmer from, I believe, Idaho Falls. He went out with the Shah on his land-distribution trips. Many of the villages were owned by absentee landowners, and the villagers were almost like serfs. Bill described for me his experiences with the Shah. They'd have a big ceremony, take the land away from the wealthy landlords and give it to the serfs. Then, the next thing you'd know, it would be back in the hands of the landlords. I'm not quite sure how. The place was filled with corruption.

So what did you recommend to alter the situation where the students were concerned?

In a final report to the Shah and the university chancellor, I recommended some vigorous action to bring the students more thoroughly into the life of the university. I submitted a number of concrete proposals for action and policies to follow; and the people in our embassy seemed pleased with them. There was some follow-through after I left, but I'm afraid it didn't last long. I'm of the opinion, of course, that if the Shah had done what I told him to do, he'd still be the Shah—if he hadn't died.

But what about Courtney Brown's observations? Did you end up agreeing with his warnings of futility?

Oh, yes. You couldn't turn around without bumping into corruption. One morning an American associated with the Agriculture Ministry in Tehran came to my hotel virtually in tears. He and several colleagues had been working for months to build up a flock of healthy productive imported chickens that could be used as breeding stock to improve the nation's poultry. Well, the Iranian government had complained to the American government that an Iranian should head the American-funded projects, so they put an Iranian at the head of this one. My American visitor had gone away for a trip; and when he got back, he discovered that the chickens were all gone. The boss had given some to friends for eating, sold the rest to butchers, and pocketed the money.

Totalitarian regimes are not only noted for their oppression of ordinary people but also for the depravity and high living of those in power. Does that square

with your observations?

I visited the Shah's palace, but I didn't observe any high living first hand. I will say that the Persians at the university and in other institutions with which I had some contact were very hospitable and would hold a banquet at the drop of a hat. The food was very good—all kinds of fruit, nuts, rice, and flat bread. But I wouldn't exactly call it high living.

Palaces aren't spartan accommodations, you know, unless the Shah's was quite the exception! What was the experience of other Americans who were at the University of Tehran with you?

There were only two American students at the University of Tehran, both of them on fellowships from the Iranian government. One was from Minnesota. He didn't understand the language and didn't bother to go to any classes. He shouldn't have been there. The other was from UCLA where he had learned Farsi and could speak it like a native. But he didn't bother with classes either. He was one of the leaders in the communist Tudeh Party. The university expelled them both. The ambassador was very unhappy about it because it looked bad to have the only two Americans at the university thrown out. In my opinion, they deserved it. So he asked me if there was some way I could get them reinstated.

What did you do?

I had dinner a couple of times with the Minnesota fellow, and it turned out that he didn't know what to do. He couldn't speak the language, had no tutoring, no language instruction, no counseling. He just stayed in his room and studied. The UCLA fellow was a plain damn nuisance. I tried to calm him down a little bit, then I took the matter up with the chancellor. I got both students reinstated. They both knew it was due to my intervention and also knew that they had to be careful about what they did or did not do in the future. The cultural attaché with whom I was associated at the embassy, a delightful person and a good friend, Mr. Ackerman, was very pleased.

How did you feel about helping an irresponsible American citizen in Iran?

I had mixed feelings about it. During the student unrest, the administration would call out the military, and there was shooting. The last time the Shah had visited the campus to dedicate the law building, someone tried to kill him. He never went back. The old campus was a safer place to be. It had a high, solid wall around it; but it had been besieged by the army before I arrived. The new campus had this fancy wrought-iron fence you could poke a gun through. This fellow from UCLA owed me one, and I collected by having him arrange a meeting with two of the leaders of the communist student party—a very mean operation.

Where did you meet?

We met in the home of some American friends of mine, the Kirks, who left for the evening so no one would be there. It was understood that I wouldn't take notes. The American interpreted for me, and the student leaders frankly told me their plans. They looked tough, and they talked tough. They had grievances and they were going to start a revolution. I asked the leader, "How do you go about starting a revolution?" He had a little trouble following the question, but finally said, "Do you mean who we're going to kill first?" "I guess so," I said, "if you start the revolution by killing someone." He just pulled an envelope out of his pocket and read the names of six people. "These are the people we will kill first," he said. These guys were tough and cold.

Was the Shah's name on the list? Did you recognize others?

No. I didn't recognize any of the names.

Were there many more Americans in Iran when you were there?

Not very many except those associated with the embassy or other U.S. government agencies. There was a large dam being built in the mountains about forty miles from Tehran by the American construction company of Idaho, Morrison-Knudson, so quite a few Americans were associated with it. And there was an agricultural team from Utah State University working with the country's agricultural college. And a BYU group involved in educational reform. The agricultural college of the University of Tehran was located about twenty-five miles from Tehran in Karaj, and I was invited to discuss educational problems with the faculty. There were six or seven Logan families there, marvelous people and real experts in agriculture. All of the Utah natives in Tehran and Karaj, whether they were Mormon or not, used to get together for Sunday school!

How did the Iranians treat Americans in general at that time?

The dean of the agricultural college in Karaj invited me to address the faculty at a luncheon held in an attractive new faculty building. The USU people who were visiting faculty for two-year terms told me that, although they'd been there for five or six months, they'd never before been invited into this building.

Any ideas why?

I don't have a clue. It was a very strange relationship. They were good, hardworking people, devoting themselves to improve the quality of that college and the Iranian agriculture—all at American expense, of course, and were being snubbed in this strange way.

What other institutions did you see in Iran?

Well, there are several universities in Iran, and I was asked to lecture to the faculty at four of them. I went to the University of Tabriz, which is up near the Russian border, the University of Shiraz, which is in the south, and the University of Isfahan, even though the lecture at Isfahan was held off the campus. This experience might interest you. At Tabriz the audience was in place—a large number of faculty members—and the chancellor of the university was about to introduce me when somebody came from backstage and whispered something to him. He said, "We'll have to go out for a moment or two." It was the secret police. They wanted to question me.

Right on the spot?

Yes. It was a friendly session. They knew I'd been to Russia before I came to Iran, and they just wanted to check it out because Tabriz is so close to the border. I went to Tabriz, incidentally, on the train—absolutely the godawfullest train I was ever on, and I've been on some bad ones. I almost froze to death. Lord Almighty, I was cold. It was a slow train, started one morning, and got there the next morning. There were six people in a compartment, three seats facing three seats, and three levels of berths. They were permanently folded down, and you either took your own bedding or rented it on the train. The embassy furnished me some bedding in a knapsack well in advance of the departure time.

I survived that cold night and got to Tabriz. The American consul in Tabriz had me to lunch, and the governor of the state of Azerbaijan—there's one in Iran as well as in Russia—held a dinner in my honor that night—a big affair. I was always a little embarrassed to be treated like visiting royalty. I stayed with a young man named Harnack, a grandson or great-grandson of the great historian Adolf Harnack. He was a Fulbright scholar at the university. We had met at the embassy in Tehran.

What about your visit to Shiraz? I recall you saying it was an adventure, too.

That's in the south, about fifty miles from Persepolis, the great Persian capital destroyed by Alexander the Great. I wanted to see it, so the head of the English department took me there with several others in two cars. Just as we were leaving Shiraz on the unpaved road, it started to snow. I said, "This is going to get bad." They said, "Oh, it never snows long here. This will melt in a few minutes." When we reached

Persepolis the snow was still coming down. I got the most amazing photographs of Persepolis in a snow storm. There was a little hotel there where we had lunch. I thought we should stay the night because of the storm, but my host insisted that it would melt off. Well, of course, it didn't. When the snow got so deep it was obvious we couldn't make it, we stopped at the next village, asked for the richest man, and he just turned his house over to us, treating us like royalty. He was in charge of a sugar beet processing factory there.

How was the night? Was it freezing cold?

I thought we'd all freeze to death. They had a big dinner for us, made up our beds on the floor, and brought in a little round kerosene heater, like a small barrel with a rim around it. We took off our shoes, put our feet on the rim, and actually got pretty warm. We sat up half the night while they quoted Persian poetry. They kind of sing it, you know. It was a memorable night. I wouldn't have missed it. Our host had several wives, but only one was permitted to associate with us. She was a beautiful woman in western dress. The others just peeked through the door.

We finally made it back the next morning after the sun came out. The snow was fifteen or eighteen inches deep. They'd never seen anything like it. I had to take a bus back to Isfahan because there wasn't any equipment for cleaning the snow off the airport runway. It was a fascinating trip past innumerable Persian ruins. At Isfahan, of course, there are great mosques with marvelous works of art. Both Isfahan and Shiraz are fascinating places. At Shiraz I was especially interested in the tombs of Persia's greatest poets, Hafez and Sa'di.

I imagine you lectured in Tehran as well?

Oh, yes, mostly on education and American philosophy. But one interesting experience occurred when the dean of the theological school in Tehran asked me to address the faculty on the subject of Mormonism. I claim to be the only Mormon in good standing who has ever given a lecture on polygamy to a faculty of Muslim mullahs. They were especially delighted to hear that the Mormon polygamists had not been limited to three wives.

That was an eventful five months in your life. And then you returned to the United States?

In a rather indirect way. You see, I was halfway around the world; and the State Department, in arranging my ticket home, said, "If you want to keep going, you can go on just as easily as coming back," so I went on—to Pakistan, India, Thailand, Hong Kong, and Japan.

Your Iranian venture, then, was really the centerpiece in a world tour that began in Europe and the Near East and ended in the various cultures of Asia. These experiences must have greatly enriched your scholarship and leadership thereafter. Your Ford Fellowship in New York and your experiences in Aspen and Iran opened the nation and the world to you.

I'm sure you are right, Jack. One of the most amusing experiences I had, however, was at an international conference in Oxfordshire, England, on problems common to the United States, Canada, and Great Britain. Now a Mrs. Burden, a comely woman, managed the great house at Ditchley Park where I stayed. She took a liking to me and put me in the Queen's Room where Elizabeth II had lodged from time to time. The first night that I slept in the Queen's bedroom, Mrs. Burden came right in after I was in my pajamas, fluffed the pillows, pulled the curtains, and then actually tucked me in bed. Then she stepped back, surveyed the scene, and said, "There, all you need now is the Queen." I was always rather fond of the Queen, but I had never quite thought of her in that connection.

11.
United States Commissioner of Education

Sterling, when did you get your first inkling that you might be asked to serve with President John F. Kennedy as his Commissioner of Education?

It was Wednesday night before Kennedy's inauguration in January 1961. As vice-president of the university, I was attending an affair of the business school in the Union Building. It was around ten o'clock and the program was about over when someone from the office called me to the telephone. It was Alvin Eurich from New York, whom I'd met when he was president of the State University of New York. At the time he called me, he was vice-president of the Ford Foundation in charge of their educational programs. He said, "Sterling, several of us are meeting here in New York. We have been asked by the incoming administration to propose someone to be United States Commissioner of Education. We want to propose you for that position and would like to know first whether you will accept it."

How did this come about? Who was involved on the other end?

I had first met Al Eurich at Princeton University, where we were introduced by Meredith Wilson. The three of us rode from Princeton to New York together. I learned afterward that John W. Gardner, who was then president of the Carnegie Corporation and the Carnegie Foundation, also recommended me for the U.S. commissionership.

What was your response to Eurich's phone call that January evening?

It seemed to me that acceptance was the proper thing to do, so I told him, "Yes, if asked, I will accept the position." I'm entirely nonpolitical, Jack, as you know. I have never had any connection with the Republican or Democratic Party, or any other party. And certainly I had no contact with the Kennedys or their associates. My Aspen experiences with Robert Kennedy came later. I did have a close friend in the government who was scheduled to become Secretary of the Interior, Stewart Udall, but apparently he had nothing whatsoever to do with this matter. I learned some time later that Stewart had a candidate for education commissioner from his own state, Arizona.

On Friday I listened to the president's inaugural address on the radio, and on Saturday morning the new Secretary of Health, Education, and Welfare, Abraham Ribicoff, called me on the telephone and said, "I understand that you and I might be able to go into business together." I said, "Yes, I've heard as much." "Well," he said, "how soon could you come to Washington to talk it over?" In those days I preferred to travel by train, and it's about a two-day trip by train. I said, "I can get into Washington on Monday. How would it be if I came to your office on Tuesday?" He said, "Fine." Monday was his first day in office.

So you went to Washington . . .

Yes, I checked into the Lafayette Hotel Monday night, not far from the White House. I hadn't set a time with Secretary Ribicoff; so about eight the next morning—I didn't know when they started things around there—I called Ribicoff's office and his secretary told me that he'd be pleased if I would come right over.

How did your discussion begin?

Mr. Ribicoff was very pleasant. He asked what I thought should be done about American education. My main response was the need to take a very good look at two things: upgrading the quality of elementary and, especially, secondary education and adapting education to the manpower needs of the nation. I had given considerable attention to both problems, the latter particularly in connection with our engineering labor force compared to that of the Soviets. Ribicoff and I discussed these matters for a short time. He then asked if I was a member of the National Educational Association. When I told him that I had no involvement with the NEA, he seemed pleased. I learned later that President Kennedy wasn't about to appoint anybody as the Commissioner of Education who was a member of the NEA.

Anyway, we had talked for maybe half an hour, when he said, "I need to call the president. I wonder if you would mind stepping into the outer office." So I went into the outer office and strained my ears as much as I could. The only fragment of conversation I picked up was, ". . . and he doesn't belong to the NEA." Then Secretary Ribicoff had me come back in, and we continued a very pleasant session while we waited for Ralph Dungan, the president's assistant on official appointments, to come over. Dungan showed up in about ten minutes and we talked for another ten or so. Then they asked me again if I would step out while they talked to the president. This time I went into a kind of foyer lobby that led into the secretary's office and sat there looking at a magazine. In about five minutes Dungan came out, put on his coat, shook hands with me, and said, "The president will announce your appointment this afternoon."

But they didn't formally ask if you would take the job!

No, they did not. If they had asked, I would have said yes. To be very honest with you, however, I had no desire to move to Washington. Natalie and I had just moved into a new home; we were settled and contented; and I was happy at the university.

Then why did you lay your reservations aside and jump in?

Well, I felt that I should. I hadn't been in military service and I thought this would be some compensation.

But you hardly escaped doing budgets, Sterling!

Sure, but I discovered that it was a simpler thing to deal with hundreds of millions of dollars in Washington than it was to deal with hundreds of thousands of dollars in the university. Anyway, the whole affair lasted no more than an hour. No one in Washington asked me, then or at any time I was in the government, whether I was a Republican or a Democrat, or even whether I voted for the president. That pleased me a great deal.

Splendid! But how had you voted—for John Kennedy or Richard Nixon?

The only person at the time who asked me if I'd voted for Kennedy was a reporter for *Time* magazine who interviewed me in Salt Lake City. I had a real hassle with him. I said, "The vote is by secret ballot, so I'm not going to answer that question." He said, "Our readers want to know." I said, "It's none of your readers' business how I voted. What's that got to do with it?" "But this is the sort of thing that we need to know. Did you favor him for president?" I said, "I'm not going to tell you whether I did or not." We went the rounds on this until he gave up. Then I said, "Now, if I have your word that you won't put it in your article, I'll tell you how I voted." He gave me his word and I said, "Yes, I did vote for the president." But that was the only time anyone ever raised that question with me. He didn't mention it in his article.

The conditions of your appointment or, more accurately, lack of conditions says something about the initial spirit of the Kennedy administration, doesn't it?

It certainly does. I did my part to keep it that way, too. I never called on Senator Frank Moss without calling on Senator Wallace Bennett and vice versa. Didn't even step inside a door unless I had time to also go to the other's office. Of course, Moss was a Democrat and Bennett was a Republican.

What did you do for the rest of that first day?

When the interview was over, it was still quite early and I had the rest of the day free. I wasn't catching my plane home until the next day, so I called on my old friend Stewart Udall, who was just starting in as Secretary of the Interior.

He was a student of yours at Tucson, wasn't he?

He always says he was. Actually he didn't take a class from me, but we spent many hours together discussing various matters and we became, and still remain, intimate friends. Stewart had been a University of Arizona basketball star before going into the Air Force. He later attended law school and became a labor attorney before he went to Congress. Kennedy appointed him Secretary of the Interior from there. He was quite close to the Kennedys.

Well, I took a cab to the Department of the Interior and found Udall's office. A very nice lady in the second or third outer office said, "Oh, it will be impossible for you to see Mr. Udall. You know, the secretary just came into this position and is so busy that he can't possibly receive callers." I wrote my name on a piece of paper and asked her to show it to him. She did, Stewart came out, and we spent about an hour and a half in his office. It was enormous. I said, "Stewart, what the hell are you going to do rattling around in a place like this? It's beautiful, but it's like a hotel lobby!" He said, "I know. I've played basketball on courts smaller than this." Harold Ickes, a former Secretary of the Interior, had built the building.

Your appointment was announced that afternoon?

As a matter of fact, the president did not announce it until the next day. I flew back to Salt Lake City, and photographers and reporters were waiting for me when I got off the plane. Later on Secretary Ribicoff told me, "You know, the president got into difficulty with the party when he appointed you. He had been making appointments without the national Democratic organization checking the candidates out with the state organizations."

You mean the Utah party headquarters couldn't have verified that you'd been passing out handbills for Utah's Democratic candidates?

I guess not! Anyway, Ribicoff said, "When the president went to make your appointment public, that's when they said, 'Now look, this has got to stop. You've got to give us time to check back with our state organizations. We can't leave them out of these things.' So you're the one who caused them to blow the whistle."

But they didn't decide to block your appointment?
Oh, no. It just held things up for a day.

What was the response to your appointment here in Utah?
The university regents and President Olpin were very pleased. President Olpin recommended to the regents that I be given a leave of absence, which they granted. The state legislature was in session and I was invited to address the Senate, which I did. It was very pleasant. They later passed a resolution unanimously congratulating me on the appointment, and the Secretary of State sent me a copy. But a motion for a resolution of congratulations in the State House of Representatives was debated for some time. Several representatives, according to the papers, voted against the resolution—one person arguing that I was not only an atheist but also a communist.

McCarthyism still lingered, didn't it? Well, onward! What about your formal Senate hearing and confirmation?
It was a pleasant occasion.

Did the NEA object?
No, I'm sure they didn't. So far as I know no one submitted any objections whatsoever.

When was the hearing?
It came with no warning in April, right after the NEA held a big reception for Ribicoff and me and our wives. Natalie and I were changing trains in St. Louis on the way to Salt Lake, and I actually had one foot on the step when a depot official came running up and said, "We have a telegram for you from Washington." The telegram said that the Senate committee would meet on my nomination the next morning. So Natalie went on to Salt Lake City, and I flew back to Washington.

How did it go?
It was very pleasant. The chair of the Senate Education and Labor Committee was Senator Lister Hill from Alabama, a Southern gentleman and a really impressive person. I later got rather well acquainted with him.

Utah's senators, Frank Moss and Wallace Bennett, were at the hearing; to my surprise they both offered generous statements in my support. There was some discussion by the committee. Senator Hill, for instance, said, "I see by your record that you're a member of Phi Beta Kappa. I said, "That's right, Senator; and I'm aware that you also are a member of Phi Beta Kappa." He said, "Yes, but I'm just an honorary member." I said, "It's a greater honor to be an honorary member than just to be an ordinary member." He laughed and said, "Commissioner McMurrin, you will go a long way here in Washington."

Everett Dirkson of Illinois came bustling in a little late, and Senator Hill said, "Senator Dirkson, as you know, our meeting today is on the nomination of Dr. McMurrin for United States Commissioner of Education." Dirkson looked down at me and said in his deep voice, "Oh, you'll be sorry, you'll be so sorry." It was all very light-hearted.

Senator Joseph S. Clark of Pennsylvania asked me whether or not, since I am a Mormon, I could support the integration of the public schools. I appreciated that question because I wanted to get my answer on the record. I responded that I did not accept the position of the Mormon church with respect to Negroes and had made my position very clear to the leadership of the Mormon church. I assured the committee that I was 100 percent in favor of desegregated schools. I didn't want to get into the priesthood ordination issue, but I felt that the church's negative position on Africans and African Americans, no matter what its roots, was wrong and I wanted to disassociate myself from it.

Yes, and it took seventeen more agonizing years for the church to right that injustice. So there was no opposition to your nomination?

Not as far as I know.

How about your swearing in?

The swearing-in ceremonies were held in April. Justice William Brennan of the Supreme Court sent word to the president that he would like to swear me in, and he did. There was a good-sized auditorium with perhaps twelve hundred people there. Secretary Ribicoff introduced me and I made a short speech.

It was all a little humorous. A couple of photographers got there too late to take pictures of the ceremony and asked us to restage the scene. But the Bible had disappeared. So Justice Brennan and I faked it, holding our hands to make it look as if they were resting on a Bible—a Catholic and a Mormon collaborating to deceive the public.

Although you have always done administrative work, you've never done it in an administrative—or bureaucratic—way. I remember, for instance, when you were dean of the Graduate School, your memoranda to the faculty were so infrequent that you would kiddingly call them Communique No. 1 or Communique No. 4. So how did a philosopher and an intellectual fit into an enormous Washington bureau like the U.S. Office of Education?

Well, strange as it may seem, it was not a problem for me. Secretary Ribicoff said to me right from the start, "You take care of the education end of things and I'll take care of the politics." He would refer to himself as a politician, which he was, of a very high order. Ribicoff was a self-made lawyer from Chicago, governor of Connecticut, then Secretary of HEW, and finally U.S. Senator. That helped the situation right from the start.

But it surely didn't solve all of your problems.

No, indeed. There were problems. For instance, I had been in Washington maybe three months when I received an edict issued from the White House that every policymaker in the administration would have to submit his or her public addresses for White House approval before they could be delivered. Well, I wasn't going to submit my stuff to somebody else for review. I didn't give a damn who they were, though I recognized the reason for such a regulation!

That's a bureaucracy, all right, whether it came from the president, one of his assistants or somebody else. Did you comply?

I sent an address to the White House only once, just once. I was to give an address at Harvard and had sent the draft over for clearance. I didn't hear back for a long time. I was actually on my way to Harvard, still without approval for my text, when I stopped along the way—we were driving—and called from a booth along the highway. They said my speech was cleared.

If it hadn't been cleared, you'd have been in an interesting position.

True, but I would simply have spoken extemporaneously. Frankly, I didn't feel I could live with that situation. Fortunately, I learned through our legal counsel that if I gave an address from notes, it wouldn't have to be cleared. From then on I just wrote my addresses for formal occasions as I always had, then simply titled them "Notes."

A small but sweet victory for the human spirit!

I never submitted another address to the White House, but I usually spoke extemporaneously anyway. Early on I was introduced to a man in the Office of Education who was recommended to me as my speech writer. He had been my predecessor's speech writer. I'm afraid he was offended when he learned that I had no use for his services. I wrote my own stuff.

Did you ever get a feeling that the White House was uncomfortable with what you said publicly?

Never had the slightest ripple either from the White House or from anyone else in the administration, not the slightest objection to anything that I said in public or things that were published. So my experience on that score turned out to be entirely pleasant. Of course, there were objections from some legislators.

You have mentioned that you were misquoted so often in Washington that sometimes you didn't even read the articles that cited your words. Were you serious?

Yes, I never got angry at the misquotes and misrepresentations; but I must say I was annoyed with Senator Barry Goldwater who had a weekly column syndicated in some eighty newspapers. In the lecture at Harvard University that I mentioned, I pointed out that the Soviet Union had created great strength through regimentation and authoritarian methods but that we must create even greater strength through our free institutions. It's all on paper. Goldwater wrote four separate columns on this lecture of mine, criticizing me for saying that we needed to do what the Soviets were doing, then adding, "I'm not saying that McMurrin is a communist, but—"

But! A big "but."

Precisely. I was astonished that a U.S. Senator would come out with that kind of stuff. Of course, after I'd been there for a while, I realized that U.S. Senators can do the damnedest things. In this case, I'm pretty sure Goldwater—or his ghost-writer back in Arizona—was just using this to get at President Kennedy. Well, a number of Senators and Congressmen got in touch with me to tell me how disgusted they were with what Goldwater had done. Walter Reuther, a very dear friend, sent me a letter saying, "All I can say is that when you have Goldwater down on you, you have arrived. There's no greater compliment." One of the highly placed people in the Office of Education was Ralph Flint, a Virginian, a courtly gentleman of such formality that he always addressed me as "Mr. Commissioner" and wouldn't get in an elevator ahead of me. When he read the first of Goldwater's columns, he came to my office and said, "Mr. Commissioner, you haven't asked for my advice on this, but I simply want to say, don't get into an argument with a man who has a newspaper column." I thought that was excellent advice.

There was no love lost between Goldwater and me anyway, because he'd done dirt to Stewart Udall when he was running for Congress from Arizona. In later years Goldwater became a moderate, and now I quite admire him as an elder statesman. But back in 1964 I really wanted one of those bumper stickers that I saw in Phoenix when Goldwater was running for president that said, "Back in the store in '64."

Whether you agreed with him or not, Goldwater was one of those rare politicians who said exactly what he believed. What kind of experiences did you have with Congress more broadly?

My relations with both the Senate and House were, on the whole, very good. But let me tell you a good story. I was testifying before the House Subcommittee on Education, on, as I recall, the National Defense Education Act (NDEA) fellowships. Recipients were required by Congressional mandate to take a special loyalty oath—not the ordinary oath of allegiance to the Constitution that every government official takes when he or she is sworn in, but a special loyalty oath. President Eisenhower had been for getting rid of it, President Kennedy wanted to get rid of it, and I testified more than once urging that the Congress repeal it because there was no justification for it.

What was the oath?

It was an oath on the order of that odious University of California loyalty oath, designed just for professors, that the California courts later outlawed. When I was being cross-examined on this oath business, some of the members of the committee began to press me. For the most part, they were doing it for the folks back home to get their patriotism on the record. Some of them would tell me this after trying to give me a rough time.

Did this acknowledged hypocrisy occur often?

Often enough. Twice when I was in long arguments with House committee members, my chief antagonist came down afterwards and shook hands. One of those who did this was a Chicago Congressman who wanted money for parochial schools and was not about to vote money for the public schools unless we came through with money for Catholic education. Well, it was quite a fracas for his two rounds of ten minutes each, but I didn't give in. As soon as the session was over, he stepped off the stand, came over to shake my hand, and said, "Nothing personal, Commissioner. This was all for the folks back home."

This sort of thing makes cynics of us all, especially students whose interest in democratic processes we can't afford to lose. Disgusting! But on this matter of the loyalty oath . . .

I volunteered that I had no objection to requiring the oath of allegiance to the Constitution, but, I said, "That's not what we're talking about here. We're talking about an additional, special oath that a person has to take simply because he's involved in education." There's always a bunch of reporters there, and the moment I said, "I have no objection—" several reporters bounced out of the room and at least one of them reported that I was in favor of these special loyalty oaths. The damnedest thing I ever heard. Well, the next day this was reported in

the *Deseret News*. Bill Smart was editor of the editorial page at that time.
I immediately wrote him a letter explaining what had happened, and he
published a correction saying that the earlier report had been a distortion
of what I said. Lord only knows what appeared in other newspapers.

*What was your feeling about the Kennedy administration's overall educa-
tional position?*

It didn't take me long to discover that I was entirely in harmony
with the educational policies of the president. He was against money for
parochial schools and in favor of federal money for public education. So
was I. I had no fundamental differences in matters of policy with the
people in the White House or with Mr. Ribicoff of HEW. So far as I
could tell, my relations in both directions, and also with other government agencies, were entirely cordial.

What other agencies do you have in mind?

Particularly the Department of State and the Department of Labor.
And also such agencies as the National Aeronautics and Space Administration (NASA), the Atomic Energy Commission, the Bureau of the
Budget, the National Science Foundation, the Department of Agriculture, and the president's Scientific Advisory Commission. Labor gets
involved a lot in education, especially through its training and retraining
programs. I served on a committee or two for the Department of Labor;
and after I left the government, the Secretary of Labor, Willard Wirtz,
asked me to chair two committees for the Department of Labor. Quite
honestly, I didn't have any clashes at all within the administration.

*By most accounts, the first year of the Kennedy administration was chaotic.
You make it sound so harmonious. What gives?*

I had problems with the bureaucracy within the Office of Education
itself and with the private bureaucracies serving education, particularly
those connected with the National Education Association.

*Now that's what I want to pursue. From the outset, you were quite critical
of the NEA—and they of you—as I recall.*

I certainly was, and I still am. They were very polite and I was polite,
but we certainly had fundamental differences.

What were your differences?

First, I should say that my relations with the higher education
associations were, as far as I was concerned, entirely positive as well as
cordial. Especially the American Council on Education, the National
Association of State Universities and Land Grant Colleges, and the
Association of American Colleges.

What were your differences, then, with the National Education Association and its leaders?

When I say the National Education Association here, I include some organizations that were in the NEA building in Washington but not officially part of the NEA. That would include such organizations as the Chief State School Officers (they just called them "the Chiefs"), which is an organization of the State Commissioners of Education, as you know, and the American Association of School Administrators (AASA). Those were the main ones that I had relations with. The National School Boards Association was located in Evanston, Illinois.

But the NEA-related associations were all of one mind, and that mind was far different from yours?

You understand that my personal relations with the people who were in the leadership of those organizations were cordial enough, with one or two exceptions. I am referring to the more or less permanent executive officers of the organization, not their annually elected officials. I should mention here Allan West, a high officer of the NEA, for whom I had the highest regard and with whom I still have a warm friendship. Allan was, in my opinion, of a different stripe from most of the others with whom I had dealings.

Back to the three organizations in the NEA building. How did the problem develop?

Well, initially there was great disappointment that a person from higher education was appointed to the position of commissioner. Most of the previous appointees had come out of public school administration. My immediate predecessor, for instance, Lawrence Derthick, had been a school superintendent. When he left the government, he became a high official in the NEA. I can understand the disappointment. At that time, however, it was a surprise to me. I got acquainted with the key people very early. My predecessor had made the deputy commissioner's position a civil service job, so I inherited Deputy Commissioner Wayne Reed. He was a pleasant person, but he had trouble handling major problems. He told me right from the start—and it turned out to be true—that the best thing he could do for me would be to act as a kind of liaison between me and the education leaders in elementary and secondary education. He was very much in their confidence and, I might say, in their pocket.

So he got you together with them?

Yes, it must have been the very first week I was in Washington. Wayne took me over to the NEA building and I had a get-together with

Bill Carr, the executive director of the NEA, and four or five of his top associates. Then on the same afternoon or evening, I met with Finis Engleman, executive head of the American Association of School Administrators, a former State Commissioner of Education, a kind of elder statesman. At that same time I met with Edgar Fuller, who was the executive director of the Chief State School Officers, a smaller organization but a very influential one. Fuller didn't like me, and I wasn't fond of him either.

And this was even before you were officially sworn into office?

Yes, before I was confirmed by the Senate. It was during my first or second stint. I would go to Washington for several days, then come back and carry on as vice-president of the university for several days, then back to Washington—a seesaw operation until I was confirmed.

Natalie and the kids stayed in Salt Lake until the end of the school year. I lived with Natalie's youngest sister, Marie, and her husband, Julian Ross, in Arlington, until June when we purchased a new home in Arlington. They were very generous with me and made things very pleasant. Without them, I would have been a very lonely person for a few months.

How long did you continue to commute between Salt Lake City and Washington?

Well, for about a month. There had to be some transition to a new university vice-president, and no one in Washington put any pressure on me to take up residence immediately. I functioned just as if I had been formally sworn in but was paid as a consultant. The Senate didn't take action on me until April because they had so many new appointments to consider. As a matter of fact, the university appointed Dan Dykstra from the law school as vice-president before I was actually confirmed in Washington.

So you started off cordially with the NEA?

Oh yes. In fact, before the Senate hearing, even, they hosted a very large affair for Ribicoff and me. Natalie came back for it. It was very impressive. Hundreds of people came. We had a reception line with Secretary and Mrs. Ribicoff, Natalie and me, the NEA president, and Bill Carr, the NEA executive officer, and Mrs. Carr. They'd asked for a list of people whom I would like to invite, and I listed the three Supreme Court Justices with whom I had had association. William Brennan and Byron White and I were good friends. I was well acquainted also with Potter Stewart. A couple of them came.

Did you invite Walter Reuther?

Yes, he was then president of the United Auto Workers and vice-president of the combined AFL-CIO. When he came in, it literally transformed the place. Bill Carr said to me, "You know, I saw Reuther's name on the list, but I had no idea he would come. We've tried for years to get him over here with no success, and by gosh, here he is."

This should have improved your standing with the NEA!

Temporarily, perhaps. The interesting thing is that before the reception was over, Reuther was in a side room with a big audience lecturing to the NEA people. Reuther was a great statesman and certainly the foremost symbol of labor that this country has had since John L. Lewis. He was a man of the highest cultivation, a statesman of the highest order. I'd vote for him for president of the United States any day in the week. We haven't had a president of his quality since Kennedy, in my opinion. Anyway, it made the NEA's day to have Reuther in their building.

One more story. As we were standing in this reception line in our black tie outfits, Ribicoff said to me, "Sterling, let's give them hell; and if it doesn't work out you can go back to teaching philosophy and I'll go back to selling ties."

Now that captures the spirit of the early Kennedy administration!

I mention this reception because it indicates that we got started off in a very good way with the NEA in spite of the fact that I already knew I was a disappointment to them.

Then what caused the deterioration in your relations with the NEA?

I'll give you two or three examples of the kind of thing I encountered soon after I arrived in Washington. I received a letter from a high NEA official whom I knew in Utah where he had been a college president. He wrote to tell me that many of his associates were of the opinion that I knew a great deal about foundations but very little about schools. I regarded this as an insulting remark and didn't reply. I was somewhat amused by the fact that most of these NEA bureaucrats hadn't taught a class for years, if they had ever taught one, while I had been teaching ever since 1937 and met classes right up until I went to Washington.

On another occasion, immediately following my swearing-in, I gave a press conference at which I made it clear that, on the whole, the American schools were not as strong as they should be—and could be. I also put in a plug for merit pay for teachers. My statements were spread all over the papers the next morning; and before many hours had passed, I received a very long telegram from the executive officer of the superintendents' association, the AASA. He let me know that he was shocked and disappointed that the U.S. Commissioner of Education had publicly criticized the American schools. I replied by letter to Mr. Engleman, saying that he could not have been as shocked by my statement as I was by his telegram, and that I considered criticism of the schools to be one of my responsibilities as commissioner. I guess that did it.

Now the picture is coming into focus, Sterling. Go on.

Not long after that I received an invitation to address the annual meeting of the National School Boards Association in Philadelphia. Wayne Reed, the deputy commissioner and liaison with the NEA and affiliated associations, came in and said, "It wouldn't be a good idea for you to address the School Boards Association." I think he told me three times that that wasn't a good idea. I said, "What do you mean it wouldn't be a good idea?" He was a little vague and said, "No, this wouldn't be a good idea. I'll write and tell them that you're busy but that you'll come and extend greetings to them." That's what I'd done at two or three organizations already. The AASA had invited me to extend my greetings at Atlantic City, for instance.

That was their way of feeling you out—having you there but not taking a chance on a full speech?

Yes, and I dug in my heels at this point. "Wayne," I said, "I wasn't invited to extend greetings to them. I was asked to be on the program and give an address."

"But this crowd will just chew you up," he said.

"Hell, Wayne," I said, "they're not going to do anything of the kind."

"Well, I know, but you're just not acquainted with a lot of these issues and you don't know this organization." He was determined that I wasn't going to address them. Now, I honestly believed that he had received his instructions from the NEA on this, and I wasn't going to back down.

"Listen, Wayne," I said, "nobody chews me up. If they raise questions that I can't speak on, I'll just tell them I'm new in this business. I taught my last class the morning I left to come to Washington. There's nobody in the NEA building as close to education as I am. I'm going up there and talk to these people."

So I went to Philadelphia, and I've never had a warmer reception. The questions the school board people raised with me at the close of my address clearly revealed why the school people in Washington didn't want me to meet with them. For instance, one question was, "How do we get rid of a superintendent?" Fire him, I said, but follow due process and respect his right to defend himself.

How were you treated by the press?

I was especially pleased by this positive reception by the School Boards Association because with me were a writer and photographer from Look magazine who were doing a feature story on me. They had been with me several days in Washington and went with me to New York where that same evening I addressed the New York Press Club at a banquet at the Plaza Hotel. The photographer had gone to Utah to take dozens of pictures of Natalie and the kids. I was treated very generously by the media, both in print and in radio and television.

Some time later, I think, you met in Atlantic City with a committee of the AASA, the superintendents' association, to discuss relations with the federal government?

I wanted witnesses for this one, so I was accompanied by Boyer Jarvis and Robert Rosenzweig, who later headed the prestigious Association of American Universities. The committee, six or seven superintendents, along with their executive officer, Mr. Engleman, handed me a series of questions that blasted me for my criticisms of the schools. The chair made it clear that they wanted me to stop making public statements about problems and weaknesses in public education. My function as the U.S. Commissioner was simply to be a representative of the schools in dealing with the government, mainly to raise money. Beyond that, I was to keep my damn mouth shut. But two of the superintendents on the committee disagreed with this—Phil Hickey of St. Louis and John Letson of Atlanta. Hickey came out flatfooted and urged me, as he put it, "to keep it up." When I refused to back down, the chair said, "We don't disagree with your criticism of the schools. What you say is true. We simply don't want you saying it in public." I told him that I represented the public and would continue to say whatever I regarded as appropriate in the interest of improving the schools. Now, Jack, I wouldn't want you to think that I went around doing nothing but criticizing the schools. Nothing could be further from the truth. But the press and television were quick to pick up anything that I said that even had the appearance of criticism. My whole approach to the schools was positive.

How did you get along with the NEA when it was all said and done?

My last encounter with Bill Carr was not especially pleasant. Some weeks after I had resigned and returned to Salt Lake, Wallace Turner, who had been head of public relations of HEW and was now at the *New York Times* headquarters in San Francisco, interviewed me regarding my work in Washington, especially my relations with the education associations affiliated with the NEA. I told him plainly that in my opinion the NEA was a great burgeoning bureaucracy that in many ways stood in the way of progress in American education, that the NEA was as much a problem for education in America as it was a solution, and that it was not as effective in improving education as the American Federation of Teachers, the AFL–CIO affiliate. I guess when they read Turner's article in the *New York Times* all hell broke loose. Bill Carr called me on the phone, terribly upset, to demand whether I had actually said such things. I assured him that I had. He was probably in difficult straits with his board and members.

That must have been a fairly brisk exchange.
    Yes, and unfortunately I never saw him again.

But there was more to this NEA conflict than that. We seem to be peeling back some layers of discord, one by one, Sterling!
    Yes, you're right. Not long before leaving Washington I addressed a meeting of NEA people from across the nation who were the experts on teacher salary problems. I challenged both the NEA and the AFT for their opposition to merit pay for teachers, especially the arguments they used against merit pay. Several who were present told me that they agreed 100 percent with me but were unable to get anywhere with the top officials in the matter of merit pay.
    In the spring of 1962 I accepted an appointment from the Secretary of State to head an American delegation to the twenty-fifth annual conference of the International Congress on Education at Geneva, Switzerland. Not long before I departed for Geneva, Bill Carr called me and asked if I was planning to attend the annual NEA convention. I told Bill that I had received no notice of their meeting, knew nothing about it, and would be out of the country. He said, I think rather sheepishly, that they thought that if I was going to be at the meeting they would put me somewhere on the program. I regarded the whole approach to be nothing but an insult. I think he was relieved that I would be out of the country.

He may have already known of your trip abroad before he called you. What was going on?
    Whether rightly or wrongly, I had the impression that the NEA was quite negative toward private education. I felt that my responsibility was to all education, not simply tax-supported schools. I rather think this

simply added fuel to the opposition that some bureaucrats in the NEA had toward me. The leaders of private schools, both parochial and independent, seemed to be very friendly toward me. I met with large numbers of them on several occasions, in Chicago, New York, New Orleans, and Atlantic City. I certainly did not do or say anything that would hurt the public schools. I have always been a strong supporter of public education.

What would you like to say about John F. Kennedy as president and as a person? He was a little younger than you, wasn't he?

Yes, I was young enough at forty-seven, and he was younger than I was. He was a very impressive person. I had seen him previously only once, when he spoke at the University of Utah before his nomination.

Did you meet him then?

No, I didn't.

What about the Kennedy charisma at close range? Did you sense it during the campaign?

To some degree, yes, but it became more obvious to me in Washington. He was very attractive and personable and obviously highly intelligent. There really was a kind of Camelot air in Washington in those days. The president was a brilliant man. My contacts with him were very pleasant. He actually had the style they write about. When I was first introduced to him in the Oval Office, he said warmly, "It's good to see you again." He'd never seen me before, but it was a nice, personal touch.

Did he sit in his rocking chair?

No, not at that time. We walked around the Oval Office and strolled into the Rose Garden.

What other times did you meet with him?

Well, I'll mention another time when it was my task to introduce the Teacher of the Year, a very attractive young woman, to the president. There was a reception in the Rose Garden, a very pleasant affair and a public event with lots of senators and representatives anxious to get their pictures taken with the president. This teacher told me that she had never been in the White House. When President Kennedy strolled up to us, I mentioned this to him. He immediately arranged to give her a tour.

He certainly made you understand the importance of courtesy and good manners. He was genteel—a much-underrated and misused word.

Tell me about your most interesting meeting with President Kennedy.

It occurred after I'd been in Washington about three or four months.

One summer morning about 9:00, my secretary came in and said, "The president wants you to come to the White House at 10:00 a.m." The rule was that you showed up at the White House ten minutes early. You might wait forever, but you were to be there ten minutes in advance. I was wearing a tie and a sports jacket, a perfectly good one—but it didn't match my trousers. I thought, "Hell, I can't go over there looking like this," so I called Natalie and asked her to bring me a suit. My office had a dressing room and bath, but I hadn't stocked it with shirts and suits and such things. After that I always kept a complement of clothes in the office.

A few minutes later Natalie called and said the battery was low and she couldn't start the car. My Lord Almighty! I called Boyer Jarvis, who was just down the hall; and we raced over to our house in Arlington, Natalie met me at the door with the clothes, and I think I changed my pants right there on the porch and finished dressing in the car as Boyer drove me back to the White House north gate. They checked me right through—they knew I should have been there already—and the head man took me right through to the president's outer office—and there was Bill Carr from the NEA.

He'd gotten there ten minutes early.

You bet he had. We shook hands, and just as I sat down, the president opened the door himself—right on the dot of ten o'clock, and—here's the point of the whole story—he was wearing a sports jacket and a pair of pants that looked like the ones I had just taken off! More stylish, of course, and more expensive than mine. He always dressed well. We went in and discussed educational matters for a half hour or so. Bill and I certainly agreed on the need for more federal funding for education, and President Kennedy was much concerned about the problem of salaries for teachers; but federal aid for education, even though he strongly favored it, was not necessarily his highest priority. After our conversation, the photographers came in for the usual photo session and snapped some pictures. The president later autographed one of those photographs for me.

You have it hanging in your hallway at home.

Yes. I didn't want to put it up but Natalie thought we should hang it somewhere. Sometimes I see it and I think, "My hell, that can't be me." I look too young. Those short haircuts, you see. Well, Bill and I were on the sofa and the president was now in his famous rocking chair. We shook hands with the president and Bill left, but the president asked me to stay.

What did you talk about?

It was a personal conversation. He said, "I'd like to talk to you about how things are in Utah." I said, "They're surviving." He smiled and said, "You know, the people of Utah didn't vote for me." I said, "I know that; but I want to tell you, Mr. President, that you have made a very profound impression on the people in Utah in the last few months. I just have an idea that when the election comes around again, they'll vote for you." And he just smiled. Then he asked about President McKay and Henry D. Moyle. He knew the latter as a leading Utah Democrat, and we gossiped a little about the University of Utah. It was a very pleasant conversation, and he asked me to extend his best wishes to President McKay. I sent President McKay a note immediately.

Another example of the personal touch.

Certainly. On several occasions one of his White House staff would ask me to draft for the president a birthday letter or a letter of congratulation about something to President McKay or other people high in the church or in Utah affairs. I got the impression that I was President Kennedy's personal letter-writer for Utahns and for Mormons everywhere.

You have mentioned JFK's intelligence several times. How was it expressed in your dealings with him?

Well, let me tell you a story that captures what I think of as his brilliance. It was a dinner meeting—about two hundred people—set up by the Committee for Economic Development. The president arrived after the dinner to address the group extemporaneously and then take questions. The way the camera lights were set up, he couldn't see much of the audience—in fact, he commented on it—but he handled the questions brilliantly, called people by their first names, and had figures and dates and events arrayed in an impressive order, totally off the cuff. It was as impressive a performance as I've ever seen, in a university or out of it.

His personal reputation has suffered somewhat in the intervening years. Has this been hard for you to deal with?

Yes, and I've found those disclosures disappointing. The president was high in my estimation, and it wasn't until after I left Washington that I learned of his alleged White House escapades. I had concentrated on my work and apparently missed the gossip. I liked Kennedy very much as an individual, and I certainly recognized that luminous quality he brought to Washington. He had style, a wonderful combination of idealism, energy, and intelligence.

You've already told me that you disapproved of Robert Kennedy's barefoot style at Aspen. What about the rest of the Kennedy family?

I've never had any use for the "royal family" stuff, the "Kennedy dynasty." I didn't ever meet Senator Ted Kennedy, but I felt that it was inappropriate for the president to campaign for him, to campaign for his brother—and I didn't like the idea of his appointing his other brother, Robert, as Attorney General. Too much of a family affair. I had a few involvements with Bobby and, frankly, as I've said, I wasn't much attracted to him. He was too arrogant. He told me once that his sister Eunice liked me. I didn't ever meet her, but I think she was pleased with some things I did in relation to the education of the handicapped. And I was all for Jacqueline Kennedy until she married what's-his-name.

Aristotle Onassis. Even so, I think she died a dignified public figure. But it sounds as if your approach to the Kennedys was personal rather than political.

That's quite true. I'm just not very political. I'll give you two examples. There was a big hundred-dollar-a-plate banquet, a Democratic fund raiser, and I bought a ticket since it seemed to be the proper thing for people in the administration to do. The president was speaking, and I would have liked to hear him, but I had no interest in going to a political rally. I gave the ticket to one of my assistants, Robert Rosenzweig, who was a political scientist. Rosenzweig was a brilliant student of Washington politics, which he loved. He was utterly delighted. He didn't waste any time getting over there and finding a good table. On the other hand, when I heard that the president was speaking to the Daughters of the American Revolution at Constitution Hall, Natalie and I took my mother and our daughter Trudy over there early to get good seats.

I've recently read a copy of your statement, "A Crisis of Conscience: The Present Condition of American Education," to the Appropriations Subcommittee of the House of Representatives on May 8, 1961, and afterwards published by the Congress and then by a number of journals and anthologies. I've been struck by the fact that, except for changing a few names, you could give the same address today and be right on the cutting edge of issues in education. For instance, you talk about racial discrimination, inequalities in opportunity, low standards of achievement, and the like.

I called it a crisis of conscience because the schools were not as good as they should be and could be, and because we knew that was so but just looked the other way. With notable exceptions, the standards and achievements were low, the expectations were low, discrimination was serious, and in general teacher education was in bad shape.

And my question is: Have we made any progress or are we just at the same point in two cycles that happen to correspond?

I don't think we've made very much progress, frankly; but I'll also have to confess that I haven't tracked national education trends carefully in the last few years. I think more attention is being given today to people who are economically disenfranchised; and that's due largely to government action which began in the 1950s. From the standpoint of the hundreds of thousands of individuals who have been personally disadvantaged in their education, I think there's probably been some improvement, but there are still many who suffer. Perhaps the curriculum has improved and teachers are generally better educated, at least in terms of certification requirements.

What, in your opinion, would constitute good teacher education?

I think the education of teachers should begin with a four-year degree in liberal education, the arts and sciences, then the equivalent of at least a graduate year of professional education work. Second, I think teachers should have genuine competence in their subject areas and on the whole should receive higher salaries based in part on merit.

I agree with you completely, Sterling. Well, let's take a break here and resume our conversation by examining the specific issues you tackled as commissioner.

12.
Controversies in Education

Let's turn to some of the tough issues, now, Sterling. You've identified three primary educational issues for that period: (1) federal aid to education, how much and under what conditions, (2) civil rights and the access of school-age children to equal educational opportunity, and (3) how to improve the quality of American education. Did they emerge in any particular order as you assumed your responsibilities in Washington?

Actually, I was involved in all of them simultaneously. There were, of course, many related issues—funding for the education of the children of migrant workers, funds for the education of Cubans in Dade County, Florida, education of the handicapped, the problems of schools in the inner cities, always the large problems of assisting college students financially and providing funds for the schools and colleges to improve scientific work, foreign language study, etc. In those days a major piece of legislation was the set of amendments to the National Defense Education Act, umbrella legislation that had been enacted earlier.

Many of these questions seem to be related to equalizing access to education.

That's quite true. There was not as strong an appreciation of the problems of the inner-city schools as there is now; but, as a matter of fact, that is one of the things that we jumped into right at the beginning. Secretary Ribicoff and I referred to it in our first conversation; and the first legislation that we sent to the Congress, a large federal aid bill for the public schools, earmarked something like $100 million in additional funds for inner-city schools—modest funds by today's standards, but it was a beginning. The Senate passed it, but it didn't survive the House.

This was part of the reawakening of the national conscience that came with the Kennedy administration—after the lull of the Eisenhower years.

Quite true. By the time I left Washington, for instance, we were all much more conscious of urban problems and discrimination. Boyer Jarvis, Robert Rosenzweig, and I, with some others, visited schools in Harlem to see for ourselves what the hell was going on. That was certainly an education for us.

Now was that something your predecessor didn't do?

It wasn't as crucial an issue at that time. My immediate predecessor, Lawrence Derthick, was a school superintendent; and I'm sure he was more conscious of this problem already than I was. However, after becoming commissioner, I soon got involved with the superintendents of schools in some of the big cities that had severe problems—Chicago, St. Louis, Atlanta, Philadelphia, and, to a lesser degree, New York and Los Angeles. I was also quite involved with superintendents in medium-sized cities. I mention this simply because I became involved very early with this inner-city problem, but we couldn't move the Congress on this. I mean we weren't able to get any money to concentrate on the central city problems while I was in Washington; but in the first package on federal aid that we sent to the Congress—which was nowhere near as large as it was when it eventually passed—as I recall, 10 percent of the total funds were earmarked for ghetto schools. As far as I know, that's the first time anything like that had been done.

Wilbur Cohen was a key man in the legislative process, Assistant Secretary of the Department of Health, Education, and Welfare for Legislation, a wonderful person, one of the creators of the Social Security system in his earlier years. Wilbur's field was social work, but he later became dean of the School of Education at the University of Michigan. I worked very closely with him in addition to the appropriate people in the Office of Education, of course, in the development of legislation for education.

What about federal aid to education?

The big controversy was we don't want our schools run by those guys in Washington; and if they give us money, they'll start to meddle. Well there's a certain amount of truth in that, no question about it. We have seen that happen with the federal financial support of research and scholarships in universities. I could appreciate this opposition to federal aid. At the same time I was very much in favor of federal aid because it was obvious that the schools needed more funds. Equalized student opportunity is as much a problem now as it was then; but the place I felt that federal aid was especially justified was in connection with areas in education where the national interest was at stake and where, without federal assistance, very little if anything could or would be done.

By "national interest," do you mean military security or social and economic well-being?

Both of those, Jack. You're on the right track. Before I went to

Washington, the NDEA—the National Defense Education Act—had been passed in 1958. This act, which provided federal funds, was pretty much geared to science and engineering education. Much that was done on legislation when I was commissioner had to do with the development of amendments and additions to the NDEA. What I undertook to do, with some success and certainly cooperation from others, was to expand the whole concept of what constitutes national defense.

Moving from national defense to national security?

Yes, whatever is necessary to strengthen the nation. I took the position in testimony before congressional committees that the strength of the nation involves much more than engineering and technology, that the strength of the nation is to be found in a sense of history, a respect for tradition, and the capacity of people to cultivate moral and spiritual values.

I remember about that time that David O. McKay said, "A citizen who loves justice is better than a battleship." It was that very perspective that you espoused in Washington.

A very fitting expression of that principle. And, yes, I wish there'd been more understanding of that matter among some Washington functionaries. Some, but by no means all, of them were just damn dumb about such ideas. All they could see was machinery—that the strength of the nation is to be found in tanks and planes and nuclear bombs. At the same time a lot of errors were made by some of the schools in their use of federal funds. We were subject to a great deal of criticism.

But you were involved in broadening their purpose and getting them more funds?

I was very committed to that. The non-governmental Council of Graduate Schools was established when I was in Washington. They held their first meeting in Washington and asked me to address them. I spoke about this problem since these were all graduate deans involved in administering NDEA fellowships and other funds in higher education. The dominant figure among deans of graduate schools was Peter Elder, at Harvard. When NDEA fellowships were being established, Elder was the chairman of the committee that worked on the question of what subjects would qualify. By the time I got to Washington, there was a great deal of energy spent by the *Wall Street Journal* and many other publications criticizing some of the fields in which these fellowships were being awarded.

These critics were pretty shortsighted. I'm surprised. And you were defending the broader use of NDEA funds?

Yes. I wasn't defending the practices simply because the grants were being handled in the Office of Education, but because I believed they needed to be defended and I wanted to expand their base even further. When I was addressing the first meeting of the Council of Graduate Schools, I stated that the strength of the nation is to be found in things other than machinery, engineering, and the physical sciences, and I referred to the fact that James Madison, Thomas Jefferson, and John Adams, among other founders of this nation, had something like a classical education. Peter Elder stood up and yelled, "Hear, hear!" I think it made a good impression on that crowd.

Certainly sounds like it! How did you go about making policies for the U.S. Office of Education?

I adopted a practice of making very sure that the people who had to live under the commissioner's regulations were parties to making the regulations. I'd see to it that every regulation was formulated with the assistance and certainly the approval of representatives of the groups that would be affected. The commissioner's regulations had the force of law. It would be outrageous if a bunch of bureaucrats in Washington formulated them alone. I tried to simplify them, too. I felt that many of the regulations governing the administration of existing legislation were far too complex. Of course, a good deal of the work of drafting regulations had to be done by the legal counsel within the Office of Education. They had to formulate the regulations in legal terms and make sure they related properly to the legislation. That was a very large task.

Could you give me an example?

I would get letters, sometimes from state school superintendents or superintendents of school districts, complaining about federal control. You see, they already had some funds from the federal government. Under the NDEA, for instance. Whenever I got a letter complaining about federal control, I would write back and say, "If you will describe the situation and tell me in what way the federal government is interfering, I will see that it is stopped." You know, in very, very few cases did they ever follow up on this invitation.

I remember one complaint from Minnesota. I said, "You let me know when you and your representatives can meet with me, and I'll come to Minnesota and we'll thrash this out." Well, I heard nothing more from them. But the Association of School Superintendents in New Mexico wrote saying that they had some very real problems with the funds that they were receiving from the federal government. Some of them couldn't live under these regulations. I think I surprised them when I called them up and said, "You set the date, and I'll come with the appropriate people who are involved in administering the regulations, and we'll work something out." I took Jack Hughes, the executive officer, a very competent man, and another specialist; and we spent a day with the New Mexico State Commissioner of Education and six or eight school superintendents. We had a first-class session, and they put before me some problems that were just outrageous.

How were they outrageous?

One of the regulations, for instance, had to do with money for the sciences in the high schools available under the NDEA legislation. One superintendent said, "We can't qualify for any of this money and we need it. The regulations require a certain sophisticated kind of book-keeping to keep track of the money. There's nobody in our county who knows how to do it." Well, that was a hell of a situation, but I took care of it.

When I got back to Washington, I appointed a committee to go over all of the regulations of the Office of Education relating to federal legislation to simplify and clean them up. That's an enormous task—couldn't be done in a short time—but it was obvious to me that some of them were so cussed complex that a lot of those people couldn't understand what was meant half the time. I couldn't either.

Did you succeed in getting them simplified?

They were working on it when I left Washington. I'm not sure they continued after I left; but if they did, I would say that's maybe one of the better things that I did—if I did any good at all—because the regulations which are established by the commissioner, now the secretary, have the force of law.

They can be a disgusting source of difficulty for those affected by them.

As can a simple lack of communication. For instance, the federal people in charge of building freeways would shoot their roads right through a school district with no concern for the effect on the schools. So I got them together with several superintendents of schools so that they'd better recognize and understand their impact on other things than traffic. I tried a number of things like that.

Now this brings us to the issue of racial desegregation to provide more equal access to American education. Did, in fact, the influence that came with NDEA funding, for example, end up being a lever in the civil rights movement?

I can see where you're going with that question, Jack. As a nation, we were just getting into civil rights enforcement when I went to Washington. I got one of the most amazing letters from Texas, addressed to me and Secretary Ribicoff. Attached to it was an article from a Texas newspaper reporting Ribicoff and me at some affair defending federal aid to education. The attached note was quite rude. It said, "You stubid asses"—spelled with a "b." I sent a copy over to Ribicoff, "from one stubid ass to another." I got more than one letter of that type. Most of them came from Texas.

Now this is only seven years after the U.S. Supreme Court's Brown v. Board of Education decision in 1954. Were you already encountering heavy resistance to federal efforts toward desegregation?

Yes. I received quite a few letters blasting me for our desegregation policies. As you well know, the Department of Justice assumed the responsibility for enforcing school desegregation. We would certainly pitch in to solve problems, but it was not the task of the Office of Education to enforce the law. In one case, somewhere in Virginia, there was a threat of violence over desegregation. A church leader wrote to me and said, in effect, "You'd better get down here, if you can, and do something about this." I thought I probably should go down, if there was any good I could do, so I talked to my associates who were involved in this sort of thing. Ralph Flint, a major player in the Office of Education, and a Virginia historian, told me that it would be unwise for me to get involved. He said, "Mr. Commissioner, you set foot in that county and your life won't be worth two cents." He meant it.

What did you do?

I consulted my legal counsel and others to determine whether there was any possibility of my being helpfully involved in that fracas. They advised against it and I didn't go.

Were there occasions where you did take direct action?

Let me give you an example. The Office of Education furnished funds to school districts that were impacted by federal installations. This was the most popular federal aid program because every state got in on it. You know the situation—federal property is not taxed, so schools for the children of people who work or live on federal property such as military bases have been financed in part by federal funds in lieu of taxes. Even Senator Goldwater, who wrote a book against federal aid, was in favor of this federally impacted type of aid. I tried to point out to some of those members of Congress and to the senators who were opposed to federal aid that they were getting federal aid to education when they made such great efforts to get federal installations and then had federal money for education.

It's only "federal aid" if somebody that you don't like or don't want to help is getting it.

I don't know whether anybody in the Congress ever opposed the law providing funds for federally impacted school districts. The administration's view was that an unjustifiable amount of money was going to that purpose—in fact, the Eisenhower administration had held the same position—so at each legislative session we recommended that that money be reduced, suspecting, of course, that it would not be reduced.

Futile but sincere! But to get back to the problem of segregated education . . .

We discovered that some segregated schools were receiving federal impact money. Now we drew up a regulation that, if the schools were on federal land and received these funds while refusing to desegregate, the U.S. Commissioner would become their superintendent. That helped to straighten them out—to my relief! I certainly didn't want to be superintendent of a bunch of local schools!

This is an example, you see, of how the federal money could be used to support the efforts of the Justice Department in desegregation. Another case was in connection with academic-year or summer institutes. These institutes, as you know, were established to bring high school teachers back to college for further study of their subjects.

Clearly the Kennedy administration was getting more assertive in the arena of civil rights.

Yes. I wouldn't have known without being told that this was the very first instance of the federal government denying funds to institutions on the basis of racial discrimination. I issued a regulation that any college or university that discriminated on racial grounds could not receive a grant for one of these institutes funded by the Office of Education. Well, several known discriminators in the South withdrew their applications immediately. This didn't force them to give up discrimination. They simply gave up the grants.

But this sort of loss eventually had an impact on them and their constituents.

There was some difficulty with several things we sought to do. We wanted to set up under the auspices of the Office of Education a kind of clearing house for information about how some school districts were desegregating successfully so that school officials could study how to do it. We would gather and disseminate information, develop model policies and techniques, develop experts, and so on. Well, we drew up a proposal to submit to Congress. Adam Clayton Powell, the flamboyant New York representative and chair of the House Committee on Education and Labor, was all for this kind of thing. I thought he was a crook and a lot of other things; but he was one of our best supporters. One day I was preparing to leave my office to testify before Powell's House committee about things we were doing to assist in desegregation, when, just before I left for the hearing, I received a call from the White House requiring me to delete the reference to a desegregation clearing house.

Why? I'm interested in the reason!

They told me that the president had been advised that Lister Hill, the Democratic senator from Alabama and chair of the Senate Education Committee, might be defeated in the next election if this clearing house on desegregation went through. Well, the president couldn't afford to lose Lister Hill. He was a powerful figure, otherwise a first-rate Democratic senator, and a strong supporter of education. So we had to throw that out.

The pragmatics of power and politics.

That was a great disappointment but something I certainly could understand. The committee before which I testified that day was delighted with the rest of my testimony relating to civil rights, but I was disappointed in not being able to add the clearing house proposal. Well, those were simply some indications of the kinds of things that we worked at in connection with the whole business of racial discrimination.

Did you get that kind of interference at other times from the White House when you were working on problems or legislation?

Very, very rarely. There could have been more interference if it weren't that the Secretary and the president and I seemed to be in full agreement on virtually all educational issues. One of the big problems, of course, was the question of how you get federal aid into public schools but not parochial schools. This was the issue that defeated the first real general federal aid bill which we sent up to Congress. This bill provided all states with general, uncategorized funds. As I recall, there was one major stipulation, that the federal funds were *not* to be used for teachers' salaries. Now that didn't make any difference, because if you used the money on remodeling or something like that, the money saved from the school budget could be used for teachers' salaries; but that stipulation was necessary to get the bill passed. The other factor, as I have mentioned, was setting aside a percentage of the total funds for inner-city schools in the larger cities. With the exception of those two provisions, it was completely a general aid bill, the first one, I believe, ever to be sent to Congress.

How was the money to be awarded?

According to the number of students a state enrolled, the number of hours the students spent in school, and so on. Every state got in on it on the same basis with every other state except for the big cities, and they got a bit more. It passed the Senate but didn't get out of the House Rules Committee. Failed to pass by one vote. That was my biggest disappointment in Washington. If it had passed, this country would have had its first general aid bill for education.

What was the snag in the House?

A member of the House Rules Committee from New York was for the bill; but, by damn, he was also going to have money for the parochial schools. He was Catholic.

One man, one issue.

Just one man. Now I didn't get into the back-room hassle with him because of my agreement with Ribicoff and Cohen that they'd worry about the political end of things. But I had hassles with other Congressmen over the parochial school issue. As you know, the president was Catholic and wasn't about to go back on his guarantees that his Catholicism wouldn't dictate his policies. But we worked at several plans to assist the parochial and other private schools indirectly.

Did this disappointment have anything to do with your decision to return to the university in the autumn of 1962?

Oh, no. That's another story. I didn't leave Washington because I was frustrated, although that was reported in some papers. I didn't suffer from frustration. It's like the fact that I don't ever suffer from disillusionment with the church. I was not illusioned in the first place. If you're not illusioned, you don't suffer from disillusionment. I took it for granted, you know, that you win some and you lose some. Well, that was the first big one and we lost it.

Tell me your views on the interplay between the two dominant movements affecting educational policy in that era: desegregation with its aim to equalize educational opportunities for Americans and the Soviet technological challenge which demanded increased excellence in U.S. education. Were those two movements contradictory or complementary?

Well, of course, it went in both directions. There's no question about that. The attempt to equalize opportunities in education can actually pull things down to a kind of dead-level mediocrity. I was very much opposed to that and made dozens of statements either in addresses or to reporters about how excellence could not, as a practical matter, be achieved across the board and that we had to concentrate on certain areas first. I learned that the hard way when I was dean of the College of Letters and Science. Departments that were willing to pay some people more to get them—mathematics, physics, and chemistry—are now the strong departments in this university, and departments that just wanted to pay everybody the same turned out to be the weaker ones.

That must not have been a popular position in Washington.

It's one of those areas where, no matter what the ideal is, the reality is pretty easy to perceive. I was completely committed to the idea that if you just spread everything around, you create mediocrity. Equal opportunity doesn't guarantee equal achievement.

Wasn't it about this time that John Gardner wrote Can We Be Equal and Excellent, Too?

I believe so. One thing I did in the Office of Education was to establish a lecture series to bring in some high-level people to address the staff on educational problems. Gardner was one of them. I hadn't met him before, but I'd read his stuff. I learned that he was one of those who proposed me for the commissioner's position. Gardner told me he'd rather talk with my immediate staff than with the whole auditorium full of staff—that would have been fourteen or fifteen hundred people—so we had lunch with a small group in my conference room. I had great admiration for Gardner; and almost immediately after I left Washington, he asked me to serve as a trustee of the Carnegie Foundation.

And you accepted?

Yes, and served for quite a long time. I guess I'd still be there, but I was on a committee of the trustees that took up the question whether the trustees should serve forever. All of the trustees except me and a couple of New York bankers were university presidents. The understanding was that their terms as trustees would end when they left their presidencies. Well, there was considerable rotation among the presidents, so I raised the question about how long I was supposed to be there. "Well," they said, "you were appointed simply because you're you and not for any position you hold, so you'll stay indefinitely." I might not have minded doing that, but I voted with the committee recommending three-year terms, so eventually I rotated off.

Back to John Gardner . . .

When he was asked to be Secretary of Health, Education, and Welfare, he asked me what problems I could see looming there. Later on he told me, "Those were just exactly the problems I faced."

You later invited Gardner to speak at the University of Utah's commencement exercises?

Yes, we wanted to give him an honorary degree and have him give a commencement address—sometime while he was secretary of HEW. President Fletcher asked me to set it up. My relations with Gardner were very warm and pleasant, so I was delighted to arrange it. I called on him in Washington and asked, "What kind of degree would you like?" and he said, "Well, what do you have?" I said, "We've never given this degree before, but what would you think of a Doctor of Humane Letters?" I coined that degree right there on the spot.

Oh, you did? I thought it was an academic tradition.

It's become one. He thought that would be great, so we've been giving them ever since. When Gardner came, they didn't have flyways—those tunnels from the terminals to the doorways of the airplane. You'd go out to the plane to meet people and they'd walk down a portable set of stairs. Well, of course, the plane was surrounded by the university's public relations people and reporters. When Gardner came off the plane, he saw me and waved, but we were inundated with all these reporters and photographers. We couldn't even get through the throng to shake hands with each other. They swept him away to the interview room at the airport and asked, "Why did you come to Salt Lake?" He said, "My main purpose in coming was to have a visit with a friend of mine, Sterling McMurrin." You know, that pleased me, because they'd just been shoving me aside when I tried to get to him.

I was greatly impressed by Gardner's work on reconciling the quests of excellence and equality.

I was determined to do something more valuable in my position as commissioner than simply spread the money around. I felt that the Commissioner of Education should pay attention to education—and not just to money.

What a revolutionary thought! How about an example or two?

Naturally I'm picking out the horrible examples, but they're important. Under the policies of the administration, you're not supposed to have any formal news conferences until you're sworn in. I was interviewed in advance by plenty of news people, but the swearing in is ordinarily followed by a formal conference with the press. Immediately following my being sworn into the office, I met the press in a rather large conference room and gave them a press release which I had written while I was still commuting back and forth to Utah. One or two of my close friends were in on it—Waldemer Read and Boyer Jarvis. I came out solidly for merit pay for teachers. I felt then and I feel now that if you're going to raise the level of American education, the first thing you do is raise the level of teaching. It's hard to raise the level of learning without raising the level of teaching; and hard to raise the level of teaching without paying for it. I concentrated on the problems of teacher education the whole time I was in Washington.

Now this was your first press conference, at least officially?

Yes, and there was quite a procedure. A couple of days before the key people from HEW's public relations office came over to drill me. The head man later became a rather close friend, but he kind of annoyed me at first. They were going to come over and put me through the paces to show me what reporters would do, you know. Hell, I'd met with plenty of reporters before; but this was well intentioned and I suppose was worth something. They ran through about fifteen minutes of difficult questions having to do with school finance, desegregation, equality, and so on; and there were staff people around to feed me information if I needed it. Well, I answered their questions; and after a little while the man in charge closed his book and said, "There's no use pursuing this any further. McMurrin can answer more questions than we can ask."

Did this mock press conference help you?

It was very useful on a couple of points. I asked how long a press conference goes on, and it goes on until the senior press person says, "Thank you." Quite informal, but that's how it's done. They told me that the press dean at my conference would be Mr. Hodenfeld, the Associated Press education writer. He later wrote an excellent book on education. As the reporters left the room, I heard one of them say, "This commissioner thinks in long paragraphs."

I welcomed this press conference, because I wanted to say some things that were, in fact, critical of American education. I wanted to urge the improvement of teacher education, highlight the lack of genuine liberal education as the foundation of the education of teachers, stress merit pay for teachers, and in general strengthen the intellectual quality of the schools by insisting on more emphasis on knowledge and the cultivation of reason.

You got to the heart of it there, Sterling.

The formal statement was carried in full in many newspapers because it wasn't terribly long; and, of course, the thing was on the national wires and was written up in the newspapers all over the country.

I understand that the National School Boards Association got snared in a paradox involving federal control of education?

Yes. The National School Boards Association made a major move to establish a National Board of Education. I was kept advised about it and Edgar Fuller, executive director of the Chief State School Officers, was pushing strongly for it. People hinted to me that he had plans to run the thing. I don't know about that, but I was invited to address their legislative body of about fifty people. It was at a national meeting, I think, in St. Louis or Kansas City. After they took action on the matter, it would then be submitted to the whole body. I talked about two things. I wanted to convert them to the idea that for certain purposes, federal aid to education was a good thing. You wouldn't have to convert people to that proposition today, but most school board members then were opposed to federal aid. I took the approach that schools were increasingly being asked to act in the interests of the nation as a whole—and cited language and sciences as two examples. Keep in mind that the Cold War was at its height. Well, I felt that I made some headway on that point. If they were doing the nation's work, then it made sense for the federal government to help foot the bill. Then I turned to the second point. I called their attention to the fact that the whole idea of a school board was a board of control. They were the very people who didn't want national control of education. I said, "You don't want the Commissioner of Education to control the schools, yet you're apparently going to create a national school board. What would be the function of that board? It would be to control the schools." I drove this point home quite forcefully. Well, when it came to a vote, they voted it down, and more than one person told me that my speech changed their minds and prevented the creation of a national board of control.

Any reaction from Edgar Fuller?

Oh, yes. He called me up the next week very indignantly and said, "I just want to tell you that you did a very bad thing." He was damn mad. And I just shot back, "I think I did a very good thing. You tried to do a bad thing." Later pro and con statements by Fuller and me on the national school boards idea were published together in some education journal.

I suppose you did a fair amount of business with the Labor Department?

Well, yes, I had repeated contacts with the Department of Labor. As you suggest, problems of education and problems of labor were very often intermixed. The Secretary of Labor asked me to serve on an interdepartmental committee that worked on such problems. Boyer Jarvis, our mutual friend, handled most of our affairs with the Department of State, especially with respect to educational matters affecting other countries and conferences with other countries.

Did Boyer enjoy that assignment?

I believe so, and he was certainly an excellent person to deal with them. He made a close friend of Carlton Savage, a very talented career man and a delightful person. Carlton was on what I think was called the State Department's Planning Commission. Boyer dragged me over to the State Department once just so I could meet Carlton. We became close friends; and as a matter of fact, the first year I was back at the University of Utah, Carlton was here as a visiting professor. Boyer also conducted certain international negotiations under the authority of the State Department. He went to Japan, for instance, on an educational mission for the government. He also represented the Office of Education in dealings with the United States Chamber of Commerce.

I had a number of connections with the Children's Bureau, another agency within the Department of Health, Education, and Welfare, and some legislative interactions with the Social Security Administration. The Surgeon General and I became involved in a variety of ways. And NASA. We shared the building with them.

What was your business with them?

NASA was financing certain scholarship and trainee programs. We also had extensive involvements with the National Science Foundation. I already had connections there because of the University of Utah's involvement with NSF programs. And then there were involvements with the Department of Defense—education on military bases or the education of American service people overseas. Some leaders in the Department of Defense wanted to transfer all these military-base schools to the Commissioner of Education, but I didn't take much to the idea and it wasn't done.

Why didn't the idea appeal to you?

It would have made the Commissioner of Education into a kind of school superintendent. A related involvement was the federal money that goes to school districts impacted by federal operations. Here are two or three other items. Under law, I was some kind of head of the Future Farmers of America and, I think, the girls' outfit—the Future Home-makers of America—because these organizations had some kind of national charters. I also sat on the District of Columbia commission that licensed M.D.'s and other professionals. When I went to my first meeting, the chair said, "You're the first Commissioner of Education who has ever bothered to show up." I went to at least a couple and found it rather interesting.

There were probably appointments that got you involved with other agencies as well, weren't there?

Yes. For instance, I was appointed by the president to the Commission for the National Culture Center, later named the Kennedy Center. Very time-consuming but quite interesting. I remember lengthy discussions about where to locate the center. We ended up putting it down along the river below the State Department, next to the Watergate—which wasn't there in those days. The president also appointed me to the Board of Foreign Scholarships, and the Secretary of State, Dean Rusk, appointed me to the United States National Commission for UNESCO.

Did all of these interconnections come about as a matter of course, or did some of them develop because of personal interests?

Many of them were just built into the job, of course; but there were real problems in the relationships among departments. Often a piece of legislation would bring us together—a bill that the Department of Labor wanted, for instance, or health in the schools would involve the Surgeon General. But with the heads of some other agencies of the government, I felt that we needed an interagency committee or commission that would be required by law or by executive order. We initiated the creation of an extralegal commission, which I chaired, and had excellent cooperation in actions involving the director of the National Science Foundation, the Surgeon General, the chair of the president's Scientific Advisory Committee, the director of NASA, the chair of the Atomic Energy Commission, and two or three others. Federal money for educational purposes was flowing through the hands of all these agencies, and it didn't make much sense for everyone to be going in his own direction without any coordination. We created this extralegal entity on the basis of our common interests, and Congress mandated the creation of such a commission after I left Washington.

So it was codified and continued?

I seem to remember reading that it had been discontinued, but I'm not sure. It turned out to be valuable for us in coordinating our efforts and putting some curbs on power grabs. I was dismayed at the hassles over territorial boundaries or "turf." It just astounded me.

For instance, there was legislation that provided funds for educational television, and the undersecretary of HEW really wanted to get hold of that operation. Highly placed people in the Office of Education frequently would tell me, "Now, we have to hang on to such-and-such.

It's our bread and butter." I heard that expression over and over. I thought, "For hell sake, these things should be where they should be, independent of whose bread and butter they are."

But if you don't watch the politics yourself, such things can well end up where they shouldn't be! Your situation was exacerbated, however, by the aftermath of the Sputnik scare?

Oh, no question about it. Science and engineering, that's where most of it was. Of course, there were funds for medical schools, but that was under the Surgeon General and the director of the National Institutes of Health, so we weren't involved in that.

Now tell me about the McMurrin Plan for the state of Mississippi.

Well, this was involved with the problems over segregation. I had picked up that expression from Henry Steele Commager, when he gave a major address at the Utah Conference on Higher Education. There was a lot of controversy over athletic programs, and Commager said, "I want to give you what is called at Columbia University the Commager Plan for intercollegiate athletics: fire the coaches." So I came up with the McMurrin Plan for Mississippi.

Wait, you had one for athletics, too, didn't you?

Yes, that was here at the University of Utah. I introduced it in the Deans' Council, back in the fifties, for half-time activities to get rid of this wasteful marching band business. The McMurrin Plan called for a large electrically powered stage or float that would move slowly around the field, with an absolutely first-rate performance of a small band or combo with singers and great sound. I thought it would be a damn sight better entertainment than these kids marching around and wasting so much time with rehearsals. I was serious, but President Olpin didn't think it was at all funny.

Universities do exist for students, you know! Well, how about the McMurrin Plan for Mississippi?

My plan was to throw Mississippi out of the Union. Just that simple. Do it in a single stroke.

If you had just come along a century earlier to advise President Lincoln . . . ! Sterling, I think I see the same theme in your relations with national educational organizations as with the Mormon church; they all have noble goals and mostly leaders of good will, but they and their organizations often run amok.

You're right. There's a kind of evil in the bureaucratic structure of any big institution—universities not excepted. It's outrageous in the federal government and very bad in the Mormon church. I suspect it's true of most churches, including the Catholic church; but at the same time I want to comment on the survivability of the Catholic church. It's simply the most impressive organization in human history because it's lasted the longest—and that makes it the wisest of all institutions. One of my great teachers, Heinrich Gomperz, a secular Jew whose ancestors had been converted to Protestantism, held that the Catholic church is organizationally superior to any institution the race has produced.

This could be because it never forgets where its bread and butter is, and it guards it well. And it only took about three hundred and fifty years to pardon Galileo!

Perhaps it errs too often on the side of caution. But I think the Mormon church should study the Catholic church—not to copy its repressiveness, but to learn from it the lessons of survivability.

Where did your lifelong resistance to bureaucracy come from, Sterling?

I suppose this sort of thing is instinctive, Jack, a love of individual freedom. I don't think it was my parents. They felt the Republican Party was on the side of righteousness, but they were really quite apolitical. We talked endlessly about religion, but the discussions concerned doctrine and the latest local sermons. The idea of a church bureaucracy never even came up. I don't think there was one then—nothing like what we have now. But you're right about resistance, Jack. Bill Carr, the executive director of the NEA, and I were being interviewed on some television program; and the interviewer commented to Bill, "Now, Mr. Carr, I take it that one of your main jobs is to keep an eye on bureaucrats like McMurrin." I thought, "My Lord Almighty, am I a *bureaucrat?*" I had never been so shocked in my life.

In one sense he was right, of course, by virtue of the office you held, even though you took steps which could be considered anti-bureaucratic.

Oh, several. I recall disbanding one organization created by a predecessor with representatives from social organizations from all over the nation who met periodically with the commissioner in an advisory capacity. I didn't like the idea of groups' representatives lobbying the commissioner, although I was certainly happy with competent advisers. It made some of those people mad as the devil when I did away with their organization.

But you had nothing against tapping experts for advice and counsel, did you?

I should say that I was interested in establishing a panel of consultants to confer with me on educational matters, experts in education and people of unquestioned wisdom and good will. I had in mind persons like James Conant, John Gardner, Meredith Wilson, James Allen, Francis Keppel, and Benjamin Willis, who would come together and work over the basic problems faced by the nation in education. This plan was not popular with some in the Office of Education, and they obviously wanted me to drop it. I got it approved, however, just before I left Washington. But my successor didn't follow my intention. Members of the panel who were appointed (not those I have listed) were consulted on an individual basis.

Returning to your aims as commissioner, what themes did you pursue in your call for excellence?

One of the phrases I found myself using quite often was the need for more "intellectual rigor." That may not have been the best word; but what I meant was that teachers should know their stuff and students should take their studies seriously—that time in schools should be devoted to important educational pursuits.

I'll tell you an interesting story about "rigor" and the reporters. I've already expressed my admiration for Hodenfeld. A brilliant person and one of the best education writers in the country. He often was associated with a Ms. Ferrer—they'd interview me together. She was the education writer for the *New York Herald Tribune,* and he was the education writer for the Associated Press.

Hodenfeld and Ferrer complained because I seldom spoke from a prepared text, which meant that when they attended a lecture by me they had to take notes. So they composed a parody of "Old McDonald Had a Farm," which went, "Old McMurrin had a school . . . with a vigor, vigor here and a rigor, rigor there . . ." They said, "The next time you give a speech without a manuscript, we're going to stand up and sing this song." Well, not long afterward I was addressing a national meeting of the AFL-CIO. Hodenfeld and Ferrer were on the very back row, and Hodenfeld held up a manuscript and pointed to it inquiringly. I shook my head, and I'll be damned if the two of them didn't stand up. I was actually afraid they were going to start singing, but they just mouthed the words and mimed it.

That sort of rapport with the press is rare and should be savored. Maybe you weren't a bad bureaucrat after all!

Thanks, but let me tell you that I discovered later that some of my critics in the NEA building thought that by rigor in education I meant simply loading more homework on students.

Sterling, how would you summarize your achievements as U.S. Commissioner?

Here I think I should mention just three or four things. In the first place, I believe that I established the independence of the U.S. Office of Education by convincing everyone concerned that the Office of Education was an instrument of the government and served the public interest, and not an appendage of private professional organizations. When I returned to Washington for the first time after leaving office, the deputy commissioner, who had been one of the chief offenders, said to me with much enthusiasm, "I want to tell you, Mr. Commissioner, that the people around here now realize that they are working for the United States government and not the NEA." That development was far more important then than it might appear to be today.

It must have been deeply satisfying to you, too.

A second and related development, in my opinion, was the breakthrough in the matter of serious analysis and criticism of the nation's educational establishment. Today, when criticism of the most radical kind comes from within the educational community itself, even the teachers' unions, it's difficult to realize that when I opened my mouth in Washington insisting that major changes were overdue, the educational bureaucrats and a large segment of the educators themselves were shocked. I wasn't greatly surprised at this because already, when I was in the administration of the University of Utah, I was held in contempt by some people in our School of Education. But things have changed—for the good.

The nation is now aware that things are not in the best of shape in our schools and no one hesitates to say so. What about policy changes?

Of course. Success in an executive post in the government is judged largely by the legislation that is enacted and here the verdict is somewhat mixed. There were comparatively minor pieces of legislation affecting education that were passed with little difficulty, and the important NDEA amendments, but the three major proposals we sent to Congress—general aid for the schools, the improvement of educational quality, and funding for facilities for higher education—were major battles; and on these we were defeated. The first I have already mentioned. The act didn't get out of the House Rules Committee because of the parochial schools issue, and the last was defeated by a last-minute drive on Congress by the NEA, which didn't want to see funds going to the colleges and universities before the public schools received a big appropriation. But we had made every effort to get general federal funds

for the schools before turning to facilities for higher education. This
finally passed at a later time, I guess during the first session under
President Lyndon B. Johnson, when he managed to get through the
Congress many things which had been turned down before the assassination of President Kennedy.

What about the "Quality Education Act"?

It didn't pass during my time there. I was anxious to get this bill
enacted into law. After revision, its provisions became parts of other
laws. I was pleased about that. It was a strategic attempt to garner support
for improved quality after the bill for direct aid failed. The HEW
Secretary and the Assistant Secretary for Legislation and the president
went along with me on this with a lot of enthusiasm. That proposal
included a provision for centers for educational research which were
later established by law.

We proposed those three large pieces of legislation: the bill for
general funding of public schools, a less general bill to improve the
quality of education in the schools, which also didn't pass, and a separate
bill for supporting higher education faculties. As you know, there was a
desperate need to finance science buildings and labs. Our bill provided
funds even for private schools, so long as the money went to basic
education, not recreation or physical plant. That bill passed the Senate
and there was every indication that it would also pass the House, but the
NEA defeated it. I learned about it while I was driving back to Salt Lake
City after my resignation. It was a great blow to me.

What was the nature of their opposition to it?

The NEA was determined—I'm going to put it that way—that
higher education was not going to get this money. They were afraid that
it might delay getting large funds for the public schools. They put on a
last-minute campaign, contacted every member of the House of Representatives the night before the vote, and told them that the NEA did
not want that bill to pass. At least that's the information given to me. I
was told that President Kennedy, who was strongly behind this bill, got
Bill Carr and some of the other key people from NEA in his office and
told them that, if they ever pulled any shenanigans like that again as long
he was president, there would be no legislation from the White House
supporting public schools. Scared the hell out of them. At least, that's
the information passed on to me.

Another effort of yours was to get federal funds for nonscientific subjects.

Yes, in the same way that the National Science Foundation was
investing federal money in school science, through such needs as science

teacher education. I began with English and history by securing additional money for education in the already-approved federal budget. From a larger perspective, even with our major legislation that failed in the Congress, we were successful, because we made some real breakthroughs in impressing Congress and the public with the broader needs of education that should be the concern of the federal government. It takes time to get things done in Washington, and we made a good beginning—some important breakthroughs.

What about some other things having to do with the structure and operations of the Office of Education?

My predecessor, Dr. Derthick, had created a committee to study the office and make recommendations relating to its policies, organization, and functions. The committee submitted its report to me and, on the basis of its findings, we radically reorganized the place. I believe and hope we improved it. But of course, it has been changed a great deal since then.

You had something to do with that, didn't you?

Yes. After I resigned as commissioner, I more than once testified before Congressional committees with the argument that education should be a department with full cabinet status.

I'm tempted to mention a rather amusing thing relating to my attempts to improve affairs in the Office of Education. Each evening after most everyone else had left my office, my assistant, Lucille Anderson, would bring in a large stack of documents for my signature, turning them over one at a time, and describing them. Many of them were materials requiring my approval for publication—pamphlets and sometimes entire books. I read enough of this stuff to convince me that much of it was at worst worthless and at best mediocre. So I assigned the task of passing judgment on publications to Boyer Jarvis when he joined me in Washington. Boyer had excellent talents for this sort of thing and waded into the task with his usual diligence. Soon the word "Jarvis" became a verb in the Office of Education. A person whose material had been denied publication would sometimes say, "It's been Jarvised."

Weren't you involved in a controversy with Admiral Hyman Rickover?

I really was not in any controversy with Rickover. Congressman John Fogarty, who chaired the subcommittee on education finance, had invited Admiral Rickover to submit to Congress a statement on the condition of American education. As you know, he was the father of the atomic submarine and one of the chief critics of American education. He was a very outspoken critic of the Office of Education. Admiral Rickover had made a study of Russian schools. His statement was a pretty good-sized book comparing American education unfavorably with Russian education. In Rickover's book American education looked very bad. Well, I thought that Rickover was naive in some of these matters, but he was a very valuable critic of American education. As a matter of fact, I invited him to lecture to the professional people in the Office of Education. Some of my staff suffered real consternation over this. The idea of bringing the enemy right there to talk to them horrified them. Some others were pleased.

At an early press conference, I mentioned that I intended to get advice from people across the country, including leaders outside of education. One of the reporters there said, "Does that include Admiral Rickover?" I said, "Yes," and that got into the news reports.

What did Rickover talk about?

He didn't come. He declined the invitation. I don't know what his motives were in declining. My contacts with him were primarily through letters and phone calls. I might just say in passing that he later put me in two of his books on education. In one of them, he stated that he liked what I was doing with education in Washington but he was quite sure that I wouldn't want to stay there very long. He said, "I hope Mr. McMurrin will stay long enough to get his ideas translated into practice. But, in any event, it is encouraging that for the first time in many decades there is someone at the head of the Office of Education who does not have the National Education Association viewpoint."[*]

Anyway, Rickover had submitted his very critical document to the House Committee in 1959. The next year Fogarty had invited my predecessor, Lawrence Derthick, to submit a statement of response. My staff had told me that he would ask me to submit one as well. Sure enough, the next time I was before Fogarty's committee, he asked me for a statement on the condition of American education. He said, "We had one from Rickover and one from Derthick. We'd like a statement from you." Of course, I assured him that I would prepare such a document.

Well, I assumed that I would write that statement; but the deputy commissioner said, "Now, Commissioner, this is the way it's done: the NEA appoints a committee, we appoint a committee, and the two committees together compose the document." I'd read Rickover's and

---

[*] Rickover, *American Education: A National Failure* (New York: E. P. Dutton, 1963), 183. He originally made this statement before the Committee on Appropriations, House of Representatives, 2nd session, 187th Congress.

then Derthick's statements. Both were entire books. Derthick's, in my opinion, was simply a whitewash of American public education. Neither paid much attention to higher education, as I recall. So I said, "If it's my views Fogarty wants, it's going to be *my* views and no one else's that he gets. I'm not going to confer with anybody. It's not going to be a whole book like Derthick's and Rickover's were. It'll be simply an essay." Some of them liked that. Jack Hughes, who was the executive officer and a kind of revolutionary, couldn't believe it at first, but I could tell that he liked what I had to say. "Now, can you do it by the deadline?" he asked. "I'll have it," I said.

And you did.

Yes. I'm not going to argue that it was good, but it was good enough that the *Saturday Review* published it; it has appeared in several books; and of course it was published in full by Congress.

How did you do it?

The way I always wrote stuff in Washington. I sat up in bed one night and just wrote it in longhand. Then I had it typed and messed around with it a little for a day or two.

What did you say in it?

I laid out what I thought was wrong with American education. Hughes came in after it was typed and said, "You wouldn't let anybody else have anything to do with writing it. Are you going to let any of us read it?" I said, "Sure, you can read it if you want to. I'd appreciate your comments on it." He read it, and so did Ralph Flint, Boyer Jarvis, and Robert Rosenzweig. I remember adding a sentence as a result of Boyer's and Rosenzweig's comments. Hughes and Flint talked with me about it. They had one recommendation—they advised me not to use the word "social" because it would make some in the House of Representatives think I was a "socialist"—but they apparently liked it.

How was it received?

Quite well, I'd say. Congress had it printed, and my secretary brought in four or five copies for me. I quite liked its looks. Two or three days later I asked my secretary, Mrs. Worsley, "Do you suppose that we could get some more copies?" She said, "I rather think we can. Congress has published over a hundred thousand copies."

If you were doing it again today, would you do anything differently?

I wouldn't take anything out, but I would add an important item. I was conscious, of course, of the problem of the inner-city schools but didn't make specific comments on them in this paper. My comments were designed to fit all schools. Beyond that, I'm afraid it simply sounds as if it were written by a university professor.

How about the same question applied to your commissionership as a whole? Is there anything you would have done differently if you were going back there again?

Well, I'm sorry we weren't able to do more with the problems of education in the inner cities. It was really James Conant's work on urban education that brought this issue to the nation's attention. Now I had some sessions with Conant. He and I were on a couple of programs together and had one or two private sessions besides that, in which we discussed these very issues. I've always been sorry that I didn't do more along those lines when I was in Washington.

Any regrets?

One thing I regret is that I lacked adequate confidence in my own judgment. I now realize that at times I yielded unwisely to the persuasions of others because of their more extensive experience in Washington. In the matter of the big-city schools, Los Angeles had an association of inner-city high school principals, and the chair was the principal of my old high school, Manual Arts. He invited me to meet with them and discuss the problems of the inner-city schools. It was a very worthwhile session. They asked me to address the student body. It was so large that they met on the bleachers of the athletic field. It had been almost entirely white and middle class when I attended, and now it was generally poor and almost completely black with a few whites and a few Asians. The demographic shift was dramatically clear. There was also a faculty luncheon, which I enjoyed very much, especially since two of my teachers were still there: James Bluet, a wonderful man, head of the physical education department, and Miss Elizabeth Mottern, the very attractive music teacher. She gave me a hug, and I said, "This is a hell of a time for us to start this sort of thing. We should have got at it when I was here as a student."

Looking back, Sterling, would you say you enjoyed working in Washington?

It wasn't unpleasant, but I wasn't there for a good time like some people who hold appointments in Washington. I took the position because I felt it was the proper thing to do. Reporters would almost invariably ask me if I enjoyed my work, and I nearly always answered, "I'm willing to do it, but I'm not required to enjoy it. I don't especially like administrative work." Some people thought it was terrible for me to say that, but it's simply a matter of being honest.

In my observation, people who go to Washington either get caught up in the headiness of being close to power or they tend to be revolted by the influence peddling. You were effective in dealing with the politics, but you also seem to have been displeased by the politicking itself.

I think that's a fair assessment. I was realistic enough not to be disenchanted with things. I must say, Jack, that when I left Washington, I didn't capitalize on my government experience to make money, though I had plenty of opportunities. I was under pressure from two lecture bureaus to let them schedule me for lucrative lectures across the country—disgusting. Even then the bureaus had plenty of ex-federal officials capitalizing on their Washington experience. But I must admit to some regret in later turning down an invitation to appear on a TV program in Honolulu where I would meet with two famous people, all three to come in blindly and discuss a variety of issues. When the TV representative became convinced that I wouldn't do it because it was an entertainment program, she revealed the secret of who the others were. Both were my two favorite movie stars—one was Burt Lancaster who died recently and the other was Ernest Borgnine. I would like to have made their acquaintance.

Perhaps one reason for your relatively low frustration is that education in some fields was getting federal money without having to fight hard to get it?

That's an astute observation. The sudden upsurge of interest in science and engineering generated a lot of money for those purposes. Such things as atomic energy for power plants, the establishment of NASA, and the very rapid growth of the health sciences in connection with the National Institutes of Health all benefitted education. To say nothing of the great problem of providing armaments to carry on the Cold War.

Not to mention the idealism of the Kennedy administration.

Oh, that's very true. I felt that idealism. I didn't go overboard on this kind of thing, as I've told you, because I'm not politically involved—

But isn't it fair to say that you have a sense of mission about making institutions more humane, more responsive?

Yes, I had a general feeling of satisfaction with what was being done and—this is what you're leading up to, isn't it?—that made it easier to avoid getting frustrated.

Yes. You did mention being disgusted by the territorial battles. Anything else?

Oh, I was disgusted when pressure was put on me a time or two to hire or fire people when there was no justification for it. Pressure was on me by Secretary Ribicoff once to appoint a Texan to be the commissioner's representative for a number of Southern states.

What did you do?

Well, I resented the political overtones. One of the Texas senators was pressuring Ribicoff on the matter. But after I'd made a thorough investigation of the man's credentials, I made the appointment. It ended well, though, since the person in question was very well qualified and it did, in fact, turn out to be a good appointment. Another incident was pressure to discipline an individual highly placed in the Office of Education because of something he'd done when Eisenhower was president.

Make him the administration's sacrificial lamb?

Something like that. In another case a highly placed man in the Office of Education was under the gun from Congressman Adam Clayton Powell, who insisted that I fire him. The man had erred unintentionally on a very minor thing and had apologized, but Powell was determined. It was a matter of race. I simply refused to give in and Powell gave up. That's the kind of stuff I didn't like. They were all quite minor, you understand, although I saw incidents in other departments that I think were absolutely disgraceful.

Now, you left the commissionership in August of 1962?

It was September or October. The president did not appoint a successor to me for some time, so the people in the Office of Education kept getting in touch with me, and I went back to Washington several times simply to carry on the work.

But you'd already relinquished the title?

Oh, yes. Though I had sent in my resignation to the president, it was a long time before I received a reply. So finally I canceled myself out; I sent the finance office instructions to quit paying me because I was leaving.

What factors contributed to your resignation?

As I said in my letter of resignation to the president, it was purely a personal matter, not work related at all. Abraham Ribicoff got hold of me one day and said, "I need to tell you that I'm planning to resign. A senate seat in Connecticut is open, so I'm going to run for that seat. I just wanted you to know." It was a foregone conclusion that he would be elected.

Well, to be very frank with you, Jack, I was tired of administrative work—not physically tired or mentally tired but just tired. When Ribicoff said that, I thought, "By damn, if he can leave gracefully, why can't I?" I instantly said, "Now, this gives *me* an opportunity to resign, too." Well, Ribicoff was very much opposed to that. He promptly called the chief of the HEW legal department, Mr. Wilcox, who came right up and the two of them started to work on me. He had Wilcox explain that since I was an appointee of the president there was no reason why I should resign just because the secretary was resigning. I listened patiently and then said, "But don't you see. It gives me an opportunity to get back to teaching, and Ribicoff's replacement can get in on the appointment of my successor." They argued very hard against this.

Flattering, all the same.

Yes, but I saw my chance. Ribicoff felt that the Department of Health, Education, and Welfare was a real problem. He was of the opinion that it could not be administered properly and that it should be divided into more meaningful units. "The first thing I'm going to do when I get into the Senate," he said—and I knew he would—"is introduce a bill to create a cabinet-level Department of Education. It'll pass, and the president will appoint you Secretary of Education."

That was his carrot to get you to stay, was it?

Yes, and frankly, it was the wrong carrot. That didn't appeal to me one bit. And, as a matter of fact, it took many years to get that department established.

What did your staff say about it?

I'll have to say that they brought every conceivable pressure to bear on me to stay. I don't know whether I was so easygoing that they had their own way or what, but they worked like the devil to get me to stay. The president appointed a new Secretary of Health, Education, and Welfare, Anthony Celebrezze. He went to work on me immediately, urging me to rescind my resignation. I liked him, and he was so persuasive that he half changed my mind. But when I got home from work on the day that I told him I might reconsider, there was Natalie half-packed, and the children were finally resigned to going home and were starting to anticipate it with pleasure. It was no good. I told the Secretary I wasn't going to change my mind.

If Ribicoff hadn't resigned, would you have stayed on for the four years?

Oh, sure, unless another good excuse had come along. But I had an even more personal reason for wanting to leave. President Olpin had asked Boyer Jarvis to come back to the university to be dean of the summer session. He also became the president's executive assistant. Natalie would greatly miss Pat Jarvis. They were and are the warmest of friends. Their relationship was very important to Natalie, who had five kids to wrangle. Boyer and I would leave for the office at 8 a.m. and usually not get home until after eleven. I had to be out of town a great deal. Sometimes I would fly back in, go to my office, and fly out again without ever going home. So Boyer's and Pat's leaving was another reason for my resigning. Natalie would greatly miss them. And I thought it wasn't entirely fair to Natalie to have the whole burden of rearing a family.

When did you actually resign?

Ribicoff told me of the date that he would resign, and I was planning to announce my resignation on the next day; but I picked up the *Herald Tribune* in Paris, and there it was. He'd jumped the gun a bit. When I returned to Washington, I called on Senator Bennett and Senator Moss to inform them of my plans. I thought this was proper, since both of them had appeared at the hearing on my confirmation and supported the appointment. When I went to Senator Moss's office, he was in Utah; but his aide said, "Oh, he's on the phone right now and he wants to talk to you." So I got on the phone and told him I was planning to resign. My resignation was leaked by someone to the press, which created some consternation over at the White House.

I'll bet it did.

Reporters began calling the president's public relations director from all over the place. Pierre Salinger got in touch with our public relations people and told them not to confirm that I was resigning. I'd sent my resignation to the White House within an hour or two after talking to the senators, but it was the president's decision when to release news of my leaving to the press.

Did you get any other reaction from the White House?

Well, I went over to the White House for a session with the president's appointments secretary, Mr. Dungan. Dungan said that the president had indicated that if I insisted on it—that's the way he put it—he would accept my resignation; but he'd like to know whom I would recommend to replace me. I gave him three names.

Who were they?

Francis Keppel, the dean of education at Harvard, was my first choice, and Dungan immediately said, "There are people in the White House who are acquainted with Keppel, and the president is not going to appoint him." So I just gave him my other two recommendations—James Allen, who was Commissioner of Education of New York, and Harold Howe, a highly successful superintendent of schools in New York State.

Did President Kennedy follow your advice?

Yes. All three of these men succeeded me as Commissioner of Education. But not in the exact order I recommended them. Frank Keppel was appointed by President Kennedy, Harold Howe was appointed by President Lyndon Johnson, and Jim Allen was appointed by President Richard Nixon. So, you see, I was bipartisan.

But there was no action from the White House on my resignation for a very long time. As I said, I couldn't get an official acknowledgment of my resignation, so I stayed as long as I could even though Lillian Ence had already rented a house for us in Salt Lake. Eventually, however, we sold our Washington home, I told them to cut off my paycheck, and we started to drive back to Utah.

Were you somewhat distressed about this?

Oh, not seriously, but the result was that I still had a lot of government business to handle. I must have carried on four or five conversations as we drove back to Utah, calling back and forth and thereafter returning several times to Washington. Eventually, at some point that fall, I got the letter from the president accepting my resignation and expressing appreciation to me. Wayne Reed, my deputy, was acting commissioner and remained in that position until Francis Keppel was appointed. I've often wondered about the details of Frank's appointment.

What honors did you receive while you were commissioner?

You know, I'm not sure, but there were several honorary doctorates and special awards. I think the first honorary degree was here at the University of Utah, at spring graduation in 1962, since I remember they had me deliver the commencement address. Another honorary doctorate was awarded in 1962 by Delaware State College, which is a predominantly black college. Quite a bit was made of the fact that I was against racism. Then an honorary doctorate at Clark College in Massachusetts, one from the University of Southern California, and others followed after I left Washington. There were a few special honors from universities, including Columbia, New York University, and the University of Southern California.

So you settled down again to teach and do scholarly work at the University of Utah. How did it feel?

I left Washington because I'd had all I wanted of administrative work and wanted to get back to teaching and writing. There were three pleasant years teaching and the next thing you know, I was involved again in administration.

You surely were.

13.
E. E. Ericksen Distinguished Professor

Sterling, when you returned to the University of Utah from your stint in Washington, what were your hopes?

My main hope was that I would have the good sense to stay out of any more administrative positions. I spent three very happy years teaching philosophy. I enjoyed teaching, but my main interest really wasn't teaching as such, but rather life in a university where I could concentrate on ideas and read and write. I'm not like some faculty I've known who couldn't live without teaching. In fact, when some of them gave up teaching and retired, it wasn't long before they died. Perhaps it won't be long before *I* die, but it won't be because I gave up teaching.

I've talked with your students and even read their evaluations of your courses, and I know your reputation as a teacher, Sterling. Whether you feel an absolute need to be in the classroom or not, you did it with a flair.

Of course I get satisfaction out of teaching, especially when students seem to be learning something; but when the system of having course evaluations came up in the first place in the Faculty Council, I was one who argued strenuously against the idea. I think the best routine I've seen is the one you developed for Liberal Education, but most evaluations didn't indicate whether the student had confidence that the instructor was genuinely competent in his or her subject. That always irritated me.

Whether the instructor is competent on his or her subject is a judgment for other faculty to make, not students! But apart from teaching, you also found great satisfaction in your research and writing?

Yes, in many ways, research and writing are fully satisfying. The problem we've always faced in philosophy at the University of Utah is that we've always been short on advanced graduate studies. We've had very good students; but by and large, the work has usually been at an undergraduate level or mixed undergraduate/graduate level. This has always been a disappointment to me.

A disappointment, but not a surprise?

No, not a surprise. I knew what I was getting into when I left USC and came here; but there's been some compensation in the general enthusiasm of our students for the subject of philosophy. Most of my students have been intensely interested in philosophical questions.

Whitehead wrote of romance as the first of three stages of learning. In this stage students have enormous enthusiasm as they discover the power of new ideas and skills. You have been romancing students in philosophy for half a century now, and then leading many of them forward.

I suppose there is a good deal to what you say. Of course, philosophical matters very often run into religious matters, and the strong interest in religion and religious issues in Utah has contributed to the enthusiasm for philosophy.

But then those pleasant years that were devoted full-time to teaching came to an end. What happened?

Well, first the Secretary of Labor, Willard Wirtz, called me up and wanted me to head up a committee on manpower for several western states, including Utah. I didn't want to do it; but I wasn't going to sit there and tell the Secretary of Labor that I wouldn't. I thought, "Oh, damn, if they want me to, I guess that's what I ought to do." And the governor of Utah, Cal Rampton, got me to arrange and chair a statewide conference on education—a time-consuming job.

That sense of public duty again?

It's really an over-developed respect for authority, you know, Jack. Wouldn't Joseph Fielding Smith snort if he could have heard me say that! Work with the Manpower Commission was rewarding in many respects, and the people I associated with were especially pleasant; but it consumed a good deal of time and effort. Later I was asked to chair the federal Commission on Instructional Technology. That took a lot of time and effort, but here again was the federal government. I've just never had the willpower to say no. For instance, I served on the board of a national organization on educational television, on the board of directors of the Northwest Association of Schools and Colleges, on the Graduate Record Examination Board.

What were your other university activities in addition to teaching?

After returning to the university, I was appointed chair of what was first called the Curriculum Committee but which we renamed the Academic Policy Committee. We were given an absolutely free hand to deal with any subject relating to the university as long as it had to do with education, and the university would supply us with a staff and any information within its power.

It's now called the Academic Policy Advisory Committee and the members are elected. What were the problems that called it into being?

Well, this committee was originally appointed by the president. In previous years there was no agency with oversight responsibility for the university's curriculum, to see that there weren't unfilled gaps or bad cases of duplication among departments and colleges. When I succeeded Homer Durham as vice-president, I gave some attention to that situation but didn't do anything about it. When I returned from Washington, Daniel Dykstra, who had taken my place as vice-president, told me that he and President Olpin had come to the conclusion that we should form a committee to deal with the problem. It wasn't the sort of thing I wanted to do, but I agreed to chair what was called the Curriculum Committee—with the clear understanding that we would *not* do the curriculum job.

So how did you define your role as a committee?

We were strictly an advisory committee, and our job was to examine and evaluate any educational program of the university independently of any administrative interference. We had no powers of action, but we did have responsibility and power to advise the administration and faculty.

So you had no control over finances, no power to change programs, but considerable influence, given the stature of the people on the committee?

Yes, that's it. By virtue of the wisdom of this group, coupled with our research and the persuasiveness of our recommendations, we had clout; but no one was under any obligation to act on our recommendations.

And what was the work of your committee?

We took as our first piece of business an examination of the College of Business, now the College of Business *and* the Graduate School of Business. I didn't think we should have an undergraduate College of Business in the first place. That's a long story, but, to make it brief, I thought we should have an undergraduate program in accounting and one or two other things but that the College of Business should be a graduate operation. After devoting some attention to the College of Business, we decided that a more acute problem, and a far more pressing one, was the College of Education. After two years of study, we submitted our first report, which recommended that the College of Education be made a graduate school.

Why did your committee decide that education was more pressing than business?

The thing that caused the shift is that the members of the committee—and I was one of them—more and more realized that the problems in the College of Education were more acute. We didn't want to rush through the thing but rather to make a thorough study, so we devoted many months to our study of the College of Education. At that time the physical education program was in the College of Education along with home economics, and we recommended the creation of a separate college for physical education and a department for home economics outside the School of Education. Thereafter, physical education became the College of Health.

Home economics is now the Department of Family and Consumer Studies, located in the College of Social and Behavioral Science. Having just come back from Washington, it was quite logical for you to have ideas about reforming education on your mind.

Yes, I thought there was nothing wrong with reforming education a little bit. As it turned out, the Faculty Senate was in favor of upgrading the college to a Graduate School of Education and splitting off physical education, modern dance, and home economics. So was the administration. The only objections that I heard were from people in the School of Education. However, the dean, Asahel Woodruff, and Reed Merrill, the education school's representative on the committee, were in favor of the committee's proposals. The main substantive thing we came up with—and this is what I personally pushed for—was elevating the status of education as an advanced professional study with a program of liberal education as its base.

Research in education is taken for granted now; sometimes it's even taken too far and diminishes our attention to other professorial duties. Explain what you see as the problem of preparing teachers and administrators for the public schools.

Educators are professionals, like doctors; and I think we should provide these people with first-class preparation. Anyone going into teaching or administration should have an honest-to-goodness liberal education as a foundation.

And thirty years later we're still talking about this, and we still haven't done it very well.

Yes, and we often talk about it as if it were something new. That's the thing that always annoys me. It is inventing the wheel all over again. So what the Academic Policy Committee favored—and I was pleased that we went in this direction—was requiring educators to get a good liberal education and then some first-rate professional education on top of that. And that the study of pedagogy should be shifted to the graduate level, like law and medicine.

Well, if you read our report, you will find that we recommended setting up an all-university committee that dealt with teacher education. Such a committee was created, the University Council on Teacher Education. Whether it ever functioned well or not, I don't know. I was so damned tired of it at the end of those two years that I didn't bother to follow through to see what happened.

It has fallen ill and been revived and renamed several times. Back to the larger matter, your old Academic Policy Committee is still doing good work, although I don't know if it tackles projects of the same scope. Its members are now elected and the name was changed about 1968 to the Academic Policy Advisory Committee.

You know what I'm really concerned about? I think that for some purposes electing committee members is a very grave mistake. It's like electing a board of regents or electing the board of education. People can get in on the basis of their popularity with the voters—a disgusting process.

This sounds like a vote of no confidence in democracy, Sterling.

I'm *not* as democratic in educational matters as a lot of people on the faculty are. I confess that. I believe in a strong department head and not somebody that is some way or other elected by a department to serve as a coordinator. I believe in strong committees, strong deans, and strong presidents at the university. If they're not any good, throw them out and get somebody else. That's the feeling that I have, and that explains my feelings about that committee. I must confess that I selected the members of the committee, with the vice-president's approval and the approval of the department heads and deans where needed. I wouldn't have taken the job if the members were to be elected. You see, I think the Utah system of an elected State Board of Education is not a good practice. Why not have it appointed as the State Board of Regents is?

How would you appraise the results of your efforts to reform the school of education?

You know, Jack, aside from the name change to the Graduate School of Education, I'm not sure there was much change. Some of the people were afraid of losing their jobs if the place were upgraded, and I think perhaps some of them should have lost them. When the school did upgrade later on, many did retire early or leave. Another argument was that the prospective teachers would go to USU or BYU to get an education if we made our requirements too stiff. The interesting thing is that the dean of education at USU told me he hoped we *would* go ahead with our reforms, because then he could upgrade things at his institution.

As you know, the argument that higher standards mean losing students still gets trotted out every time a college thinks about raising its expectations. But it actually doesn't work that way. Higher standards mean a higher quality of student because their degree is worth more. Raising standards raises interest.

I think you're right, Jack. The education faculty has been complaining for years that not enough first-rate students want to go into education. I keep hearing it from the students' perspective. They feel that they won't get a good education if they go into the School of Education. I think that's pretty much true all over the country and it's unfortunate.

It once was, but the University of Utah School of Education and some others around the country now have very high admissions standards for prospective teachers.

Yes, and the task of educating a teacher is a task for the whole university, not just one college. I always tried to break down the isolation of the School of Education. I gradually realized the extent to which the School of Education would not recognize high-quality teaching by other departments relating to teacher education. At times in the past it wouldn't even let students earn credit toward certification when they took legitimate education work from professors in other colleges.

Could you give me an example?

James Jarrett in the philosophy department was first rate and very interested in the philosophy of education. His first degree was in our education college, his doctorate from the University of Michigan. After he left us, he became president of the Great Books Foundation, president of Western Washington College, and professor of the philosophy of education at Berkeley. He's as good a man as there is in this country in the philosophy of education. For a number of years, Jim taught our philosophy department's course in the philosophy of education. But the School of Education would not let a student taking Jarrett's course receive credit for that course toward teacher certification! It had to be someone on their own payroll, teaching their own course.

So it was just a territorial concern, not an intellectual matter? What nonsense.

Absolutely. Well, when they were getting around to appointing a

person in the philosophy of education in the sixties, I let them know
that the philosophy people had a great interest in the subject and would
be very pleased to be present when their candidates read papers. Well,
Mike Parsons was one of those under consideration. When he gave his
seminar, more people came to hear him from the philosophy department
than from the School of Education. He was very, very good. We liked
him, and I like to think that our favoring him helped him get the
appointment.

*Mike became a major figure in the School of Education, but he recently
moved on to head the education department at Ohio State. In the meantime
what steps did you take toward breaking down these territorial walls?*

Asahel Woodruff was very interested in this problem. When he was
dean, he worked very hard to see that the School of Education was really
integrated into the university, recognizing that people all over the
campus had as much interest as the education faculty in seeing that
prospective teachers got a good liberal education.

*One reason for the barriers, Sterling, is that education faculty never feel
they're in control of their own affairs because, to do their job right, they have
to coordinate and draw on the talents of faculty campuswide. Other
departments can be much more autonomous. They don't ask the School of
Education how to run their programs. But to get back to our topic—your
contributions to the university. Did you have your appointment in the faculty
of education when you were on the Academic Policy Committee?*

No, that came much later. The people in the education school had
a very negative opinion of me, generally speaking. I became aware of
this when I was vice-president. I was once invited to address them and
spoke in essentially critical terms, and it was obvious to me that they
didn't like me. Now, not everyone. I'd been involved in Ashael
Woodruff's appointment as dean when I was vice-president, and I always
felt he was not opposed to my views; but it was fairly clear to me that
the rank and file of the education school—and I hope I'm not saying
this too irresponsibly—had a kind of contempt for me. Not simply a
negative attitude toward my views on education, but a personal contempt for me which, by the way, matched the opinion I had of a couple
of them.

*Contempt is a strong word. What was the source of this mutual enmity?
You were critical of some things going on in education, I know, and I expect
they saw you as rather arrogant.*

Perhaps so, and some of them were highly critical of my policies in
Washington. Vice-president Jack Adamson told me that one education

professor claimed that he got me fired from my position as Commissioner of Education. This amused me, of course, in view of the difficulty I had in getting out of Washington.

This was a very long-standing disagreement you had with these people? But you were seriously interested in teacher education.

Yes. In the 1950s, when I was still dean of the college, the National Science Foundation got involved in the funding of summer institutes for high school teachers of science. Some of us, including Thomas Parmley in physics, got busy and formulated an application for an academic year institute for high school science teachers. Ours was the second one funded in the nation. When we received the grant, I appointed Parmley to head the program. More than one person in the National Science Foundation told me that they regarded it as the best program of its kind in the nation. It continued for years. We had several of these summer institutes; in the mathematics department, too. Allan Davis in mathematics headed those up. He was interested in teacher education.

In the physics department you appointed a person specifically in connection with teacher education?

Yes. That was Robert Kadesch to teach physics and astronomy. Parmley and his committee were from all across the university, including education. But we wanted high school teachers—if they were able to put in the time and had the credentials—to get a master's degree. Not in education where they would be bogged down with more education courses, but in the sciences that they taught.

How did you manage that?

We had biology, chemistry, physics, and mathematics teachers, so we invented a new degree which the Faculty Council and the board of regents approved—Master of Science Education. That degree was awarded in the education school, you see, but it was under the administration of a broader entity. Some people over in education didn't like the idea, but we worked it out. Most of the students were not fully qualified for a master's degree in physics, for instance, but they were for a degree in the teaching of physics. I don't know whether they still have that degree or not, but that was a damn good thing. Well, I want to establish myself, you see, as a person interested in the preparation of teachers.

Your criticism of the College of Education, then, was over their wish to devote too much time and energy to pedagogy rather than academic content, as you see it?

Absolutely. But that doesn't mean that I am opposed to pedagogical research and study. I wanted to put pedagogy on an advanced level.

Sterling, you've been affiliated with three different academic departments on this campus. You began in the Department of Philosophy, you had connections with the School of Education, and the latter years of your career were in the Department of History. Could we turn now to your disaffection with the Department of Philosophy and your intensifying ties with education and history?

As you know, I had fulfilled the requirements for a degree in history and political science as well as philosophy as an undergraduate, but all of my graduate work and faculty appointments were in philosophy. When I came here in 1948 as full professor in philosophy, I didn't have the slightest expectation of ever becoming affiliated with any other department, although I was sorely tempted at one time in the 1950s to do some things in the law school. But that would not have involved my joining its faculty, even as an adjunct professor.

But your branching out reached first toward the School of Education?

It started in the 1950s and the problems with teaching the philosophy of education. Jim Jarrett had left and Charles Monson, who had earned his doctorate in philosophy from Cornell, was appointed to teach the philosophy of education. He was intensely interested in teaching, just as you are, Jack. Monson was later head of the philosophy department and associate academic vice-president. Well, at some point Monson went back to Cornell on an American Council of Education grant, so they asked me to teach his course in the philosophy of education. This was never a specialty of mine, as you know, and never anything that I was very interested in until I was in Washington. When I was Commissioner of Education, I was asked to address a meeting of professors of the philosophy of education in New York City—I can't remember its name. I asked the executive officer of the Office of Education to have the specialist on the philosophy of education give me a good sampling of the books these people would use. Well, the Library of Congress delivered to me about eighteen books, and, to be very frank with you, I was horrified with some of the stuff that I encountered.

Can you give me a sample?

Usually, the first part of a text was an introduction to philosophy, sometimes well done and sometimes done by people that didn't know a damn thing about it. Usually the authors described different schools of thought—idealism, realism, pragmatism, phenomenology, positivism, existentialism—and then launched into an attempt to deal with education in terms of these philosophical schools. Well, much of what I saw really amused me and, in an intellectual sense, disgusted me. So I went up to Queen's College and told them so.

You told them you were disgusted by the quality of the major texts in their field?

That's right. Disgusted that they seemed to think there should be a separate philosophy of education for different theories of epistemology, metaphysics, and logic—because that's the way a lot of this stuff was written. I told them I thought this was just a lot of damn nonsense. Well, there were some very competent people in that crowd with whom I had had previous philosophy connections. I got along famously with these people. A little later they sent a delegation to Washington to ask if I would take the lead in creating a national organization in the philosophy of education. Well, I told them no because it would be a very bad thing to have this done by the federal government.

There is such an organization now. Did you associate with it after you left Washington?

Yes, in fact, I later gave an address to a regional meeting at Berkeley.

Now all of this was preparatory to your becoming involved in the School of Education?

The American Philosophical Association holds separate regional meetings rather than a single national one. Although I had never attended their meetings, the nominating committee of the Central States Division contacted me and said they would like to nominate me to be vice-president; then the following year I would become president. Well, I told them that they hadn't better do it, as I associated with the Pacific Division. But the same year the Eastern Division asked me to do a paper on the philosophy of education, and the respondent would be a man of considerable stature in the philosophy of education. I was embarrassed because I was so busy that I didn't get the paper to him very far in advance. This all happened just as we were coming back to Utah, and President Kennedy hadn't replaced me, so I still had one foot in Washington. Nevertheless, I read the paper and the respondent was very gracious, more gracious I think than I deserved. Well, my paper was primarily a criticism of the most widely used philosophy of education book—though I didn't name it—and the *Journal of Philosophy* published my essay. Since then, of course, I have published numerous papers on education.

A number of years later you and Jim Jarrett, who was then at Berkeley, decided to do a book on the philosophy of education together, didn't you?

It was after I became dean of the Graduate School, so it would have been about 1969 or '70. It was Jarrett's idea that we do a text for classroom use in courses in the philosophy of education. We worked on the book, but I didn't have time. I finally had to throw in the towel, and Jarrett carried on alone with *Philosophy for Educators*. It's a Houghton Mifflin publication, now out of print. Too bad, because it's an excellent book.

What approach did you and Jim take in the book?

There are sizable studies of people of very real competence as philosophers, like Plato, Whitehead, Dewey, and others, dealing with educational matters. And the very man who wrote the awful book that I criticized so severely at the meeting of the Philosophical Association was the editor of the series in which this book appeared.

So your book with Jarrett was to be largely an anthology?

Our idea was that if you want to study the philosophy of education, take a good look at the ideas on education held by the major philosophers. One of the best things about the academic pursuit of philosophy is that you are concerned almost exclusively with the work of scholars of great intellectual stature. There isn't time to waste on second-raters. But all of this is background to your question about my appointment in the School of Education. During the 1960s we made it pretty clear in the philosophy department that we were very much interested in the philosophy of education from the standpoint of the university's interest in the education of teachers. Now this, you see, was after the work of the Academic Policy Committee, which stressed that the education of teachers was a responsibility of the whole university.

So you were pleased to offer your support to Michael Parsons, who had joined the education faculty in the philosophy of education. It was after Michael was hired that you received your appointment?

Yes, I was asked to join the education faculty to offer a course in the philosophy of education. I agreed to accept an appointment as professor of the philosophy of education, not professor of education, because I couldn't lay any claim to that title.

Now that was a full appointment, not adjunct?

That was an appointment as a full professor. They didn't ever have to pay me anything, you understand, so it was simply a matter of their picking up some free teaching. This was shortly before you came to the university, Jack.

That's right. The philosophy of education was in the area called Cultural Foundations of Education in the Department of Educational Administration.

Not the proper place for Cultural Foundations, but that's where it was. I really took an active part in faculty affairs in that department. I regularly attended meetings of the faculty and took a lively interest in its procedures. I felt that it was a worthwhile thing to do. I taught only one class each year; I was still in the administration and teaching two classes in the philosophy department. Shortly afterward they were interested in expanding and asked Charles Monson to teach some education courses. I advised Charles to do it only on one condition—that he have a regular appointment as professor of philosophy of education.

How did things work out for you, Sterling?

My situation was pleasant enough. I had two or three good classes and some rather advanced people, and then the thing just fell off. It became fairly evident to me—and by this time I had come to the history department—that there wasn't really much interest in my teaching in education. On two different occasions they simply failed to list my course. I found out about it the first time because some students who were interested in taking the course came to see me about it and I discovered I wasn't even in the schedule for that quarter. When I called this to the department's attention, the chair said, "Oh, that's too bad. We'll just cancel it out this time." I thought, If they're not interested in my holding the class, why should I worry about it? There was still time to announce the class.

What response did you have from the administration of the School of Education?

None. The associate dean of the Graduate School, Richard Kendall, was in the School of Education, and it bothered Kendall some—the lack of any particular interest in seeing that I even taught over there after I had agreed to be on the faculty. He got involved one year, and, through his influence, they put together a first-rate class of advanced students. That class was a very real pleasure. But after that Kendall left the university and the thing dwindled down to the point where the last time I went up to meet with a class there was only one student. Parsons canceled it, and I went back to my office and wrote a letter of resignation.

Canceled your appointment as well.

Yes, I canceled my appointment. It didn't make any difference to them. Nobody objected one bit to my resigning. I don't think I as much as received a reply.

That's surprising. I can't understand how that could have happened unless there were residual hard feelings in the School of Education that made the faculty and dean deliberately uncooperative. How did you feel about it? This amounts to a serious and painful personal rejection!

You see, I wasn't on their payroll. When you're not on the payroll, nobody gives a damn about you. Anyway that was the end of my short-lived career as a teacher in the field of education.

But you had other important involvements in education that continued to bring satisfaction.

Yes, I should mention that during this period I devoted a great deal of time elsewhere to the problems of education. From 1963 to 1975 I directed three projects on schools and colleges for the prestigious Committee for Economic Development of New York, which yielded a number of influential policy statements which I wrote and books which I edited. And I served on several national committees on education, including the chairmanship of the federal Commission on Instructional Technology.

Well, what about your disaffection with philosophy? It occurred about the same time.

It was very early in the seventies while I was dean of the Graduate School. I had some problems with the philosophy department—mind you, the problems were not what you would regard as serious in a personal way, but I always had a sense of disappointment that we were not creating a first-rate department of philosophy. This was the big problem.

It was just maintaining the status quo, so you quit?

Yes. The philosophy department was once the intellectual hub of the campus. I don't think you could point to any single department that is the hub now. When I was first on the faculty, any number of faculty people would take my courses. The dean of the law school took a course from me in medieval philosophy, two people in the engineering school took a course in the philosophy of history. I had people from the Department of English, two or three of whom are still on the faculty, professors from the departments of psychiatry, psychology, and history. The same thing can be said of Jarrett, Read, and Tanner—they all attracted other professors.

Why did you choose to stay at the University of Utah? You could have gone to USC or a variety of other distinguished institutions to pursue your reading, research, and writing.

Well, I simply have to say that I like it here. It's home to me. I would rather live in Salt Lake City than anywhere else I've been in the world, and I've been to a lot of places. I simply don't want to live anywhere else. I've turned down a considerable number of very attractive offers, both in administration and teaching or research. In every instance, from a monetary standpoint I would have gained if I had left here—sometimes more than twice the salary that I was receiving here. But I just like it here. I'm a Westerner and I can't get this terrain out of my system—don't intend to. I like the people. They aren't any better than people anywhere else, but they're my crowd; and the University of Utah, as I've said on many occasions publicly, is a far better institution than the people of Utah have any idea that it is. I'm at home in this university. It is a very, very good university. There is genuine academic freedom here. There is a zest for knowledge. Natalie and I have felt that this is a good place to rear a family.

For the scholarly pursuit of philosophy, as I've said, it has not been a particularly good thing for me to remain at the University of Utah.

I can see that you were disillusioned with the philosophy department here, and then reminded by the USC offer of greener pastures, but just how did your break with philosophy and your appointment in history come about?

It was back in the sixties, when strange things were happening in the universities. In the philosophy department there was a lot of faculty bickering and I simply became disgusted with it. There wasn't anything personal about it, but I just felt let down the way things were going. There's no point in dragging it all out now as it was many years ago and the faculty has changed greatly since then. When I decided to leave the philosophy department in 1970, the tenured people in history seemed anxious to have me, so I joined them. Several years later I resigned from the graduate deanship and moved into Carlson Hall, the history building. I was treated well by my history colleagues, but I always felt like an illegitimate child at a family reunion. I had classes in the philosophy of history and the history of ideas, but the history faculty had changed considerably since I joined the department, and I think many of the new people regarded me as an interloper.

But for ten years or more you enjoyed the best years of your university work.

Yes, partly because they left me alone and I had complete freedom, but also because I had the support of a wonderful assistant, Jacqueline Jacobsen. I had previously enjoyed the assistance of two other women in the university who had made my administrative work both bearable and pleasant, Lillian Ence and Helen Hyer. I am of the opinion that the secretaries of an institution are the ones who make it work. Without them things would go to hell.

When I resigned from philosophy, I wrote a letter resigning as

E. E. Ericksen Professor of Philosophy and also as Distinguished Professor. But the president advised me that the "Ericksen Chair" and the "Distinguished" title both belonged to me and not the Department of Philosophy, so I became E. E. Ericksen Distinguished Professor and Professor of History. Several times after that I was urged by the philosophy department chair to rejoin them. I agreed to teach one class a year as adjunct professor at no cost to the department. As a matter of fact, most of my salary was in the vice-president's budget, not the history budget.

When were you originally appointed E. E. Ericksen Distinguished Professor? What were the circumstances of this change for you, this step for the university?

It was, as I recall, a short time after I agreed to turn down the latest USC offer. There was no bargaining, and my salary was not affected. But the regents created the Ericksen chair in honor of E. E. Ericksen, and at the same time I was appointed Distinguished Professor, the first person to ever hold this rank at the University of Utah. The Ericksen chair, I was told, was the university's first chair since the early days when we had the Deseret Professorship of Geology. That chair was discontinued many years earlier. Since my appointment, there have been a number of distinguished professor appointments. Henry Eyring was the second person to hold this rank. Now there are quite a few of us, and proposals for appointment as distinguished professor are submitted to this group for their approval before any action is taken. It is now a rigorous screening procedure. I guess it's a good thing that I got in before there were any rules and tough standards.

It is a fairly common practice today for a rising faculty member to elicit an offer elsewhere and then see if his or her dean can match it. Do you think offers from USC or elsewhere resulted in your being appreciated more here, materially?

I doubt it. I didn't ever use offers elsewhere to elicit salary increases here; besides, no one in the administration ever knew about most of the offers I received. I think the university paid me what it could. After my service as Commissioner of Education in Washington, the University of Utah gave me a $500 raise. And that's not a $500 raise over what I made in Washington, but what I made in Utah before I went to Washington. I would have been better off financially if I had not gone to Washington. It was about $4,000 a year less than the Washington salary. I was being paid $16,000 here as vice-president when I left. The salary in Washington was pegged, I think, at the same salary as people in the House of

Representatives—then about $20,000. According to the papers, the
Secretary of Education now makes about $148,000 a year. I returned to
Utah on a salary of $16,500, but this was what I wanted to do and we
could live on it. I never did discuss salaries with my superiors either here
or in Washington. I learned about the salary after I took the jobs. I came
here as a full professor of philosophy in 1948 not knowing what the
salary was until after I had accepted the position. The same was true in
Washington. I didn't know what my salary would be until just before
my Senate confirmation. No one had bothered to tell me, and I wasn't
about to ask.

*So you chose to stay here as a professor but got sucked back into admin-
istration anyway.*

Yes, that's where I made my big mistake. I should have stayed out of
administration. I had already paid my dues in administration. I ended up
with twenty years in the Park Building, in the university administration!

*That chapter of your life put you at odds once more with your own nature.
Before moving on to that phase, however, let's turn to Obert and Grace
Tanner's generosities, large and small, and your role in shaping some of
them. Where did their remarkable philanthropies begin?*

Well, the first large contribution that I was aware of may have been
the gift of a philosophy library to Stanford University. I think it was
shortly after the gift of that Tanner Library to Stanford that he made the
gift of the Tanner Room in Orson Spencer Hall at the University of
Utah. Obert's business had to be in pretty good shape then or he couldn't
have made that gift because it was very expensive. That library and
meeting room in Spencer Hall had its own ventilating system, its own
heating and air-conditioning system (before the rest of the building was
air-conditioned), fine-furniture book shelves and cabinets fashioned
from imported wood, and decorating done by one of the state's leading
decorators.

*There is an interesting story behind the funding of the Grace Tanner Dining
Room in the Alumni House, is there not?*

Yes, David Gardner who was then president of the University of
Utah called me on the phone one day and said, "We're in the business
of planning an alumni house and it's going to be a very beautiful thing."
He said, "You know here at the university we have no place to hold
fine dinners, a truly beautiful place for official dinners, and it has occurred
to me and perhaps to others that we have nothing on the campus that
is named for Grace Tanner. We have things named for Obert and Grace's
children, and for Obert's mother, so now a lovely dining room named

for Grace Tanner would be a marvelous thing. Is there any likelihood that Obert might be interested in funding such a room? I said, "I think he would." "Well," Gardner said, "how do you think we should go about it?" I said, "It's very simple. What you need to do is get an appointment with Obert down at his office on State Street. Go down and just say to him what you've said to me." He said, "We'll have to ask him for at least a hundred thousand dollars." I said, "The figure's not going to bother him, I'm sure of that. Just go down and ask him for it." David said, "All right, I will." Not long after that, he called me up and said, "I thought I should tell you that I went down, asked Obert for the money, and he gave it to me." I said, "I'm not surprised." About a week or ten days later I was with Obert and I said, "Obert, I see you're still spreading your money around the university." He said, "What do you mean?" I said, "I know about that hundred thousand dollars you've given to Gardner for a dining room," and—now this is the point of my telling you the story—he said, "Well, what could I do? There's David Gardner, the president of that great university, as busy as he is, with all of the things he has to think about, and he took the time to come clear down to my office on State Street to ask me for the money. The least I could do was give it to him."

As things developed, I think the price went far beyond the hundred thousand because Obert also gave them the tableware and the silverware and the whole shebang.

Obert and Grace were both an amazing mixture of humility and generosity. The many fountains he and Grace donated are surely symbols of life-giving water in a desert region. I'm aware of a list of forty-two of their fountains. Is that the total?

I believe there were more than fifty. The problem is, I'm not sure that Grace knows about them all!

At some point Obert shifted from fountains to endowing lectureships. How did the renowned Tanner Lectures on Human Values get started?

This is an example of how Obert worked. They were dedicating the fountain that he gave to Dixie College in St. George, and the president asked me to come and offer some remarks about Obert at the ceremony. Obert and Grace were there, of course, and after the affair Natalie and I and Grace and Obert all lodged at the same inn. Obert invited us over to talk; so we went to their room. I'd had an idea for some time, so I said to Obert when the time seemed right, "Obert, I think you've given enough fountains now," and Grace interjected, "I think so, too!"

All the colleges and universities in Utah had at least one Tanner fountain by then, and other public institutions in Utah had been given fountains by the Tanners, too.

Yes, and I said, "Obert, I think you should put your money into something else now." He said, "Well, what?" I said, "I think you should establish a world-class lectureship." Now I had in mind a lectureship on the order of the Gifford Lectures in Scotland—given at the University of Utah with several lectures by the same person. I said, "I think you should establish a very high-level lectureship: The Obert C. Tanner Lectures on Moral Philosophy." "Well," Obert said, "let's do it, but it is not to be named for me. What do you think it will take to get it started?" I said, "Well, it'll take an initial endowment of about one hundred thousand dollars." "Fine," he said, "We'll do it."

What happened next?

In less than a week the money was in the hands of President Gardner and the planning for what was to become the Tanner Lectures on Human Values was underway, engaging the efforts of David Gardner, Meredith Wilson, Obert Tanner, and me. The Tanners subsequently donated millions of dollars to create these remarkable lectureships. Today the lectures are established and funded in perpetuity at some of the world's great universities, including Cambridge, Oxford, Harvard, Stanford, Yale, Princeton, University of California, Berkeley, Michigan, and the University of Utah. Annually, they provide a forum for the finest scholars and statespersons in the world. The Tanner Lectures on Human Values are held in high esteem wherever you go today. Obert regarded these lectures as his most important achievement.

Obert and Grace also gave generously to BYU and to many other educational institutions. In 1995 the Tanner Foundation gave $1.5 million to endow the Humanities Center at the University of Utah. It was a marvelous decision.

Yes, they are continuing with Obert's notable generosity and spirit.

And there is the Sterling M. McMurrin Distinguished Visiting Professorship, which President Gardner asked me to establish in the late 1970s when I was dean of Liberal Education. I chaired the selection of the first ten incumbents. It has been a real boon to the undergraduate programs all over campus to have these people come for a quarter. The position has been occupied by leaders as diverse as Herbert Kelman, Cabot Professor of Social Ethics at Harvard University, and Jacques d'Amboise, the great ballet artist and teacher. Running that program was one of the great satisfactions of my deanship.

I remember those distinguished visitors with respect and affection. Reginald Cane's work in the history of science was of great interest, as was anthropologist Marvin Harris's.

Fountains of water and fountains of knowledge. Those symbolized Obert's approach to life. He truly believed in and acted on the great ideas he taught as a philosophy professor all those years—liberty and justice, beauty and goodness. He brought ideas to life.

We could go on, of course, and I wish we could. We've hardly done justice to Obert and Grace's benefactions, at home and abroad, to individuals and to institutions.

Your six-decade rapport with Obert played a significant role in shaping the flow of his instinctive generosity and plentiful resources to many good causes. The two of you, really the four of you including Natalie and Grace, enjoyed a friendship from which tens of thousands have already benefitted.

14.
Senior Statesman

President Ray Olpin's retirement from the University of Utah presidency precipitated a host of administrative changes and got you involved again. How did this happen?

When I came back from Washington in 1962, President Olpin was already preparing for his departure from office. When he did retire in 1964, the regents used what I think proved to be a very unwise procedure to search for his successor. They established their own search committee and also a separate faculty search committee, chaired by Fred Emery of the Law School. I met a couple of times with the regents' committee at their invitation, but don't recall ever meeting with the faculty committee.

This dual arrangement sounds like a recipe for inter-tribal conflict.

Oh, it certainly was. But in my consultations with the regents, I strongly urged the appointment of someone who had not only academic credentials and experience but who also understood business, industry, and economics. It seemed evident at the time that the university must get tied more closely into the economy of the state. I mentioned James C. Fletcher, whom I knew slightly, as someone who seemed to fit this bill. I had met him in California, knew he was highly successful, had a doctorate in physics from Cal Tech, and had studied at Columbia. He was a leader in the aerospace industry and a person of considerable sophistication. As you know, Jack, he is the candidate the regents eventually appointed.

Were you a disinterested party in this process, aside from making the initial recommendation?

Well, I actually had a little more to do with it than that. I was in New York when I got a phone call about midnight from Jim Fletcher. He was calling from Salt Lake City, where the regents had just offered him the presidency of the university. He wanted my advice about whether he should take the job. I told him that he certainly should, that the university was in desperate need of someone who could have the

confidence of the business and industrial people in the state. Then he
said, "But you know, the faculty is opposed to me." I said, "I didn't
know that *you* knew that." Then I tried to convince him that the faculty
committee's opposition was not personal but represented their strong
preference for an academic candidate. I told him that after he'd served
as president a very short time, the faculty would come to respect him.

Which, in fact, happened.

Yes. Fletcher was highly successful and built exactly the kind of ties
with the community that I felt were necessary. He acquired the land for
the Research Park, for instance, which has proved to be an excellent
cooperative effort with industry.

*Shortly afterwards you were appointed Fletcher's provost. How did that
happen?*

Jim had been president for about a year when Jack Adamson, who
had been academic vice-president since Olpin's final year, decided to
leave the administration even though he liked Fletcher a great deal. Jack
got a year's leave of absence to do postdoctoral work in English at
Harvard. When it became clear he was going to leave, Fletcher bludg-
eoned me into going back into the administration. I didn't want to. I'd
been out of the administration for three years, ever since returning from
Washington. I didn't want to have anything more to do with it.

But you've done it much of your life, Sterling!

Yes, over twenty-two years' worth.

There have been some rewards, at least intrinsic ones, that kept you at it.

Well, the main one is that you do what you think you should do,
what you feel you owe to your university or to your nation. And of
course, the people with whom you associate are the best reward.

How did President Fletcher persuade you?

I held out for several days. Fletcher wanted to create the position of
provost or chancellor, and this officer would be in charge of the internal
functioning of the university—its educational program—while he handled the outside stuff like legislative relations, public relations, and
business and community relations. The business vice-president would
report to both Fletcher and the provost, but the academic vice-president
would report to the provost. I didn't want to do it.

What was it, however, that you couldn't resist?

A secretary! I needed a secretary! I was completely and totally
swamped in the philosophy department, which had one typist for the
entire faculty. I gave the commencement address at the University of

Chicago, for instance, and the president asked for a copy so they could publish it. But I couldn't get it typed in a reasonable time.

So you took that job with Fletcher.

Yes, and we ended up calling the position "provost" rather than "chancellor." I was to have Lillian Ence again as my secretary. She had been Jack Adamson's secretary and was a marvel of organization and efficiency.

Did your life then became easier?

No! That's what's so ironic. Fletcher and I had to choose an academic vice-president to replace Jack Adamson, and I suggested Fred Emery. There was no doubt about his qualifications, but he chaired the faculty committee that had gone on record as opposing Fletcher's presidency. But Fletcher instantly said, "That's the person I'm thinking of!" He immediately phoned Fred and asked him to come up. Fred was due for a leave, to teach either at Berkeley or Stanford, and had his plans all made; but he agreed to come on as vice-president.

But you lost Lillian Ence to Emery.

Right. He insisted that he couldn't function without Lillian, so Lillian remained as secretary to the vice-president and I lost out. The appointment of Emery indicates Fletcher's broad-gauged tolerance. He held no animosity toward Fred for his opposition. He held no grudges. In fact, not long after we'd both accepted these new positions, Fred and I were in Fletcher's office arguing about something. I can't remember what the issue was, but Fletcher and I agreed and Fred opposed the position. It was a pretty stiff conflict of opinions. When the meeting ended, just as Fred was walking out the door, Fletcher said, "You just remember that I became president over your dead body." We all laughed, and any difficulty that might have remained as a result of the exchange just dissolved. I always thought this incident captured Fletcher's character and leadership ability.

That's a powerful testimonial, and well deserved. Would you care to comment on your experiences as provost?

This was a busy but rather confusing year. There were countless things relating especially to research, graduate work, and government contracts that had to be straightened out. Emery and I divided up a good deal of the work, he taking the regular departments and I the rest, such as libraries, television, radio, continuing education, the graduate school, and a host of others. I had an assistant, Keith Wilson, who was a pleasure to work with. With him I was involved in the abortive effort to create an Aspen-like cultural center in Deer Valley and Park City. With

Brigham Madsen in Continuing Education, I oversaw the establishment of the Repertory Dance Theatre, and I became involved with Ardean Watts in the formal creation of a university opera program that eventually became the professional Utah Opera Company. The university's reaccreditation took a great deal of time—the list goes on and on. One of my main interests was bringing some kind of order into the whole process of establishing and administering graduate programs and graduate degrees.

You were involved in setting up the Distinguished Teaching Awards. What do you think of that program after thirty years?

I've seen instances of their being given to teachers who really didn't know very much about their subjects, but they convinced the students. I'm afraid that sometimes it has been a popularity contest. But I think overall that the awards have been given to people who genuinely deserve them.

Now you were in the administration during Fred Emery's presidency, too?

Yes, when Olpin retired, the question of the presidency was brought up with me by the regents' committee and I said, "Absolutely not." Then when Fletcher left to direct NASA, the National Aeronautics and Space Administration, I was part of an informal group that the regent's chair brought in to discuss how they should proceed. The regents decided to give Fletcher a leave of absence.

The idea was that Fletcher would come back?

Not exactly. The regents planned to appoint a president for a term of two years; and at the end of the first year, they would establish a search committee. They might find for Fletcher or they might recommend that the two-year appointee—who turned out to be Fred Emery—continue. Or it could be someone else—as it turned out to be.

You were all for Fred's appointment?

Yes. My name was thrown into the hopper, and I got it out damn fast. Fred was an excellent president at a time when a legal mind was needed in the leadership. Before his time was up, the regents appointed a proper search committee with several of their own members plus administrators, faculty, alumni, and a representative of the public at large. Pete Billings was chairman, and I represented the administration. Again some wanted to push me for the job, and I said, "No." When they persisted, I wrote a letter to the chair saying that under no circumstances would I be willing to serve as president of the university. That took care of that. David Gardner was appointed president. I had decided after a few months in the provost position that it was a bad idea, and I recommended to Gardner when he came that he drop that position, which he did immediately on assuming his office in 1973.

You've convinced me, Sterling, about your lack of executive ambitions!

Hell, yes, Jack. I hired on as a schoolteacher, and I wanted to be a good scholar, but I put so damned much time in on administrative work that I never became a good scholar.

You can't say that.

I can say it. It takes time.

But you did always hang on to your teaching.

Yes, and that was a real satisfaction. During the whole twenty-plus years as dean, vice-president, provost, and later dean of the Graduate School, I always taught classes—at least one class per term except when I was away on a leave of absence. Incidentally, clear back when I was dean of the college, Homer Durham told me about a department head in the fine arts college who didn't teach at all. He was really outraged. I was, too.

Today most deans teach rarely, if at all. It is a real loss for them, their students, and the university. Some don't publish, either; they become academic managers and that's it.

I published quite a lot of stuff in my field, and each year I wrote the philosophy articles for the *Britannica Book of the Year,* which kind of kept me up to date, even though it was a problem to find the time and energy to do it. I was expected to read the major philosophical works that had come out that year—an impossibility. Even when I was in Washington, I wrote that article and gave some lectures in philosophy.

How long did you continue to write the Britannica articles?

I started in 1952, so the first article came out in '53. I finally quit because they kept cutting down the amount of space they allotted to me. I thought it was outrageous when they gave more space to the attempt of Evel Knievel to jump the Snake River on a motorcycle than they gave to my article on philosophy. That was the straw that broke the camel's back. I wrote to the editor and said, "This is the end."

We've referred several times to experiences you had as dean of the Graduate School. How did you get into that job?

I was searching at the time for a person to take the graduate dean's position. Henry Eyring was turning sixty-five the next year, so we'd need a new dean by 1 July 1966. I was looking very hard for a person to replace him, and I wanted to get a Nobel Laureate. Henry was no help. He'd say, "Quit looking for someone else. It's the best job in the university. Take it yourself."

And President Fletcher said to me twice, "You shouldn't have trouble finding the person you want. It's the best job in the university." The second time Fletcher said that, I said, "Jim, if you say that again, and Henry Eyring keeps saying it, I'll just take the job myself." Well, I was just kidding; but I told him I was resigning from the provost position at the end of the year and not long afterward, he asked me if I *would* take the Graduate School on. He said, "I'll let you out of the job of provost if you'll take the position of dean of the Graduate School for five years." Well, hell, I thought, that was a decent enough trade. So I agreed. I had convinced him that I wanted to get out of the provost position.

Five years? But you were dean for twelve.

Yes, that's another story. At the beginning of the fifth year, I told the vice-president, "I understand that you review deans every five years." He said, "That's right." "Well," I said, "don't review me because I'm through at the end of this year." I was very serious. Well, he didn't want me to leave, and Fletcher had no recollection whatever of any five-year understanding. I had this battle every year for seven years or so, seriously wanting to retire from administration. But I held that job until I was sixty-five.

How did you finally manage to leave?

Well, Rick Davern became vice-president; and the first piece of business he found on his desk the first day was my letter of resignation, explaining that I had taken the job for five years and, since this was my twelfth, it was certainly my last year. He said, "Will you reconsider?" I said, "Hell, no." He said, "Will you hold up your decision for a while?" I said, "I'll tell you what I'll do. I'll hold up my decision until January 12th. That's my birthday. And on January 12th, I'll give you my decision, but it's gonna be exactly what it is now." And it was. My resignation became effective at the end of the 1978 academic year.

Anyway, when I agreed to take the graduate deanship, it was with the idea that I'd do something about the proliferation of graduate programs and degrees, a problem that greatly concerned me.

How about a little history here, Sterling.

The University of Utah launched into Ph.D. programs starting in the 1950s with utter abandon, without any regulations governing the appraisal of its resources or even of the needs of the students to be given Ph.D. degrees. There'd been master's degrees for some time, but the first Ph.D. was established in chemistry when Henry Eyring came as dean. Chemistry was a field in which we were highly qualified. But we added many other Ph.D. programs after that in some fields where I didn't think we were qualified or had any business preparing scholars at that level.

About a week or ten days after I became dean of the Graduate School, I asked the secretary, who had been Henry's secretary, to give me a list of the dates on which all of the doctor's degrees were established. She looked through the files and told me she couldn't find any such list. I said, "Dean Eyring can direct you to it."

The next day Henry came over to the office to pick up some mail; and when he left, I walked out of the building with him. He said, "You know, there's no need for you to look for the dates when those degrees were established. We didn't take any formal action to create them." I gasped. "Henry, what are you talking about?" He said, "No, if somebody showed up with a program for a Ph.D. degree that was approved by five people who had Ph.D. degrees, then I approved it." Well, I had known that the decision to have a Ph.D. program in philosophy was approved simply by a telephone call from the department head, Waldemer Read, to Dean Eyring.

Those were certainly simpler times in organizational life everywhere. Today we have the opposite extreme in universities and almost every other institution. Gridlock.

Certainly. And I should say that no faculty member has made the contribution to this university that Henry did. But this situation was extreme. I had been on the Graduate Council while Henry was dean, and some quarters we wouldn't even meet. I immediately set up regular monthly meetings, as a step in the right direction. Every school and college had one representative on the Graduate Council, and that person was selected by me in consultation with the head of the school or the college. Everyone was appointed for three years, and every year a third of them went off, although they could be reappointed.

Didn't you also have students on the Graduate Council?

I did my damnedest to include students. I took up the idea with the dean of students and the student body president, and, do you know, I couldn't get the students interested. They're always complaining that they aren't included in everything; but it was three or four years before I could get the student leaders even interested in appointing students to the Graduate Council. I wanted them to be graduate students, and there was then no graduate student organization. You understand I didn't lose any sleep over it; but even when we finally got some students, I think only one ever bothered to come to the meetings more than once.

That's interesting. In the years I worked with the Liberal Education Council as dean—1974 to 1990—we generally had three students appointed and two would drop out after the first meeting or so. It was very difficult, even with an undergraduate program, to have consistent student representation.

I know what you mean.

How did you approach the job of establishing procedures for internal review of graduate programs? You really put us on the map in that regard.

Well, I just sort of eased into that. I was, for a number of years, a member of the Higher Education Commission of the Northwest Association of Schools and Colleges; and while I was provost, the commission was preparing to examine us for reaccreditation. The chair of the fourteen-person committee, Henry Hanson, who was dean of the graduate school at Oregon State at Corvallis, called on me to apprise me of their intentions. He said, "I'm just going to tell you that one of the things that we are going to examine very, very carefully is graduate degrees."

Well, I thought that was wise. Fletcher insisted that I take on the job of doing the university's report to the accreditation commission, which I did. It's a book three inches thick, but I was at least able to show that we were working to improve the situation. We came off all right. Ten years later, damned if I didn't get tied into that job again and produced the accreditation report for 1976. It was a time-consuming task.

I served on that committee with you. I believe that was the first occasion that we really worked together on something, Sterling.

That's right! And a hell of a lot of work it was, too, wasn't it?

Back to the review process . . .

Well, with the Graduate Council I set up a two-fold system. The first was to develop a regularly scheduled review for graduate degrees and programs to determine their quality and whether they should be continued. The second was to develop a set of policies, rules, and procedures under which new degree programs and new degrees would be established. It took a little time, but we got both of these procedures on the road.

And they're still being followed today. Did you run into any opposition? I imagine some of these degree programs were considered private fiefdoms.

No difficulty with the departments but some with the council itself. I had an unfortunate experience at the start. The representative from the medical school had an intense interest in these new procedures. He was very active, all for it; and I thought, "He's the guy to appoint as chairman of the committee to work with me." But he was a disaster. He wanted everything to be secret. I think he had been on the faculty at UCLA before he came here—at any rate, he knew a lot about UCLA, or he thought he did; so he insisted that when we conducted the review of a department that it be done secretly. Hell, I couldn't believe what I was listening to! Unfortunately that held us up, because I refused to go along with his kind of stuff. So I just marked time until the end of the year when he left the Graduate Council. That kind of slowed up the process.

It's difficult to believe that he thought they'd get any cooperation with that system.

That's right. He didn't believe that everything should be open, with people knowing what was going on. I needed money to hire a person at least half-time to direct this operation under my supervision and deal with the departments in getting the reviews done. Of course, we needed money for secretarial help, to pay travel and honoraria for outside reviewers to examine proposals for new programs and degrees, to review the departments, and to appraise dissertations. The system that I worked out was to have outside reviewers from leading universities as well as internal reviewers—from inside the university but outside the department being reviewed.

How did you choose them?

The department would not select the reviewers, but it could make nominations. Outside reviewers were appointed by me, in each case one from a list of three submitted by the department. If I didn't approve of anyone on the list, then the department could submit another list. And it was understood that we wouldn't bring in a person that the departmental faculty seriously objected to. An outside reviewer was appointed in each case to read doctoral dissertations picked at random and sent to him or her. That saved on travel, even though we paid quite a substantial fee to the critic. Some of them would just blast those dissertations all to hell.

What about the internal reviewers?

We selected three people from outside the college. Again we didn't select anyone the faculty under review was absolutely opposed to. Later we also paid them a small honorarium. The response of the administration in providing funds was excellent. We always had all of the money that we needed, though we were careful in the way we spent it.

So you had some staff?

Yes and no. I did appoint a person half-time with a decent half-time salary, and he proved to be completely unsatisfactory. He was from outside the university, highly recommended, and I thought he would do a first-rate job. When he proved to be incapable of the job, I assigned it to the assistant dean, who later became associate dean. I suppose that's the way it's still done.

What was your procedure?

The reports would come to me, I'd see that the departments got copies and they would consider them and give me their response. I'd take the report and response to the Graduate Council for action. The department head and anyone else he or she wanted to include would come in for the hassle—and sometimes those meetings became very heated and the discussion on a particular subject would last for several meetings.

What kind of results did you get?

The reviewers could recommend dropping a program or a degree, putting them on probation, not taking any disciplinary action but blasting general hell out of the faculty or their teaching capability or their lack of research . . .

Or commend them?

Or commend them. Lots of commendation. Some of them came through beautifully. After the Graduate Council made its judgment, the decision went to the academic vice-president, who normally took it to the Faculty Senate, the president, and the Institutional Council (Board of Trustees). They all took a serious interest in what was going on. Everything we ever recommended was endorsed by the administration when I was dean. If we recommended dropping something or putting something on probation—then that's what happened. Over a period of years we dropped a number of degrees and programs. The State Board of Regents approved our actions, but they'd always announce it in their reports and in the newspapers, by hell, as if they were cleaning up the University of Utah—making it appear as if the actions had been initiated by the board.

I have heard that on one occasion you were quite unhappy with the state board on the matter of a degree.

The Board of Regents, which had the final say on degrees, wanted to assign the Ph.D. in education to Utah State in Logan. So they abolished our broad powers to offer a Ph.D. in education, gave it to USU, and assigned us the Ph.D. in educational administration. I, as dean of the Graduate School, first learned about this board action by reading it in the newspaper.

That's astonishing. Did you know this deal was under consideration?

No. But some higher-ups in our administration knew about it, and they didn't even bother to tell me.

How did some of those reviews go?

They went very successfully. The first two set the precedent. Pete Gibbs, chair of the physics department, said they'd like to be first; and, of course, they came through with flying colors. The next department we selected was the theater department. Keith Engar, who was the chair later, said, "I didn't take this thing very seriously," and I said, "Hell, Keith, you'd better take it seriously. This is serious business." The theater department didn't do too well in its review. The Graduate Council was ready to vote to throw out their Ph.D.

What happened?

Two of the three outside reviewers felt it didn't have a satisfactory program. One reviewer from the University of Colorado took that position very strongly. I said we'd better hear from the students, so I asked Engar to send me over a list of his Ph.D. candidates who lived nearby; and I picked out two men and a woman at random and invited them to come in. All three of them argued in favor of keeping the degree, and, believe it or not, they did a better job of it than the faculty. The woman, especially. Her name was Marilyn Holt, and I learned later she had been Miss Utah. She later became professor and then head of our theater department. My hell, she made such a case for the Ph.D. program that the department won the day.

It was an interesting case. One question was whether operating a community theater was a proper activity for a university theater department—whether it was genuinely academic. I took the position at the time that the university's Pioneer Theatre was built in part as a community theater.

Otherwise I doubt very much that organizations like the Mormon church and Kennecott Copper and the Utah legislature, all contributors to the building of the Pioneer Theatre, would have had much to do with it.

Exactly. So I defended the program as long as they were doing high-level creative work, whether it got on that big stage or not. There was a minority opinion that it shouldn't be doing popular musicals, but I defended it because I knew its history and its value for the community. Actually, they were turning out quite a few degrees, which is more than you could say for some departments like the philosophy department.

Did the philosophy department come under review during your tenure?

Yes, more than once; and it had trouble. I really saved the department, although several faculty members thought I was trying to do them in. I did my damnedest to save them while being perfectly honest with the Graduate Council. It really came down to two issues. First, productivity. There was very little demand from the students for a Ph.D. in philosophy. I used to urge masters' students to go somewhere else for their Ph.D. I didn't ever encourage them to stay. I thought we were perfectly competent to award a master's degree, but I was concerned about getting into a Ph.D. program at that time. I don't mean to imply that we gave the degree loosely.

What was the second issue?

The second problem was the faculty's lack of research. I was never strong on this "publish or perish" business; but, still, in a philosophy faculty, you needed more research activity than we were then having. On the other hand, the outsider reviewers, though critical of the department, were not in favor of dropping the degree. They felt it would cripple the department, and I agreed. So, on that basis, it was saved. Let me mention one more department.

The Department of Education?

Yes, with the college reorganization, that would be the Department of Educational Studies. The dean, Robert Erdman, was on the Graduate Council, and he was a strong critic of this department. As far as we were concerned, it was in educational shambles, and we used the term "bankrupt" in our report. We recommended it should be put into receivership, which it was. The dean administered it directly—or, at least, he assigned Michael Parsons to do it until it pulled itself together.

The same term—receivership—was applied to the sociology department and the same solution—an outside chair—was applied in 1985 or 1986. So that was terminology you invented?

Well, we borrowed it.

What do you remember about the other departments?

The mathematics department came through in fine style. There were complaints in the biology department that undergraduate work was being neglected in favor of graduate work. These reviews really put the departments on their toes. The Graduate School administered degrees in several Medical School departments—masters' degrees and Ph.D.s. But the Medical School was interested in having us do the whole damn works. I can't remember what we decided there, but, of course, we were not involved in the professional medical work. We had no direct authority in the case of the law school, and they didn't want us to review them. They said they were adequately covered by the

American Bar Association and the Association of Law Schools and so on. My recollection is that later they gave in and were reviewed just like all the other departments.

What about the other professional schools?

No problem. We did reviews of business, engineering, and so forth, as well as the departments in fine arts.

And you set out to review each department and degree every five years?

That was our original intent, but we couldn't get around to them in that length of time. We lengthened the review cycle to seven. There were always three or four going on at once.

Did you also work with undergraduate degrees?

In general, I'd have to say that undergraduates display a remarkable lack of interest in their own education. After the graduate review process had been going for some time, the University Senate created a committee to review undergraduate programs. I had nothing to do with it; but it was apparently not very successful, so the committee gave up on it.

Did they turn it over to the Graduate Council?

No, the committee just recommended abolishing it. When they made their report to the University Senate, the senate said they'd be willing to abolish the committee if the Graduate Council would take on the task of undergraduate reviews. I wasn't interested in doing it, but the Graduate Council considered it very seriously, and we decided to tackle it, to add undergraduate reviews to our graduate reviews.

Did you have strong support from all of the presidents during this period?

I'd say so. Fletcher was very interested, of course; and Gardner liked what he saw. The budget was already making them consider what they should keep and what to drop. These reports became very important in making central administration decisions about what to fund.

Did your recommendations include funding?

I should have mentioned that earlier. From the beginning we decided not to make any financial recommendations, because I saw us functioning simply as an educational operation. We had no central administrators on the Graduate Council. I was very opposed to that idea. In fact, I usually avoided having deans on it—and just a few department heads. David Gardner urged us to make any kind of recommendations we wanted to, including funding; and after that we became more involved in financial matters.

Were you comfortable with that?

Well, to the extent that a good percentage of the things we had to deal with involved money one way or the other, yes. But I would have been happier to just deal with education without worrying about the damn money. Fletcher had a tendency to say, "Look, you go ahead and say what ought to be done, and I'll worry about the money."

That'd be nice for anybody, wouldn't it? To what extent was this review process being used elsewhere?

I was astonished, Jack, that we were the pioneers. As soon as I was appointed graduate dean, I sent out letters to at least fifteen major institutions, asking their graduate deans or vice-presidents about their review procedures and policies. Not all of them answered; but from those who did, without exception, they said, "We're not doing any- thing, but if you develop something, we wish you'd let us know."

So you were acting without precedent.

Yes, but it didn't take me long to decide the kind of thing we should do. It worked out exactly as I hoped it would, and I consider it a plus in my administrative legacy. We began to get inquiries from all over the country, and I was asked to describe our system at graduate school meetings. I addressed the national body of graduate school deans in Williamsburg, and we were so flooded with requests that we ran off materials and had packets ready to send to other institutions who requested information.

A mail-order operation! It sounds to me as if you affected the entire system nationally.

I believe it did. Any number of people told me so, especially graduate deans.

Given your ties to USC, you must have had some conversations with David Gardner when he was being considered for the presidency down there about 1978.

Yes, I did; I had conversations also with members of the USC search committee who consulted me about Gardner. They wanted him and thought they had him. But he went to California instead, later on, of course.

Yes, I thought it was a pretty close decision from this end. Sterling, you've frequently been involved in making important personnel decisions yourself. What criteria have guided your judgments when you've chaired search committees?

Well, I take it for granted that a university is a teaching and research enterprise. Take teaching. I don't want to see anybody on the faculty who doesn't thoroughly know his or her subject. People say, "I teach students." Well, I must say, I *don't* teach students. I teach subjects and hope that some students come around once in a while and profit from my teaching. I think the "I teach students" attitude is quite appropriate for an elementary school, but a university is a different matter. An on-going, up-to-date knowledge of the field is absolutely essential for appointment as a teacher. You appoint a person to teach physics because he or she is a highly competent physicist—not because of a good attitude toward students.

But as essential as such knowledge is, you still have to teach it, and the processes developing it, to students!

I'll grant you that, Jack. But you still have to have a person who is involved in continuing research. I suppose there are some exceptions, for instance, ancient history, where our knowledge doesn't grow very rapidly, but still that scholar must be involved in continuing research in the field or related fields to broaden his or her understanding and perspectives.

What about teaching methods?

You hear a lot of people talking about how the lecture method is bad. You've got to get into discussions they say. This is a lot of nonsense, as far as I'm concerned. If a person handles his or her subject best by lecturing, let him lecture. I'm reminded that Alfred North Whitehead, after he came to Harvard in the 1920s, made the statement that he had tried very hard to be a good American and use the discussion method of teaching, but he finally had to abandon it. Most teachers actually teach the way their own teachers taught them; and I must say very honestly that I've learned the most myself from teachers who lectured and really knew their stuff.

Whitehead was clever there, Sterling. He should have said the Greek way of teaching, instead of the American way. Socrates invented it! I've heard you praise Ephraim Ericksen and Obert Tanner for engaging their students in discussions. Isn't this a matter of style rather than value?

Well, yes, that's true. Ericksen wasn't a good lecturer. He was a fine discussion leader, and I've gained more from Ericksen than from any teacher I ever had. But it was not what you would call knowledge. What I gained from Ericksen was a capacity to look critically at ideas and examine them carefully. I've learned other things from people who discuss—but the main value there was in arguing with my teachers. They, on the one hand, were able to show what a poor arguer I was and stimulate my desire to engage more skillfully in critical thought.

Weren't they, then, masters at pushing you—goading you—to discover and develop knowledge yourself? Didn't they make you a more perceptive reader and a keener listener even to lectures?

Yes, though of course no one can do much with the Socratic method in a class of four or five hundred students or fifty or seventy-five. You don't engage in much discussion in those circumstances. More advanced students should probably be "discussed with" more than "lectured to," but many beginning students don't know enough about the subject to carry on a very intelligent discussion.

My courses at the University of Utah have usually been ten and fifteen students. Most of the time I have lectured in a very informal way, but the students always knew that they could interrupt me at any time to interpose ideas, agree with me, or deliver their own sermonettes. I tried to keep their sermonettes down in length, and to argue my own views, unless they really wanted to get into the act. My presumption is that the teacher is the teacher because he or she knows more about that particular subject than the students. Granted, that's not always a safe assumption.

I hear you, Sterling, and I agree up to a point. But one of the reasons undergraduate students don't know enough to engage in serious debate is that they have rarely been expected to think for themselves. All that most of them have ever done is take notes and spit the stuff back. What sort of motivation does that endless process provide? Why do we blame the students? Well, what kind of research do you think teachers should be involved in?

That varies according to the teacher's field. Creative work in the arts is equivalent to research—although it's stretching it a bit for me to call a symphony or a sculpture research. There are more appropriate words. I think of a scientist in a laboratory or the scholar in the library as engaged in scientific and scholarly research.

How do you define scholarship or research and how are they related to publishing? Is publishing in scholarly journals the best or only tangible evidence of scholarly achievement?

As I've already mentioned, I really don't go along with that "publish or perish" stuff. Now if someone is doing first-class intellectual work, whether it's in history or poetry, chances are he or she *will* publish a great deal. But I wouldn't judge scholarship on the basis of whether it gets beyond the scholar and out to the educated public. At the same time I'd say that the institution's responsibility is to add to the world's knowledge. I'm not opposed to the idea of putting pressure on people to do research; and in fields where research output takes the form of writing—it seems most appropriate to get it published. History and philosophy are both examples. I could name people who have been among the most prized professors in this university, who were first-rate teachers and real scholars, but who rarely published anything, and then only under protest!

For example?

Louis Zucker in the English department. He was a man of immense learning and monumental scholarship, a scholar of major proportions. But, hell, you couldn't get him to write anything. His name appears on no books. I couldn't name more than three or four articles he published, and I was acquainted with him from about 1934. He had so many books in his office that his desk, side chairs, and floor were stacked high. He could hardly get in there himself. Now I'm not saying it's necessarily a mark of virtue to fill your office with books. He would have never been promoted beyond instructor if it depended on publication. But his students would swear by him. I had him as a teacher. I'd swear by him. He was great.

One of our dilemmas today is that we put enormous pressure on new faculty to publish, so they pick out a very narrow specialty and make it even narrower, but they publish! That is a wholly different kind of scholarship than a Louis Zucker or a Jack Adamson whose knowledge is broad and deep and for whom integration and meaning are the point—and the joy of it all.

Exactly. Where do we find the generalists today who can synthesize things for us and engender genuine wisdom? I sense you have a pessimistic concern about the future of academic scholarship, which I certainly share. However, Bertrand Russell says that you can't love everyone in general unless you love someone in particular. So I think it's appropriate for everybody in academic life to have a specialized field or fields in which they are very competent. I think a scholar has to know some things very well in particular, otherwise he can't know very much in general.

If you were to suggest university policies that would encourage wise generalists—people who are very liberally educated but also have a great depth somewhere—what would you change about our current practices?

I think I would drastically change the financing of higher education. Now most of the funds for research go to the sciences, engineering, and medicine. Faculty in the sciences are paid more than faculty in the social sciences, humanities, and arts.

Which has caused artists and humanists to behave and talk like scientists, sometimes betraying their own gifts. This sort of thing shows the power of market conditions.

Market conditions, yes, but also the temper of the culture. It is not just how universities wish to use their money, but where the government and industry are willing to invest. It involves such things as the miserably low pay scale for teachers in elementary and secondary education. If we want great teachers in the public schools, we're going to have to pay them more. Otherwise, they'll be picked off by private industry and business. During the 1960s I met with an assistant superintendent of Salt Lake City schools to discuss staffing problems. I remember he was specifically concerned about finding first-rate physics teachers for high school. I asked, "How much do you pay a B student from the university to teach driver education?" He told me the pay scale according to seniority. "Now," I said, "if you have a straight-A student from mathematics and physics, with the same service record, etc., how much do you pay him?" "Exactly the same," was the reply. "Well," I said, "you're just going to have to set up differential pay scales, the way we do at the university."

I don't know what faculty pay scales are now at the university; but when I was dean of Letters and Science, in general we paid our mathematicians more than we paid our language teachers. And if we hadn't done so, we probably wouldn't have had a mathematics department at all. Mathematicians were as scarce as hen's teeth.

So how can we finance the humanities, Sterling?

That's a problem. Much of the research money comes from the federal government, and many of the people in Congress can't see that the humanities are of much value. When I met with congressional committees, I was frankly appalled at the ignorance of some people, especially in the House of Representatives, of the value of the humanities. They kept saying they wanted federal money to strengthen the nation, but that meant two things: engineering armaments and manufacturing armaments. That's what they thought strengthened the nation. To make a nation more intellectually literate didn't impress them much.

For most citizens the best reasons to support education are jobs, defense, and industry.

Sure. The idea of having a literate, educated society for the sake of having a high-quality intellectual, spiritual, and moral life in the nation is completely overlooked. My predecessor in Washington had just approved NDEA fellowships for the study of folklore, and I had to defend that decision before a committee in the House of Representatives. Now I admit it's not particularly easy to make a case for the positive effects of folklore research on the strength of the American people, but I argued that such knowledge has an impact on the moral and spiritual quality of the nation. That meant nothing to one member of the committee. I argued and argued, and all he would say is "I don't see it." All he *could* see was guns and ammunition for strengthening the nation.

Do you think of researchers as creating knowledge or discovering knowledge? Is truth lurking there someplace, waiting for us, or do we make meaning, wisdom, and knowledge?

I personally think we create knowledge on the basis of discovering what the facts are, but we don't create the facts. I'd say that achieving knowledge of the world—a more extensive, more accurate understanding of it—is 50 percent of the function of a university. It's not the function of a secondary school. The primary function of a secondary school is to communicate knowledge, generate rationality, and encourage learning, but the university has an immense responsibility to advance knowledge through research as well as to communicate knowledge through teaching.

I like the notion of "advancing" knowledge because it allows room for both discovery and creation. This whole issue has become so politicized, so ideological, in universities today.

That's very true. It's also true—and very unfortunate—that those who tend to be less involved in research simply don't want to do it. And, of course, some first-rate researchers who have a lot to offer as teachers just don't want to teach. I recall, when I was dean of Letters and Science, appointing a very good young man as assistant professor, I believe in chemistry. He told me that he was a research man and didn't want to teach. I told him, "Unless you take a position entirely on soft money, you will have to teach." Well, he was very good as a teacher and still is. He just didn't want to do it. He loved working away at his subject and really produced research, so he was a very valuable person to the university.

I don't think, however, that the chief problem is to encourage research. Lots of money is pouring into it in some fields, and that appears to be incentive enough. The real problem is guaranteeing that every person who goes through a university comes out with at least a liberal education.

It is indeed. And that takes inspired teaching by liberally educated professors.

And that, of course, brings us to the core question of what constitutes a liberal education.

The great dilemma, practical as well as philosophical, is whether we can go back and assemble a new canon of enduring ideas and works that represent the global human heritage, humanistic, scientific, and artistic. If students were exposed to this sort of core curriculum—assuming the faculty could come to some agreement on what it would be—we could at least claim to offer a liberal education for the twenty-first century.

Yes, I think it's an error to think of liberal education in terms of the great books. Now I have nothing against the great books, but they're too focused on the past. I know you agree with me that liberal education is the type of education that liberates the mind, that overcomes ignorance, superstition, and prejudice.

Wholeheartedly.

Let me give you an example. When I first joined the university faculty, I was rather active in Phi Beta Kappa which is, of course, for students in liberal studies. I remember a real hassle over whether to classify journalism as a liberal study. I don't now recall how it came out; but I'm prepared to say that one might find liberal studies anywhere in the university. Certain business courses in labor and management might qualify. National and international problems in finance should qualify as liberal subjects. Therefore, I think it's a very bad approach to liberal education to describe it in terms of university departments or disciplines. The key question is: to what extent are these things essential to a high quality culture and a strong social order?

So much depends on how a course is taught—the attitude and approach of the teacher is everything. I've seen literature taught as a narrow vocational skill and school finance taught as an exploration of equality and justice and a quest for human dignity—a truly liberating experience for students. You see, I like to think of it as distinguishing between great books and noble ideas—such as liberty, justice, mercy, the good, the beautiful, and so forth. These might well be manifest in a whole variety of applied fields. The field of labor relations is an excellent place to explore ideas about justice.

Quite right, Jack. I'd like to hear more about your noble ideas.

I like to define noble ideas as the enduring concepts that nobody can live one day without having to confront, either consciously or unconsciously. Someone who may give no thought at all to the notion of equality is still making decisions every day that advance or assault human equality. How do you treat a little sister? Who do you vote for? Do you laugh at a racist joke? And on and on—everyday stuff. A liberal education ought to help students come to grips with truly important ideas in a way that anchors their own thoughts and informs their actions daily and for a lifetime.

I certainly like that approach; and what you say suggests that a person would not be liberally educated unless he or she has actually developed the habit of critical thought—not just that he or she recognizes it but that he or she habitually does it. You don't have to advertise what you're thinking all the time, but you have to *think* all the time. The liberally educated person has learned to examine himself, or herself, his society, and the world, and to do it intelligently, critically, and positively.

I'd go farther than that, Sterling. I think noble ideas and critical thought must be reflected in the way a person lives and acts before I would agree that the individual is liberally educated.

15.
At Home in the World

Sterling, in addition to your rich personal life, three institutions have been the focus of your lifelong interest: religion and the Mormon church, education and the University of Utah, and government in the form of cultural policy. Start wherever you like, and let's look at your conclusions about each institution after eight decades on this planet.

Well, Jack, I'll begin by reflecting on my life as a whole. Looking back over the years, I can easily see where I should have done things differently and might have steered clear of some things that didn't pan out. But there are other places where I overcame an obstacle or removed one, or successfully advanced an idea, or effected changes in an organization.

If it were simply a matter of doing it all over again, what might you have changed?

I would rather have written two or three good books on philosophic problems, in the hope of making a contribution to learning and human values, than to have done what I did in the university's administration or in the federal government. It gave me far more pleasure to sit in my own study and try to run down some basic idea in ancient Greek thought than to sit in a meeting of the Graduate Council or a federal commission and hassle over regulations and financial problems. I found more pleasure and satisfaction in dealing with university students than in working with members of Congress.

Are you saying that you found no satisfaction in academic leadership or national policy making?

Of course, we gain some satisfaction from administrative work, but seldom a sense of intellectual accomplishment. I have found far more pleasure in scholarly activities than in institutional leadership.

Sterling, how would you appraise the development of your philosophical interests over the years?

My interests have changed a good deal in research and writing.

When I was an undergraduate and graduate student, my interests were primarily in the theory of knowledge, and that lasted right through my doctoral studies and dissertation, which was on the logical analysis of value judgments. Then I got over the epistemological syndrome and began to pay attention to other things. I was never much interested in the study of ethics or aesthetics, but I gave more attention to problems in metaphysics. For many years my main interest has been the philosophy of history and the history of philosophy. Recently I've gone back to the history of religion, which was another major interest of mine as an undergraduate.

But that's not the sort of course you taught at the university until toward the end of your career?

When I first came to the University of Utah, I taught courses in Asian philosophy and religion, and also in the history of philosophy. I didn't teach the philosophy of religion or the history of occidental religion. Obert Tanner was in the latter field—and later Max Rogers. In the sixties I began paying attention again to the history of Christianity, and I've probably spent more time there than I should have. This has been due in part to my involvement with Rogers and Tanner in the volume *Toward Understanding the New Testament.*

Why do you say you have spent too much time on the history of Christianity?

I can think of so many other things that I should have devoted more time to, that's all. I would like to have devoted much more time to the study of logic and, among other things, the history of philosophy. At one time I was under agreement with two publishers to produce two books, a history of philosophy and a volume on Mormon philosophy, neither of which materialized because of lack of time.

You have mentioned several times that you wish you had spent more time studying languages. Which languages and where would you have fit this pursuit into your education?

I should have studied more Latin and Greek as an undergraduate, along with more mathematics and logic. I could always have used more competence in modern languages, too.

Most doctoral programs don't require any foreign languages now. Is this a step backward?

Actually, eliminating the standard all-university language requirement for the Ph.D. was my gift to graduate students across the country. My predecessor as dean of the Graduate School, Henry Eyring, a great scientist, had a typical iron-clad rule about languages. He used to say, "They've got to know French and German if they're going to get a

Ph.D. from this institution." Well, I was no sooner dean of the Graduate School, replacing Henry in 1966, than I learned that as dean he had wisely made all kinds of exceptions—often on the recommendation of a student's doctoral committee. For instance, if a student were doing something related to Russia, he could use Russian for one of his languages. That made perfectly good sense. I felt that if a departmental committee could be trusted with determining what the person should study for the degree, it should also be entrusted with decisions regarding what languages are pertinent. In some cases it might even be a requirement of advanced statistics or, more recently, a computer language.

At about this time you were invited to address the national meeting of the Council of Graduate Deans?

Yes. Well, the chair of that plenary session was Peter Elder, dean at Harvard and a scholar of very high order in the humanities. I had a feeling Elder wasn't going to like what I was about to say. My paper was on the standard all-university language requirement, and I went right down the line opposing this requirement. I insisted that it has created a tyranny of language departments over graduate students and tends to be a mechanical requirement rather than one geared to the best education of the student.

Well, Peter Elder was a classicist, and I was sure he would just hit the ceiling. Instead, he got up after my address and said that he wanted to know, by a show of hands, how many of the deans would go home and do the right thing—and the right thing was what I had recommended: get rid of the all-university language requirement for graduate degrees and open it up so that requirements could be designed that fit each student's particular needs.

How did the audience respond?

A few hands started to come up, but Elder wasn't satisfied. "More, more," he insisted, and you know pretty soon he had most of those hands up. I walked out of there as a kind of hero of the day. That's why I say it's my gift to graduate students. Now I didn't intend, of course, nor did Elder, that language requirements simply be dropped—just that they be tailored to the student's scholarly work. I also argued, Jack, for more undergraduate language as a requirement for admission to graduate school.

In your own case, you studied Latin in high school and college, but where did you pick up Greek?

I never had a formal course in Greek. A Latin teacher who wanted me to know Greek spent a lot of time tutoring me. I can wade through

Latin, but Greek is another matter.

Sterling, you have written several books of enduring value. Your two "Foundations" pieces on Mormon philosophy and theology created quite a stir in the 1950s and sixties and still enjoy high respect. We've talked previously about the unusual circumstances that led to you, as a nonbeliever, writing them, but I want to hear more about official and personal responses to these works.

As you know, the first of these, *The Philosophical Foundations of Mormon Theology*, is an extensive essay that I wrote for delivery in a lecture series on religion that was established cooperatively by the major universities in Utah in 1958. I read the lecture at those institutions, and then, when Ohio State asked the LDS church to provide a lecturer on Mormonism for its religion week, Apostle Harold B. Lee asked me to give it at your alma mater, Jack.

How was this essay received when it was published by the University of Utah Press in 1959?

President Olpin of the university sent published copies of the address to the general authorities of the LDS church. He received several letters in reply, which he passed on to me. One, from President David O. McKay, concluded by saying: "I am glad [McMurrin] is on the faculty of the University of Utah and also a member of the church. I hold his name in high regard."[1] Another letter, from J. Reuben Clark, the second counselor to President McKay, stated that "there is a great deal of difference of opinion regarding [McMurrin's] address and its usefulness to us. . . . A lot of people are troubled about a lot of things about which they know nothing."[2] So, you see, it all depended on the reader. This little book was still in print the last time I checked. I see it once in a while in the bookstores and still occasionally receive letters that have been prompted by it.

Now, about the other volume, **The Theological Foundations of the Mormon Religion?**

It arose from a series of lectures on Mormon theology that the Extension Division of the university asked me to give during the winter of 1965. I offered my lectures with the understanding that they would initiate a larger series of lectures on world religions—featuring Judaism, Buddhism, Islam, Protestantism, and Catholicism. Unfortunately, the larger series never materialized.

1. David O. McKay to A. Ray Olpin, May 15, 1959.

How did your lectures go? I know they were published very soon after you gave them.

They were well attended, even though there was an admission charge. In 1965 the University Press published the lectures as a single volume, just as I read them for the public audience. I added an additional lecture treating the question of whether God is a person which I had given on the Great Issues Forum sometime earlier. The book was published first in hardback, and then in paperback. This book is not an argument either for or against Mormonism, or religion, for that matter. It is entirely expository and was intended to call attention to the more important facets of Mormon theology.

What about your 1982 book Religion, Reason, and Truth: Essays on the Philosophy of Religion?

It's a volume of essays that I had written earlier, together with several that I wrote especially for this publication. The essays are both analytical and substantive and, as with most things that I write, they have a pronounced historical flavor. I was pleased that Charles Hartshorne, whom I regard as the foremost contemporary philosopher of religion, commented favorably about this book in his essay in *The Library of Living Philosophers* volume on his philosophy. Hartshorne, as you know, was a leader in the process theology movement.

How extensive is the body of your published work?

I think my work to date, including books edited or co-authored, comes to a total of about twenty-three volumes. That includes three things that I wrote for the Committee for Economic Development with the assistance and support of a number of research scholars, and which did not actually carry my name as author. I am listed simply as the director of the educational projects in which the volumes were issued. My bibliography lists about 250 or 300 published papers and many unpublished writings.

Of your major published works, Sterling, which ones have brought you greatest satisfaction?

Oh, hell, I don't know. I'm not sure that any of them have brought a lot of satisfaction. What I would really like to do, my main interest now, is to write a good book on the philosophy of history. I have a manuscript on this subject in the works. Perhaps it will represent what I have really wanted to say.

Speaking of satisfactions, Jack, one of the things about the pursuit of academic philosophy is that you are concerned with minds of the highest order. There isn't time to spend on minor ones. This has meant for me some association with a few of the world's leading thinkers. Sarvepalli Radhakrishnan, for instance, later became president of India and who was the foremost philosophical scholar of Asia. When he visited Utah in the 1950s, President Olpin and I were his hosts. I arranged for him a meeting with President McKay, a special concert in his honor by the Tabernacle Choir, and a luncheon with the governor. His lecture at the university was published. It was a memorable association. We even went to the Bingham Copper Mine across the valley.

When Brand Blanshard, the nation's foremost rationalist and a philosopher of great distinction, visited the university from Yale, I did a series of televised interviews with him. I think you've seen the tapes, Jack. Both Radhakrishnan and Blanshard are in the prestigious *Library of Living Philosophers*, along with Martin Buber and nearly twenty others. I serve on the board that selects the world's leading philosophers for inclusion in this series. It has been my good fortune to have associated with a surprising number of truly great scholars, including Jewish theologians Louis Finkelstein and R. H. Pfeiffer.

What about the personal side of living, Sterling, your social life and your cultural interests?

I have sometimes been asked, especially in the East, how I can survive in Utah—by which they imply that we live in an intellectual and cultural wasteland. Of course, nothing could be further from the truth. Although here we are quite isolated geographically, we live in a state that is unmatched for its physical variety and beauty, in a culture that encourages imagination and action, and in a place where human relations are strong and lasting, and where there is an authentic commitment to the pursuit of humane values. I don't know what you think about it, Jack, but I've seen a lot of places and I wouldn't want to live anywhere else.

Of course you were born here, and partially grew up here, so you can't be objective, Sterling! Now I came here to the University of Utah at the age of thirty-five, with the aim of staying only a few years and moving on, but after two decades Linda and I have not found a place we'd rather live and work. This is our home. So perhaps you're right after all. Let's talk about your social life next, Sterling.

Natalie and I have had a rather wide, far-reaching social life in Utah. When we were living in California in the late 1940s, we did very little but associate with a few close friends and members of my family. Natalie had no relatives living in that part of California. After we came to Utah in 1948, however, our circle of friends expanded greatly. Our social life has been primarily through the university and other colleges in the state—though we have had many pleasant connections through the LDS church, and we have wonderful neighbors. Of course, we have also made numerous friendships beyond the boundaries of Utah and the mountain west. The serious discussion group that you and Linda and Natalie and I belong to—the so-called "Monday Nighters"—includes some of our most intimate friends. Several who were original members of the group have died, and we have replaced them with younger people like you and Linda. It has been a delightful experience for Natalie and me.

What are Natalie's special interests?

Natalie belongs to the Daughters of the American Colonists and has been regent of the Utah Chapter. She has the qualifications for membership in the Daughters of the American Revolution (the DAR), and her great-aunt Mattie and her mother, who were both active in the DAR, insisted that she join that organization. But she didn't like some of their group prejudices, so she settled for the Colonists. Natalie's Aunt Mattie once said to her, "Natalie, your prejudices have been sadly neglected."

And, happily, they have remained so! What cultural events do the two of you especially enjoy?

We have always held season tickets to the Pioneer Theatre at the university, the Utah Opera, Ballet West, and the Utah Symphony. The fine arts have always played a large role in my life with Natalie—especially music. I sometimes hear of people who spend a week or two in some "retreat" to "renew" their souls. A two-hour concert of the Utah Symphony is all it takes to renew mine. Or a half-hour concert of the Tabernacle organ will do the job. As a matter of fact, I am a "Tabernacle organaholic." When we were students at the university, Natalie and I were fixtures at the Tabernacle organ concerts. In later years we were close friends of the great organist Alexander Schreiner, whom I first met as a student at UCLA when he was the organist in Royce Hall. Alex did a Ph.D. in music composition at the University of Utah, minoring in philosophy. He took all of my classes. He was a delightful person. On several occasions he gave special concerts for distinguished visitors at our request, taking them back into the heart of the organ and sometimes into the roof of the Tabernacle to examine its unique "cowhide" construction.

What is it about music that speaks to your soul?

Like music itself, musicians have always seemed to me to be inhabitants of an ideal world. If I had several lives to live, I would want one of them to be in music—not as a performer, but as a composer of symphonies. I have been more deeply impressed by the music that I have heard than by the books I have read. My deep sense of the tragedy and triumph of life, expressed in the world's greatest literature, for example the Book of Job, is a living experience in the world's greatest music.

Natalie and I had a warm friendship with Maurice Abravanel, the chief creator of the Utah Symphony, whom we admired not only for his great artistry but as well for his becoming a sincere and understanding member of his adopted community. We have had many friends in the world of music, including Aaron Copland, Leroy Robertson, the celebrated Mormon composer, Harry Rickel, a brilliant pianist and harpsichordist in Arizona; Lowell Durham, a composer and music critic whose honesty and humor never failed to delight his audiences; Ardean Watts, who can produce a symphony on the piano; and the highly talented choir director Jay Welch. More recently, we have become close friends of Russian-American violist Mikhail Boguslavsky and his wife, Nina, who are mines of artistic and literary culture. All of these people have given dimension to our daily lives.

Do the visual arts inspire you, too?

I think Natalie is more sensitive to the visual arts than I am. We are both addicted to ballet, partly through the influence of Willam Christensen, the creator of Ballet West. I am affected emotionally by great architecture, such as the Salisbury and Chartres cathedrals, the Brooklyn Bridge, the basilica of Saint Peter's and the Pantheon in Rome, the Parthenon in Athens, and the Taj Mahal. On one occasion we went from Rome to Istanbul primarily to see the interior of the dome of the Hagia Sophia. Natalie and I are both pleased that our second son, Sterling James, turned to architecture, and that our youngest daughter, Melanie, is now pursuing painting, for which she has real talent.

I know you have also visited some of the world's great museums . . .

Yes, we have always been drawn to great art museums and have visited many of them, from the Prado in Madrid to the Hermitage in St. Petersburg. I am personally overwhelmed by these collections, and I'm aware that I don't have the capacity to appreciate what I am seeing. The University of Utah is fortunate to have a small but very high-quality art museum whose director, Frank Sanguinetti, is a man of most unusual talent and sophistication.

Friends have always been central to your life and work—to the kind of life that you and Natalie live. How do you think about friendship? What is it?

Of course, Jack, there are friends—and friends—family friends, friendly neighbors and colleagues, and casual friends. True friendship, the real thing, however, is more restrictive and intense. For me, such friendships are an ineffable experience that cannot be adequately defined or described, but they affect the whole qualify of a person's life—attitudes, pleasures, and general temperament.

Among our intimate friends there have been many of uncommon talents and achievement. None has been more celebrated than the portrait artist Alvin Gittins. He was a wise and highly sophisticated person and without question an artist of supreme talents. He did a portrait of me for the university when I returned from serving as U.S. Commissioner of Education, back in the sixties. He and I retreated to a hilltop villa for a week near Puerto Vallarta, Mexico, a favorite spot of his, to do the portrait.

It hangs in the Winder Board Room in the Park Building. During long and boring meetings there, I have often contemplated your youthful bearing in that somber brown suit. Now I must picture you posing in that dark wool coat under a palm tree in the sweltering heat of the tropical sun!

Just two or three weeks before his untimely death, Al told me he was planning another portrait of me because, being older, I would make a better subject. I was very pleased with the first one.

Gittins was a master. I think his portraits of Jack Adamson, Brig Madsen, and David Gardner were among his best. His use of light, and his ability to capture subtle personality traits, were truly awesome.

Great poets make me feel the same way Gittins's paintings do. I have no talent whatsoever for poetry, and I'm afraid I have an inadequate appreciation for it, but I think I know great poetry when I hear it. I have had at least some connection with two major poets, Brewster Ghiselin at the University of Utah and Carl Sandburg when he visited the University back in the late fifties. Sandburg was scheduled to lecture at the university, and he called me by telephone from Provo and asked if he could stay with Natalie and me while he was in Salt Lake. I had never before had any contact with him. Natalie and I with our daughter Trudy drove to Provo to bring him to Salt Lake. He was a delightful guest, so long as we had him, but we learned that the student body president who had invited him to lecture had planned to have Sandburg stay with him at his parents' home. So we gave him up for the night. But we had a delightful time with Sandburg and delivered him to the airport when he left.

I've heard many colorful accounts of Sandburg's presentation at the university. You have mentioned a number of artists, Sterling, but I know you are equally fascinated by the sciences.

I have had friends among scientists, even though I am not a scientist and know far too little about science. Natalie and I have had a warm relationship, since our student days, with the linguist and anthropologist Charles Dibble, one of the world's foremost authorities on Aztec language and culture. I can't resist telling you of my first meeting with Charlie back in early 1935. He had seen Natalie and me together on the campus, and he came into a classroom where I was sitting and said, "Say, if you decide you don't want that girl I saw you with, I wish you'd let me know." Of course, that was before he met his wife, to whom he is greatly devoted. I decided to keep Natalie, and she me, but the three of us became and have remained close.

Your predecessor as graduate dean, Henry Eyring, was one of the world's celebrated physical chemists. I know he was expected more than once to win a Nobel Prize. Here at home, of course, he was revered by the Mormon community as a scientist who never lost his Mormon beliefs.

We had countless conversations on matters relating to science and religion. Henry was, as is well known, religiously orthodox, and though we found areas of agreement, for the most part we were miles apart on religion. He wanted me to join him in doing a volume on religion and science, but that was out of the question for me. He could hold his magnificent scientific understanding separate from his theology, but that sort of compartmentalization never worked in my case. Henry was truly a great treasure for the university, the church, and, indeed, for the nation.

Your writing and teaching have been primarily in the humanities—what about your associates near your home base in academe?

I have talked already at great length about people in philosophy at the University of Utah, especially E. E. Ericksen and Waldemer Read, teachers and friends from my student days, and about my long and fruitful friendships with Louis Zucker, Boyer Jarvis, and Obert Tanner. But I must tell you about my daily associations with two or three others at the university. There aren't many first-rate scholars in these parts in the field of religion, but you are well acquainted with Lewis M. Rogers with whom I worked on the book on the New Testament. Max is a highly competent scholar, and I regard him as the leading living biblical scholar in the Mormon community. Stan Larson at the Marriott Library is also a meticulous scholar and strong contributor in this domain.

Two other friends of mine, major university figures as teachers and writers, were Jack Adamson, who died at the height of his powers in 1975, and William Mulder, who writes elegant and insightful prose. An unsung Utah scholar who deserves to be remembered in the humanities was Brigham Young University professor P. A. Christensen. P. A. was for many years head of the BYU department of English and he mentored many fine teachers and writers. Teachers of his stature too often get lost from history.

What about friends outside the halls of academe?

In recent years I have enjoyed the friendship of George D. Smith of San Francisco, a historian and writer of considerable capabilities, and a publisher of books. Through his company, Signature Books, he and others have made great contributions to the understanding of Mormon history and sociology. The Mormon church really owes them a great debt of gratitude for what they have done and are doing, but it's a debt that will probably never be acknowledged.

We have also had wonderful neighbors here near our home of more than thirty years. Natalie and I have spent many hours discussing religion with two of them, Talmage and Dorothy Nielsen, who are now serving as missionaries in Germany for the LDS church. And, at Natalie's eightieth birthday party, given by Pat and Boyer Jarvis, you met James and Beth Fillmore from Arizona, intimate friends for many years.

What are the bases of your closest friendships today?

For the most part, my friendships have been based on common intellectual interests. One of my chief pleasures in recent years has been a close association with four intimate friends who are interested in Western history: Brigham Madsen and Everett Cooley, both historians and authors of high competence, and Ernest Poulson and Richard Smoot who, like me, delight in the company of historians who know where the forts were located and the massacres took place. Each year the five of us take a couple of extended trips together to study early events in the American West.

Speaking of history, Sterling, you have a more complete grasp of the annals of the University of Utah than anyone alive. What were the real turning points as you see it? Who have been the key people in our development?

Jack, I have personally known every president of the University of Utah except its first, John R. Park. Two or three of them should go down as heroes of the university. George Thomas, who in the twenties and thirties fought the battles that yielded an intellectually free institution, and A. Ray Olpin, who catapulted the place into the ranks of strong research universities. Ever since Thomas, in fact, we have had strong presidents who knew what a university is for. More recently, I enjoy a warm personal friendship with David Gardner, who deserted us after leading the University of Utah from 1973 to 1983 and accepted the presidency of the University of California. I'm glad he's coming back to Utah in his retirement.

Arthur Smith, our current leader and first non-Mormon president, is building on the foundation of intellectual freedom that his predecessors built and defended. Speaking of university presidents and what they can do for their institutions, you knew Daryl Chase long before he served as president of Utah State University.

Our friendship with Daryl and Alice dates back into the early forties. He was an accomplished scholar in the history of religion, belonging to that small group of scholars the Mormon church sent to the University of Chicago to study in its distinguished divinity school, back in the days when the church was not afraid of advanced education in religion. Speaking of religious education in the church, I should mention two people who have had a very significant influence on others: Lowell Bennion and George T. Boyd. We've talked a lot about Lowell, who is widely known and highly respected as a teacher and writer, and as a selfless worker among the poor and disadvantaged. Lowell's great contribution to Mormon thought has been his insistence on the moral grounding of theology and religion. George Boyd and I taught together in Arizona, where with our wives we developed a warm and lasting friendship. George has been a tremendous influence on his colleagues in the church institute system and has always been an excellent teacher and a highly competent theologian.

The friends whom you have mentioned seem to have come largely from the arts, education, and the professions. But you have had considerable involvement with leaders from business and industry, especially through your work with the Aspen Institute and the Committee for Economic Development. We have talked often about Obert Tanner, but what about others?

There are too many to name here, although we have mentioned many of them along the way; people like Walter Paepcke, who transformed Aspen, Colorado, into a culture and recreation center, and Walter Reuther, the great American labor leader. Closer to home, I'll mention Marriner Eccles, the chief creator of the Eccles banking and industrial empire, former chairman of the Federal Reserve Board, and his wife, Sallie. Marriner died several years ago, but we continued to have a most pleasant relationship with Sallie until she died in 1995. She was an institution in herself, a delightful bundle of talent and personality. Marriner was a great man in the world of finance and a public servant of the highest order. When I was graduate dean of the university, he gave the university more than a million dollars for graduate fellowships.

A little later Joseph and Evelyn Rosenblatt gave their beautiful home to the university to serve as the president's house.

I know you and Linda have been at many events at Rosenblatt House. Quite apart from that and other generous gifts to the university, however, Joseph Rosenblatt's name has been known and respected far and near. He is a dedicated civic leader, a remarkably generous benefactor, and a man of great wisdom. Obert Tanner, Marriner Eccles, and Joseph Rosenblatt would be a powerful triumvirate to set the standards and give leadership to any community. Utah has benefitted greatly from their combined vision, generosity, and high idealism.

Looking farther afield, you and Natalie have been friends of Theodore Hesburgh, who recently resigned after many years as president of Notre Dame University.

Yes, he is a very dear friend of ours, a truly remarkable man. Our friendship with Father Ted developed when he and I were trustees of the Carnegie Foundation, of which another friend, John W. Gardner, was then president. Hesburgh holds the world's record for honorary doctors' degrees—more than a hundred. We gave him one a few years ago. He is truly a citizen of the world. I must tell you a little story. He is a very handsome man, the type that everyone finds attractive. Natalie is fond of him, and he of her. He always kisses her when we meet. A few years ago in New York, Father Ted, Meredith Wilson, and I were in a conversation on the subject of priestly celibacy in the Catholic church and the resulting shortage of seminarians preparing for the priesthood. Met Wilson said to me, "Sterling, you could enter a seminary and prepare for the priesthood and have a second career. All you would need to do is give up Natalie." Father Ted said, "When Sterling gives up Natalie; that's when I give up celibacy."

Sterling, let's turn to what you believe about the world today. Are you optimistic about the trends you see emerging here and abroad?

I am inclined to be somewhat pessimistic about the world—and I guess pretty much about everything else. The world is in terrible confusion at the present time. There is a great deal of chaos in our own country as well, and countless problems in our own immediate cultural environment.

The population of the earth has doubled since I was born in 1938, and I suppose the destructive power of weapons and the speed and reach of communications have multiplied a hundred-fold. No wonder we are confused.

Is your pessimism part of our times or of your nature?

When I was young, I was somewhat optimistic about the future. I inherited the optimism about human history that developed especially in the eighteenth and nineteenth centuries. It was very strong in America, and especially in western America. There was a pervasive faith that with more education, more science, more democracy, and more people going to the polls to vote, things would get better and better. Human beings would become freer; there would be greater economic prosperity, and so on. This was a manifest destiny type of thing—that there is some kind of inevitable progress in history that was decreed by God or built into the very structure of the universe.

But in the last fifty years we have come face to face with two threats to human survival—both of our own making—nuclear bombs and environmental degradation. Who can escape the irony that the dreams inspired by technology have turned partly into nightmares in the twentieth century?

Overall, there is probably more freedom in the world now than there ever has been, and less slavery. But there has been so much war and so much evil in this century—evil that is symbolized by the Holocaust and the atomic bomb—that it's difficult anymore to have that sanguine faith in human progress—the kind of faith that became very strong right up to the beginning of the First World War. Of course, there has been real progress in technology, which becomes more startling every day in the fields of electronics, communications, medicine, transportation, and food production. But, as you said, Jack, also great increases in the production of the weapons of war and in the toxic byproducts of our material prosperity. We don't seem to be getting one bit better as human beings.

I agree with you on that ironic point. The disintegration of the Soviet empire since 1989 has brought some new hope for human freedom and some new worries about who or what may move into the power vacuum. Anarchy, civil war, and organized crime lurk everywhere in that sphere—and beyond it—as the Oklahoma City federal building bombing reminded us so tragically.

When one considers the evils of mass starvation, the new political and military oppression that we are experiencing in many different parts of the world, the decentralization of the nuclear threat, the corruption and incompetence in our own government and in virtually all governments, and the specter of terrorism, it is difficult to believe that things are going to greatly improve in the foreseeable future. We fail to learn from history. That's one source of my pessimism. The great music and the great art of the world are, I think, more a product of the tragic than of the positive side of the human condition.

Knowing you as I do, Sterling, I can think of few friends who enjoy life more fully, who laugh more easily or more frequently! Is this the countenance of a doomsayer?

For myself and my own experience, I have no complaints whatsoever. I am now eighty-two years old. I have a wonderful wife and family and extended family and friends—everything has been a source of happiness in my experience. I've never been without work. I applied only once in my entire life for a job. That's when I went to see Lynn Bennion and applied for a job teaching in the LDS education system. I'm not sure that that proved to be a wise thing to do, but it was the beginning of a great friendship with Lynn Bennion. I've never aspired to positions of influence or wealth. I've always had at least enough to get by on from the time that I became independent. I've never had a lot, but I've had enough to live on with a certain amount of comfort and some of the amenities of life, enough to feed my kids. My personal experience in this world has been a very happy one.

But as you look at the lives of others around the globe, do you see any reason for hope?

I have a sense of ultimate sadness about the general condition of the world—the way in which we are progressively destroying the biosphere and destroying one another. I do place hope in democracy and in the United States of America. This country can point the way for the future—though I'm not of the opinion that all peoples or all cultures should fashion their social and political lives after ours—not by any means. I'm not of the opinion, however, that everything is necessarily going to turn out right. Consider the overwhelming blunder and tragedy of the Vietnam War. I don't believe that democracy as we have it now, or as it may become in the future, is written into the ultimate structure of the world—or that it will necessarily prevail. But I believe that the future is open and undetermined, that human beings have free will, that anything might happen. In this sense, Jack, I am hopeful.

Hopeful, but not too confident! Even so, I have often sensed that you feel quite disillusioned by the contemporary American political process.

Yes, politics has become all too negative in the United States. It shows up in Utah. It shows up everywhere. When I went to Washington I functioned entirely on a nonpolitical basis. I have contempt for the way the major political parties go at each other, the way they frequently line up purely on party lines on matters that are crucial to the well-being of the nation. I have never had any political aspirations. As a young man, when I first started in college, I thought I would like to get into the diplomatic service of the federal government. But I've never been interested in holding political office.

Were you ever asked or urged to do so?

When I returned from Washington, there were efforts among some leading Democrats to get me to run for governor. Frankly, I didn't take this at all seriously. I had no interest in such a thing, and I was well aware that the probability of my ever being nominated or elected to political office was absolute zero. So that didn't last very long. I talked them out of it.

It may not be your thing, or mine, but I have great admiration for good people who will put themselves through the trauma of running for high office and face the possibility of defeat.

But I think that in some ways it is a kind of tragicomedy in America—the way people fight and spend money for high office. In the early years of the nation, the offices searched out the people, instead of the people searching out the office. I think the possibilities of statesmanship such as we saw in George Washington or Thomas Jefferson are long gone. I believe our country is still producing people who could become great leaders, but they simply aren't interested in becoming involved in the kinds of things that go on in government. Or the kinds of things that you have to suffer through to be elected to high office. Occasionally, we have major figures in high office, such as Franklin Roosevelt, but by and large I think that we are subject to a great deal of mediocrity in the leadership of our cities, counties, states, and the federal government. This is not to ignore the fact that there are some people in office, of course, with real political talents, high morality, and obvious commitment to their work. I have known some of both kinds.

Religion has been your most persistent interest over the years—the study of it and the exploration of it in thought and practice. Why has this been so?

I think I have always, even from my childhood, been strongly inclined toward religion. When I was young, in high school, I was at times somewhat emotional—too emotional—with respect to religion. But over the years I overcame that, as I became more rational and more critical in my approach to religious matters. I guess it was a simple case of maturing.

What were your earliest religious instincts or feelings?

I think Alfred North Whitehead said, "Religion is what you do with your solitude." I like that. When I was young I seemed to crave solitude; I wanted to be alone. And when I was alone I sometimes had very

profound emotional experiences that now seem to me to have verged
on the mystical—not genuine mystic experience, you understand, but
simply something a little like that in the presence of great art, especially
music, or in encountering cases of great suffering or profound moral
achievement. In these matters I am sure that I am like everyone else,
moved by tragedy and triumph, by the superb beauty of nature, or by
the supreme goodness that can be found in the human soul.

*But have you really changed that much, Sterling? It sounds to me like you
never left the simpler religious perspective of your childhood, that foundation
laid well before your graduate philosophical and theological study. The values
and feelings you have just described as childhood experiences are still at the
core of your life and the heart of your philosophy. You've never identified
the religion experience with theology. You have lived one and studied the
other!*

I'll grant you that religion is a sentiment; we experience it. Theology
is just words and ideas. I think that most theology is nonsense—it simply
doesn't make any sense. Too much of it is wishful speculation that has
very little, if any, factual grounding and little connection with genuine
religion.

*What about recent trends in theology? Are you attracted to them, or are they
just more nonsense?*

I will say that the kind of non-absolutistic theology which is
emerging now, with a finite, temporalistic conception of God—and the
belief that process is at the foundation of reality—has more to commend
it than the traditional theology where God is a timeless absolute being
who embraces the whole universe and its total history.

*Theology, then, can serve to orient us in a baffling world by giving us an
interpretation of how things work in the universe and where we fit into the
larger scheme of things. But don't our individual conclusions, based in part
on theology we may choose to embrace, give rise to religious feelings and
meaning to our personal experiences? If this is so, then might not theology
be the underpinning of at least some religious experiences?*

I certainly can't argue with your proposition that theology can serve
religious ends, Jack, but theology doesn't necessarily lead to these ends.

And with respect to your own religion, Mormonism?

I have very strong attachments to Mormonism, but they are largely
matters of sentiment and habit. These attachments certainly do not spring
from my understanding of Mormon doctrine. There is a great deal of
nonsense, in my opinion, in the corpus of Mormon belief, but there are
notable strengths, too, especially in its non-absolutistic nature and its

grounding in process, universal process. Mormon theology is temporal-istic and intensely moral. In my opinion, that is all to the good. Despite the fact that much of it is rough and crude and obviously false, the basic theology of Mormonism is strong and commendable.

Mark Twain said that "Wagner's music really is better than it sounds!" Is something like this also true of LDS theology?

Very true, but my *personal* views are essentially agnostic, naturalistic, and humanistic. This isn't to say that I don't have a genuine appreciation for the more liberal forms of theism, especially where there is a serious attempt to ground theism in scientifically verifiable fact. But I'm not of the opinion that it's possible, for instance, to establish any kind of rational, factual proof of the existence of God—or, for that matter, the nonexistence of God. For the latter reason, I'm certainly not atheistic. My views are essentially agnostic, but with strong inclinations toward religion—religious attitudes, religious sentiment.

Unlike many people, some of whom you and I have known and care deeply about, you've never had a crisis in your religious experience.

I think this is due to the fact that, from my childhood on, a free discussion of religion was commonplace in my home. My father was well informed on matters of theology—especially within the LDS framework. We used to talk very freely. It was a very common thing for us to go to church when I was a kid and then go home and criticize the speaker's ideas. I simply grew up with that kind of critical, analytical attitude toward church and religion, without being at all opposed to religion. So whatever views I have that are different from my early childhood or adolescence are views which have developed quite unob-trusively and without my even being aware of any radical changes taking place. I can't remember a time when I didn't have doubts, for instance, about such things as the authenticity of the Book of Mormon, which I have never accepted as a genuine historical document or scripture, or of the divinity of Christ, or the factual truth of much that is found in the Bible. So I've never gone through any kind of religious crisis—either in my attitudes or my beliefs.

You have been criticized severely by defenders of the faith for dismissing the Book of Mormon without having made a thorough study of it. How do you respond to this charge?

I haven't made a thorough study of whether Santa Claus lives at the North Pole either. I'm simply convinced that we don't get books from angels and translate them by miracle. And such things as the narrative of Christ in the Book of Mormon, especially the prophecies of his coming and the descriptions of his very teachings centuries in advance of his birth, reveal that it is not an authentic document.

Quite apart from its doctrines, how do you feel now about the LDS church as an institution?

The church is very strong and efficient in its pursuit of practical affairs, but now it faces great problems as it becomes more and more a worldwide religion. It has a parochial mentality and seems incapable of turning its attention very far outside of itself. Its concern is to get more members, but there's a question of what it's going to do with them—people from other cultures grafted on to a Utah-Southern Idaho-California mentality. The intellectual leadership of the church has declined a great deal since the deaths of B. H. Roberts and James E. Talmage in the early 1930s.

What are the strengths and weaknesses of the LDS church leadership today?

By and large, I think it is strong and effective. In my opinion, with very few exceptions, the central leaders, the so-called general authorities, have in recent years been men of unquestioned integrity and completely devoted to the good of the church and its people. But they are often lacking in the experience, knowledge, and wisdom to refrain from exerting political domination, especially in Utah and Idaho. Today the rapid expansion and internationalization of the church poses difficult problems with which the church leadership has had comparatively little experience. I'm afraid there is still a strong parochial mentality among the leaders that makes it difficult for them to deal with intercultural problems.

Are you optimistic that things will improve in this regard under President Gordon Hinckley? Do you expect any changes?

President Gordon B. Hinckley is a leader of the highest order. I only wish that he and other twentieth-century Mormon presidents could have taken office at an earlier age. Starting your administration at the age of eighty-four, just to take the case of President Hinckley, means that much of your energy and ideas have been spent and, even under the best of circumstances, you don't have much time left. On another matter, I wish the church would face its own past honestly and with more understanding of the efforts of those who want to be a part of it while at the same time maintaining their own integrity.

The church has a highly efficient and effective organization, with enormous power and wealth, that is seriously adrift when it comes to concern for the dignity of those outside its circle—be they on the edge or far away—intel-

lectually or geographically.

Yes, the central leadership of the church is very weak when it comes to tackling large intellectual issues. This shows up, for instance, very clearly at the time of the general conferences, when most of the time is taken up with simplistic, moralistic anecdotes. The conferences are a very tame and boring affair now, compared to what they were in the old days when the Mormons produced great orators and independent thinkers.

Church authorities' speeches are practically always designed in part to get the people to accept them as their leaders.

God's own chosen deputies, as they see themselves. Never think for yourself! Following the leaders is the basic rule in the church, a rule which has produced a massive congregation of sheep. The leaders' other ever-present message is pay tithing to build up the financial empire of the church. All in all, however, the rank-and-file members of the church seem uplifted by whatever their leaders say.

Ironically, a noble virtue like humility is now defined as obedience to leaders, and obedience has superseded love as the anchor of a good life. Attend your meetings, pay your tithes, say no to tobacco, coffee, and liquor, and all is well with you, now and forever!

Jack, it couldn't be put better. I fully approve of a strong moral emphasis in religion, but the people need exercise in the meaning and foundations of morality that goes beyond being told over and over and over again to behave—and just how to behave. The church has gone through a remarkable expansion, and it has increased its top bureaucracy accordingly. If there is anything the Mormon church knows how to do, it's how to manage things. I suspect it's doing a remarkable job of managing the growth of the church. But the big problem is really not one of management. It's a question of the imposition of Mormonism on cultures utterly foreign to the basic elements of this American religion.

It's a question of what's actually happening in the religious lives of these people who are being converted.

In Latin America it's obvious that a large number of the converts come out of a pseudo-Catholicism combined with a certain amount of primitive animism. And I raise the question as to what the LDS church is interested in achieving with these people—whether it wants to convert them into American-type Mormons, which is what it has always attempted in the past, or whether it is simply interested in some kind of accommodation with their religion—which has been the case with the Catholic church—or something else.

Do you think half-baked Mormonism would be better than the fully-cooked kind?

I don't at all recommend what the Catholic church has done in this respect. But the great success of the Catholic church in dealing with people has been its accommodation to their cultures. This is a carryover of a practice of the Roman government which allowed conquered peoples to rule themselves as long as they went along with Imperial requirements to pay taxes, keep order, and recognize Roman authority. The Catholic church inherited that general attitude of accommodation as it spread around the world.

I'm inclined to think that the Mormon religion is going to become a strange hybrid or aggregate religion, which may or may not be all right. I'm afraid the church is moving into territory that it does not fully understand and may not be able to control to its satisfaction. But that's a matter for the leaders to worry about, I suppose.

As a prominent and outspoken heretic, you have been treated very decently by the church.

Better than I really deserve, considering that some people get excommunicated for heresies that don't begin to compare with mine. It's outrageous when they excommunicate believing, practicing members simply because of some of their theological views or because they are taking an honest look at church history. The church's effort to control the thought of the people, to destroy genuine intellectual freedom in matters pertaining to religion or church history, is a great evil.

They seem to excommunicate others for less critical statements about church doctrines and policies than you have made, while leaving you pretty much alone. Does it ever bother you to be getting what appears to be special treatment? Is it your university status, your family heritage, or your history of public service?

I'll be damned if I know. Of course, by the time this is published I may be out on my head, and you may be, too! But you know, Jack, excommunication, in many cases, is a function of geography. It depends on where you live—among bigots who will try to get you thrown out, or with people of mature experience, understanding, and compassion. Now for over thirty years we have lived in the only true ward in the church, where the people are intelligent, decent, and all you could ask for. Besides, though I am a total heretic, I'm not an apostate. I'm not running around trying to make trouble for the church.

As you know, however, in the last several years some general authorities of the church have called on local leaders to try feminists, historians, intellectuals, and others for heresy, resulting in a number of excommunications. Yet you continue to be spared.

I guess it is because I don't fit into any of those categories. Anyway, I'm what should be considered a "good heretic." A good heretic is one who doesn't believe, but who nevertheless likes the church. I like the church. It brings happiness to countless people, sometimes through devious means, but often in ways that are generous and in every way commendable.

For many people your age this is a time to consider the meaning of death and the question of immortality. Do you ponder these things?

No, I don't think in those terms at all. The prospect of dying doesn't bother me. It doesn't seriously concern me, though I realize that I am getting close to it. I want to be the first one in my family to die so that I won't have to experience the death of any of the others. And I want to finish a few things I'm working on.

As for immortality, I simply am not a believer in the resurrection of the body or the immortality of the soul. I think it would be great if what the churches teach about immortality were true—at least for those who are among the saved. I wouldn't want to end up with the damned—but that's always a possibility. To me, personal immortality has meaning only as something that I read about and respect in the beliefs and teachings of others. I am not banking on immortality in any way.

This being the case, Sterling, the balance of your life takes on even greater significance. What's next? What do you hope for in the coming years?

Of course, I hope that the world will have less evil and suffering and more freedom. We can at least hope. For myself, I am concerned that I finish up some of the things that I have wanted to do before I die. I have three or four books partially written that I should complete. I really don't need to travel much anymore. Natalie and I have been around the world together; I've been around it twice. I've been in all fifty states and forty different countries. But I do like to travel around the western United States. Natalie and I have never been to New Zealand and Australia, and I think such a trip would be a very pleasant experience. I envy your recent visiting professorship at the University of Auckland.

We surely enjoyed it. But you and Natalie both like best to travel by train. You can't get to Auckland that way.

There aren't many good trains left anyway. Natalie and I traveled through Russia and virtually all of Europe by train, and that's a wonderful way to see the country. We went back and forth across the United States many times in the days when we had the great trains, and we still do an Amtrack trip occasionally. But I like to drive with Natalie to see our children and grandchildren, and enjoy the countryside.

I recently read Ernest Becker's prize-winning book **The Denial of Death.** *He struggled mightily with the plight of humans living in our time. With science and technology having objectified so much of our existence, we have lost our life-enriching myths. He believes we search in vain for the meaning of life and death, faith and doubt, hope and despair. Surrounded by material wonders, we grope to escape the fear of oblivion and death.*

That anything at all exists is an unsolvable mystery. There is much happiness in the life of some people, but very little, if any, in the life of an equal or greater number. But the end, of course, is always death— sometimes with great travail and sorrow as well as mental anguish and physical pain.

Isn't religion primarily an attempt to overcome this sense of the tragic in human existence?

Yes, and I think it does so not by argument from evidence but by genuine human sympathy and compassion, by the perpetuation of myth, belief in immortality, and the promise of a felicitous salvation of souls in eternity. Christianity, of course, traditionally has believed in the salvation of some souls, but not all. The main Christian belief is that the souls of the elect—those whom God has created for salvation, or those who accept Christ as their savior—will be saved and the rest of us will be damned. I regard the Christian religion generally as a sublime myth. It brings comfort, happiness, and joy to countless millions, but I cannot accept as the final truth the claims of the Christian religion, or of any of the other theistic religions.

Did this myth bring you comfort or confidence as a child, Sterling? Must a myth be "true" to enrich culture, provide solace to a suffering child, or moral courage to a leader under fire?

I think you are quite right in suggesting the religious value of myth. Cultures depend to a great extent on their myth-making capabilities, and I have no objection to that. The Mormon myths are fascinating and for some they may be necessary, you know, gold plates and all. But I don't think there were any gold plates; and while myths can be beautiful and profound and moving, if they are myths basically, they are not true, even though they may express profound feelings and attitudes. As you know, Jack, some of us want the truth. I have always felt that we can have an effective symbolism in religion without mythology. No society can function without a certain amount of symbolism.

In your book Religion, Reason, and Truth, *at the end of a long passage on the meaning of religion, you wrote: "Religion should bring consecration to life and direction to human endeavor, inspire men and women with faith in themselves, dedicate them to high moral purpose, preserve their natural piety in the presence of success, and give them the strength to live through their failures with nobility and face with high courage their supreme tragedies." That says it all, but it also sounds as if you see life as a struggle between faith and despair. Is this true?*

You are quite right, Jack. That is the nature of human life. It is a struggle between faith and despair.

Sterling, we have uncovered the nub of your philosophy. But where do you come down personally on the prospects of life on earth as we close in on the twenty-first century?

I am discouraged enough by the suffering and agony I have seen in the world and by the likelihood for greater human suffering in the future that I cannot escape the awful judgment that it would have been better if human life had never existed or, for that matter, any kind of life. On balance, suffering has greatly outweighed joy in the total human experience. And our century, the century of science and technology, has been history's most abject failure in its totality of human suffering.

But, Sterling, no one seems to enjoy life more than you do.

Well, as long as we are here, we should make the most of it. The future is not determined and the human spirit has magnificent strength. In the worst of times we create visions of the best of times. And no matter what happens, we look to the future with faith that good will ultimately prevail.

Is the irrepressible human spirit only a kind of naiveté born afresh with each new generation?

Perhaps it is. While I see no cosmic purpose or divinely ordained meaning in human history, I believe we can invest our lives with purpose and value and build meaning into history. We can always hope that I am wrong in believing that we are alone in an indifferent world, keeping alive the faith that the things that matter most are not ultimately at the mercy of the things that matter least.

Thank you, Sterling, for this abundant and challenging conversation.

Epilogue

L. Jackson Newell

With powerful whinnies, Bridger and Isis took their liberty as we unfastened their halters. In seconds they were racing across the high pasture toward their companions on Kolob Plateau. Bill and I watched in the morning light, then settled without words on a big log to savor our thoughts.

We each knew what the other was thinking: Sterling McMurrin and his brother Keith, Bill's father, had died this past spring of 1996 within three weeks of each other. They had loved these horses and this place where they had come together every summer for decades. Sterling had even remarked not long before he died that if he were granted another life, he would choose to be a horse in southern Utah, wintering near St. George and summering on Kolob.

This scene captured the spirit of Sterling McMurrin. He was a man of intense loyalty to family and friends, he loved horses and Utah ranch country, and he exercised his freedom with uncommon delight. He was, of course, also a man of distinction—many distinctions.

In the larger world of affairs, he served his country as U.S. Commissioner of Education—a position from which he advocated racial integration of the public schools, broad elevation of academic standards, and more serious teacher preparation in both liberal and vocational education. He raised a stir, and he made a difference. At other times in his long career, McMurrin spent five months in Iran as an official envoy, represented his country at many international conferences on education and economic development, and served as a director of the Carnegie Foundation for the Advancement of Teaching. Many of these opportunities—and others—grew out of lifelong friendships he forged with business, labor, and government leaders whom he taught as a bright young philosopher at the Aspen Institute in the 1950s and 1960s.

In his native Utah, McMurrin was known as a brilliant writer and teacher and a fearless exponent of reason and justice in human affairs. He said what he thought, and he thought deeply and often. He believed religious and educational leaders and their institutions have a special duty to set high ideals and to live by them every day—after all, these public institutions, more than any others, shape the values and inform the minds of each rising generation.

Sterling served on the faculty of the University of Utah for forty years, often in high academic offices, and he turned down its presidency more than once. More important, he was appointed E. E. Ericksen Distinguished Professor of Philosophy in 1964 and held that chair for nearly a quarter of a century. His memory was almost photographic, and he never lectured from notes—although he occasionally carried a fistful of blank pages to the podium to forestall criticism that he had not prepared properly. In his later years the university endowed two professorships and a lectureship in Sterling McMurrin's honor.

McMurrin's relationship with the LDS church was especially complex. He was born and reared in the faith, he taught in the seminary and institute system for a half-dozen years between earning his master's degree and his doctorate, and he was widely recognized as the foremost authority on Mormon theology—which he described as "much stronger than our leaders make it appear." Two of his early works are without peer: *The Philosophical Foundations of Mormon Theology* (1959) and *The Theological Foundations of the Mormon Religion* (1965). Sterling was Mormon, through and through.

McMurrin regarded himself, however, as a "good heretic," which he defined as someone who loved the church but could not accept all of its claims. For Sterling, loving the church meant caring enough to speak out if he thought it was making a mistake—and to speak in its defense if he thought it was being attacked unfairly. Few critics do both, but Sterling did.

He expected the church and its leaders to live up to their ideals, and he spoke and wrote courageously when he thought the institution failed morally, as it did until 1978 in withholding the priesthood from men of African descent. His was also a clear and strong voice against church intolerance (either official or rank-and-file) of free thought—including the use of excommunication and other sanctions intended to suppress the expression of creative thought or thoughtful criticism.

The moral leaders of every generation choose their duties—embrace their special challenges. The removal of racial barriers in religion and education was one of McMurrin's major aims in life. And he and his peers achieved a measure of success. Sterling and others like him, however, whose consciences helped to carry the moral burden of the 1960s and 1970s in Utah and in the church, were sensitive to the unresolved manifestations of discrimination.

They knew that church policies and federal laws can change without changing people's attitudes, and that it is within individual minds and hearts that the real problem must be solved. They were also aware that priesthood barriers to women are as offensive as those to African Americans. While they left this challenge for another generation, Sterling offered special encouragement and extended heartfelt support to women writers and leaders in the church. He was especially offended whenever these women were punished for expressing unpopular views.

Sterling McMurrin's life and work revealed an uncanny capacity to reconcile the competing demands of duty and freedom, loyalty and principle, self and society. He not only reconciled these often conflicting but fundamentally complementary values, he also lived and expressed them with a flourish. In an era when tensions among these values are increasingly ducked by an escape into cynicism and alienation, or simply ignored by acceptance without question of institutional demands as a necessary good, Sterling McMurrin reminded us that there is another way. He lived with uncommon delight for eighty-two years—running free, while packing powerful messages about truth, and justice, and integrity. No wonder he was controversial. No wonder we loved him.

Index

Bowen, Lucy Gates, 21
Bowne, Borden Parker, 131-32, 378
Boyd, George, 106, 117, 181, 197, 203, 362
Bradford, William, 23
Bradley, Francis Herbert, 135
Brennan, William, xxiii, 244, 262, 268
Brigham Young University (BYU), xv, 114, 179, 182, 188, 206, 211, 239, 242, 253
Brightman, Edgar Sheffield, 129, 131, 138
Britannica Book of the Year, 333
Brown, Courtney, 248, 251
Brown, Hugh B., 200-201, 209
Buber, Martin, 356
Budge family, 151
Burned-Over District, 182
Bush, (President) George, 2

C

California State University at Northridge, 102
Calvin, John, 173
Campbell, Roald, 222
Can We Be Equal and Excellent, Too?, 288
Cane, Reginald, 327
Canning, Ray, 180
Carnap, Rudolph, 146, 149, 152, 176
Carnegie Foundation, x, xxiv, xxix, 98, 257, 375
Carr, William, 268, 271-72, 274-75, 295
Catron, David, xiii, xv
Celebrezze, Anthony, 305
Chamberlin, Elliott, 68
Chamberlin, Ralph, 48, 60, 66-69
Chamberlin, W. H., Philosophical Society, 70
Chamberlin, William Henry, 67-69, 80, 87

Chase, Alice, 362
Chase, Daryl, 123, 234, 362
Children of God, The, 120-21
Chipman, W. Drew, 47
Christensen, Carl, 205
Christensen, P. A., 68, 181, 361
Christensen, Willam, 78, 101, 358
Christ's Ideals for Living, 237
Civil rights, 284-87
Clark, J. Reuben, Jr., 114-16, 201-202, 354
Clark, Joseph F., xxiv-xxv, 262
Clayton, Desmond, 211
Clemson University, 159, 184-85
Cohen, Morris, 236
Cohen, Wilbur, 280, 287
College of Wooster (Ohio), 176
Collin, Henry F., xvii, 9-11, 87
Columbia University, xxi, xxiii, 73, 138, 141, 162, 176, 178
Commission on Instructional Technology, 310
Committee for Economic Development, xxix, 362
Conant, James B., 296, 302
Contemporary Philosophy: A Book of Readings, xxi, 225
Conversations with Wallace Stegner, xiii, 99
Cook, Melvin, 183-84
Cook, Merrill, 184
Cooley, Everett, 8, 361
Copland, Aaron, 358
Corwin, Norman, 244
Cotterel, Clyde C., 92
Cotterel, Mattie Alice Easley, 92, 120
Cotterel, Samuel, 91
Cowles, LeRoy, 49, 51, 81-83, 86-87
Creative Skeptics, 144
Crellin, Janice, xv
Cross, Whitney, 182

About the Editor

L. Jackson Newell, professor of higher education and former dean of liberal education at the University of Utah, is currently president of Deep Springs College in California. He is a celebrated teacher and widely published author on the philosophy and history of higher education. His honors include the Joseph Katz Award for distinguished leadership in American higher education and selection of the State of Utah's first CASE Professor of the Year. He is a Presidential Teaching Scholar at the University of Utah. With his wife, Linda, he served as editor of *Dialogue: A Journal of Mormon Thought* from 1982 to 1987.